THINKING THEOLOGICALLY
ABOUT MASS INCARCERATION

THINKING THEOLOGICALLY ABOUT MASS INCARCERATION

Biblical Foundations and Justice Imperatives

EDITED BY
ANTONIOS KIREOPOULOS,
MITZI J. BUDDE, AND
MATTHEW D. LUNDBERG

NATIONAL COUNCIL OF THE CHURCHES
OF CHRIST IN THE USA

FAITH & ORDER COMMISSION
THEOLOGICAL SERIES

Paulist Press
New York / Mahwah, NJ

Cover image by klss/Shutterstock.com
Cover and book design by Lynn Else

Library of Congress Cataloging-in-Publication Data
Names: Kireopoulos, Antonios, editor.
Title: Thinking theologically about mass incarceration : biblical foundations and justice imperatives / edited by Antonios Kireopoulos, Mitzi J. Budde, and Matthew D. Lundberg.
Description: New York : Paulist Press, 2017. | Series: National Council of the Churches of Christ in the USA Faith & Order Commission Theological Series
Identifiers: LCCN 2017021087 (print) | LCCN 2017040385 (ebook) | ISBN 9781587687464 (ebook) | ISBN 9780809153725 (pbk. : alk. paper)
Subjects: LCSH: Imprisonment--Religious aspects--Christianity. | Discrimination in criminal justice administration—United States. | Social justice—United States.
Classification: LCC HV8687 (ebook) | LCC HV8687 .T45 2017 (print) | DDC 261.8/336—dc23
LC record available at https://lccn.loc.gov/2017021087

ISBN 978-0-8091-5372-5 (paperback)
ISBN 978-1-58768-746-4 (e-book)

Published by Paulist Press
997 Macarthur Boulevard
Mahwah, New Jersey 07430

www.paulistpress.com

Printed and bound in the
United States of America

CONTENTS

CONTENTS

CONTENTS

PREFACE
The Churches and the Incarceration Epidemic

Antonios Kireopoulos, Mitzi J. Budde, and Matthew D. Lundberg

PART ONE: WHY MASS INCARCERATION MATTERS

Why does the issue of mass incarceration matter? Why is it of concern to churches in the United States? And why is it a topic of theological inquiry, especially for theologians who participate together at a dialogue table that is designed to look at issues at the heart of ecclesial division and unity?

These questions are the basis for this book. When the National Council of the Churches of Christ in the United States of America first identified mass incarceration as a priority for its work and witness, the Convening Table on Theological Dialogue and Matters of Faith and Order (formerly the Faith and Order Commission) carefully considered what it would mean in terms of theological dialogue. Admittedly, it appeared the issue was perfect for, and needful of, the churches' joint advocacy work—mass incarceration was looming large on the national agenda, and its connections to racism and the violence impacting the African American community were undeniable. Bringing the moral weight of the churches to the handling of this issue in terms of advocacy was critical.

But theological *dialogue*? It would be an understatement to say that, at first, there was some hesitation to delve into this topic. Few envisioned more than a repetition of historical analyses of incarceration and liberation, or perhaps clichéd foundational arguments in support of advocacy initiatives, as the outcome of our efforts. In addition, some were skeptical that the topic would be fruitful in terms of fostering church unity. After all, which churches were not already united in the view that racism, mass incarceration, and related incidents of violence were a scandal? It was only after the participants at the table began to look at what it was *within* the issue of mass incarceration that could be church dividing (and church uniting) that fruitful discussion started to take place. It was clear that mass incarceration was a stain on the soul of the country. The line from slavery to Jim Crow laws to the "War on Drugs" initiative to mass incarceration was straight and unbroken. But what of the voice to challenge it? Was there another straight and unbroken line, this one from the abolitionist movement to the civil rights struggle to the present day? Certainly there were individual prophetic calls to break the bonds of injustice reflected in the statistics. But was there something the churches of the United States could say together—precisely as the one Church of Christ—about this alarming reality? Heeding the scriptural imperative "to proclaim release to the captives...[and] to let the oppressed go free" (Luke 4:18), this book is one attempt to raise this united voice.

PART TWO: SEEKING JUSTICE TOGETHER

The Convening Table on Theological Dialogue and Matters of Faith and Order (henceforth Faith and Order) organized itself into three study groups to approach the mass incarceration topic from three distinct theological perspectives. The first group, Biblical Foundations, looked at various biblical and historical markers for what justice is as it relates to mass incarceration. This group also sought out experiential testimony. The essay by Michael Richardson in this collection is an invited contribution from this group to offer the firsthand account and theological perspective of one formerly incarcerated. The second group, How Theology Informs Justice, sought to use theology as the starting point to inform faith's understanding of the ethical demands of various approaches to justice. The third group, How Justice Informs Theology, utilized experiences of justice and injustice as the starting point for their claim that the current

U.S. criminal justice system is not an expression of God's justice. The group then sought to provide a theological framing around that assertion that interpreted and offered an alternative vision for the churches' vocation for dialogue, action, and advocacy.

Over the course of 2014 to 2016, members presented papers to their study groups and engaged in lively theological debate and dialogue around each other's perspectives. While not all Faith and Order members contributed a paper to this collection, each contributed significantly to this work through their participation in the study group process. For example, Faith and Order member the Rev. Dr. Ray Kibler III presented a paper for dialogue that encouraged us to consider how mass incarceration could be a church-dividing or church-uniting issue at different levels within the ecclesial life of the churches here in the United States. These discussions, as well as many others, helped the larger Faith and Order Table think through the topic and helped to shape this publication.

This work on mass incarceration coincided with the themes of the Ecumenical Advocacy Days (EAD) events in 2015 and 2016. Faith and Order offered preconference theological workshops for Ecumenical Advocacy Days around the themes of "Breaking the Chains: Mass Incarceration and Systems of Exploitation" (2015) and "Exploring the Theological Basis for Lifting the Voices of the Marginalized" (2016). It was at the former workshop that the Rev. Dr. Stephen Ray, also a Faith and Order member, in a moving and even shocking way, urged us to grapple with the "commodification of dark bodies," thereby leading us to see what was at stake by the undertaking of this theme by U.S. churches. At the latter workshop, the U.S. context was broadened by the participation of Dr. Agnes Abuom, the moderator of the World Council of Churches, who presented a paper on the WCC's Programme to Combat Racism and helped us to link related issues of racial injustice globally to those we identify with mass incarceration.

Throughout this Faith and Order work, the study groups have kept ever before them the key question, "How does this work on mass incarceration reveal and advance the visible unity of the church?" We do not want solely to be Christians working alongside one another on a matter of shared social concern—even on as vital an issue as this one. Rather, in line with the Faith and Order vocation to advance the ecumenical agenda for justice, reconciliation, and unity through this work, we are very clear that living into Christian unity means that each voice represented here in these essays contains a *charism* that is a gift to other Christians and churches.

The papers in this book are the result of this multiyear, multilateral dialogue process. These essays address mass incarceration in our society as an issue in need of radical reform, and do so from the theological perspectives of multiple Christian traditions committed to Christian unity and to the pursuit of a common witness for justice. We know that these papers do not provide all the answers our society needs to the complex theological and ethical issues surrounding mass incarceration. But maybe the greatest gift that we can offer here is to gesture toward a common ground for constructive theology, inviting Christians and churches to wrestle theologically with God's call to justice and mercy.

PART THREE: THINKING THEOLOGICALLY ABOUT MASS INCARCERATION

The commitments of the American churches to seek greater unity with one another in the face of a grave injustice have produced this book's concern with mass incarceration. That is, the churches simultaneously find this issue to represent a troubling reality in our country, one that has divisive effects in society and church, and an opportunity for us to speak and work together for repentance, liberation, and justice. As such, this book intends to be an expression of shared Christian commitment to healing, even as it hopes to urge the churches forward in their common quest for justice in the face of the incarceration epidemic in the United States today.

Part 1 of this book sets the stage by surveying the contemporary situation from both experiential and historical angles. Authors of these chapters take on questions such as: Where are we with respect to the justice and injustice of mass incarceration today? What historical forces and attitudes, including those embedded in American Christianity, have contributed to today's situation? How are real people's lives affected by the acceleration of incarceration rates over the past forty years? Perhaps most painfully, how have structures and attitudes of racism contributed to the problem? What roles do Christians and their churches have in both the problem and in possible solutions?

Part 2 explores the primary source and norm of Christian witness, the Bible. The contributors to this section of the book look to various dimensions of the biblical text—the words of Jesus, the theology of Paul, and the Book of Revelation—to shed theological light on realities of mass incarceration, both at the level of analyzing the problem and seeking constructive ways for the church to move forward. As the ecumenical movement has found over the years, listening to the Word of God together is a key first step in seeing our unity as Christians and seeing our shared way forward on the journey of faith, especially on vexing issues such as mass incarceration.

Part 3, in turn, offers a set of theological reflections on various dimensions of today's reality of American mass incarceration. From the experience of immigrants to the prophetic dimension of Christian theology, from themes of divine justice to the cross and atonement, from the theological task of proclamation to the daily task of discipleship, contributors in this section offer ways to deepen our appreciation of the systemic problems involved with mass incarceration, including theological attitudes that have contributed to those problems, and also point to theological resources that can help to direct the American churches to more faithful responses.

The shortest of the book's sections, part 4, employs mass incarceration as a lens through which to understand the theological purpose of the ecumenical movement whose work, through the National Council of the Churches of Christ in the USA, led to this book. Ecumenism flows from the double-sided recognition of the lamentable divisions that afflict the Body of Christ and awareness of the rich degree of unity the churches already share in Christ. Accordingly, these chapters examine ways in which mass incarceration is not merely an issue of social injustice but also an ecumenical problem, while also exploring ways in which shared and sustained Christian work on mass incarceration, as on other ethical issues, can witness and contribute to the unity of the church that the ecumenical movement seeks.

Part 5, the final section of the book, returns to experiential and practical perspectives on mass incarceration, with the goal of giving Christians and churches in the United States ways to move forward constructively on this issue. As with other sections of the book, the issue of race appears frequently in these chapters. Only as we take seriously the experiences of those on both sides of the racial element of the problem can we progress in an honest and constructive way. This section of the book draws from the perspectives of preachers, activists, and prison ministers who aim to provide the American churches with practical steps to take toward improving the justice of our criminal justice system while dismantling its evident injustices.

As this summary shows, there is a productive tension pulsing through the book between repentance and hope, lament and transformation. On the one hand, we deeply grieve the pain and injustice of the systems of racialized mass incarceration that have made the land of the free into the nation with the highest incarceration rates in the Western world. But, on the other hand, precisely as we express our lament and repent of the churches' complicity in the systems, attitudes, and practices that constructed our incarceration system, we simultaneously glimpse and work toward a better way. Our shared conviction is that the reconciling work of Jesus Christ through the energizing presence of the Holy Spirit can empower God's churches in this land to contribute to that better way through our Christian witness.

To this end, we invite Christians and other interested persons to read this book and reflect theologically on these questions. In addition, the Christian Education, Ecumenical Faith Formation, and Leadership Development Convening Table of the National Council of Churches in the USA has constructed a "toolbox" or "starter kit" of resources and readings, available online (http://www.nationalcouncilofchurches.us/images/CEEFFLD_2015_SKTL_MI.pdf). This tool kit is a resource for parishes and readers to build upon what they have encountered in this book and to work for action and advocacy in their own local communities. We offer the present book in hopes that it will spur us all on to small and large actions of faithfulness, both spiritual and political, both theological and practical, that will help to liberate and bind up the wounds of those who have been unjustly impacted by mass incarceration.

I THE SITUATION TODAY

1

AN EPISTLE TO THE AMERICAN CHURCH

"Set the Captives Free"

Michael C. Richardson

My dear fellow clergy and saints,

I greet you in the matchless magnificent name of Jesus. It is my sincere prayer that you are continuously refreshed in mind, body, and spirit as you labor in the ripened fields of our Father's harvest. There are a variety of challenges that confront the twenty-first-century church from within and without. Religious pluralism, immigration, environmental issues, Muslim-Christian relations, and poverty are among the myriad pressing concerns of the church globally and locally. In light of these many challenging issues, I can understand you may be puzzled as to why I am raising concerns here about the liberty of individuals convicted of crimes through seemingly due process of law. I can imagine that the liberation of convicted drug dealers, addicts, thieves, and other felons does not rank high on your list of priorities. The matter does not rest solely on the matter of guilt or innocence, but in the motivation behind the punishment and the degree of scrutiny given to the perpetrator. When the punishment is by one individual against another based on race, social status, or ethnicity, it is called a hate crime. However, when a race is singled out by a country to be punished for their offenses against society, too many rest complacently in naming it "justice." This methodical mutation of justice is part and parcel of the unrighteous mass incarceration system in America.

My beloved brothers and sisters, maybe you have been anesthetized by the dismal statistics and grotesque facts concerning the plight of all incarcerated persons. Such statistics and their historical

3

background can desensitize you to the reality that we are talking about the lives of human beings, people created in the image of God.[1] Maybe if I can give you a glimpse into the harsh reality of these men, you might find the compassion in your heart to take up the mantle of our Lord and Savior and endeavor to set the captives free.[2]

So where do we begin? How did we get here? The mass incarceration problem in America has its roots in racism, slavery, and white supremacy. American history has been steeped in oppressive practices targeting minorities and particularly African Americans. There is little difference between this twenty-first-century tyrannical scheme and the segregation that Martin Luther King Jr. condemned. Slavery, segregation, and mass incarceration devalue human life. Dr. King asserted that "segregation substitutes an 'I-it' relationship for the 'I-thou' relationship, and relegates persons to the status of things."[3] What are we to do about more than a million African American men and women—and indeed all persons imprisoned—who are being dehumanized in the current system?

As an African American man who continues to struggle to be emancipated from the mass incarceration system, I would like to share my own story, hopefully to provide my perspective on the matter at hand. In 2000, I was a young man with a couple of minor encounters with the criminal justice system. One January morning I found myself on a Philadelphia street corner where I had no business being and subsequently was arrested for possession with the intent to deliver a ten-dollar bag of heroin. I was charged with selling to an undercover police officer, even though the marked money was found on another individual and no drugs were found in my possession. I remained in pretrial detention for almost two years before I was convicted based on police testimony contrary to the physical evidence. As my mother and ten-year-old daughter watched from their courtroom seats, I was sentenced to ten to twenty years in prison for this nonviolent offense. My sentence was ten times the twelve-month sentence prescribed by the sentencing guidelines. My only hope was that the court would appoint me an appeal attorney that would be less inept than the trial attorney appointed to me.

I was quickly transferred to Graterford State Correctional Facility to be processed into the system. I would like to share with you the details of the intake process. As you will see, the description of the intake process for Pennsylvania state correctional institutions eerily mirrors the inspection and labeling process of the slave trade, with both culminating in the individual being deemed property. I invite you to imagine the psychological impact of such an experience.

An ominous tension permeated the air as a sea of brown skin slowly meandered down the cold, cramped corridor. The deafening murmur of hundreds of men scuffling along the pale grey, steel bar-lined passage was only quieted by the bellowing commands of the escorting correctional officers. Each one of the new arrivals had been stripped of all personal items, identification, clothes, and any ounce of dignity that remained. Our lives had been reduced to the contents of a cardboard box that we carried, wearing nothing but a pair of skivvies and shower shoes. We were herded single file to the intake room where we turned over our possessions to be shipped back home. "Next!" the officer bellowed. "Your number is EV2256," he said as he took my paperwork and directed me to the next intake station. Disoriented, confused, and demoralized, I was instructed to strip naked in a room full of officers and inmates. As I stood in front of an officer, he belted out a series of commands, "Open your mouth, lift your tongue, hands out, turn them over, lift your arms, lift your penis, lift your scrotum, turn around, lift your foot, lift the other one, bend over, and spread your cheeks!" This was only the beginning of the humiliation. I was given a shampoo to rub in my hair and deloused with a powdery substance. After being escorted through a communal shower, I was given three sets of undergarments. I approached the intake desk and reality set in with this question, "Where do you want your body sent?" I struggled to swallow the knot in my throat and reluctantly replied, "I don't have a life sentence." I will never forget the response, "No one is guaranteed to get out of here alive, but until then you're state property." This would be my reality for a decade of my life.

I was one of a million men created in the image of God who are methodically deprived of their dignity, self-worth, and freedom. Dr. King declared that "deeply rooted in our political and religious heritage is the conviction that every man is an heir to a legacy of dignity and worth."[4] The mass incarceration system in America seeks to defraud African American men of their

5

birthright. As you can see from my story, the main culprit in this fraudulent divestment of liberty and legacy is the woefully biased criminal injustice system. There is a bevy of injustices that perpetuate mass incarceration. Discriminatory sentencing, racial profiling, prosecutorial misconduct, ineffective legal representation, and racially biased juries are all contributors to mass incarceration in America. Tokunbo Adelekan argues that "the average citizen now believes that there are two Americas: one rich and one poor, a two-tiered system of laws, one of which exists for rich whites and the other for poor people of color, largely male, who serve mandatory sentences for petty crimes."[5]

So what is to become of individuals like me who have been found to be prisoners of this system? Is there deliverance for the people languishing in the cold concrete gyves of America's capitalist machine? Unfortunately for many, this is only the fount of a life of captivity. After ten years in prison, I was paroled and reunited with my then eighteen-year-old daughter. I returned home like many, hoping to put this nightmare behind me. But to my chagrin, as Michelle Alexander reminds us, "this caste system extends far beyond prison walls and governs millions of people who are on probation and parole, primarily for nonviolent offenses. They have been swept into the system, branded criminals or felons, and ushered into a permanent second class status—acquiring records that will follow them for life."[6] Millions of black men have been permanently branded felons and convicts. Regardless of sincere reformative efforts, they have been estimated to be only the sum of their failures. Interview after interview, job after job, background check after background check, these men are turned away, virtually unemployable. Today, sixteen years after my last crime, I am still denied positions due to my criminal record.

Joblessness, stringent probationary restrictions, societal and domestic pressures, blighted communities, psychological bondage, and scarce reentry assistance all contribute to high recidivism rates. Many of these nonviolent offenders return home with addiction problems. A 2004 U.S. Department of Justice survey showed that drug use prior to incarceration is common in both state and federal prisoners.[7] I can personally attest to this reality. The existence of substance abuse among incarcerated individuals is most evident in county prisons when they are first introduced to the system. This is the period when these individuals must adjust to life without the addictive substance that had become their motivation for life. I remember during the initial county prison intake process how fifteen to twenty men were placed in one cramped holding cell with nothing but two metal benches lining the walls. Individuals would find a place on the cold, dirty floor to get some rest during their two-day long intake process. In this constricted space, about half the men began their withdrawal from drugs and alcohol. As I tried to mask the pungent stench of vomit, feces, urine, and other body odors, I watched as the shivering, convulsed bodies of individuals combated the physical and mental withdrawal from heroin, alcohol, cocaine, and other substances.

The same 2004 survey that documented the substance abuse among state and federal prisoners showed that 40 percent of state and 49 percent of federal inmates took part in some kind of drug program, but most were self-help or peer counseling groups. Only 15 percent of state prisoners and 17 percent of federal prisoners took part in drug treatment programs with a trained professional.[8] In my experience, there were various mandatory programs for those who had a substance abuse history; however, they were facilitated by individuals like me without any formal training to address the various issues addiction presents. So often under the pressures to assimilate into society, these men seek to numb the pain of their hopeless state through substance abuse. Because of these moments of decrepitude and lapses in judgement, they find their way back through prison's revolving door as parole or probation violators.

Many of these individuals carry the ignominy of being imprisoned and the perception of unemployability home to children who need their financial support. Now we begin to see the ripple effect of the systematic enslavement of the African American male and other incarcerated individuals. Families and communities are torn apart because of this unrighteous system. Mass incarceration is a dehumanizing industry that has a far-reaching impact on individuals, families, and communities. These men and women are more than the number assigned to them or the bottom line on a company's income statement. The collateral integration consequences and issues that plague those individuals who are attempting reentry into society are tremendous. The clear majority of individuals who have been incarcerated are parents. It has been estimated that roughly three million children have parents who are currently incarcerated or have been recently paroled.[9] The separation from a parent due to incarceration has become highly likely in the lives of African American children due to the disproportionate incarceration rates among African American men. These splinters in the family unit have adverse effects on all the interpersonal family relationships within the family. The separation due to incarceration often leads to infidelity in romantic relationships and eventually to severed ties. Additionally, it has been determined that parental incarceration has an adverse effect on children's social skills. "The psychological bearing on the children of incarcerated individuals can manifest in a medley of ways such as, poor socialization, faint aspirations, and diminished self-worth due to the stigma of incarceration."[10]

Lastly, mass incarceration has a profound effect on the communities of the individuals incarcerated. Mass incarceration harms the communities by returning these former prisoners as disenfranchised individuals without voting privileges and prospects of employment. The lack of voting privileges leaves these communities with a sector of their populace unable to vote for policymakers in that community. The lack of employability limits the communities' spending power. "Concentrated incarceration in impoverished communities has broken families, weakened the social control capacity of parents, eroded economic strength, soured attitudes toward society, and distorted politics."[11] There is far more damage this unrighteous caste system has done in the lives of the declared guilty and the victimized innocent; this letter only serves as a glimpse into the abyss. I question whether we are still to believe that mass incarceration is a matter of inmates lawfully adjudicated within a justice system. A better question would be whether we are compelled to act on behalf of these poverty-stricken, disenfranchised, marginalized individuals.

I stand with Dr. Martin Luther King Jr. in his declaration that "it has always been the responsibility of the Church to broaden horizons and challenge the status quo. The Church must move out into the arena of social action….It must take an active stand against the injustices which Negroes confront in housing, education, police protection, and in city and state courts."[12] The mass incarceration system is an incursion against the social, economic, psychological, and political freedoms of an entire demographic. The deprivations of these freedoms are diametrically opposed to the mission of God in Christ. Christ's liberating mission has been passed on to the church. If the church is to indeed prove to be faithful to the *missio dei* ("mission of God"), it has a responsibility to be a facilitator for liberty. I can only offer the words of our Lord and Savior Jesus Christ as a clarion call to action.

> The Spirit of the Lord is upon me,
>   because he has anointed me to bring good news to
>   the poor.
> He has sent me to proclaim release to the captives
>   and recovery of sight to the blind, to let the
>   oppressed go free,
> to proclaim the year of the Lord's favor."
>
> (Luke 4:18–19)

I implore you, brothers and sisters, to resolve to liberate the oppressed. I dare to venture that the church has more in common with these marginalized outcasts of society than initially conceived. Christians have experienced the joy of deliverance, the hope evidenced by the gospel of grace, the mercy showered upon us from on high, and the joy of being set free from the power of sin. I aspire to arouse your compassion for those on the fringes. My friends, I hope to incite your passions and invigorate your courage as I bare my soul. I have shared with you the stresses and impediments I have experienced through my incarceration. Six years ago, I was liberated from the bowels of that concrete leviathan unscathed following a ten-year incarceration. Against all odds, over the ensuing six years, I would graduate with a Bachelor of Science in Business Administration *magna cum laude*, obtain a Master of Divinity with honors, own and operate a successful business, and become an ordained elder in the Lord's church.

Considering the seemingly pervasive trappings of this deplorable system, you might wonder how I could achieve these victories and others like them. The clear answer would be Christ, the Body of Christ, the church. Because of the presence of God in the form of church prison ministries, where others' leaves withered, mine flourished. Because of the support of a church community upon reentry, I have been able to avoid the many pitfalls present in urban communities.

I dare not purport that my journey was one of smooth thoroughfares and unobstructed passages. I still deal with the stigma of a convicted felon as I navigate life. These rebuffs emanate from worldly sources and even from the called out ones. At my orientation interview for seminary, I was told that I would be given a chance but that I represented all ex-convicts. I understand I had a responsibility to God to excel in my seminary career; however, my success or failure could never represent such a diverse group of individuals. As I sought to complete my clinical pastoral internship as a chaplain, I was turned down multiple times after a background check was performed. I want to remind you that we are referring to a crime that is sixteen years old. The brand of convict or felon has proven to be a formidable challenge for even a man who has excelled academically, professionally, and, I humbly pray, spiritually. The sad truth is that often my trepidations are about sharing my testimony with believers rather than unbelievers. Beloved, I stand unveiled before you cloaked only in the righteousness of God to urge you to act and set the captives free. As Dr. King so aptly declared, "As guardian of the moral and spiritual life of the community the church cannot look with indifference upon these glaring evils."[13]

The question remains, what is the church's ethical response to mass incarceration? What can be done to curtail the escalating numbers of African American men being torn away from their families and communities? How do we help to make reentry into society a successful assimilation? What does the church offer as a healing balm to the psychological abuse experienced by these individuals? The answers are available, but none of them is a quick fix. To turn the tide of this mass incarceration epidemic, we will need to have diligence and perseverance. The other chapters in this volume are doubtless an important contribution from many different scholars and church leaders to ask similar questions and to persevere toward God's justice.

The greatest weapon that the church has to assist and heal inmates is the gospel. Churches need to actively engage in prison ministries to build these men and women up through the good news of Jesus' sacrificial death and resurrection. They need to hear that they have value to God. They need to know that if they were the only sinner on the face of the planet, he would still take the punishment to be reconciled to them. They need to know that no matter what they have done, God loves them and has forgiven them. The gospel message is an antidote to low self-esteem and a diminished sense of self-worth. For me, it was the outside ministries that reminded me of my worth. This is what the church has been instructed to do in Holy Scripture. "Remember those who are in prison, as though you were in prison with them; those who are being tortured, as though you yourselves were being tortured" (Heb 13:3). We must remember that whether incarcerated or on parole, each one of these individuals is beloved of God and counted among the number of lives that Christ died to restore relationship with the Father.

Second, the church must begin to champion the cause for justice and equity in the criminal justice and penal systems. There must be an active voice that will challenge the policymakers to balance the scales regarding the disproportionate incarceration of black men. Additionally, there must be public support for the Second Chance Act and rehabilitation initiatives. Returning citizens will be able to utilize the benefits of the Second Chance Act through job readiness programs, job placement, substance abuse treatment, education, and other reintegration assistance. The families of these returning citizens can also receive support in order to improve communities as a whole.[14] The church must also be a support system for those who are attempting to reenter society.

Finally, the church must make efforts to mend the communities to which these men and women will be returning. The light of the church must not be hidden behind sanctuary walls. We must take our light into our communities to offer hope to the fatherless, undereducated, and impoverished youth. We must sponsor after-school programs, volunteer at organizations that provide reentry assistance, and support families and children of incarcerated individuals. Within our church walls, we must develop effective youth ministries that seek to give our youth a biblical perspective of their value and worth. Our men's and women's ministries must teach biblical principles about marriage, parenting, and civic responsibility. Additionally, we must develop programs and collaborations among local businesses that will help with the employability of those reentering society.

I pray that I have offered you a clear snapshot of the ugly truth that is America's mass incarceration system. There are many evils that we face in the world, but none as cunning and resilient as the one that has found its home on this country's soil. It seeks to disinherit humanity of its divinely vested freedom and its supreme identity. An identity that is not divided into ranks based on race, social status, ethnicity, gender, or any other schismatic factor. An identity that exemplifies the unifying freedom found in the divine community of the Godhead. This evil has made its way from the Garden of Eden, across time and across oceans, and seeks to enslave those who have been set free. It is constant in its nature, but capricious in its modality. It has reared its cunning head as slavery, Jim Crow laws, segregation, and now as mass incarceration. Beloved, it is my belief that this evil's head was crushed at Calvary. The Body of Christ must securely replace its foot on this enemy and deracinate it with the authority vested in the church. It is my hope that you will stand with me and for me in the liberation of the captives. I leave you with these words of encouragement from Dr. Martin Luther King Jr: "When we are in the darkness of some oppressive Egypt, God is a light unto our path. He imbues us with the strength needed to endure the ordeals of Egypt, and he gives us the courage and power to undertake the journey ahead."[15] May God bless and keep you my beloved brothers and sisters in the faith.

In His Image,
Rev. Michael C. Richardson

Notes

1. A few statistics may nonetheless be instructive to share. Five hundred twenty-six thousand African American men were serving time in state or federal correctional facilities in 2013. That is 37 percent of the overall 1.5 million imprisoned men. The National Council on Crime and Delinquency identified similarly disturbing statistics for Native Americans' incarceration rates, which is often underreported by mainstream media. Native Americans are incarcerated at two times the rate of whites in the United States. This is higher than any other ethnic group except African Americans. Christopher Hartney and Linh Vuong, *Created Equal:*

Racial and Ethnic Disparities in the US Criminal Justice System (National Council on Crime and Delinquency, 2009), 3.

2. The growth of numbers of women imprisoned in the United States is also disturbing, and I do not intend to minimize that fact by focusing on male incarceration.

3. Martin Luther King Jr., *Strength to Love* (Philadelphia: Fortress Press, 1963), 141.

4. Martin Luther King Jr., *A Testament of Hope: The Essential Writings and Speeches of Martin Luther King Jr.*, ed. James M. Washington (New York: HarperCollins Publishers, 1986), 118.

5. Tokunbo Adelekan, *A Charge to Keep: Remissioning the Urban Church for the 21st Century* (Chicago: MMGI Books, 2014), 120.

6. Michelle Alexander, *The New Jim Crow: Mass Incarceration in the Age of Colorblindness* (New York: The New Press, 2012), 101.

7. Christopher J. Mumola and Jennifer C. Karberg, *Drug Use and Dependence, State and Federal Prisoners 2004*, U.S. Department of Justice, Office of Justice Programs (Washington, DC: Bureau of Justice Statistics, 2007).

8. Ibid., 9.

9. Holly Foster and John Hagan, "The Mass Incarceration of Parents in America: Issues of Race/Ethnicity, Collateral Damage to Children, and Prisoner Reentry," in *Race, Crime, and Justice: Contexts and Complexities*, ed. Lauren Krivo and Ruth D. Peterson (Thousand Oaks, CA: SAGE Publications, 2009), 180.

10. Bruce Western and Christopher Wildeman, "The Black Family and Mass Incarceration," in *The Moynihan Report Revisited: Lessons and Reflections after Four Decades*, ed. Douglas S. Massey and Robert J. Sampson (Thousand Oaks, CA: SAGE Publications, 2009), 24.

11. Amy Levad, *Redeeming a Prison Society: A Liturgical and Sacramental Response to Mass Incarceration* (Minneapolis, MN: Fortress Press, 2014), 37–38.

12. King, *Testament of Hope*, 141–42.

13. Ibid., 142.

14. Lior Gideon and HungEn Sung, *Rethinking Corrections: Rehabilitation, Reentry, and Reintegration* (Thousand Oaks, CA: SAGE Publications, 2011), 27.

15. King, *Testament of Hope*, 85.

2

CHRISTIAN UNITY FOR A FRACTURED SOCIETY
The Problem of Mass Incarceration for the Churches

Antonios Kireopoulos

I

Where to begin on such an important and extensive topic as the Christian witness, and specifically the *ecumenical* Christian witness, as churches seek to bring about justice? Especially in matters having to do with race relations in a time of Sanford, Florida; Ferguson, Missouri; and even Staten Island, New York?

In addition to this, I could expand my analysis to include, among other things, the ecumenical Christian witness on gender- and sexuality-based discrimination, which is not a thing of the past; economic disparity, which on account of its growth is causing increased tensions between classes; religious intolerance, which shows signs of increasing again despite years of intense relationship building among different faith communities; community disharmony, which flares up in debates over immigration and other policy debates having to do with Mexico, Central America, the Caribbean, and even Cuba; and global warming and environmental degradation, which still threaten whole populations. Unfortunately, space does not permit me to explore these and other areas, and the ways Christians are living out the imperative to bring healing to these situations. But

An earlier version of this chapter was delivered on November 10, 2014, in the O'Neill Lecture Series at the Ecumenical Institute of the School of Theology and Ministry at St. Thomas University in Miami Gardens, Florida.

even though we will not focus on these issues here, let us not forget that they, too, require us to work for justice.

On these and all such concerns, Christians (almost in a clichéd way) take as their inspiration the words of the prophet Micah: "He has told you, O mortal, what is good; / and what does the LORD require of you / but to do justice, and to love kindness, / and to walk humbly with your God?" (6:8). Yes, God requires us to see wrong, and to "do justice." But what I find interesting, almost humorous were it not for its seriousness, is that Christians typically forget to read the two preceding verses (6–7), which talk about repentance: "With what shall I come before the LORD, / and bow myself before God on high? / Shall I come before him with burnt offerings, / with calves a year old? / Will the LORD be pleased with thousands of rams, / with ten thousands of rivers of oil? / Shall I give my firstborn for my transgression, / the fruit of my body for the sin of my soul?" These verses indicate that doing justice, while an ideal in and of itself, is also the *act of repentance*—of "turning"—for which God is asking, or perhaps better, that God demands. Which begs the question: What "sin of my soul" are we who look to this verse for insight and inspiration to repent of? We need to turn from our complicity in precisely the injustices that require remedy. And while we turn away from this sin, we are also required to turn toward love of kindness so as to walk humbly with God. Repentance involves a continuous turn, in the Greek of my own religious tradition, *metanoia*, not only in mind and heart, but also toward acts of fairness and justice that have been seeded with love.

II

It would be a very complex assignment if I were to attempt to dissect the complicity of the churches in all the injustices I've named, and others to be sure. The exploration would necessarily go back centuries, it would have to examine different cultural contexts, and it would of course cut across geographical boundaries. I would therefore ask you to go along with me on this assertion, to accept the premise that to one degree or another, and at one time or another, every church tradition—and indeed every religious tradition—and often with theological justification, has been complicit in injustice, sometimes directly, and sometimes indirectly; for example, by being aware of an unfair situation, but with an ability to oppose the wrong, and yet failing to do so. To support this assertion, I could cite, among only various relatively recent Christian examples, Anglican complicity in the slave trade, Methodist complicity in the destruction visited upon Native Americans, Lutheran complicity in the Holocaust, Catholic complicity in the Rwandan Genocide, and Orthodox complicity in the massacre at Srebrenica. As you can see, no Christian tradition writ large is exempt from complicity in injustice.[1]

However, what I can do here is talk about the Christian complicity of another kind, and the commitment and ongoing effort to repent of this sin. The sin I am talking about is no less than the weakening of the powerful message of the gospel through ecclesial divisions. It is no secret that the churches are divided. It has been so almost since the beginning. Over the centuries, these divisions have led to estrangement, ill will, and even war. More profoundly, they have led to the inability to celebrate our common confession in Jesus Christ around the same eucharistic table. But most tragically, in my opinion, is that they have led to a fracturing of the gospel proclamation. How can we Christians proclaim with full integrity the reconciliation of the world to God when we cannot reconcile among ourselves and proclaim the gospel as one?

This has always been so. And throughout the history of estrangements, and even heresies and schisms, the divisions have been drawn with hard and fast boundaries. But in our context, in our country today, when society seems more fractured than ever on every level, it seems that our sin is more pressing. What word can the churches bring to such a fractured society when our own proclamation is likewise fractured?

At the same time, over the last century we have seen what repentance for this sin looks like. And thankfully, for the sake of the world in which we find ourselves today, we are still engaged in this act of repentance. And what comprises this repentance? The search for Christian unity. The search for Christian unity is the goal and work of the ecumenical movement. While seemingly abstract, and with a seemingly eternal timeline, it is nevertheless the only thing that will in the end make our proclamation whole. It is, in fact, what Jesus prayed for in the Garden of Gethsemane the night before he was crucified (see John 17), when he knew his followers were certain to run in different directions, and when he no doubt foresaw that the church they would establish would eventually divide into separate churches and likewise run one from another in different directions.

By the early part of the last century, the churches saw the consequences of the lack of unity—one of which was competition in the mission fields—and saw the need to seek together that for which the Lord had prayed. The 1910 World Missionary Conference in Edinburgh, which is commonly thought of as the beginning of the modern ecumenical movement, was inspired by such a realization, and had as its aims "to avoid competition, to realize better stewardship of resources, and to provide more effective witness to non-Christians."[2] Indeed, it is not surprising that the ecumenical movement started out of a concern for mission. As this concern was further reflected upon and addressed, at Edinburgh and afterward, the realization was precisely "that it was inconceivable to divorce the obligation of the church to take the gospel to the whole world from its obligation to draw all Christ's people together; both were viewed as essential to the being of the church and the fulfillment of its function as the Body of Christ."[3] And so the search for Christian unity began, precisely as an attempt to make whole our proclamation of the gospel.

But this search for unity has a corollary. While the search for unity is the goal, commonly affirmed as theological unity as reflected in fellowship around the same eucharistic table, the recognition of the degree of unity that we already have, even as we are divided, by virtue of our common confession of Jesus Christ as Lord and Savior, is what compels us in very real ways to seek together to establish justice in his name even as we continue toward our eternal and seemingly elusive goal. And this is what I wish to focus on here: the ecumenical witness, as a reflection of the unity we seek, to bring about justice in a world rife with injustice. In doing so, I will center my remarks primarily on matters of race.

III

In talking about justice in the face of injustice, particularly having to do with matters of race in early twenty-first-century

America, in some ways we take as our starting point 2014's commemoration of the fiftieth anniversary of the Civil Rights Act. That landmark piece of legislation in 1964 marked a turning point in race relations in this country. Many Americans had been horrified in the years leading up to that year, and continued to be so afterward, by the bigotry and violence suffered primarily by African Americans, even if they weren't as attuned to the institutionalized and pervasive discrimination that underlay the abuse. Before his assassination, President Kennedy, who called it "a moral issue…as old as the scriptures and…as clear as the American Constitution,"[4] sought to bring an end to this violence and suffering through legal remedy. Picking up the mantle, and basing it on these same moral, religious, and constitutional principles, President Johnson carried on the fight for its passage as it wound its way through the legislative process.

As we know, this law outlawed discrimination based on race (and what many may not realize, also on religion, sex, and national origin). While it proved to be the baseline for equality among the races, the Civil Rights Act did not end racial inequality or discord. It did ban discrimination in public places and school segregation, but it did not ban job discrimination or housing discrimination. It did not end brutality against African Americans, nor did it end racial tensions more broadly, as exemplified by the events of Selma, Alabama. But as the baseline, it went on to influence the passage of the Voting Rights Act in 1965, and the Civil Rights Act of 1968, which mandated fair housing and sought to end the legitimacy of violence against people because of race.

As the events of the 1960s proceeded, religious voices were among the loudest calling for change. Of course, we all know the influence of Martin Luther King Jr. But we can lift up so many more people of faith, some of them in the historic black churches that accompanied King on the African Americans' march to equality, and consequently to his own martyrdom, some of them in predominantly white churches who, likewise, saw the injustice as a violation of their scriptures and a warping of their theology. These people drew moral authority and strength from their religious traditions to battle against the injustice. Many, and perhaps most, of the Christian religious leaders who joined this battle had met in the ecumenical movement and drew inspiration from this fellowship.

18

I will mention only a few here, and will recall some of those during that period who were connected in some way to the National Council of Churches (and not in addition, for example, those standing in the ranks of the long and honorable social justice tradition of the Catholic Church and other church communities). For example:

- Eugene Carson Blake, an ordained minister of the Presbyterian Church, was president of the NCC in the 1950s. He helped organize the 1963 March on Washington and spoke a few minutes before Martin Luther King Jr. delivered his famous "I Have a Dream" speech.
- Andrew Young, ordained in the United Church of Christ, would go on to become president of the NCC (among his other prominent positions for which he is well known) in the early 2000s. But back in the late 1950s and early 1960s, he was on the youth staff of the NCC before he became a "lieutenant" of King, his longtime friend, in the campaign for civil rights.
- Archbishop Iakovos, of my own Greek Orthodox Church, marched with King in Selma, Alabama, in 1965, just days after another white clergyman was brutally killed by segregationists for promoting civil rights. The photographs capturing the moment, including the one on the cover of *Life* magazine, with the archbishop dressed in his long black robes and veiled episcopal hat, seemed to convey the truth that all Christian history and tradition was on the side of civil rights.
- Arthur Sherwood Fleming, a United Methodist Church layman, was president of the NCC in the late 1960s, and he spoke forcefully about confessing guilt when it came to racism. He was present on behalf of the churches of the NCC to mourn King's assassination.

Perhaps it was William Sterling Cary, a United Church of Christ clergyman who was president of the NCC in the early 1970s, and the first African American president of the NCC, who gave the most powerful theological reflection on that period. In reflecting on these events he said, "We, as churchmen, recognized the need to become engaged in an effort to empower a people.... And so, we felt it important to say that the will of God was that people be engaged in this struggle against the powers and principalities that were oppressing them....Racial injustice [is] a legacy of the slave period...and...continues even to the present day."[5]

Cary made these comments in 2008. Whether merely an observation of the times or a prophetic witness, his comments certainly resonate when thinking about Trayvon Martin and Michael Brown today. Indeed, what Cary said highlighted the fact that such racial tensions are not the stuff of ancient history, and the ecumenical witness similarly not relegated to past periods of church history. Today's events reveal that the sin is still with us, and that the healing witness of the churches is still necessary.

IV

When theologically considering the sin of racism, many believe that there is no such thing as race to begin with. If God created the one human race, then separations within that one race are false creations.[6] Instead, they see race as a "social construct," with "prejudice" and "bigotry" being based on the belief in the superiority of one group over another, and "racism" itself being "the abuse of power by a 'racial' group that is more powerful than one or more other groups in order to exclude, demean, damage, control, or destroy the less powerful groups," and the conferral of "benefits upon the dominant group that include...social privilege, economic position, or political power."[7] I would add to these aspects one other, namely fear, fear of others outside one's group.

These diverse groups within the one race of humankind are rarely self-defined, and commonly defined by the dominant group within the whole. And herein lies the root of the sin, as articulated by a longtime ecumenical colleague, Leonard Lovett, of the Church of God in Christ. As he writes in an essay as part of a volume published in 1998 called *Ending Racism in the Church*, which partly evolved out of the work of a study group of the Faith and Order Commission of the NCC in the 1990s: "The roots of racism lie deep within the soil of human pride and the pervasive will to be different and superior....Because racism is grounded in pride (hubris, which is the exaltation of the self), it may very well be classified as one of the sins of the spirit....It is the perverse worship of the self, rooted in spiritual pride...self-deification in its purest form...the worship of the creature rather than the Creator."[8]

Lovett's observation—again, might this be considered prophetic?—is that "to break down the divisive walls of hostility will require a different kind of solution from any that Congress can provide."[9] This is a helpful observation, given the recitation a moment ago of the ecumenical witness during the civil rights struggle surrounding the passage of the Civil Rights Act and other pieces of legislation. But herein lie the twin aims of ecumenism made real: to provide a common witness to justice in everyday contexts of injustice even as we seek unity to proclaim the Gospel of reconciliation in all its fullness. Or, as we noted earlier, Christian ecumenism's conviction that we cannot separate living the gospel in the world from the obligation to unite all Christians, but instead that we see them both, necessarily intertwined, as essential to being the embodiment of Christ.

As the deaths of Trayvon Martin and Michael Brown show us, we have a long way to go on both counts.[10] Without going into the details of either case, what should be evident are aspects of the sin of racism—whether personal, cultural, or institutional—and our complicity in it. What should also be evident is that the churches have a role in bringing about justice, healing, and reconciliation to a society plagued by such brokenness.

V

The persistence of racism, and the tentacles of this sin, go beyond the individual and tragic events that make the headlines. Indeed, they point to a systemic problem.

In a recent series of three articles, *The New York Times* columnist Nicholas Kristof enumerated some of the places where these tentacles reach. The net worth of the "average black household in the United States is $6,314, compared with $110,500 for the average white household...and the United States now has a greater wealth gap by race than South Africa did during apartheid."[11] Life expectancies are shorter among blacks than whites, educational failure is greater, and mass incarceration rates are higher. With regard to the latter, "nearly 70% of middle-aged black men who never graduated from high school have been imprisoned";[12] "black men get sentences one-fifth longer than white men for committing the same crimes";[13] "similar percentages of blacks and whites use illegal drugs [while] blacks are arrested for such drug offenses at three times the rate of whites";[14] and "blacks [make] up 16 percent of observed drug dealers for the five most dangerous drugs and 64 percent of arrests for dealing those drugs."[15]

These latter statistics and others reveal why racial "inequity is embedded in our law enforcement and criminal justice system."[16] And this is why mass incarceration has become such a burning issue in the minds of people in all sectors of society, including religious communities. This includes the NCC.

I confess that I was ignorant of the state of this issue when (in 2013) the NCC chose mass incarceration as one of its priorities for the current period. I had heard anecdotally that the U.S. incarceration rate was highest in the world. But I didn't know that (for 2012), this meant that there were 2.2 million adults in U.S. prisons, and that "close to 25 percent of the world's prisoners were held in American prisons, although the United States accounts for about 5 percent of the world's population, [or that] the U.S. rate of incarceration, with nearly 1 of every 100 adults in prison or jail, is 5 to 10 times higher than rates in Western Europe and other democracies."[17]

I also didn't know that (for 2011), according to The Sentencing Project, while "38% of people in state or federal prisons were black, 35% were white, and 21% were Hispanic," it was also true that "1 in every 13 black males ages 30 to 34 was in prison, as were 1 in 36 Hispanic males and 1 in 90 white males in the same age group," that "black males have a 32% chance of serving time in prison at some point in their lives, Hispanic males have a 17% chance, [and] white males have a 6% chance," and that "the rate of prison incarceration for black women was 2.5 times higher than the rate for white women [while] the rate for Hispanic women was 1.4 times higher."[18] In broad terms, this means that (in 2010) "blacks were incarcerated at six times and Hispanics at three times the rate for non-Hispanic whites."[19]

I'm sure you find these statistics as shocking as I do. While it is difficult to find causal relationships in terms of other social factors—in the age-old childhood theological question, "Which came first, the chicken or the egg?"—it is nevertheless true that, with changes in criminal justice policy over the last few decades, including most pertinently the increased punishment related to the "War on Drugs," the problems associated with mass incarceration fall disproportionately on communities of color.

VI

In her seminal book on this subject, Michelle Alexander calls mass incarceration the "new Jim Crow."[20] More than just the criminal justice system itself, which gives rise to the statistics just highlighted, she argues that mass incarceration includes legal postprison discrimination in housing, employment, voting rights, and social benefits that together provide systemic reinforcement of the kind of double standard that leaves the black community forever at the bottom of the social hierarchy. In her words, looking at the evolution from slavery to Jim Crow to mass incarceration, "we have not ended racial caste in America; we have merely redesigned it."[21]

Whether one agrees with her conclusions or not, it is difficult to look at the evidence and not agree that she is onto something, and that something is radically wrong. For example, she states that she "came to see that mass incarceration in the United States had, in fact, emerged as a stunningly comprehensive and well-disguised system of racialized social control that functions in a manner strikingly like Jim Crow."[22] It would seem that the evolution of this system, according to her assessment, had been guided by some sort of intention and planning.

Might she be right? Citing the "War on Drugs," she notes that "sociologists have frequently observed that governments use punishment primarily as a tool of social control, and thus the extent or severity of punishment is often unrelated to actual crime patterns."[23] Referring to the statistics above, that despite relatively equal drug use, blacks are three times as likely as whites to be arrested for such offenses, it would seem that the statistics bear her out. Again, I am not asking that we necessarily agree with her conclusions, especially when it requires an acceptance of intention and even collusion in designing this system to be able to say, as she does, that "mass incarceration…is the most damaging manifestation of the backlash against the Civil Rights Movement."[24] Still, there seems to be truth in the notion that rules and laws designed to protect against crime reinforce this reality.

Whether we accept her conclusions or not, we must still recognize the damage that informs her conclusions. Especially when we consider the perpetuation of the situation for generations to come, we cannot turn a blind eye to it. When "more than half of the young black men in many large American cities are currently under the control of the criminal justice system (or saddled with criminal records),"[25] the exponential progression of the problem becomes almost unimaginable. If these young men are or become fathers, this means that their children become fatherless for a good amount of time in their childhood. If these fathers return to their households, they are consigned to unemployment rolls, marginalization from society, and likely a return to crime, if not to prison. All of this and other factors breed ongoing poverty, and the cycle begins again, within the same generation, and from one generation to the next.

This is not only a social concern. It is a moral and pastoral concern. The challenge to the churches is huge. If the task of the churches includes a turning toward loving-kindness and walking humbly with God, then affirming the dignity of each person, responding with compassion, and building a positive future in concrete ways are equally part of the task. If this isn't a spiritual imperative, I'm not sure what is.

Michelle Alexander is urging a building effort of another kind, that of a social movement to cultivate the necessary changes in society that will ensure this type of positive future for all. It is a worthy call, quite frankly for any situation of injustice. And, as just intimated, there is a role for the churches here. The role, the imperative, *the calling* is to name the injustice, to affirm the dignity of those around us, to work for change, and to provide a vision of what can be.

At the risk of being repetitive, the kind of change that is needed is moral, spiritual, and practical. Therefore, one of the practical things church communities can do, even as they minister to the incarcerated and their families, is to advocate for sensible policies that can alter the criminal justice system. One of the recommendations of the National Research Council is the following:

> Given the small crime prevention effects of long prison sentences and the possibly high financial, social, and human costs of incarceration, federal and state policy makers should revise current criminal justice policies to significantly reduce the rate of incarceration in the United States. In particular, they should reexamine policies regarding mandatory minimum sentences and long sentences. Policy makers should also take steps to improve the experience of incarcerated men and women and reduce unnecessary harm to their families and their communities.[26]

There's a lot of work to be done if this recommendation is to be implemented. But for the churches' words and actions to be most meaningful in such actions, their first act is to acknowledge ways in which they may be complicit in the problem, and then move in positive directions.

Is mass incarceration the "new Jim Crow"? Maybe, maybe not. Is it a morally unacceptable situation? Most definitely.

VII

A half century ago, Martin Luther King Jr. famously said, "History will have to record that the greatest tragedy of this period of social transition was not the strident clamor of the bad people, but the appalling silence of the good people."[27] He was talking in the midst of the civil rights struggle.

Today, his words are being echoed by others when it comes to the racial divide. As Nicholas Kristof puts it, "Today we sometimes wonder how so many smart, well-meaning white people in the Jim Crow era could have unthinkingly accepted segregation.

The truth is that injustice is easy not to notice when it affects people different from ourselves; that helps explain the obliviousness of our own generation to inequity today. We need to wake up."[28] More specifically related to mass incarceration, Michelle Alexander has written along the same lines: "Racial caste systems do not require racial hostility or overt bigotry to thrive. They need only racial indifference."[29]

The churches are waking up to the problem, and are joining hands with others to provide solutions. This is part, dare I say it, of the *prophetic* word to be said in our time, in our place. Personally, I don't like to use the word *prophetic* when talking about ourselves as Christians, or about our own communities as churches. It is up to others to see in a person's words and actions, and in our churches' words and actions, what is prophetic. If our words and actions don't reflect a divine judgment on a situation of injustice, then they aren't prophetic; if they don't reflect a divine response to that situation of injustice, then they likewise aren't prophetic. Still, in this case, in this time and place, what is needed from the churches, and from every one of us, is a prophetic word, both as a judgment on the injustice and as a vision of what can be. In the face of this moral, religious, and spiritual problem, we cannot be silent, oblivious, or indifferent.

VIII

The ecumenical community—those churches who are formally part of the ecumenical structures within the movement, and those who are perhaps not formal participants but ecumenical partners nonetheless—has long been concerned with racism, and has likewise long been concerned with aspects of the criminal justice system. These concerns arise from the theological convictions these churches hold regarding the human person and our treatment of one another.

Mass incarceration is the new face of this racism. It links racism as a general sin with the particular sins we visit upon one another through an otherwise legitimate attempt at criminal justice. By highlighting this phenomenon, the ecumenical community is witnessing to justice in the face of injustice. Time will tell if this witness is prophetic.

I would issue a caution here as well. The problem of mass incarceration came about largely with the War on Drugs. We are now also engaged in a War on Terror. Drugs are evil. Terror is evil. But as we contemplate the implications of our self-described wars on these evils, what sins related to religious intolerance might we, as a society, commit against one another—I'm thinking of our Muslim neighbors now—even as we appropriately address the terrorism that has marked the last decade and a half? We've already committed some sins in this regard. Torture and Guantanamo immediately come to mind. Let us not allow the tactics of this War on Terror to continue to take us down a path where we become less than we are, or less than we are called to be, as we have in the War on Drugs.

What makes this more difficult is the extent of the fracture in society. The increasing gap between rich and poor; the growing chasm between immigrant and native; the unprecedented inability to compromise between Democrats and Republicans; the persistent distance between people of different faiths: these contribute to the fracturing of our society. This reality calls for a united witness for justice among Christians, and together with people of other faiths. But more so, it calls for vigilance in the search for Christian unity, so that the gospel of God's reconciliation and salvation we proclaim resonates fully in the hearts and minds of all.

Notes

1. I have referenced these examples based on a consultation sponsored by the National Council of Churches in New York in 2007 that I convened on precisely these acts of violence and the complicity of the churches in them.

2. Gerald H. Anderson, "American Protestants in Pursuit of Mission: 1886–1986," *International Bulletin of Missionary Research* 12, no. 3 (July 1988): 102.

3. David J. Bosch, *Transforming Mission: Paradigm Shifts in Theology of Mission*, 20th anniv. ed. (Maryknoll, NY: Orbis, 2011), 470.

4. From an announcement on June 11, 1963, related to the presence of the Alabama National Guard to implement the desegregation of the University of Alabama. For a transcript of the speech, see John F.

Kennedy, "Report to the American People on Civil Rights," https://www
.jfklibrary.org/Asset-Viewer/LH8F_0Mzv0e6Ro1yEm74Ng.aspx.

5. William Sterling Cary, interview by Michael Martin, "Civil
Rights Leader on Race, Religion and Politics," April 2, 2008, http://www
.npr.org/templates/story/story.php?storyId=89302902.

6. Jack W. Hayford, "Confessing What Separates Us," in *Ending
Racism in the Church*, ed. Susan E. Davies and Sister Paul Teresa Hennessee (Cleveland, OH: United Church Press, 1998), 15.

7. Susan E. Davies and Sister Paul Teresa Hennessee, "Introduction: What is Racism?" in *Ending Racism in the Church*, 1.

8. Leonard Lovett, "Color Lines and the Religion of Racism," in
Ending Racism in the Church, 24–25.

9. Ibid., 25.

10. This is true also for other similar cases that have lamentably
happened in subsequent months and years since the original version of
this paper was delivered.

11. Nicholas Kristof, "When Whites Just Don't Get It," *The New
York Times*, August 30, 2014, https://nyti.ms/2jAE285.

12. Ibid.

13. Kristof, "When Whites Just Don't Get It, Part 2," *The New York
Times*, September 6, 2014, https://nyti.ms/2k1x3lF.

14. Kristof, "When Whites Just Don't Get It, Part 3," *The New
York Times*, October 11, 2014, https://nyti.ms/2kuy4CY.

15. Ibid.

16. Ibid.

17. Jeremy Travis, Bruce Western, and Steve Redburn, eds., *The
Growth of Incarceration in the United States: Exploring Causes and Consequences*, National Research Council of the National Academy of Sciences
(Washington, DC: National Academies Press, 2014), http://www.nap
.edu/catalog/18613/the-growth-of-incarceration-in-the-united-states
-exploring-causes, 2.

18. The Sentencing Project, "Facts about Prison and People in
Prison," January 2014, http://www.sentencingproject.org/publications/
facts-about-prisons-and-people-in-prison/.

19. Travis et al., *Growth of Incarceration*, 2.

20. Michelle Alexander, *The New Jim Crow: Mass Incarceration in
the Age of Colorblindness*, rev. ed. (New York: The New Press, 2012).

21. Ibid., 2.

22. Ibid., 4.

23. Ibid., 7.

24. Ibid., 11.

25. Ibid., 16.

26. Travis et al., *Growth of Incarceration*, 343.

27. From an address delivered at Oberlin College, October 22, 1964. It was echoed in his famous sermon at the Washington National Cathedral on March 31, 1968, in which he questioned the U.S. war in Vietnam. For the version of the quotation in the latter speech, see King, "Remaining Awake Through a Great Revolution," in *A Testament of Hope: The Essential Writings and Speeches of Martin Luther King, Jr.*, ed. James M. Washington (New York: HarperSanFrancisco, 1991), 270.

28. Kristof, "When Whites Just Don't Get It, Part 3."

29. Alexander, *New Jim Crow*, 14.

3

ON INCARCERATION
For the Sake of Our Shared Future

Michael Reid Trice

INTRODUCTION

Do you believe that we can transform the present system of incarceration for the sake of our shared future? On a Thursday in 2001, I sat in a cold, utilitarian room at North Carolina Central Prison, peering through the hard, translucent barrier between myself and the inmate, David Junior Ward. The imprint of David's face was reflected over my own against the barrier due to a strange trick of light refraction and the dimming sun that pierced through a small window behind me and across the room. I had to look directly through his face, superimposed over mine against the glass, to see David's eyes on the other side. It was a restless way to end the afternoon, with David just hours from his execution on Friday, October 13th, and the public tensions hanging heavy in the country, only one month after the 9/11 attacks.

That afternoon, David and I spoke of his daughter, who desired to be a doctor and a ballerina, of his fear of hell, and of Michael Jordan, nearly in that order. David's fear of hell was palpable, with his description of the "little red man" spoken in somber tones. Recently graduated with my second master's degree in theology, my listening was shrouded in inexperience. At first, faced with the certain execution of a client and a friend only hours away, I could feel the lump in my larynx. "How did I get through seminary without an education in the churches' moral stance on the tentacled system of incarceration in this country?" I thought.

David's dread of hell was something like Anna Mercedes's interpretation of personal formlessness in the face of an execution;

his was a dread over social and familial death too.[1] In David's mind, death was an uncrossable separation from his daughter and living his last hours with hell as a specific, final incarceration, locked away and alone. David was a disaffected, dissolute crest of silence in the pain of these moments. There was no persuading him otherwise. And then, out of my mouth came these words: "David, when you get to hell make sure to save me a place right next to you." That slowed his mind. "What?" His head lifted. "Why?" That was a good question. As Christians, we trust the infusion of the Spirit, as that pneumatological moment where the light we cannot conjure by ourselves breaks into a painful place and illuminates it. "Because," I continued, "Scripture tells us that where two or three are gathered we are never separated from the love of God. So... you save a place right there next to you. And where we are, God will be there too."

David leaned back in his chair, staring at me through the refraction as I searched to find the pupils of his eyes. "But David," I said, "when you get to heaven, do me a favor, do us all a favor. We need it. When you speak with God, tell him that we need help here, all of us, and to send us that help. Can you do that?" After a moment, the vertebrae in David's back straightened. "I can do that." He coughed. His demeanor elevated slightly. David held onto what connected him to the land of the living, to his daughter, and to a hope far beyond the final act of capital incarceration in death. Hope spoken in these moments has the power to transcend finality. I can still see that light in David's face, even clearer now. Hours later he was gone.

This is a story of humanizing the incarcerated and of seeing through societal death to the hope for the living. The church has a role in assisting society to peer beyond societal convention and ambivalence to witness the humanity within the incarcerated in the United States. The United States is burdened with at least two mortal sins. One of these is our denial of the liberty of others within incarcerated communities. And yet, Christian liberty preexists the nation-state; indeed, freedom is the Judeo-Christian bedrock upon which the moral imperatives to love and be loved are moored. Cherishing the liberty of others is the ground of love itself because loving the other begins in experiencing human otherness in the neighbor, as an inviolable portion of God's image; impenetrable, unassailable, and to be cherished. From that existential floor only, our earliest texts beckon us to care for the widow and orphan, for the sick, for the homeless and dispossessed, and for the imprisoned. Cherishing human liberty is a barometer for the health of the kingdom of God on earth.[2]

And yet our responsibility to cherish liberty is often eclipsed by a public belief that incarceration in the United States is a reasonable feature of contemporary life. Nothing in our society is farther from the truth.[3] In fact, the restriction of the liberty of U.S. citizens is more often in contradiction with the Supreme Court's Eighth Amendment juridical positions, which prohibit cruel and unusual punishment. In brief, the severity of punishment must not degrade human dignity, as the rulings prove time and again. But punishment in the incarceration system in the United States does degrade human dignity, which is the factual lodestone of this essay.

The first part of this essay aims to untangle the aforenoted public perception of incarceration with an emphasis upon the best and most recent interdisciplinary assessment of the penal system in the United States to date. Second, I will summarize how the Christian churches have responded to the system of incarceration in the United States, particularly in the past forty years, yet with attention to the last ten. And third, the essay will assess the normative principles that shape the churches' responses to prison policy reform, and incarceration broadly, in the present. With a view to the future, this essay will conclude with a way forward in the churches as a response to the challenges of incarceration.

PART ONE—THE GROWTH OF INCARCERATION IN THE UNITED STATES

In 2014, the most comprehensive study to date was completed on the rate of incarceration growth in the United States; the study was convened by the National Research Council (NRC) of the National Academies. The NRC was first organized in 1916 with the responsibility for advising the U.S. public and the federal government on matters of national interest. Advisors in the study included criminologists, sociologists, political science experts, and additional relevant, cross-disciplinary experts. Two separate and independent committees were convened for the study. These included The Committee on Causes and Consequences of High Rates of Incarceration and The Committee on Law and Justice. I discern three notable points relevant to our analysis of the rise of incarceration rates within the United States.

First, between 1973 and 2009, both state and federal prison populations rose from around 200,000 to 1.5 million, not including 700,000 individuals held daily in local jails across the country.[4] Taken together, the United States penal population as of 2012 is the largest in the world, with over 2.23 million people imprisoned; in global quantitative terms, approximately 25 percent of the world's prisoners are imprisoned in the United States, even as the U.S. accounts for only 5 percent of the global population.[5] In domestic quantitative terms, 1 in every 100 adults in the United States is in prison or in jail.[6] Consider this growth when current homicide rates, motor vehicle theft, and burglary rates are the lowest since the mid-1960s, even as imprisonment at the federal and state levels has grown.[7] And percentages of incarceration have grown exponentially: in 1973, approximately 161 residents per 100,000 in the general population were in prison; today, over 707 people are incarcerated for every 100,000 in the general population.[8]

A second point pertaining to the rise of incarceration rates in the past forty years involves two trends. The first trend is a multidecade enterprise of criminal justice policy reform that is focused on a retributivist philosophy for managing the consequences of illegal activity in the United States.[9] At its core are successive U.S. presidential administrations, beginning with the Johnson administration, which committed themselves to a "War on Crime" (or a corollary "War on Drugs"). These successive retributivist wars take place amid a second trend: the national rise and concentration of socioeconomic zones of opportunity exclusion, with an emphasis on urban areas that discriminate (not exclusively and yet determinatively) on the grounds of race and ethnicity in this country.[10]

These two trends are caught in each other's gravitational pull, whereby an increasingly punitive political context pursues criminal justice policy reform, even as the citizenry most affected by this policy reform are residents living in poor or minority communities, particularly in urban areas predisposed to socioeconomic disadvantages, and overwhelmingly within African American and Latino communities in the United States.[11] A sobering result of these two trends is poverty, whereby "those sent to prison tend to come from the poorest, most violent, and segregated communities, and imprisonment tends to leave them even more likely to remain poor, unemployed, and socially isolated."[12]

These trends are not new information to the churches. What is new is how a recent national study of this depth and clarity is evidentially and factually based and confirms the brokenness of the incarceration system in this country. Of equal importance to the future, this study breaks through a popular deniability hypothesis in which the first trend is seen to be caused by the second. We see dark skin everywhere. And because we do, the public assumes that issues around race (second trend) justify the retributivist policies of incarceration (first trend) today.[13] But correlation is not the same as causation, and race is not a cause for prisons. Yet by assuming causation, society faces a moral dilemma in the conflation of race to structural racism in incarceration within the United States.

Third, the study warns of the unassailable ditch along racial lines between full citizens and partial citizens, or "internal exiles."[14] The consequences of this broad ditch "pose a significant risk to achievement of the nation's aspirations for democratic self-government and social and racial justice."[15] A free and democratic society cannot rationalize a racist incarceration complex without undermining the core principles, ideals, and values that shape western democracy itself, beginning and ending with the liberty of an active citizenry.[16] When values are undermined on the backs of its own citizenry, and in the name of protecting democracy for the citizenry in general terms, this is a perfect storm for western democracy.

And finally, the study concludes by appealing to future discussion on incarceration in the United States that identifies the clear, self-evident normative principles for shaping state and federal incarceration policies and practices in the United States. It is the case that the Christian normative principles regarding incarceration are evident in the statements and activities of the churches in this land. Identifying these normative principles is helpful in declaring the way forward into this collective future.

34

PART TWO—THE CHRISTIAN RESPONSE TO INCARCERATION IN THE UNITED STATES

Taken together, the churches within the United States do have transparent normative principles pertaining to incarceration in this country. Decades prior to, and now inclusive of, the 2014 study, the churches have identified the failings of the U.S. system of incarceration and have declared a viable way for addressing these failings. Statements were consulted from organized Christian responses in the United States, including from Christian Churches Together, the National Council of Churches of Christ, the United States Conference of Catholic Bishops, and the National Association of Evangelicals; likewise, statements from individual communities of faith were also consulted, ranging from the Evangelical Lutheran Church in America to the National Baptist Convention.

Of immediate notable distinction within these agencies and churches is their differentiated starting points on incarceration. Whereas the National Association of Evangelicals focused in 2013 and 2014 on sentencing alternatives for punishment of nonviolent crimes and capital punishment, the Orthodox Church in America emphasized effective prison ministry from the local parish context. The Alliance of Baptists called for a halt to the criminalization of race (2014), focusing on the "lower caste of individuals" being people of color already on the margins of society.[17] These statements overwhelmingly rejected the privatization of the criminal industrial complex and resoundingly supported a decrease in sentencing for drug-related charges following the War on Drugs (as a war ranging from the U.S. presidential administrations of Reagan to Clinton).

Some ecclesial or church-related responses are more helpful than others for discerning the normative principles that address incarceration, such as the insightful response by Christian Churches Together to Dr. King's "Letter from Birmingham Jail," and the challenge of bringing injustice to light.[18] Other approaches are less helpful, for instance in pronouncing that "mass incarceration must stop!" and yet no strategic process is fitted for the reform its drafters have in mind.[19]

Two of the church responses that identify normative principles for defining the future of prison policy reform are found in the

National Council of Churches of Christ's *Social Creed for the 21st Century* (2007) and within the statement and report of the United States Conference of Catholic Bishops (USCCB) titled *Responsibility, Rehabilitation, and Restoration: A Catholic Perspective on Crime and Criminal Justice* (2000), and likewise *Criminal and Restorative Justice* (February 2014). Both documents predate the study of the National Research Council by seven to ten years, and provide clear normative principles that the report calls for; they likewise serve as ample evidence of the broad Christian response to the challenges of incarceration today.

PART THREE—SEEKING NORMATIVE PRINCIPLES

Liberty of the Person: First, the *Social Creed* begins with the liberty or "dignity of every person" and their "intrinsic value"[20] within society, whereas the USCCB report on *Criminal and Restorative Justice* directs the reader to Pope Francis's statement of affirmation that none are outside of the sustaining love of God—"No cell is so isolated as to exclude the Lord."[21] Both of these attest to the liberty of the person as essential and unfalsifiable.

For Christians, the first normative principle of human liberty begins with the freedom of the subjective individual before God.[22] In fact, God's restoring of human freedom in Christ is the simplest expression of a two-millennium midrash on this theme. Every act thereafter involves human generosity as a response to freedom. Themes of restoration of freedom are the only viable Christian responses to prison reform. Retributivist policy contradicts the gospel;[23] Christians, from Mennonites to Orthodox, experienced centuries of oppression. The theologies and principles of societal formation that arose in these experiences inform a theological response to imprisonment by placing liberty first.

Mercy is the First-Order Virtue: Next, some of the most fruitful current discourse on liberty before God begins in Christian reflections on the public virtue of mercy. Mercy is the first public virtue that arrives in recognition of mutual human liberty, grounded on Scripture and Jesus' moral imperative to "go and learn what this means, 'I desire mercy, not sacrifice'" (Matt 9:13).[24] For Christian self-understanding, mercy is a virtue rooted in a singular form of generous agency between human beings toward one another, and in response to the first creative act of God who brings life into the world.[25] As a first-order virtue in society, it is not surprising to see Latin American Catholic Liberationist theologian Jon Sobrino or Evangelical popular theologian Ron Sider both writing about the filaments of generosity and mercy that begin with human dignity and that are essential to overcoming the diversity of humanity's ills.[26]

Christian statements on incarceration begin with liberty and then seek the virtue of mercy and its capacity for unprecedented restraint in the world. For Christians, mercy is not equal to permissibility as a form of immediate clemency and requisite amnesia of past trespass. Rather, mercy is a vanguard public principle that seeks restoration over retribution as an end.[27] Rooted in Christian consciousness from Jesus' teaching and elevated in Medieval theology is the truism, commonly attributed to Aquinas, that "mercy without justice is the mother of dissolution; justice without mercy is cruelty." Too much cruelty and lack of mercy poisons society at the root of liberty.[28]

Actionable Witness: Every Christian act is a witness of freedom and mercy. At the Christian best, our valuation of neighbors and strangers, our estimation of ourselves, and our care for the society in which we coexist alongside others, requires faith active in love for the world.[29] All the churches in the United States that responded to incarceration in the past few years do so through the aspirational hope in Christ that aims for healing, restoration, and new life within community or society.[30]

In terms of actionable witness, experts in the NRC study were specific about the four principles that must shape any future public effort to reform the prison system in the United States. These four principles are proportionality, parsimony, citizenship, and social justice. In brief, proportionality refers to sentencing and confinement in both proportion of the offense and the necessary goals for achieving aims of sentencing; parsimony is a term used in early jurisprudence (1830), still salient today, that acts as a restraint on punishment that otherwise succumbs to a public sentiment of retributivism. Parsimony reminds society that limiting retributivism can advance the public welfare where otherwise crime flourishes as justice institutions falter.[31] Aligned to these first two principles (proportionality and parsimony), two more principles are recommended to the nation. These are citizenship and social justice. Citizenship as a principle reminds a nation not to violate one's status as a citizen of society. And, the last principle, social justice, aims to promote society's aspirations for fairness in the distribution of rights, resources, and opportunity.[32]

A future response to incarceration in the United States benefits when the statements of the churches are aligned to the findings of the NRC study. Consider the following alignments, which are evident in the statements of the churches. First, the Christian appeal to a liberated conscience has a corollary relationship with the human subject not unjustly constrained within society. Second, the invocation to mercy that prohibits revenge can be correlated with the appeal to parsimony, which seeks restraint and restoration as a benefit to social well-being; third, Christian servanthood as one's self given freely for others can be correlated to the public service anticipated by an active citizenry. Taken together, the beneficial correlation between freedom and liberty, mercy and parsimony, and servanthood and service, will be necessary for the successful revisioning of incarceration in the United States.

Consider the contours for an activist faith in the future where churches in the United States cooperate out of a gospel-based conviction to unity, whereby they publicly endeavor to reconfigure the current system of incarceration as a condition for a shared future.[33] Imagine that, from a place of unity, these churches designed, operationalized, and orchestrated an integrated response to incarceration that was tailored to their shared, aforenoted key normative principles, and that was aligned to the findings of the NRC study, as the most comprehensive of its kind in U.S. history.

The best of our communities—from local to national—and from every conceivably useful profession, may gather from local municipalities to state and national corridors of power, toward a multiyear effort to force a bipartisan reconstruction of the current system of incarceration in society, which, by wide agreement on all reasonable and professional accounts, is institutionally bloated, ill-conceived for the twenty-first century, and unmoored from transparent operational normative principles. In specialized and differentiated yet congruent efforts, the Christian churches call for a national discernment toward change on matters of crime prevention, rehabilitation, education, substance abuse treatment, probation programs, parole and reintegration, smarter sentencing, privatization of prisons, reentry programs, racial discrimination, the general overuse of the prison system, and more. In so doing, Christians in the United States, working within additional evolving religious and political partnerships, could be finally able together to turn a corner on race and structural racism so intertwined in incarceration practices. Indeed, we discover that by reconstructing incarceration together, numerous societal conflagrations and ills come within our capacity to address more fully.

CONCLUSION

Is it possible to disentangle incarceration from race? No, I don't believe so. As a case in point, when I shared the narrative of David Junior Ward at the start of this essay, and explained in some detail the Thursday afternoon when his face was transferred atop mine on the translucent barrier, what was the color of the face you saw in your mind's eye? Was it a black face? Societal conditioning often prescribes color to us, even as I never wrote that David was an African American.

David was a tall, imposing African American man. That's true. And, it was clear that his race was a directly relevant circumstance at his trial, particularly during the sentencing phase, which contributed to his receiving the death penalty.

I am convinced that our only viable future pertaining to incarceration reform is to disentangle its reconceptualization from race and structural racism first. That may seem an insurmountable effort to the reader; and yet, the alternatives for not addressing race and structural racism in the United States, and the consequential conflation of race in incarceration reform, are simply and unassailably dire. We must see this reform for what it is—a societal reconfiguration. This essay is committed to aligning principles from the best resources of our moment, returning us again to our starting sentence: Do you believe that we can transform the present system of incarceration for the sake of our shared future?

Notes

1. Anna Mercedes, "Who Are You? Christ and the Imperative of Subjectivity," in *Transformative Lutheran Theologies: Feminist, Womanist, and Mujerista Perspectives*, ed. Mary J. Streufert (Minneapolis: Fortress Press, 2010), 87–95.

2. The best most recent scholarship I've read on the connection between love and justice, or *agapism*, comes from Nicholas Wolterstorff, *Justice in Love* (Grand Rapids, MI: Eerdmans, 2015), esp. 75–92.

3. Jeremy Travis, Bruce Western, and Steve Redburn, eds., *The Growth of Incarceration in the United States: Exploring Causes and Consequences* (Washington, DC: The National Academies Press, 2014), 33.

4. Ibid.

5. Ibid., 36.

6. Ibid., 13.

7. The study does clarify the more recent dip in state prisons in the past twenty years.

8. Travis et al., *Growth of Incarceration*, 27, 34, 70–129. Chapters 3 and 4 assess the policies and practices that contribute to high rates of incarceration, including the underlying causes of rising incarceration, relative to crime, politics, and social change.

9. Howard Zehr, "Retributive Justice, Restorative Justice," in *A Restorative Justice Reader: Texts, Sources, Context*, ed. Gerry Johnstone (Portland, OR: Willan Publishing, 2003), 69–82. Zehr provides an intelligent analysis and useful diagrams for assessing the current retributivist justice system in the United States alongside a potential restorative justice alternative.

10. Travis et al., *Growth of Incarceration*, 104–29.

11. Ibid., 31.

12. Ibid., 339. See also Michelle Alexander, *The New Jim Crow: Mass Incarceration in the Age of Colorblindness* (New York: The New Press, 2012), 140–77. Alexander's narrative rehumanizes the fight to reclaim a life, family, and community after prison.

13. Alexander, *New Jim Crow*, 185–90. From the War on Drugs to incarceration and color, this section demonstrates "how it works."

14. Travis et al., *Growth of Incarceration*, 318.

15. Ibid., 104–29, 281–302, and 318. For evidence of these societal trends, I encourage the reader to consult chapters 4 and 10 of the study.

16. I recommend reading Mark Lewis Taylor's *The Executed God: The Way of the Cross in Lockdown America* (Minneapolis: Fortress Press, 2001), 48–67. What the NRC terms "internal exiles" delivers on

a prominent theme for public theologians: permanent margination of the post-citizen.

17. Alliance of Baptists, 2014 Statement on Mass Incarceration, http://allianceofbaptists.org/documents/2014-Statement-on-Mass-Incarceration_mar_2014.pdf.

18. Christian Churches Together: "CCT's Response to Dr. King's Letter from Birmingham Jail," 2011, http://christianchurchestogether .org/letter-from-birmingham-jail/.

19. 2014 Mass Incarceration Press Release: "National Christian Leaders Oppose Mass Incarceration," http://christianchurchestogether .org/2014-mass-incarceration-press-release/.

20. National Council of Churches of Christ, *A 21st Century Social Creed*, (2007), http://ncccusa.org/news/ga2007.socialcreed.html.

21. United States Conference of Catholic Bishops, *Criminal and Restorative Justice* (February 2014), http://www.usccb.org/issues-and -action/human-life-and-dignity/criminal-justice-restorative-justice/ index.cfm.

22. The Christian self-understanding of liberty is reliant upon the individual not only within society, but for the Christian actor, as one within the greater kingdom of God. Ethics is a responsiveness and activity within that kingdom, which includes but is not exhausted by the church. For a primer on this, see Stanley Hauerwas, *The Peaceable Kingdom* (Notre Dame, IN: University of Notre Dame Press, 1983), 96–102.

23. Christian freedom and individual liberty in the eyes of a nation-state are not identical, even if they are not fully semiotically distinct. It is essential to do a critical reading whenever conversing on this topic. An excellent start is Han Joas, *The Sacredness of the Person: A New Genealogy of Human Rights* (Washington, DC: Georgetown University Press, 2013) in particular, 140–72.

24. Walter Kasper, *Mercy: The Essence of the Gospel and the Key to Christian Life* (Mahwah, NJ: Paulist Press, 2013).

25. *Misericordiae Vultus*, the Bull of Indiction of the Extraordinary Jubilee of Mercy, 2015, 1–5.

26. Jon Sobrino, *The Principle of Mercy: Taking the Crucified People from the Cross* (Maryknoll, NY: Orbis Books, 1994); Ronald J. Sider, *Just Generosity: A New Vision for Overcoming Poverty in America* (Grand Rapids, MI: Baker Books, 1999).

27. For greater awareness of a restorationist approach to incarceration, I recommend beginning with Gerry Johnstone, ed., *A Restorative Justice Reader: Texts, Sources, Context* (Portland, OR: Willan Publishing, 2003), from variations to rationales and models, in 245–352.

28. Michael Reid Trice, *Encountering Cruelty: The Fracture of the Human Heart* (Boston: Brill, 2011), 315.

29. Much is written in the past twenty years particular to peoples' movements and countering state terrorism; some models are more effective than others. Prior to advocacy, people of faith must locate their political voice around whether and how a new prison paradigm can be constructed. Read Laura Magnani and Harmon L. Wray, *Beyond Prisons: A New Interfaith Paradigm for Our Failed Prison System* (Minneapolis: Fortress Press, 2006), 159–87.

30. In the United States, John Adams's inclusivist vision of cooperation between civic and religious leadership endured until post World War II; thereafter, the emergence of Jeffersonian separatism reveals the history of the uncertain relationship between government and religion. Knowing this history assists in how the churches continue to work with government on matters of incarceration. See John Witte Jr., *God's Joust, God's Justice: Law and Religion in the Western Tradition* (Grand Rapids, MI: Eerdmans, 2006), 243–62.

31. Travis et al., *Growth of Incarceration*, 327.

32. Ibid., 320–33.

33. Charles Marsh, *The Beloved Community: How Faith Shapes Social Justice, From the Civil Rights Movement to Today* (New York: Basic Books, 2005), 207–16. I owe much to this section of Marsh's work: "The pursuit of beloved community is not finally about the redemption of America's soul, nor even about the achievement of interracial community. To the Christians in our story, it is rather about bearing witness to the Prince of peace in a violent and suffering world" (207).

4

WHITE SUPREMACY AND THE CHURCH

How White Christians Created and Perpetuate the Ideology of White Supremacy

Douglas A. Foster

> Since, then, we have such hope, we act with great bold-
> ness, not like Moses, who put a veil over his face to keep
> the people of Israel from gazing at the end of the glory
> that was being set aside. But their minds were hardened.
> Indeed, to this very day, when they hear the reading of
> the old covenant, that same veil is still there, since only in
> Christ is it set aside…but when one turns to the Lord, the
> veil is removed. Now the Lord is the Spirit, and where
> the Spirit of the Lord is, there is freedom. And all of us,
> with unveiled faces, seeing the glory of the Lord as though
> reflected in a mirror, are being transformed into the same
> image from one degree of glory to another; for this comes
> from the Lord, the Spirit. (2 Corinthians 3:12–18)

Two points strike me from this passage. The first is that even people of God can be kept from a full comprehension of the gospel—to
have, figuratively speaking, a veil over their understanding. The
second is, that though the veil that clouds our vision is taken off
in Christ, it does not happen all at once. Christians are in a process
of being transformed into the image of Christ "from one degree of
glory to another." Little by little, as Christ removes whatever veils
cloud our understanding, we come to see things as they are.

This study has as its aim "removing the veil" obscuring the truth about the white church's role in the creation and perpetuation of the ideology of white supremacy. There is no pretension that this can be fully accomplished in one essay. With the power of God's Spirit, however, perhaps the process may be begun or furthered. This paper is not intended to stir up white guilt or incite anger among persons of color.[1] Though guilt warns us when we violate God's nature, we can alleviate it by superficial action and avoidance. And while righteous anger can stir action against evil, anger is too easily subverted to vicious and destructive hatred.

The intention here is to confront *Christians* with the role of the white church in creating an ideology contrary to the nature of God and the purpose of the gospel. It is to describe the suffering inflicted on peoples deemed unworthy of the rights and freedoms of the "superior" race. It is to push white Christians to view and embrace all people the way God embraces us—the God who has made of one blood all races of people, and is no respecter of persons.

White supremacist ideology is evil and destructive at both the individual and corporate levels. The struggle "is not against enemies of blood and flesh, but against the rulers, against the authorities, against the cosmic powers of this present darkness, against the spiritual forces of evil in the heavenly places" (Eph 6:12). It is not possible to prevail against such powers with mere education or moral entreaties. Sin is vanquished only by the power of God's Holy Spirit. May these words enlighten us, but more importantly humble us, to allow God to use us in bringing in the kingdom "on earth as it is in heaven."

INTRODUCTION: THE IDEOLOGY OF WHITE SUPREMACY

The story of the creation of white supremacist ideology is astounding and largely unknown, one that, in the words of Charles W. Mills in his 1997 book *The Racial Contract*, has largely written itself out of existence.[2] Yet the data is abundant and overwhelming.

The study is divided into three periods: (1) from the colonial and early national periods through the Civil War (when slavery was white supremacy's chief embodiment), (2) from Reconstruction to the civil rights movement (when the ideology was embodied in Jim Crow laws and practices in every part of the United States[3]), and (3) from the civil rights movement to the present (when white supremacy moved underground, operating mostly at subliminal levels and denied until resurfacing toward the end of the Obama administration).

In the words of theologian James Cone, "It is a sad fact that the white church's involvement in slavery and racism in America simply cannot be overstated. It not only failed to preach the kerygmatic word, but maliciously contributed to the doctrine of white supremacy....Racism has been part of the life of the Church so long that it is virtually impossible for even the 'good' members to recognize the bigotry perpetrated by the Church."[4]

Cone speaks from experience and from history partly documented in this paper. It is important to be clear, however, about what the study is *not* saying. It does not claim that no white Christian leaders have been allies of black citizens in causes like antislavery, antilynching, civil rights, and mass incarceration. Drick Boyd's November 2015 book, *White Allies in the Struggle for Racial Justice*, for example, catalogs powerful stories of white Americans who joined their black sisters and brothers to fight for racial equality.[5] Nor can we ignore initiatives for racial justice and unity undertaken by predominately white churches such as the Presbyterian Church, USA, the United Church of Christ, the Evangelical Lutheran Church in America, the Christian Church (Disciples of Christ), and the Mennonite Central Committee. The National Council of Churches in the USA has long championed antiracism and equality for all. None of these ongoing efforts is inconsequential.

Yet despite the work of some white Christian leaders and members, the racial divide not only still exists, it has worsened. In the words of Daniel Little, philosopher of social science and Chancellor of the University of Michigan—Dearborn:

> Pick almost any category where you'd rather have more than less—income, health status, property and home ownership, likelihood of having health insurance, life expectancy, or likelihood of having a favorable outcome

in the criminal justice system. In all of these categories there is a wide gap between black and white Americans. And this remains true even when we control for income—the health gap between white and black Americans earning more than $80,000 remains significant. So America has embedded a set of economic and social institutions that reproduce racial disadvantage. America remains a deeply racialized society.[6]

The question remains: If, in fact, the white church was fundamentally committed to doing whatever it takes to eradicate white supremacy, why does it remain very much in place?

I. THE CREATION AND IMPLEMENTATION OF THE IDEOLOGY OF WHITE SUPREMACY BY WHITE CHRISTIANS IN THE COLONIAL AND EARLY NATIONAL PERIODS THROUGH THE AMERICAN CIVIL WAR

White supremacy did not originate in North America.[7] The Europeans who colonized North America brought the idea.[8] Early contact between white Europeans (particularly English) and dark-skinned persons of Africa evoked emotions of contrast. "White and black connoted purity and filthiness, virginity and sin, virtue and baseness, beauty and ugliness, beneficence and evil, God and the Devil."[9] Explanations for the darkness of the Africans' skin varied from geographical and natural to a curse of God. The so-called "curse of Ham"[10] as an explanation for blackness was feeble at best. Yet the idea among whites that blackness must be a curse persisted, and this scriptural explanation seemed to justify the idea for many.[11]

Furthermore, the vast differences between "Christian" white English and "pagan" black Africans and Native Americans solidified the assumption of white supremacy. They were defective in their religion—heathens that inherently contradicted Christianity. They were savages—uncivilized in dress, language, government, and morals. Whites came to equate savagery with blackness. Early

British colonists seem to have viewed Native Americans as more "culpable" for their savagery than Africans because they were not so different in appearance from Europeans.[12] The equating of apes and black people in the minds of the English, and attributing beast-like sexual behavior to blacks and Native Americans deepened assumptions of white supremacy, notions that have morphed but have seldom been identified and challenged. All were based on white Christian assumptions that defined whiteness as good and blackness as evil and to be feared.[13] Colonial laws toward Native Americans restricted their movement and access to land in ways that disregarded their culture and assumptions about land use. The laws often showed utter disregard for the value of Native American lives.[14]

The fundamental assumption of white supremacy by the European colonizers shaped the nature of forced labor (slavery) in North America. The language of slave laws reflected European Christian belief. For example:

> Virginia Law 1662: If any Christian shall commit forni-cation with a negro man or woman, he or she so offend-ing shall pay double the fines imposed by the former act (for aiding a runaway slave).

> Virginia Law 1680: If any negro or other slave shall pre-sume or lift up his hand in opposition against any Chris-tian, shall for every such offence, upon due proof made thereof by the oath of the party before a magistrate, have and receive thirty lashes on his bare back well laid on.[15]

The laws equated *negro* and *slave*, and contrast *negro* with *Christian*. The language, reflecting white assumptions of black sav-agery, implicitly raised the question of whether slaves who become Christians were still slaves. The answer, codified in a 1667 Virginia law, was that "baptism does not alter the condition of the person as to his bondage or freedom."[16] As white fear increased with the growth of the black population of North America, legal codes began to place a growing set of restrictions on all blacks—slave or free. In 1723, for example, the Virginia House of Burgesses passed laws denying the right to vote to free blacks and forbidding them to carry weapons. A 1732 statute stated that though some negroes and Native Americans who professed Christianity had been allowed to testify as lawful witnesses, they were "people of such base and corrupt natures, that their testimony cannot be depended upon." They were therefore denied the right to be witnesses in trials except in capital cases involving a slave.[17]

White Christian understandings in the 1800s viewed black Africans as assigned to slavery by God. Since the enslavement of blacks was the divine order, we must not change it. Once accepted, the position required scriptural justification. One often used proof text was Genesis 9:20–27, mentioned above, called the "Curse of Ham." When Noah's son Ham failed to cover his drunken father's nakedness, Noah cursed Ham's son Canaan and his lineages to be servants of the other brothers and their descendants. White scriptural interpreters discerned from descriptions of the dissemination of Noah's family that the descendants of Ham had gone to Africa. Descriptions of Old Testament patriarchs as slaveholders and New Testament admonitions to slaves to obey their masters seemed clear to whites. The Scriptures never condemned slavery; rather they assumed it, blessed it, and regulated it. Anyone who believed Scripture would do the same.

Perhaps even more striking is the clear evidence that even white Christians who opposed slavery almost without exception operated out of deep-seated white supremacist beliefs. Thomas Jefferson, while not a traditional Christian, reflects the attitude of most white Christian antislavery leaders. While slavery was evil, it was because it created destructive attitudes of dependency and dominance among white citizens charged with ruling the country—not because it was a moral sin to hold human beings in bondage.[18] He opposed government imposed uncompensated abolition and strongly believed that black inferiority precluded blacks and whites from ever living together on equal footing. He held that if and when blacks were emancipated, they would have to be expelled from the country.[19]

Alexander Campbell provides an example of a prominent white American Christian leader who held Jeffersonian ideas of race. Leader of the reform movement that produced Disciples of Christ, Churches of Christ, and Christian Churches, Campbell insisted, like Jefferson, that slavery was an evil that impeded the progress of the nation and of his own religious reforms. Yet he was clear that he believed white citizens were the ones being harmed:

> Much as I may sympathize with a black man, I love the white man more. As a political economist, and as a philanthropist, I have many reasons for preferring the prospects and conditions of the Free to the Slave states; but especially as a Christian, I sympathize much more with the owners of slaves, their heirs, and successors, than with the slaves which they possess and bequeath.[20]

Black abolitionists like Frederick Douglass despaired over the lack of white Christian commitment to end slavery and the gross racial inequality in every part of the country. He increasingly questioned his commitment to Christianity as he realized the role of the white church—even of his fellow antislavery lecturers who refused to eat with him at meals—in the preservation of slavery and white supremacy.[21] Asked to speak in Rochester, New York, on July 5, 1852, on "The Meaning of the Fourth of July to the Negro," Douglass expressed his deep hostility toward white Christianity's failure:

> The church of this country is not only indifferent to the wrongs of the slave, it actually takes sides with the oppressors. Many of its most eloquent Divines,...have shamelessly given the sanction of religion and the Bible to the whole slave system. They have taught that man may, properly, be a slave; that the relation of master and slave is ordained of God;...and this horrible blasphemy is palmed off upon the world for Christianity. For my part, I would say, welcome infidelity! welcome atheism! welcome anything! in preference to the gospel, as preached by those Divines!...The sin of which [the American church] is guilty is one of omission as well as of commission.[22]

Pervasive images in popular culture depicted blacks as ugly, violent, servile, and of low intelligence. The film *Ethnic Notions* documents how white America created images of black people as docile, loyal, and simple (the mammy and uncle), incapable of self-direction (pickaninny and Sambo), childishly entertaining or viciously brutal (coon and black brute). These images saturated American culture and continue to in many ways.[23] Such depictions became common features in popular culture—including in church papers of predominantly white denominations—well into the twentieth century, and continue to appear in more subtle ways today.[24]

The nation's most complete articulation of the dogma of white supremacy, however, is embedded in the 1857 Supreme Court ruling known as the Dred Scott decision. Politically the ruling effectively declared the Missouri Compromise of 1820 to be unconstitutional, thereby eliminating the existence of "free states." Historians and legal scholars almost universally regard the decision as one of the worst in the history of the Supreme Court because of its twisted logic and poor interpretation of the Constitution.[25]

The document's most far-reaching significance, however, is its articulation and codification of the myth of white supremacy at the highest levels of power in the nation. While scholars have vilified the defective political, legal, and constitutional aspects of the decision, the document's ideology of white supremacy, upon which the nation's founders and its subsequent leaders had always operated, continues to function:

> [The negro African race] had for more than a century before [the Declaration of Independence] been regarded as beings of an inferior order, and altogether unfit to associate with the white race, either in social or political relations; and so far inferior, that they had no rights which the white man was bound to respect; and that the negro might justly and lawfully be reduced to slavery for his benefit....
>
> The men who framed [the] [D]eclaration [of Independence] were great men—high in literary acquirements—high in their sense of honor....They perfectly understood the meaning of the language they used (that is, "All men are created equal"), and how it would be understood by others; and they knew that it would not in any part of the civilized world be supposed to embrace the negro

50

race, which by common consent, had been excluded from civilized Governments and the family of nations, and doomed to slavery.[26]

Every one of the justices who produced the decision identified as a practicing Christian. Among the majority were Roger B. Taney (Chief Justice), Roman Catholic; James Moore Wayne, Episcopalian; John Catron, Presbyterian; Peter Vivian Daniel, Episcopalian; Samuel Nelson, Episcopalian; Robert Cooper Grier, Presbyterian; and John Archibald Campbell, Episcopalian.[27]

The Civil War resulted in the abolition of slavery, which had been the chief embodiment of white supremacy. Yet Congress hotly contested passage of the Thirteenth Amendment to end the institution. The amendment failed in the House of Representatives on the first vote on June 14, 1864, opposed entirely by Northern congressmen—the Southern states were not present.[28] Though it finally passed the House seven months later and was sent to the states for ratification, its success was based on the argument that the action would be the final blow to the Confederacy and end the war more rapidly. Though some maintained the evil of slavery, the arguments for abolishing it overwhelmingly assumed black inferiority and its harm to white society.[29]

Much has been written to vilify or praise Abraham Lincoln as both white supremacist and believer in equality of the races. He seems, however, consistent in his belief that blacks and whites could never live together as equals. In his fourth debate with Stephen A. Douglas on September 18, 1858, for example, he was clear:

> I am not, nor ever have been, in favor of bringing about in any way the social and political equality of the white and black races, that I am not nor ever have been in favor of making voters or jurors of negroes, nor of qualifying them to hold office, nor to intermarry with white people; and I will say in addition to this that there is a physical difference between the white and black races which I believe will forever forbid the two races living together on terms of social and political equality. And inasmuch as they cannot so live, while they do remain together there must be the position of superior and inferior, and I as much as any

51

other man am in favor of having the superior position assigned to the white race.[30]

Some contend that Lincoln changed his mind during the war. Yet during his presidency, he engaged in serious efforts to arrange for transport of freed blacks out of the country. In June 1863, after the Emancipation Proclamation in January, he conducted secret negotiations to transport emancipated slaves to British Honduras (Belize). Recently discovered evidence shows this to be only one part of a "colonization" effort to remove formerly enslaved blacks to the British West Indies. During the Civil War, Lincoln apparently used the promise of black colonization as a political maneuver to appease congressional leaders who opposed abolition. Yet these efforts and his views of the impossibility of blacks and whites living together on equal footing reflected the white conviction that removal of blacks from the nation was necessary for its survival.[31]

II. THE RECONFIGURATION OF THE IDEOLOGY OF WHITE SUPREMACY BY WHITE CHRISTIANS IN AMERICA FROM RECONSTRUCTION TO THE CIVIL RIGHTS MOVEMENT

The high hopes of the formerly enslaved Africans for "equalization"—full citizenship and equal rights before the law— were not without reason. Slavery as an institution was now abolished. The rhetoric of radical Republicans gave blacks a sense of anticipation of true equality. Yet white citizens in both the North and South, including most Republican leaders, viewed as absurd the notion that the formerly enslaved people would be allowed to participate equally with whites in the governance of the nation.[32]

J. M. Sturtevant, president of Illinois College at Jacksonville and congregational minister, reflected the attitude in an 1863 article titled "The Destiny of the African Race in the United States." "The negro is, to a large extent, a barbarian in the midst of civilization," he asserted. Emancipation would be a disaster. The English colonies had prospered in contrast to those established by the Spanish, French, and Portuguese because the English had refused to mix racially with "their savage neighbors."[33] Virtually all whites, North and South, held similar ideas at the time slavery was abolished.

Despite significant gains politically and socially by blacks after the Civil War, virulent white supremacist ideology championed by white Christians consistently thwarted "equalization" of the races. Some overt attempts to maintain the separation and subordination of blacks can be seen in white supremacist organizations like the Ku Klux Klan. The first Klan arose in the immediate aftermath of the Civil War and was designed to terrorize blacks and stop the "equalization."

But the most consistent and widespread institutions to preserve the purity of the white race and stop the erosion of civilized white rule were the white churches.[34] White Christians were fully convinced that the racial hierarchy of white over black (and all other "colored" races) was divinely created. During Reconstruction, they organized their churches and all social institutions for "redemption" from the possibility of black domination—drawing overtly from the Christian concept of redemption from sin and destruction. This was a "cosmic struggle between order and disorder, civilization and barbarism, white and black."[35] By 1877, President Rutherford B. Hayes had withdrawn all federal troops from the former Confederate states and Reconstruction ended, leaving blacks with no national support for their civil rights. Redemption had come. New Orleans Methodist leader W. J. Sullivan exulted in 1880 that no blacks had been at the polls during a recent election. "Let Negroes and Chinamen and Indians suffer the superior race of white men to whom Providence has given this country, to control it."[36]

Black Christians who were members of white churches in the South before the Civil War began forming new black denominations, partly because it was apparent that they would never be allowed to function as equals. Whites encouraged the separation. At an October 1874 consultation meeting in Murfreesboro, Tennessee, white Disciples of Christ leaders passed a resolution recommending that "our colored brethren who have membership with the whites, whenever practicable, to withdraw themselves and form congregations of their own, believing that by doing so they will advance the cause of Christ among themselves."[37] When blacks remained in predominantly white denominations, white leaders created new black jurisdictions that remained under white supervision. New black denominations included the Colored Methodist Episcopal Church, formed out of the ME Church, South in 1870; and the National Baptist Convention, USA, that coalesced in 1880. While separation provided institutions in which black Christians could develop and exercise leadership, it also meant the virtual elimination of meaningful contact with white Christians.[38]

White church leaders defended their separation from and subordination of black Christians as they had justified slavery—biblical interpretations of a cursed race, pseudoscientific data that "proved" the inferiority of blacks, and the deeply visceral fear of black sexuality and miscegenation that would lead to the pollution and weakening of the white race. After Reconstruction, the Southern "Redeemer" governments rewrote state constitutions, passed legislation to exclude blacks from political involvement, and created Jim Crow[39] laws designed to enforce "God's order of the races." Poll taxes, literacy requirements, and "grandfather clauses" eliminated virtually all blacks from the voter lists. White leaders at local, state, and national levels enforced by law and custom the racial segregation of schools, transportation, housing, and public facilities like restaurants and hotels.

Though many of the discriminatory laws originated in the post-Reconstruction South, racist laws and practices were not confined to one part of the country. Anti-miscegenation laws banned the marriage of whites with any persons of color, for example, in over half of the states, and where such laws did not exist, there were extremely small nonwhite populations.[40] National legislation consistently reflected white supremacist convictions, with decisions that completely eroded advances made by blacks during Reconstruction.[41]

Perhaps the most overt recommitment of national legal policy to white supremacy in this era was the 1896 Supreme Court decision known as *Plessy v. Ferguson*. Like *Dred Scott* almost forty years earlier, *Plessy v. Ferguson* unequivocally reiterated white supremacist ideology underlying American society. Homer Plessy, one-eighth black, refused to vacate his seat on a whites-only train car in Louisiana and was forcibly removed and arrested.[42] The legal question was, did segregation laws violate the Fourteenth Amendment's guarantee of equal rights of citizens?

The majority ruled that segregation laws were constitutional, provided the races were each provided equal accommodations. Yet, as in *Dred Scott*, the decision reflects in an almost matter-of-fact way the overtly racist ideology of the nation:

> If...a white man [be] assigned to a colored coach, he may have his action for damages against the company for being deprived of his so-called property. Upon the other hand, if he be a colored man and be so assigned, he has been deprived of no property, since he is not lawfully entitled to the reputation of being a white man.
>
> We consider the underlying fallacy of the plaintiff's argument to consist in the assumption that the enforced separation of the two races stamps the colored race with a badge of inferiority. If this be so, it is not by reason of anything found in the act, but solely because the colored race chooses to put that construction upon it....If one race be inferior to the other socially, the Constitution of the United States cannot put them upon the same plane.[43]

As with *Dred Scott*, the Supreme Court justices who decided *Plessy v. Ferguson* were professing Christians. They were Melville Weston Fuller (Chief Justice), Episcopalian; Stephen Johnson Field, Congregationalist; Horace Gray, Unitarian; Henry Billings Brown, Congregationalist; George Shiras Jr., Presbyterian; Edward Douglass White, Roman Catholic; Rufus Wheeler Peckham, Episcopalian; and David Josiah Brewer, Congregationalist, who did not participate because his daughter had just died.[44]

White Christians in the Jim Crow era continued to debate the origin and nature of black persons. Charles Carroll, author of *"The Negro a Beast" or "In the Image of God,"* published by the American Book and Bible House in 1900, contended that God created blacks as beasts to serve whites.[45] The older idea of blacks being human descendants of Noah's cursed son Ham also persisted. Still others viewed blacks as human but created in a separate creation (the polygenesis debate of the nineteenth century), and inferior to whites. Defenders of white supremacy presented pseudoscientific physical evidence through careful comparisons of skull size and other physical characteristics to back the notion.[46] Philadelphia medical doctor Samuel George Morton, the chief formulator of nineteenth-century scientific racism, had been raised a Quaker but later became an Episcopalian.[47] He insisted that God was the source of racial differences, with the "Caucasian type" always at the top, "God's will expressed as natural order and verified by empirical science."[48] In his quest to prove the hierarchy of races empirically, between 1830 and his death in 1851, Morton amassed what many believe was the largest collection of human skulls in existence at the time. His careful measurements showed, he insisted, that the white "Caucasian" race had the largest cranial capacity and therefore the largest brain, highest intelligence, and most developed civilization.[49] Furthermore, Morton claimed that the biblical account of creation explained the origin only of the Caucasian race, and that the other races were the result of different creations, the polygenesis theory. Again, the "white race" existed in a place of special favor with God.[50]

Other white Christians insisted that all humans came from the common ancestors described in the Bible. Nevertheless, God's differentiating of the races made it imperative for those clearly at the top to "care for" the less advanced. For example:

> If God has made certain peoples inferior to others, as we clearly have proven, it does not mean at all that the stronger have the least right to be unkind to their weaker neighbors....If each and every color could realize his own God-given sphere, and be willing to serve in it as God has so wonderfully appointed,...this would be a great world in which to live.[51]

While this "benevolent" attitude might have allowed for a level of kindness and even protection of persons of color, it still embodied the ideology of white supremacy and the inherent necessity of separation, subordination, and protection (control) of "nonwhites" by whites.

Whether manifested in benevolence or open hostility, the dogma of white supremacy in the post-Reconstruction era resulted in the de facto reinstatement of slavery. Douglas Blackmon's remarkable 2008 study, *Slavery by Another Name: The Re-Enslavement of Black People in America from the Civil War to World War II*, later made into a documentary film by PBS, charts the criminalization of blackness and the imprisonment and forced labor of blacks in the late nineteenth and twentieth centuries. The Thirteenth Amendment had abolished slavery and involuntary servitude, "except as a punishment for crime whereof the party shall have been duly convicted." The procedure, then, was to pass laws making blackness a crime. States and local governments passed laws—mostly enforced on blacks—making it illegal to be unemployed (vagrancy), walk along railroad tracks, carry concealed weapons, and use profanity or speak loudly in the presence of a white woman. The number of arrests rose whenever there was a need for more laborers in industries like coal and iron mining. Local governments profited from leasing "convicts" to such industries that worked them in horrific conditions, with a mortality rate approaching 30 percent in places.[52] Thousands of blacks, along with a small percentage of poor whites, were convicted of illusory crimes and leased out to corporations like U.S. Steel to spend years in hard labor, abuse, torture, and often death. The law enforcement and industrial leaders who benefited from this new slavery were professing Christians.[53]

The practice of lynching was another tool of white "Christian" society to intimidate and eliminate blacks at will. Such violence was used against those who would pollute white blood—the most common charge against black men executed by lynching was rape. One Georgia Christian stated frankly in 1901, "The spirit which upholds lynch law as the only proper answer to the infamous outrage on female inviolability...is part of the religion of our people."[54] Anti-lynching crusader Ida B. Wells, in her 1895 book detailing stories of lynchings, reflected another reason—perhaps the real one—for such illegal executions when she exclaimed, "The blood chills and the heart almost loses faith in Christianity when one thinks of...the countless massacres of defenseless Negroes, whose only crime was their attempt to exercise their right to vote."[55]

While Northern white Christians sometimes decried the horror and violence inherent in lynching, they often justified such action because of what they asserted was the lawless nature of uncivilized blacks. J. H. Garrison, editor of the Disciples journal *The Christian-*

Evangelist, published in St. Louis, effectively endorsed lynching in an 1899 editorial. Northerners, he said, could not understand the conditions that led white Southerners to such extreme measures. "The sudden emancipation of the negro race, together with their enfranchisement, has precipitated a condition of things in many parts of the South which is responsible for these appalling crimes." Southern women had suffered "brutal abuse by the negroes," and Southerners were doing what they had to do to preserve the social order.[56] Similar statements by Northern leaders of other denominations appear, despite anti-lynching resolutions passed by several national assemblies. Frances Willard, longtime Methodist and president of the Woman's Christian Temperance Society from 1879 to 1898, expressed the sentiment of many white Northern Christian leaders in 1890:

> I pity the southerners, and I believe the great mass of them are as conscientious and kindly-intentioned toward the colored man as an equal number of white church-members of the North [but] the problem on their hands is immeasurable. The colored race multiplies like the locusts of Egypt. The grog-shop is its center of power. The safety of women, of childhood, of the home is menaced in a thousand localities at this moment, so that men dare not go beyond the sight of their own roof tree.[57]

The creation of the "second" KKK in 1915 by ordained Methodist minister William J. Simmons, with its overt white supremacist agenda, was saturated in Christian symbolism and the rhetoric of racial and religious purity. That the second Klan appropriated the cross as its chief symbol of intimidation and violence against blacks is a striking indication of the group's self-identification. By 1924, the Klan rose to a national membership of four million and exercised tremendous political clout. Its membership consisted of the chief members of many communities, including doctors, lawyers, and Christian ministers.[58] The second Klan developed a technique of demonstrating its "Christian character" by entering white Christian revival services and presenting a certificate of approval and cash donation to the minister in front of the congregation.[59] The Klan's strength extended across the South, Midwest, and

West, with its largest membership in Indiana, claiming as many as a third of the state's white male Protestants.[60] Half the membership of the Klan was in urban areas like Chicago, Detroit, Philadelphia, Denver, and Portland, Oregon.[61]

Though the second Klan's national political power peaked in the mid-1920s and began to decline, even its white opponents did not object to its commitment to white Protestant rule, but to its secretive nature. For example, Methodist Henry J. Allen, Governor of Kansas, in a 1922 address to the U.S. Governors' Conference explained that his opposition to the Klan was "not in the fact that it fights the Catholic Church, or expresses its antipathy to the Jew or to the negro, but in the fact that it does this under the protection of a mask and through the process of terrorism and violence."[62] Clearly, the Klan was only one manifestation of a white Christian agenda to protect America from a perceived threat to white dominance by foreigners, Jews, Catholics, and blacks. According to Kelly Baker, "The Klan was not a movement of the right-wing fringe but a movement of white Protestant citizens who wanted to protect their dominance and their culture."[63]

Congress passed the first citizenship law in 1790, granting that right to "free white persons." Not until 1882 did Congress pass laws placing restrictions on immigration: the "Act to Regulate Immigration" and the "Chinese Exclusion Act." The fear of economic harm to white citizens was the presenting reason for the new immigration policies. Chinese immigrants in California were blamed for a rise in unemployment and declining wages, and the Chinese Exclusion Act barred virtually all immigration from China for ten years. Behind the law, however, was the fear of weakening white dominance by people of inferior bloodlines and culture, including religious beliefs.[64] In 1892, the Geary Act extended the prohibition for another decade, and in 1902, the ban was made "permanent."

Subsequent immigration laws targeted "undesirables" from Asia as well as Eastern and Southern Europe in 1917, 1921, and 1924. Quota systems strongly favored Northern and Western Europeans. Even when Congress repealed the Chinese Exclusion Act in 1943 when China became a U.S. ally in World War II, only 105 immigrants per year could enter the country. Eugenics, the pseudoscience that, like Morton and others in the nineteenth century, gathered "scientific evidence" for the superiority of the Northern European founders of America, justified the restrictive policies.[65]

White supremacy underlay the creation of all governmental social programs in the twentieth century. In 1934, the National Housing Act provided Depression-era, low-income families access to mortgages and loans for construction and home improvement. A new appraisal system accompanying the new law linked property value and loan eligibility to race. These new policies effectively locked persons of color out of home buying just as many white Americans were getting in. It also helped create the legacies of segregated communities and a substantial wealth gap between whites and nonwhites that still exist today.[66]

In addition, the 1935 Social Security Act exempted agricultural workers and domestic servants (predominantly African American, Mexican, and Asian) from receiving old-age insurance, while the Wagner Act for guaranteeing workers' rights did not prohibit unions from discriminating against nonwhites. Combined, these two acts locked most persons of color out of higher paying jobs and union benefits. Minorities were at the lowest levels of the income chain and had the greatest need for union benefits like medical care, job security, and pensions; yet they were systematically denied these benefits that white Americans came to take for granted.[67]

The cumulative effect of the laws and practices of white Christian culture in the United States that targeted persons of color for discrimination, marginalization, and exclusion from many of the benefits of citizenship, were devastating and long-lasting. Explicit white supremacist convictions had operated virtually unquestioned for over four centuries in the United States. As the nation entered the civil rights era in the 1950s, these deeply held beliefs remained as strong as ever.

III. THE SUBMERSION AND REEMERGENCE OF WHITE SUPREMACY FROM THE CIVIL RIGHTS ERA TO THE POST-OBAMA ERA

Growing numbers of persons of color and their white allies increasingly challenged the ideology through courageous action.

Blacks had always resisted the system of racist discrimination in powerful ways in the previous periods through courageous individual action and through the establishment of organizations like the National Association for the Advancement of Colored People (NAACP) and the Urban League. In many ways the culmination of previous action, especially by the NAACP, federal laws and Supreme Court decisions would begin to strike down blatant white racist laws and practices.

Yet the ideology of white supremacy did not die, nor arguably diminish. No longer supported by Jim Crow laws and state constitutions that blocked voter registration, restricted access to public services, and prohibited interracial marriage, it was forced to go covert, subliminal, partially invisible, and deniable. But it never went away, and it seems to be gaining strength and boldness in the twenty-first century.

While white Christian allies joined forces with Martin Luther King Jr. in the civil rights movement, deeply embedded, often unconscious white supremacist attitudes inhibited the dismantling of white power. Martin Luther King, like Frederick Douglass over a century earlier, expressed his deep frustration with his supposed allies in the church:

> I must make two honest confessions to you, my Christian and Jewish brothers. First, I must confess that over the past few years I have been gravely disappointed with the white moderate. I have almost reached the regrettable conclusion that the Negro's great stumbling block in his stride toward freedom is not the White Citizen's Counciler or the Ku Klux Klanner, but the white moderate, who is more devoted to "order" than to justice; who prefers a negative peace which is the absence of tension to a positive peace which is the presence of justice; who constantly says: "I agree with you in the goal you seek, but I cannot agree with your methods of direct action"; who paternalistically believes he can set the timetable for another man's freedom; who lives by a mythical concept of time and who constantly advises the Negro to wait for a "more convenient season."[68]

King's white Christian sympathizers often reflected the common white Christian attitude—that blacks were not ready for the full rights of citizenship—with the implication that they never would be.

The idea of the superior "white race," documented by Nell Painter in *The History of White People*, combined with scientific racism and eugenics to form the rationale for the prohibition of interracial marriage. *Miscegenation*, the term coined in the mid-nineteenth century for interracial marriage, implied dilution of pure white blood. State anti-miscegenation laws at the beginning of the civil rights era usually made interracial marriage a felony.[69]

The U.S. Supreme Court upheld the constitutionality of such state laws in 1883 in *Pace v. State of Alabama*. Tony Pace, a black man, and Mary Cox, a white woman, were convicted of the misdemeanor of "living together in a state of adultery or fornication" and each sentenced to two years in the state penitentiary. Pace appealed based on the equal protection clause of the Fourteenth Amendment, alleging the judgment was discriminatory because he was black, since the penalty for two persons of the same race convicted of the offense was considerably less. The Alabama Supreme Court and the U.S. Supreme Court upheld the original ruling, asserting that because the crime was between races, it had to be punished more severely.[70]

That ruling was not overturned until 1967 in the case of *Loving v. Virginia*. Richard (white) and Mildred (black) Loving were legally married in the District of Columbia in 1958, but when they returned home to Virginia were tried, convicted, and sentenced to one year in prison for violating the state's anti-miscegenation law. The sentence was suspended on the condition that they leave Virginia for twenty-five years. In 1963, the couple appealed to the state trial court, the U.S. District Court, and finally the Virginia Supreme Court to overturn their conviction and Virginia's anti-miscegenation law. The courts upheld the constitutionality of the law and the Lovings' conviction. The Virginia judges were clear that the ruling was "to preserve the racial integrity of its citizens," and to prevent "the corruption of blood" and "a mongrel breed of citizens."[71]

Upon appeal to the U.S. Supreme Court, the justices ruled unanimously that the "Fourteenth Amendment requires that the freedom of choice to marry not be restricted by invidious racial discriminations. Under our Constitution, the freedom to marry, or not marry, a person of another race resides with the individual and cannot be infringed by the State."[72] Though several states continued to have anti-miscegenation laws on the books and in their constitutions, the laws were no longer enforceable.[73]

Though no longer legal, the stigma against interracial marriage remains strong. After the Loving decision, the percentage of all marriages in the United States between persons of different races was a little over 1 percent. Forty-six years later in 2013, only 7 percent of all whites who married for the first time married a person of a different race.[74] Obviously, marriage is an intensely personal decision that cannot be dictated by law. Yet the numbers would seem to indicate either continued negative views of interracial marriage or the continued racialization of the country so that meaningful social relationships between persons of different races remain relatively rare.[75]

While data indicate positive attitudinal shifts among white Christians concerning interracial marriage, attitudes resulted in no significant change.[76] White Christians who were loyal to a specific religious tradition viewed interracial marriage for their children in a significantly more negative light.[77] Even though arguments against the "dilution" of white blood have been discredited, powerful antipathy toward interracial marriage remains—especially in the white Christian community.

The years since the civil rights movement have witnessed increasingly diverse manifestations of white supremacy. One of the most disturbing is the de facto resegregation of a significant segment of American public schools. This resulted partly because of the creation of a widespread system of alternative private, often Christian, schools to avoid school integration during the civil rights movement.[78]

While the trend is affected by multiple complex economic and social factors, a study by researchers at Stanford University showed that medium and large school districts released from civil rights era court-ordered desegregation in the 1990s and 2000s had a significant increase in racial segregation, growing faster "in districts where the prerelease school segregation levels were lowest."[79] Another study by the National Center for Education Statistics in 2012 noted that in the 1968–69 school year, the year the U.S.

Department of Education began enforcing desegregation orders, "approximately 77 percent of Black students and 55 percent of Latino students attended public schools that were comprised of 50 percent to 100 percent racial minorities." Forty years later, 74 percent of Blacks and 80 percent of Hispanics attended schools that were 50 percent to 100 percent minority, and "more than 40 percent of Black and Latino students were attending schools that were 90 percent to 100 percent minority."[80]

According to a 2013 study, economic disadvantages frequently found in schools with a high minority population, often reflecting the legacy of economic discrimination described in previous sections of this study, often have "lifelong negative consequences." Gregory J. Palardy of the University of California, Riverside, contends that

> students who attended high-SEC [socioeconomic composition] schools were 68% more likely to enroll at a four-year college than students from low SEC-schools. Because educational attainment is associated with several important life outcomes—access to careers, income, and even health—this finding suggests that attending a low-SEC high school may have lifelong negative consequences."[81]

As stated, the trends are complex, with direct conscious racial motivation difficult to document. Nevertheless, numerous studies show the reality of increased school segregation after the end of court-ordered desegregation. Though the 1954 Supreme Court decision *Brown v. Board of Education* declared the unconstitutionality and inconsistency of the "separate but equal" doctrine established by *Plessy v. Ferguson*, segregated schools are an increasing reality in many places.

The complex and inflammatory debate over affirmative action in higher education and the workplace has generally ignored the "affirmative action" that consistently favored whites during most of American history and, as indicated earlier, still reverberates in the American experience.[82] Most whites assumed that merely abolishing centuries-old discriminatory laws and practices would remedy all previous problems. Suddenly ceasing to exclude (in theory) those who had been banned from access to certain employment, educational, and economic opportunities to step into those places amid continued hostility and resentment with no support system to counterbalance the centuries of exclusion, was a setup for failure. Among many whites, it created a mentality that now they had become the targets of racial discrimination in favor of what they saw as ill-equipped and incompetent persons of color.[83] Whites overwhelmingly oppose affirmative action policies and insist that their opposition has nothing to do with race. Such a stance, however, fails to acknowledge the continuing effects of centuries-long white supremacist policies.[84]

In chapter 5 of his book *Racism Without Racists*, Eduardo Bonillo-Silva analyzes numerous interviews of whites concerning affirmative action policies. The clear majority used some variation of the following: "I don't think we can make retribution for things that happened in the past. I don't think it serves any purpose today to try to fix something that happened a long time ago that doesn't affect anyone today. All it does is bring up to the surface that there was a problem."[85] Bonillo-Silva concludes that "for whites, remedial policies are inherently divisive, hence white's insistence on forgetting the past."[86]

Some white Christians have given significant support to affirmative action policies, including progressive Evangelicals like Jim Wallis.[87] Yet others, including most Evangelicals, view race problems as individual rather than systemic, seeing the solution as reconciling personal relationships rather than providing structural remedies. Because of this, affirmative action has received relatively little overt support from these groups.[88]

Amazingly, scientific racism has reappeared in recent years, reflected both in publications with a thinly disguised white supremacist agenda as well as more "respectable" ones. In Richard D. Fuerle's 2008 book *Erectus Walks Among Us*, the author, a retired patent attorney from upstate New York, compiled data from evolutionary anthropology to claim that blacks were of the "less advanced" *homo erectus* species rather than the white *homo sapiens*.[89] Highly selective in his use of data, Fuerle reveals his agenda in the final sections of the book—to argue against "race mixing." Though garnering practically no attention in mainstream media, the book has been distributed free on the Internet with little attempt at refutation.

A more disturbing version of evolutionary racism is Nicholas Wade's 2014 study *A Troublesome Inheritance*. Wade contends that race, contrary to the current consensus that it is essentially a social construct, is a biological reality that over time evolved genetic links to, among other things, traits such as thrift, nonviolence, economic prosperity, and intelligence. The rise of the West, he insists, can be explained by evolutionary development and the genetic embedding of traits that led to its success:

> Why are some countries rich and others persistently poor? Capital and information flow fairly freely, so what is it that prevents poor countries from taking out a loan, copying every Scandinavian institution, and becoming as rich and peaceful as Denmark? Africa has absorbed billions of dollars in aid over the past half century and yet, until a recent spurt of growth, its standard of living has stagnated for decades. Economists and historians attribute the major disparities between countries to factors such as resources or geography or cultural differences. But many countries with no resources, like Japan or Singapore, are very rich, while richly endowed countries like Nigeria tend to be quite poor. The brisk and continuing pace of human evolution suggests a new possibility: that at the root of each civilization is a particular set of evolved social behaviors that sustains it, and these behaviors are reflected in the society's institutions.[90]

Though many scientists have denounced Wade's thesis as racist, Wade denies the charge. He insists that he does not contend that westerners are superior to others, and that success is provisional.[91] And Wade is certainly no Christian. His 2009 *The Faith Instinct: How Religion Evolved and Why It Endures* contends that religion became hardwired into the human psyche through the struggle for survival.[92] Nevertheless, the implications of his contentions are clear, and the Christian community has given little notice.

The powerful continuing effects of segregated and inferior housing, employment discrimination, inaccessibility of federal programs and bank loans, and limited access to quality healthcare and education affect the economic, social, psychological, and political well-being of large portions of the country's nonwhite population. The centuries-long, race-based discrimination has devastating psychological and physical consequences.[93] The so-called John Henry Syndrome, identified by epidemiologist Sherman James in the 1970s and named after one of his subjects, John Henry Martin, shows how constantly having to prove one's capability and worth leads to high blood pressure, arthritis, ulcers, and other serious disabilities.[94] These pressures and other factors mentioned below have produced the phenomenon of "black rage" so unfathomable to most whites.[95]

In this era of the often-covert nature of white supremacist ideas, the ideology has arguably been most operationalized through what have been labeled microaggressions. Derald Wing Sue and fellow researchers defined racial microaggressions in a 2007 study as "brief and commonplace daily verbal, behavioral, or environmental indignities, whether intentional or unintentional, that communicate hostile, derogatory, or negative racial slights and insults toward people of color." They explain that often those who engage in such actions are unaware of how they are communicating to people of color. From extensive examination of social psychological literature, as well as accounts of the "racial awakenings" of white and black counselors, the authors identify three forms of microaggression: microassault, microinsult, and microinvalidation.[96]

Despite the still early stages of the study of microaggression, data reflect indisputable and devastating consequences on persons of color. Citing dozens of studies, Sue and his colleagues conclude, "When one considers that people of color are exposed continually to microaggressions and that their effects are cumulative, it becomes easier to understand the psychological toll they may take on recipients' well-being." In fact, Sue asserts from an earlier study that because such manifestations are mostly invisible and can be easily ignored, "this contemporary form of racism is many times over more problematic, damaging, and injurious to persons of color than overt racist acts."[97]

The 2013 U.S. Supreme Court decision in *Shelby County (AL) v. Holder*, striking down provision 4(b) of the 1965 Voting Rights

Act, struck a serious blow at stopping states from changing voting laws to restrict the right to vote.[98] Section 5 of the Act required certain states and voting jurisdictions to receive "preclearance" from the federal government for any changes in voting laws and practices. Section 4(b) defined which jurisdictions had to obtain the preclearance based on past discrimination and percentages of citizens registered to vote. The court did not declare Section 5 to be unconstitutional, but by striking down Section 4b as not reflecting current realities, it effectively made Section 5 inoperative—no one must get preclearance. Based on the historical realities detailed in this study, the opportunity for laws to be passed that, while never mentioning race, restrict access to voting for citizens historically at the margins of power in the nation, has increased immensely.[99]

The systemic pattern of police discrimination toward minority populations, most strikingly seen in the multiple incidents of the fatal shootings of black males in recent years, is another reflection of the deeply embedded white supremacy that has engendered fear of nonwhites in general and of black males in particular. It would be easy to simply equate these murders by law enforcement officials as a remnant of the lynchings of the pre-civil rights era. Certainly, attitudes behind lynching are likely involved in some of the cases—that is, simple raw white supremacist attitudes that view blacks and other persons of color as threats and deserving of imprisonment or elimination. But that does not account for those whites who, by all accounts, are good police officers conscientiously trying to protect their communities. Nor does it explain how black officers themselves could have been involved in these deaths. Three of the six law enforcement personnel charged with the 2015 death of Freddie Gray in Baltimore are black.

One explanation for this can be seen in the Harvard Race Implicit Association Test (IAT).[100] Described in Malcolm Gladwell's 2005 book *Blink: The Power of Thinking Without Thinking*, the test measures one's subconscious attitudes by having test takers respond instantaneously to match a series of pictures and words with appropriate descriptions. Photos of European Americans and African Americans flash on the screen, and test takers simply press the "e" or "i" key on their computer keyboard to match with the correct descriptor. The same is done with words that would be considered good, like "glorious" or "wonderful," and others that would be seen as bad like "hurt" or "evil." When asked to associate only one item at a time, it is relatively easy to make the correct association. But when the computer pairs the ethnic and qualitative tests and asks test takers to do the same rapid association, things get more complex. Gladwell describes the first time he took the Race IAT:

> In the back of my mind was a growing sense of mortification. Why was I having so much trouble when I had to put a word like "Glorious" or "Wonderful" into the "Good" category when "Good" was paired with "African American" or when I had to put the word "Evil" into the "Bad" category when "Bad" was paired with "European American?" Then came part two. This time the categories were reversed. Now I was having no trouble at all….Does this mean I'm a racist, a self-hating black person? [Gladwell is "half black."] Not exactly. What it means is that our attitudes toward things like race or gender operate on two levels. First of all we have our conscious attitudes. These are our stated values which we use to direct our behavior deliberately. But the IAT measures something else. It measures our second level of attitude, our racial attitude at an *unconscious* level— the immediate, automatic associations that tumble out before we've even had time to think.[101]

Gladwell makes the point that such attitudes are formed in the "giant computer" of our mind by the millions of pieces of data fed into it by everything we experience, including books, TV shows, movies, newspaper articles, news shows, music, advertisements— even the way clothes and toys are presented in stores. The verbal and spoken images of persons of color that have permeated American society for four hundred years and continue to exist in more subliminal yet real ways form these unconscious attitudes. Seventy to eighty percent of whites who take the Harvard Race Implicit Association Test (IAT) show a moderate to "automatic preference" for whites. Approximately 50 percent of blacks who take the test show the same preference.[102] The IAT demonstrates "that our unconscious attitudes can be utterly incompatible with our stated conscious values."[103]

CONCLUSION

The story partially told in this essay is one that seems overwhelming at times. It serves as backdrop for the current devastating problem of mass incarceration. Michelle Alexander and others have documented in stunning detail the shift from the de facto criminalization of blackness in the Jim Crow era to the so-called War on Drugs, in which African Americans are vastly disproportionately imprisoned.[104] More African Americans are jailed today than were enslaved in 1850. The extensive documentation of the development of mass incarceration and its perpetuation of racist social and legal policies reflects the reality of attitudes toward black Americans present since the beginning of the nation and has serious implications for action by the church.[105]

The overt expression of white supremacy has been shoved to the fringes, to radical hate groups who become easy scapegoats for the rest of us to denounce.[106] Yet even this brief and incomplete discussion of the ideology's current operations provides ample evidence of its continuing presence. Reflecting Frederick Douglass's quote from Albert Barnes over a century ago, white supremacy could not stand if the white church acted decisively and in solidarity to stop it.[107]

There is rising awareness among parts of Evangelical Christianity of the white supremacy operating at the heart of the nation and its institutions. Soong-Chan Rah's *The Next Evangelicalism: Freeing the Church from Western Cultural Captivity*, for example, provides an incisive call to white Evangelicalism to acknowledge white supremacy and a description of changes already underway.[108] Evangelical justice activist Jim Wallis's *America's Original Sin: Racism, White Privilege, and the Bridge to a New America* is a compelling call to Christians to destroy the white supremacist ideology that produced white privilege and white power.[109] Serious efforts by Catholic and mainstream Christians also continue, as mentioned above. And so there is hope. As Paul says in 2 Corinthians 4:8, "We are afflicted in every way, but not crushed; perplexed, but not driven to despair."

I end as I started. As humans, we wear veils that obscure the fullness of the gospel. White Christians have had a veil that clouded their understanding of the evil ideology of white supremacy. Yet Gladwell ends his chapter on the Race IAT with a word of hope. "We are not helpless in the face of our first impressions...just because something is outside of awareness doesn't mean it's outside of control."[110] He goes on to explain how changing our experiences and our environment—the things that have unconsciously created these attitudes—can change the ways we think and respond. This is the message of the gospel. People can be transformed "by the renewing of [their] minds" (Rom 12:2).

White Christians (I am one) must be involved actively and relentlessly in the exposure and breaking down of white supremacy wherever it exists. This involves raising the consciousness of white Christians to the history of white supremacist ideology in the church so that we can confess the sin and repent of it—bringing forth fruit worthy of repentance. Forgiveness and radical reconciliation must follow, along with a conscious rejection to perpetuate the sins of the past. May God help us to do so.

Notes

1. See Alexis Robinson, "The Convoluted Spectrum of White Guilt Reactions: A Review of Emerging Literature," *The Jury Expert* 22 (July 2010): 47–52, see http://thejuryexpert.com/wp-content/uploads/TJEVol22Num4_Jul2010.pdf; Shelby Steele, *White Guilt: How Blacks and Whites Together Destroyed the Promise of the Civil Rights Era* (New York: HarperCollins, 2006).

2. Charles W. Mills, *The Racial Contract* (Ithaca, NY: Cornell University Press, 1997), 19, 27, 73.

3. James Baldwin, *Nobody Knows My Name: More Notes of a Native Son* (New York: The Dial Press, 1961), 68. "Whenever a significant body of Negroes move North, they do not escape Jim Crow; they merely encounter another, not-less-deadly variety."

4. James Cone, *Black Theology and Black Power* (Maryknoll, NY: Orbis Books, 1997), 72; original, New York: Seabury Press, 1969.

5. Drick Boyd, *White Allies in the Struggle for Racial Justice* (Maryknoll, NY: Orbis Books, 2015).

6. Daniel Little, "Can America Overcome Racism?" CHANG-INGSOCIETY: New Thinking about Justice in a Global World blog (January 1, 2009), http://changingsocietyblog.blogspot.com/2009/01/can -america-overcome-racism.html.

7. Two books that carefully trace the creation of the idea of white supremacy are Winthrop Jordan's *White over Black: American Attitudes toward the Negro, 1550–1812*, published first in 1969; and Nell Painter's *The History of White People*, published in 2010. The first is a classic compilation of documents charting the creation of white supremacy by Europeans and the way it functioned legally and socially in the American colonies. The second traces white race theory from ancient Greece to twenty-first century America.

8. The concept had its modern roots in seventeenth century pseudoscientific racism. See, for example, David Hurst Thomas, "A Short History of Scientific Racism in America," in *Skull Wars: Kennewick Man, Archaeology & the Battle for Native American Identity* (New York: Basic Books, 2001), 36–43.

9. Winthrop D. Jordan, *White over Black: American Attitudes toward the Negro, 1550–1812* (Chapel Hill, NC: The University of North Carolina Press, 1968), 7.

10. Refers to the incident in Genesis 9:20–27 in which Noah's youngest son Ham did not cover his drunken father's nakedness. In the text, Noah curses Ham's son, Canaan, saying he would be a servant of his brothers.

11. Jordan, *White over Black*, 19.

12. Ibid., 27, 89.

13. Ibid., 20–43.

14. See, for example, Bacon's Laws of Maryland at the Archives of Maryland Online, http://aomol.msa.maryland.gov/megafile/msa/speccol/sc2900/sc2908/000001/000075/html/index.html, and John R. Wunder, ed., *Native American Law and Colonialism, before 1776 to 1903*, vol. 1 of Native Americans and the Law: Contemporary and Historical Perspectives on American Indian Rights, Freedoms, and Sovereignty (New York: Garland, 1996).

15. June Purcell Guild, *Black Laws of Virginia: A Summary of the Legislative Acts of Virginia Concerning Negroes from Earliest Times to the Present* (Richmond, VA: Whittet & Shepperson, 1936), 46.

16. Ibid., 42.

17. Ibid., 154.

18. Thomas Jefferson, *Notes on the State of Virginia* (Boston: Lilly and Wait, 1832), 169–71, 144ff. Available at https://catalog.hathitrust.org/Record/008584184.

19. Thomas Jefferson to Jared Sparks, February 4, 1824. Transcription available at http://founders.archives.gov/documents/Jefferson/98-01-02-4020.

20. Alexander Campbell, "Our Position to American Slavery—No. V," *Millennial Harbinger* (May 1845): 234.

21. Wu Jin-Ping, *Frederick Douglass and the Black Liberation Movement: The North Star of American Blacks* (New York: Garland Publishing, 2000), 92–93; William S. McFeely, *Frederick Douglas* (New York: W. W. Norton & Co., 1991), 84–85, 92–94, passim.

22. Frederick Douglas, "The Meaning of July Fourth for the Negro," a speech given at Rochester, New York, July 5, 1852. Available at http://www.historyisaweapon.com/defcon1/douglassjuly4.html.

23. *Ethnic Notions*, California Newsreel, 1987, full transcript available at http://www.newsreel.org/transcripts/ethnicno.htm.

24. Robert M. Entman and Andrew Rojecki, *The Black Image in the White Mind: Media and Race in America* (Chicago: University of Chicago Press, 2001); Catherine Squires, *African Americans and the Media* (Cambridge: Polity, 2009).

25. See, for example, David G. Savage, "How Did They Get It So Wrong?" *ABA Journal* (January 1, 2009), http://www.abajournal.com/magazine/article/how_did_they_get_it_so_wrong/.

26. Excerpted from *Dred Scott v. John F. A. Sanford* (1857), the "Dred Scott Decision," http://www.ourdocuments.gov/doc.php?flash=true&doc=29&page=transcript.

27. Two justices, Benjamin Robbins Curtis (Unitarian, then Episcopalian) and John McLean (Methodist), dissented on constitutional and legal grounds, but still reflected white supremacist attitudes. See Earl M. Maltz, "The Last Angry Man: Benjamin Robbins Curtis and the Dred Scott Case," *Chicago-Kent Law Review* 82 (December 2006): 265–76, http://scholarship.kentlaw.iit.edu/cgi/viewcontent.cgi?article=3577&context=cklawreview.

28. See the transcripts of the Congressional debates in the *Congressional Globe* at the Library of Congress website: https://www.loc.gov/rr/program/bib/ourdocs/13thamendment.html.

29. Michael Vorenberg, *Final Freedom: The Civil War, the Abolition of Slavery, and the Thirteenth Amendment* (Cambridge: Cambridge University Press, 2001), 79, 99, 112, 160, passim.

30. "Fourth Debate with Stephen A. Douglas at Charleston, IL," full text available at https://www.nps.gov/liho/learn/historyculture/debate4.htm.

31. Phillip W. Magness and Sebastian N. Page, *Colonization after Emancipation: Lincoln and the Movement for Black Resettlement* (Columbia,

MO: University of Missouri Press, 2011), vii, 10–11, 118–28; Michael Vorenberg, "Abraham Lincoln and the Politics of Black Colonization," *Journal of the Abraham Lincoln Association* 14, no. 2 (Summer 1993): 22–45.

32. Thomas Bahde, *The Life and Death of Gus Reed: A Story of Race and Justice in Illinois During the Civil War and Reconstruction* (Athens, OH: Ohio University Press, 2014). See especially chapter 4, "A White Man's Country."

33. J. M. Sturtevant, "The Destiny of the African Race in the United States," *Continental Monthly* 3 (May 1863): 600–610, quoted in Bahde, *The Life and Death of Gus Reed*, 77.

34. Paul Harvey, "'That Was about Equalization after Freedom,' Southern Evangelicalism and the Politics of Reconstruction and Redemption, 1861–1900," in *Vale of Tears: New Essays on Religion and Reconstruction*, eds. Edward J. Blum and W. Scott Poole (Macon: University of Georgia Press, 2005), 73–92.

35. Ibid., 91.

36. W. J. Sullivan, "The Color Line," *New Orleans Christian Advocate*, June 17, 1880; quoted in Harvey, "Equalization After Freedom," 92.

37. *Christian Standard* (November 7, 1874): 356. Petitions also came from black members to be allowed to separate and form their own churches. Arnold H. Taylor, *Travail and Triumph: Black Life and Culture in the South Since the Civil War* (Westport, CT: Greenwood Press, 1976), 142–45.

38. Paul Harvey, *Through the Storm, Through the Night: A History of African American Christianity* (Lanham, MD: Rowman & Littlefield, 2011), 71–77; Taylor, *Travail and Triumph*, 145–47.

39. Refers to a character in antebellum minstrel shows that represented an exaggerated comical black figure. See "Who Was Jim Crow?" Jim Crow Museum of Racist Memorabilia, Ferris State University, http://ferris.edu/HTMLS/news/jimcrow/who/.

40. James R. Browning, "Anti-Miscegenation Laws in the U.S.," *Duke Law Journal* (March 1951): 26–41.

41. Lawrence Goldstone, *Inherently Unequal: The Betrayal of Equal Rights by the Supreme Court, 1865–1903* (New York: Walker & Company, 2011).

42. Plessy could "pass" for white and had purchased a first-class ticket. The "colored" car had no first-class seats.

43. *Plessy v Ferguson*, 163 U.S. 537; Argued: April 18, 1896; Decided: May 18, 1896. Available at https://www.law.cornell.edu/supremecourt/text/163/537#writing-USSC_CR_0163_0537_ZD.

44. John Marshall Harlan, a Presbyterian, dissented based on constitutional rights of citizens to full access to public highways, but in his dissenting opinion he stated, "The white race deems itself to be the dominant race in this country. And so it is, in prestige, in achievements, in education, in wealth, and in power. So, I doubt not, it will continue to be for all time, if it remains true to its great heritage and holds fast to the principles of constitutional liberty."

45. Full text available at https://archive.org/details/thenegrobeastori 00carrrich.

46. Thomas, "Short History of Scientific Racism," 36–43.

47. George B. Wood, *A Biographical Memoir of Samuel George Morton, M.D.* (Philadelphia: T.K. and P.G. Collins, 1853), 4–7.

48. Thomas, *Skull Wars*, 41. See "Timeline of Scientific Racism," compiled by the Asian Pacific American Institute at New York University, accessed on August 13, 2017, http://www.nyu-apastudies.org/hauntedfiles/about/timeline/.

49. Samuel George Morton, *Crania Americana* (Philadelphia: J. Dobson, 1839). Available at https://archive.org/stream/Craniaamericana00Mort #page/n9/mode/2up.

50. Painter, *The History of White People*, 177, 191–94.

51. John W. Tyndale, *The Origin of the Black Man* (St. Louis: Metropolitan Correspondence Bible College Book Department, 1927), 57–58.

52. Douglas A. Blackmon, *Slavery by Another Name: The Re-Enslavement of Black Americans from the Civil War to World War II* (New York: Doubleday, 2008), 53–57, 99–103, passim; Sam Pollard, director, "Slavery by Another Name," documentary movie, http://www.pbs.org/tpt/slavery-by-another-name/watch/ or http://www.slaverybyanothername .com/.

53. See, for example, Wayne Flint, *Alabama Baptists: Southern Baptists in the Heart of Dixie* (Tuscaloosa, AL: University of Alabama Press, 1998), 230–31; "The Convict Lease System," in Robert W. Rydell, ed., *The Reason Why the Colored American is Not in the World's Columbian Exposition* (Urbana, IL: University of Illinois Press, 1999), 23–28.

54. Quoted in Donald G. Mathews, "Lynching is Part of the Religion of Our People," in *Religion and the American South: Protestants and Others in History and Culture*, ed. Beth Barton Schweiger and Donald G. Mathews (Chapel Hill, NC: University of North Carolina Press, 2004), 166; Amy Kate Bailey and Karen A. Snedker, "Practicing What They Preach? Lynching and Religion in the American South, 1890–1929," *American Journal of Sociology* 117 (November 2011): 844–87; Amy Louise Wood,

Lynching and Spectacle: Witnessing Racial Violence in America 1890–1940 (Chapel Hill, NC: University of North Carolina Press, 2009).

55. Ida B. Wells-Barnett, *The Red Record: Tabulated Statistics and Alleged Causes of Lynching in the United States*, 1895. Full text at http://www.gutenberg.org/files/14977/14977-h/14977-h.htm.

56. "The Problem of the Negro," *The Christian-Evangelist* (June 1, 1899): 677. The alleged widespread sexual abuse of southern women by black men was cited repeatedly in justifications of lynching, though data showed such to be false. Philip Dray, *At the Hands of Persons Unknown: The Lynching of Black America* (New York: Random House, 2002), 60–68.

57. Frances Willard, *The Voice* (October 1890), quoted in Phillip Dray, *At the Hands of Persons Unknown: The Lynching of Black America* (New York: Modern Library, 2003), 106–7.

58. Kelly J. Baker, *The Gospel According to the Klan: The KKK's Appeal to Protestant America, 1915–1930* (Lawrence, KS: University Press of Kansas, 2011), 8–9.

59. See, for example, Nancy K. MacLean, *Behind the Mask of Chivalry: The Making of the Second Ku Klux Klan* (New York: Oxford University Press, 1994), 15; JoEllen McNergney Vinyard, *Right in Michigan's Grassroots: From the KKK to the Michigan Militia* (Ann Arbor, MI: University of Michigan Press, 2011), 55; Kenneth T. Jackson, *The Ku Klux Klan in the City: 1915–1930* (New York: Oxford University Press, 1967), 98.

60. Leonard J. Moore, *Citizen Klansmen: The Ku Klux Klan in Indiana, 1921–1928* (Chapel Hill, NC: University of North Carolina Press, 1997).

61. Jackson, *Klan in the City*, 236–39.

62. Cited in Henry J. Wallace, "The Ku Klux Klan in Calvin Coolidge's America," Calvin Coolidge Presidential Foundation, July 14, 2014, https://coolidgefoundation.org/blog/the-ku-klux-klan-in-calvin-coolidges-america/, note ix.

63. Baker, *Gospel According to the Klan*, 212–13.

64. Andrew Gyory, *Closing the Gate: Race, Politics, and the Chinese Exclusion Act* (Chapel Hill, NC: University of North Carolina Press, 1998); Erika Lee, *At America's Gates: Chinese Immigration during the Exclusion Era, 1882–1943* (Chapel Hill, NC: University of North Carolina Press, 2003).

65. Edwin Black, *War against the Weak: Eugenics and America's Campaign to Create a Master Race* (New York: Four Walls Eight Windows, 2003); Wendy Kline, *Building a Better Race* (Berkeley, CA: University of California Press, 2001). See archives of the Eugenics Records Office at http://www.eugenicsarchive.org/eugenics/.

66. Melvin L. Oliver and Thomas M. Shapiro, *Black Wealth, White Wealth: A New Perspective on Racial Inequality* (New York: Routledge, 2006).

67. Ira Katznelson, *When Affirmative Action was White: An Untold History of Racial Inequality in Twentieth-Century America* (New York: W. W. Norton & Company, 2005), 42–49; see especially the "Go Deeper: Race Timeline," in *Race: The Power of an Illusion*, available at http://www.pbs.org/race/000_About/002_03_i-godeeper.htm.

68. Martin Luther King Jr., "Letter from a Birmingham Jail," April 16, 1963. Available at https://www.africa.upenn.edu/Articles_Gen/Letter_Birmingham.html.

69. Peggy Pascoe, *What Comes Naturally: Miscegenation Law and the Making of Race in America* (Oxford: Oxford University Press, 2009), 30, 53–69.

70. *Pace v. State of Alabama*, January 29, 1883. Text at https://law.resource.org/pub/us/case/reporter/US/106/106.US.583.html.

71. Quoted in 388 U.S. 1 (1967), *Loving et Ux v. Virginia*, No. 395, Supreme Court of United States. Text at https://scholar.google.com/scholar_case?case=5103666188878568597.

72. Ibid.

73. Alabama did not amend its state constitution to eliminate the prohibition until 2000 when 40 percent of voters opposed the change. Alabama Interracial Marriage, Amendment 2 (2000), https://ballotpedia.org/Alabama_Interracial_Marriage,_Amendment_2_(2000). A feature movie telling the story debuted in November 2016; see http://www.focusfeatures.com/loving.

74. Robert Acquaye, "Interracial Marriage: Trends since *Loving v. Virginia*," *The Network Journal* (May 2007); Wendy Wang, "Interracial Marriage: Who Is 'Marrying Out'?" Pew Research Center FactTank News in the Numbers, http://www.pewresearch.org/fact-tank/2015/06/12/interracial-marriage-who-is-marrying-out/.

75. Andrew Hacker, *Two Nations: Black and White, Separate, Hostile, Unequal* (New York: Scribner's, 1992); Rajini Vaidyanathan, "Why Don't Black and White Americans Live Together?" BBC News, http://www.bbc.com/news/world-us-canada-35255835.

76. Samuel L. Perry, "Religion and Whites' Attitudes toward Interracial Marriage with African Americans, Asians, and Latinos," *Journal for the Scientific Study of Religion* 52 (June 2013): 425–42.

77. Melissa R. Herman and Mary E. Campbell, "I Wouldn't, But You Can: Attitudes toward Interracial Relationships," *Social Science Research* 41 (March 2012): 343–58; Samuel L. Perry, "Hoping for a Godly (White) Family: How Desire for Religious Heritage Affects Whites'

Attitudes toward Interracial Marriage," *Journal for the Scientific Study of Religion* 53 (March 2014): 202–18.

78. John Wihbey, "School Resegregation, Race and America's Future: Recent Research," *Journalist's Resource*, Harvard Kennedy School Shorenstein Center on Media, Politics, and Public Policy, May 5, 2014.

79. Sean F. Reardon, Elena Grewal, Demetra Kalogrides, and Erica Greenberg, "Brown Fades: The End of Court-Ordered School Desegregation and the Resegregation of American Public Schools," *Journal of Policy Analysis and Management* 31 (2012): 876–904.

80. Quoted in Dana N. Thompson Dorsey, "Segregation 2.0: The New Generation of School Segregation in the 21st Century," *Education and Urban Society* 45 (September 2013): 533–47.

81. Gregory J. Palardy, "High School Socioeconomic Segregation and Student Attainment," *American Educational Research Journal* 50 (August 2013): 746.

82. Ira Katznelson, *When Affirmative Action Was White: An Untold History of Racial Inequality in Twentieth Century America* (New York: W. W. Norton & Company, 2005).

83. Russell Nieli, *Wounds That Will Not Heal: Affirmative Action and Our Continuing Racial Divide* (New York: Encounter Books, 2012).

84. Khiara M. Bridges, "Class-Based Affirmative Action, or The Lies That We Tell about the Insignificance of Race," *Boston University Law Review* 96 (January 2016): 55–108.

85. Eduardo Bonilla-Silva, *Racism without Racists: Color-Blind Racism and the Persistence of Racial Inequality in America*, 4th ed. (Lanham, MD: Rowman & Littlefield, 2013), 126.

86. Ibid.

87. See Brantley W. Gasaway, "'Glimmers of Hope:' Progressive Evangelicals and Racism, 1965–2000," in *Christians and the Color Line: Race and Religion after Divided by Faith*, ed. J. Russell Hawkins and Phillip Luke Sinitiere (New York: Oxford University Press, 2013), 91.

88. Michael O. Emerson and Christian Smith, *Divided by Faith: Evangelical Religion and the Problem of Race in America* (New York: Oxford University Press, 2001), 79, 87.

89. Richard D. Fuerle, *Erectus Walks among Us: The Evolution of Modern Humans* (New York: Spooner Press, 2008). Available at https://analyseeconomique.files.wordpress.com/2012/12/richard-d-fuerle-erectus-walks-amongst-us.pdf.

90. Nicholas Wade, *A Troublesome Inheritance: Genes, Race and Human History* (New York: Penguin, 2014), 13–14.

91. Ibid., 250.

92. Nicholas Wade, *The Faith Instinct: How Religion Evolved and Why It Endures* (New York: Penguin Press, 2009).

93. See, for example, Elizabeth A. Klonoff, Hope Landrine, and Jodie B. Ullman, "Racial Discrimination and Psychiatric Symptoms among Blacks," *Cultural Diversity and Ethnic Minority Psychology* 5 (November 1999): 329–39; Tiffany Yip, Gilbert C. Gee, and David T. Takeuchi, "Racial Discrimination and Psychological Distress: The Impact of Ethnic Identity and Age among Immigrant and United States–Born Asian Adults," *Developmental Psychology* 44 (May 2008): 787–800; Shelly P. Harrell, "A Multidimensional Conceptualization of Racism-Related Stress: Implications for the Well-Being of People of Color," *American Journal of Orthopsychiatry* 70 (January 2000): 42–57.

94. See, for example, Sherman A. James, David S. Strogatz, Steven B. Wing, and Diane L. Ramsey, "Socioeconomic Status, John Henryism, and Hypertension in Blacks and Whites," *American Journal of Epidemiology* 126 (1987): 664–73; Sherman A. James, "John Henryism and the Health of African-Americans," *Culture, Medicine and Psychiatry* 18 (June 1994): 163–82.

95. The classic explanation was by William H. Grier and Price M. Cobbs, *Black Rage* (New York: Basic Books, 1968; reprint ed., 1992).

96. Derald Wing Sue et. al., "Racial Microaggressions in Everyday Life: Implications for Clinical Practice," *American Psychologist* 62 (May–Jun 2007): 271–86.

97. Ibid., 279.

98. Shelby County, *Alabama v. Holder, Attorney General, et. al*, accessed at http://www.supremecourt.gov/opinions/12pdf/12-96_6k47.pdf.

99. Jess Bravin, "Court Upends Voting Rights Act: Justices End Nearly 50 Years of U.S. Oversight of Election Laws in Much of the South," *Wall Street Journal*, June 25, 2013, available at http://www.wsj.com/articles/SB10001424127887323469804578521363840962032.

100. Available at https://implicit.harvard.edu/implicit/takeatest.html.

101. Malcolm Gladwell, *Blink: The Power of Thinking without Thinking* (New York: Little, Brown and Company, 2005), 83–85.

102. Guy Harrison, *Race and Reality* (Amherst, NY: Prometheus Books, 2010).

103. Gladwell, *Blink*, 85.

104. Michelle Alexander. *The New Jim Crow: Mass Incarceration in the Age of Colorblindness*, rev. ed. (New York: The New Press, 2012).

105. See especially Eugene Jarecki and Christopher St. John, *The House I Live In: The War on Drugs Has Never Been about Drugs*, 2012 documentary, http://www.thehouseilivein.org/; Matthew Pillischer, *Broken*

on All Sides: Race, Mass Incarceration & New Visions for Criminal Justice in the U.S., 2012 documentary, http://brokenonallsides.com/.

106. David Fleer, "Scapegoating and Truth-telling," in *Reconciliation Reconsidered: Advancing the National Conversation on Race in Churches of Christ*, ed. Tanya Smith Brice (Abilene, TX: Abilene Christian University Press, 2016).

107. Douglas, "The Meaning of July Fourth for the Negro."

108. Soong-Chan Rah, *The Next Evangelicalism: Freeing the Church from Western Cultural Captivity* (Downers Grove, IL: InterVarsity Press, 2009).

109. Jim Wallis, *America's Original Sin: Racism, White Privilege, and the Bridge to a New America* (Grand Rapids, MI: Brazos Press, 2016).

110. Gladwell, *Blink*, 96.

5

ON THE OTHER SIDE
OF THE DIVIDE

Reginald D. Broadnax and Kenneth Q. James

"Hear my voice, O God, in my complaint...."
—*Psalm 64:1*

Rage. It is a feeling, an emotion, a sentiment, or a reaction that is not well tolerated in our nation, particularly if you are a black citizen. You can be enraged or outraged about ISIS, the economy, the "War on Terror," local or national politics even. But if you dare express rage—or anything even remotely close to such a thing—you are silenced, marginalized, ostracized, or ignored. The message, subtle but obvious, is that you have no right to feel this way. Rage is not acceptable. It is scary to most other Americans, and it is therefore not welcome or well tolerated.

But what exactly are we as a nation to do with the long, simmering hurts and offenses accumulated by our citizens of color? Is it really our intention to sweep them under the collective national carpet and either pretend they do not exist or hope that no new powder keg of violence will set off the explosion that is a long time coming and one day sure to explode? Is it the expectation that we can appease just enough people who might be otherwise injured under the same or similar circumstances with trinkets of success that they will get so wrapped up in the spoils and take the side of the oppressor, telling the masses who are pained to keep quiet and be grateful that they are not...somewhere else instead of here? Do we who bear the brunt and shame of these acts of cruelty, subjugation, and violence merely want to settle for a "hashtag" to express our frustration and outrage, only to return to business as usual, back to how things were, and complain of how we can't get ahead because of "The Man"?

What shall we do about this rage? James Baldwin wrote powerfully of this:

> I first contracted some dread, chronic disease, the unfailing symptom of which is a kind of blind fever, a pounding in the skull and fire in the bowels. Once this disease is contracted, one can never be really carefree again, for the fever, without an instant's warning, can recur at any moment. It can wreck more important things than race relations. There is not a Negro alive who does not have this rage in his blood—one has the choice, merely, of living with it consciously or surrendering to it. As for me, this fever has recurred in me, and does, and will until the day I die.[1]

Please don't rush past this comment. In fact, just let these words sit here. Think about them. Sure, it is going to be uncomfortable for a moment, but try not to squirm. The discomfort you feel may in a short time go away. For some others of us, it won't. It can't. It will, as Baldwin says, be with us on a recurring basis until the day we die. Perhaps more importantly and to the point, maybe this rage shouldn't leave any of us, no matter where you stand or what you believe.

We realize it is hard to imagine anyone living with rage. It is detrimental, some would say, to one's being and psyche to live with such emotion bottled up inside. Some will dismiss the rage and even suggest that one who should feel such aggravation or sentiment is either ungrateful or unpatriotic—and by the way, how dare they, given the many advantages of living in this "exceptional" country called the United States of America?

A number of issues in every area and facet of our lives, from sports to politics, have both informed this rage and the responses to it. Discussions around theological circles, conversations in homes and churches, even what once may have been polite "watercooler" talk, could not possibly allow us to move past this matter. Our theology is informed by these matters at hand. In fact, it is hard to imagine how there could be two more significant topics that "go together like a hand in glove" like theology and justice. Theology and justice are twins, inseparable, indivisible, intertwined. Well, at least most of us thought so.

Two years ago, when I (Kenneth) attended my first National Council of Churches Christian Unity Gathering meeting, a comment was made that both stunned and electrified me. The comment pointed out and brought into sharp relief the difference between some in the faith community who act out of a sense of charity and those in the faith community who act out of a sense of justice. I had not quite thought of it on those terms, but since I heard the remark, I have not been able to let go of the thought.

Please understand, in no way do we doubt or question the sincere charity of those who see the injustices heaped upon persons in our community, the African American community. We fully believe they are concerned. We would have to believe they are callous and heartless to be unaffected by the horrors so many are facing, and not for one second do we believe they are. If we tried to cite instances where outrage is appropriate, what we discover is that every time we start a list, another outrage emerges. There have already been too many names of too many people who would surely much rather be anonymous and alive than dead and famous, a reason for a cause that continues to add names and victims without resolution or resolve. What we (and certainly their families) wouldn't give to have never heard the name Trayvon Martin. Or Sandra Bland. Or Eric Garner. Or Tamir Rice. Or...have you any idea how *exhausting* it is to try to count all those names?

But what spurs us to act, to write, to think of ways to address the matters that challenge and impact those marginalized by the issues we discuss in the safety of conferences at well-appointed hotels is that charity, well-meaning and well-intended as it is or might be, is just not enough. We are convinced, sure and certain, that the proximity one has to tragedy or trouble influences and shapes the way they see it. And on the matter of the mass incarceration of people of color, most Americans, dare we say most Christians, ourselves included, are standing on the other side of the divide.

That there is a divide, even among the best and well-meaning among us, is undeniable. Here is what proves the point for me. Engage someone from another culture other than your own living in America about any one of these issues and you will see what we mean. Bring up over lunch or dinner (assuming you have a friend of another culture or race that you regularly dine with) the shooting by Dylann Roof in Charleston, South Carolina, at the Mother Emmanuel AME Church on a Wednesday night during Bible study. Raise the issue of the flying of the Confederate flag over a state capital in which African Americans live. Bring up the subject of #BlackLivesMatter. Discuss the recent election of Donald J. Trump, and how black people see this outcome versus how white people see it. And then try to convince us that there is no divide. Again, we are not saying that anyone who is not an African American is uncaring. This is just meant to say what the late AME Zion Bishop Alfred G. Dunston Jr. was known to frequently say: "Where you stand determines what you see."

What do we see? Most of us have never been to jail, or had any adverse dealing with American justice. In the main, this American justice system works for us; at least that's what we believe and are told. Most of us would like to think that if a person ends up in jail that the American "justice" system works fairly and well for everyone; in the end, we all get what we deserve. There is, after it's all said and done, "liberty and justice for all." Right?

Well, here is where we encounter a problem. The problem we encounter is a legal problem, it is a social problem, it is a cultural problem, and most of all it is a theological problem. It is at this level of the problem—the theological level—that we should find the urgency to address the matter.

The legal, social, cultural, and theological problem that is manifest and is continuing to metastasize must be clearly on our radar for the damage it has done and is continuing to do. For one thing, it cannot be a positive development to consider the continuing and growing mistrust that the African American community has (in general) for the legal system. You may have heard the joke Richard Pryor used to tell about going to jail. Pryor quipped that when you look at the American legal system, "If you are looking for justice, that's what you find—just us." Whether that joke makes you laugh or cringe, let us accept the challenge to examine it for its theological implications. Those implications are racial, uncomfortable, disturbing, and dangerous. And they cannot be ignored.

We don't ignore the implications of mass incarceration. We

just handle them or address them differently. Let us take, for example, one of the more interesting developments of late, the question of whether felons in Virginia should have their voting rights restored after they have served their time. Estimates given suggest that as many as 200,000 freed felons would be able to vote if the measure proposed by Governor Terry McAuliffe stands. The argument against this move is that Gov. McAuliffe made this move as a blatant political stunt to assist the election of former Secretary of State Hillary Clinton in her bid for the presidency, that he is showing, some have said, "flagrant disregard for the Constitution of Virginia." That sounds hauntingly familiar to many, and it seems to fall back on the "law and order" argument of a few decades ago (which has resurfaced in the 2016 presidential campaign), whose design and purpose was alleged to keep people in certain communities (minorities?) in check.

Let's be clear that no one we know is arguing for lawlessness or anarchy. All of us, regardless of race, color, or creed, want to live in safe, secure, decent neighborhoods. But this matter of felons voting in Virginia and what is seen from one side of the divide versus the other raises this question—would, say, G. Gordon Liddy get to vote in Virginia? Or does this opposition against felons voting only apply to "certain" felons?

This is an issue that matters, theologically and politically. Even Senator Bernie Sanders, candidate for the Democratic Party nomination for president in 2016, has acknowledged (even if awkwardly and perhaps a bit ineptly) that poor people don't vote. And some can't even if they wanted to because they are restricted from voting due to a past felony on their record.

This is the reason for hope that we can understand why we have a problem. We cannot ignore this because the values we honor as a society or as a people of faith are the values we cultivate. Freedom is supposed to be a cherished American value, but it is apparently available only to a few, and those few to whom it is most readily available are those who can be counted among the privileged. They are the persons who get to frame the discussion, to shape the conversation, and make up the rules. Policies, culture, laws, and wars are determined by those who have a seat at the table and a voice in the discussion. This is the culture we have and live with, hesitant though we might be to admit it. And what we are cultivating in the matter of mass incarceration, particularly as it impacts the poor of our society, is doing extraordinary damage to an extent that we may not ever have considered. This is not just an issue of cruel injustice; it is a national liability, and we ignore it at our peril.

As we speak to this, we do so in respect to the degree to which this impacts the black community. This is not intended to be an exhaustive analysis; nor is it intended to be exclusive or ignore the problems of other communities. The example of using the black community and black people as a template for our pain is instructive because, as Baldwin says,

> The Negro tells us where the bottom is: *because he is there*, and where he is, beneath us, we know where the limits are and how far we must not fall. We must not fall beneath him. We must never allow ourselves to fall that low....In a way, if the Negro were not here, we might be forced to deal within ourselves and our own personalities, with all those vices, all those conundrums, and all those mysteries with which we have invested the Negro race....We would never, never allow Negroes to starve, to grow bitter, and to die in ghettos all over the country if we were not driven by some nameless fear that has nothing to do with Negroes.[2]

Nevertheless, we confess to only offering a perspective. In 1903, W. E. B. DuBois famously wrote in his seminal work *The Souls of Black Folk* that "the problem of the Twentieth Century is the problem of the color line."[3] We have long thought of that quote and its implication and meaning. Two things strike us quite differently now as we think of what DuBois wrote at the dawn of the twentieth century. First, we wonder how could a man as intelligent as DuBois—one graciously afforded with the talents, gifts, and skills of a brilliant mind and sharp intellect—and who, despite the obvious hurdles of race and discrimination he faced, excel to the degree he did, manage to succeed in the American experiment and yet, despite his successes, grow or remain so cynical about the state of American cultural matters? We recognize that it is easier to dismiss persons who disagree with or stand on the other side of the divide from where we stand, but we also think it should be of grave concern that any person, not to mention someone with the resumé of DuBois, could so easily be so disillusioned with the American system. We also think we should count it as no small miracle that even more persons, despite their disillusionment, have remained hopeful and optimistic of the chances of "liberty and justice for all" when in so many cases those hopes have been severely disappointed.

But what else strikes us as interesting as we think of DuBois's comment is how he could have been so right for so long. He made this observation about the problem of the *twentieth century* being the problem of the color line in the early years of the twentieth century. Over a century later, this is still the problem. Despite the election—twice—of a black man as president, despite every and all other gains made by persons of color, this one problem persists. It reshapes itself and takes on new forms, mass incarceration being one that we address as our concern here.

It is the challenge incumbent upon us all to look at what is happening on the other side of the divide. We thought to address this topic in this way because others of our colleagues have written elsewhere in this book of this matter as a "church-dividing issue." That phrase struck me (Kenneth); it seemed a good way to frame the discussion. We are divided, and we must work together, cohesively and in unity, to address this manifestation of a racist seed that grows and won't be easily uprooted.

This is going to be a challenge for us, something that will stretch us and make us uncomfortable. Good! If we content ourselves to only see what we can see from where we stand, there are so many opportunities that we will miss. And for the sake of the kingdom, this will be most unfortunate.

It is most likely, maybe even probable, that we will not do justice to the impact that poverty has on the issue of mass incarceration. Here is what we know—and if we did not know this before, the O. J. Simpson trial proved it. Paul McCartney was almost right; no, money can't buy me love, but it can buy me justice. If I can pay for a lawyer, hire a smart and aggressive legal team to investigate fully and thoroughly, I can get justice American style. If I am G. Gordon Liddy, I can get a president to commute my felony sentence and even go on to influence politics as a radio commentator and pundit. Even if I am an Ethan Couch and I am responsible for the death of four people in Texas because I was driving while drunk, my parents can arrange for good enough legal counsel to allow me to plead "affluenza" as a defense, and get probation as a penalty for my crime, and even abscond from the state and country in disguise for a while hoping to avoid any penalty such as jail for my crime. No, money can't buy me love, but it can sure buy me justice.

And we also recall something Jim Wallis said in his outstanding book *America's Original Sin: Racism, White Privilege, and the Bridge to a New America*. Wallis offers this challenge: "It's time for white Christians to be more Christian than white."[4] That sounds like a tall order, even if it is a lofty goal. Frankly, maybe there is not a salient argument to be made against it. After all, the belief that binds us and the hope that buoys us is the hope that we might be one—unified, unanimous, and undivided in our concerns for justice—as Christians, as brothers, and as sisters. But it also gives us pause, because we are both black *and* Christian, *both* undeniably, *both* unashamedly, and *both* unmistakably. Raised in the inner city, in the black community (Kenneth in New York City, Reginald in Detroit), we cannot be otherwise. Furthermore, we do not wish to be diminished in our own perspective or in the way we are regarded, given the cultural and historical factors at play, by making any attempt to be less black because we are now Christians.

What does our theology say to this? What does our theology say about us when we say what it says about this? What impression or understanding will those who do not know have of God when we construct a theology that allows for the systemized subjugation of the poor? What are we to say about the will of God when the judicial system we endorse supports the suppression of the downtrodden and relishes the benefits of the "prosperity gospel" and those who stand to benefit from this, even while we pray, "Thy kingdom come, thy will be done on earth, as it is in heaven"? Is this to be understood as the will of a good and gracious God?

Still, I can't see poverty. I am sad to say this. I can't see it because I don't want to. I turn away from the television commercials that show me images of poor children. Leave me alone; I'm trying to binge watch *Game of Thrones*.

Blackness is then a useful metaphor for how this issue of poverty and the injustices in the system of American jurisprudence can be addressed. Blacks are at the bottom, and we do not want to be at the bottom, not while we are trying to "make America great again." But to be the church for which Jesus died, the church that is in pursuit of the goals of the kingdom of God, we may see how the black church has led the way toward a theology of hope and for justice, and thus follow a course already chartered for us. And as Lester Agyei McCorn wrote,

> The African American community has long relied on the Black Church as an agent and advocate of stability within a hostile society. Currently, however, there appears to be a lack of concrete strategy of action from the church because of a perceived lack of information, interest and involvement.[5]

The black church, long in the vanguard of issues of justice, is tempted by the lure of the "prosperity gospel," losing members of our community and society in its quest for success, and in danger of being perceived as irrelevant. The church at large faces the dilemma of being an institution seen and populated by the "upper crust" of the society, an institution with a grand legacy and no one to leave it to. Yet, despite these apparent obstacles, there remains great opportunity, for the fact is that for all our discussions of unity and mutuality, there is not a single person who would want to trade places from our position of affluence and opulence to be in the place of the downtrodden, those we deal with charitably rather than justly. This fact need not discourage us to inaction. It can spur us to make bold decisions—and it should—in Jesus' name! Because it is with the downtrodden that Jesus has chosen to take up his lot:

> The basic fact is that Christianity as it was born in the mind of this Jewish teacher and thinker appears as a technique of survival for the oppressed. That it became, through the intervening years, a religion of the powerful and the dominant, used sometimes as an instrument of oppression, must not tempt us into believing that it was thus in the mind and life of Jesus....Wherever his spirit appears, the oppressed gather fresh courage.[6]

Thus, the challenge we present, and one that we hope each person will accept in God's name as well as we trust you will accept us, is that we bring our blackness and our experience, which is sometimes painful, as black men in America, to the discussion, and we invite you to see what we see from the other side of the divide.

> "Therefore confess your sins to one another, and pray for one another, so that you may be healed. The prayer of the righteous is powerful and effective." (James 5:16)

Notes

1. James Baldwin, *Notes of a Native Son* (Boston: Beacon, 1955), 96.

2. James Baldwin, *Nobody Knows My Name* (New York: Dell, 1961), 133–34.

3. W. E. B. Dubois, *The Souls of Black Folk*, in *Three Negro Classics* (New York: Avon, 1965), 209.

4. Jim Wallis, *America's Original Sin: Racism, White Privilege, and the Bridge to a New America* (Grand Rapids, MI: Brazos, 2016), xviii.

5. Lester Agyei McCorn, *Standing on Holy Common Ground: An Africentric Ministry Approach to Prophetic Community Engagement* (Chicago: MMGI, 2013), 11.

6. Howard Thurman, *Jesus and the Disinherited* (Richmond, IN: Abingdon, 1976), 29.

II BIBLICAL REFLECTIONS

6

SEVENTY TIMES SEVEN
Offenders, Victims, and Jesus' Extravagant Call to Forgive

Gayle Gerber Koontz

If God were not forgiving, heaven would be empty.
—*Zimbabwean proverb*

When family members and loved ones of the nine members from the Emmanuel African Methodist Episcopal Church Bible study, killed by Dylann Roof on June 17, 2015, in Charleston, South Carolina, said to him several days later that they had forgiven him, not everyone rejoiced. Some worried that this was "cheap grace," given too quickly and without repentance, and that it focused attention on the violator rather than on the long-term process of healing for the victims.[1] This critique echoed some of the concern voiced in 2006, when Amish families in the village of Nickel Mines, Pennsylvania, quickly forgave Charlie Roberts, who shot ten children in the local Amish school, killing five and severely wounding the others. Yet, doesn't the God known through the long biblical story call Christians to forgive others with extravagant mercy?

As profoundly true as this bottom line conviction is, it seems to run roughshod over those who have lost property, families, or friends through the violent actions of others. Because my Mennonite tradition has upheld a strong commitment to forgiveness for the sake of peacemaking, it has had to face challenging questions. What about justice? Doesn't an emphasis on forgiveness privilege the welfare of offenders over that of victims? Isn't readiness to forgive an integral part of a pacifist orientation that tends to ignore the need for interpersonal and structural justice while focusing on love of the enemy?

This critique along with other developments, including work with offender-victim reconciliation initiatives since the 1970s, has led many American Mennonites to a more holistic theology and practice of peacemaking, and an emphasis on *restorative justice*.[2] This term, now used widely in different fields, is an approach to criminal offending "that concentrates on relational, emotional, and material repair more than on conviction and punishment," and offers a third way between "the retributive and rehabilitative models that have long dominated penal philosophy."[3] It affirms values and commitments such as respectful dialogue, honesty, acceptance of responsibility, compassion, confession and forgiveness, acts of reparation, reconciliation, and social transformation. When possible, focus on restorative justice for *both* the injured and offenders is one way to emphasize that love *and* justice, forgiveness *and* repentance are critical aspects of a reconciling process.

While this approach has been most often used in situations where lesser crimes have been committed, in a few unusual cases a family member of someone who was murdered has over time met with and built relationships with the one who killed while the offender was serving long years in prison.[4] Occasionally time and events, including mental and emotional stability, do bring offenders to honest repentance. And many victims can and do forgive enough to move on with their lives without being bound by bitterness or the need to seek revenge.

Theological foundations for practices that encourage restorative justice are based in biblical narrative and faith. Christian Scripture testifies to a God who in relation to humankind expresses and embodies a rich understanding of restorative justice. "All have sinned and fall short of the glory of God" (Rom 3:23), yet Christians trust that God's saving purposes include not only judgment but also the restoration of a planet full of offenders, a creation groaning with violation and violence. Jesus' life and teaching, death on the cross and resurrection are critical keys to God's intent for a "new creation" marked by both love and justice.[5]

Jesus' parables of the Good Samaritan and the prodigal son, among many other parables and symbolic actions, are striking examples of teaching that honors practices of restorative justice for victims and for offenders.[6] And in his life, even in the face of suspicion, criticism, and violent death, Jesus held fast to God's reconciling purposes and call, demonstrating this quality of divine love. Looking back, Jesus' followers came to understand that God had "retrieved from the event of the death of Jesus the means of reconciliation precisely with those who killed him." That God "rendered the crime scene a place of mercy and grace was the surprise love sprang on humanity caught in the act of rebuffing the messenger" of God's new creation. "Remarkably, such love is nothing other than God's justice (*dikaoisunē*) at work in the faithfulness of Jesus (Rom 3:21–26)."[7]

Conviction that God raised Jesus from the dead and that the Holy Spirit was continuing to empower the early followers of Jesus in a myriad of ways led the early church to understand that God's purposes on earth included the creation of an outward moving, healing, justice-seeking, reconciling community of Jews and Gentiles, men and women. Two thousand years later it remains clear that our world desperately needs communities of faith committed to reconciling work. But human reconciliation—setting human relationships right before God and with each other—requires more than justice, defined as getting what one deserves, or love, defined as naïve grace. Adequate restitution for unjust acts or interpersonal wounds often cannot be made, and grace without accountability is shallow. The possibility for reconciling relationships, therefore, depends finally on the gift of *costly* forgiveness. But isn't that exactly the problem? Forgive an unrepentant shooter who kills innocent people? How can this happen with integrity?

The Emmanuel AME members and Amish families who spoke of forgiving the men who killed those they loved had been formed by straightforward biblical teaching and by theology and practices that had been developed in their church traditions. A central practice is the Lord's Prayer, which includes the words, "Forgive us our debts, *as we forgive our debtors*." This is one of the first prayers that the parents of the Amish children in the Nickel Mines community had learned as children. It is repeated at every one of their church services, and at meals, inscribing it in their spiritual orientation.[8] Elizabeth Alston, a longtime member at Emmanuel AME, also mentioned the shaping force of the Lord's Prayer in her orientation toward forgiveness: "It took me awhile. If somebody shot my mother I didn't think I could be as forgiving, but now I could. I just felt that I've been praying 'forgive those who trespass against us' (from The Lord's Prayer) for years, and now it was time to re-examine those words and practice it."[9]

In Matthew, the prayer Jesus gave us is followed by the warning that if we forgive others their trespasses, God will also forgive us; but if we do not forgive others, neither will God forgive our trespasses (Matt 6:14–15). Even more direct are those verses in Luke: "Be on your guard! If another disciple sins, you must rebuke the offender, and if there is repentance, you must forgive. And if the same person sins against you seven times a day, and turns back to you seven times and says, 'I repent,' you must forgive" (Luke 17:3–4).

Jesus' teaching in the Sermon on the Mount addresses not only relationships among disciples but also responses to enemies. The Gospel of Matthew remembers Jesus moving beyond an understanding of justice that limits retaliatory violence to "an eye for an eye" toward creative actions that seek not only to break the cycle of retaliation but potentially to move the relationship to a different level of human interaction (Matt 5:38–48). In the New Testament context, turning the other cheek, going the second mile, and offering one's cloak as well as coat, as Walter Wink has suggested, could have startled an enemy into recognizing the humanity of the person they were injuring, while also giving the less powerful person an option for response other than violence or passive acquiescence.[10] Interim pastor Novel Goff Sr., at the Emmanuel AME Bible study one week after the shooting, exemplified this active possibility as he declared that "this territory belongs to God." In facing trouble—their violent enemy—the members of the community were not powerless; they refused to contribute to the racial war the shooter hoped to initiate. Though they would never be the same, "God gives us the ability to let it go," Goff said. Compared to the hatred displayed last week, "We are better than that."[11]

A Christian orientation toward forgiveness is not primarily a strategic response to those who commit evil acts, for there is no guarantee that enemies will repent or stop violent activity, though it leaves open that possibility. Rather, it is part of a spiritually formed character that trusts in God's care of the lost, power to heal, and ultimate vindication of those who follow Christ's way of facing evil through the power of the Holy Spirit.

Nor is an orientation toward forgiveness a stance that ignores justice, as it might first appear. A theology of forgiveness and reconciliation that has integrity within a framework of restorative justice *looks forward* toward a human community in which justice and love embrace. God's desire for just and loving relationships among humans—rather than an apparent harmony that hides injustice—suggests several important actions when injury has occurred: the truth about what has happened must be told, those who commit crimes must be confronted with the wrongness and results of their actions and steps taken to hold them accountable for ongoing actions; and resources for healing must be directed to the needs of those who have been injured. In addition, it is important to address power dynamics between the injurers and injured. Injured ones are likely to feel extremely powerless and often are quite powerless economically, legally, socially, or physically in relation to those who injure them. Offenders who are apprehended may be vulnerable in a variety of ways as well. Often they are themselves victims of neglect, bullying, unstable family life, addictions, systemic poverty, racism, or mental illness. Companioning, advocating for, and empowering those who have less access to power is part of a process of restorative justice. The call to forgive is not the first or only word when Christians face injury.

Part of the confusion that plagues talk about forgiveness in the context of violent crime is differing understandings of what it means to forgive. Forgiveness is not a single, onetime act; it is an orientation and an ongoing process. It is not as simplistic an action as the media initially might have made the acts of the Nickel Mines Amish and the Charleston AME members appear. When interviewing Nickel Mines families five years after the tragedy, family members made it clear that "the path to forgiveness is ongoing and must be walked every day." One father said, "I can say I forgive Charlie Roberts, and I mean it, but that doesn't mean I don't have to revisit the issue next time."[12]

Further, without a nuanced understanding of forgiveness as a process, we might assume that it is impossible to be both forgiving and angry. Christian ethicist Beverly Harrison's essay "The Power of Anger in the Work of Love"[13] has been helpful to injured ones who have rightly felt anger and blame toward offenders but have then felt shame for feeling angry. This shame is intensified when others in the church criticize the injured persons for allowing the sun to "go down on your anger" (Eph 4:26). A cycle ripe for the growth of resentment has begun. Harrison suggests that one way to break this cycle is to recognize the valid role that anger and blame play *in the work of love*. If injured ones can accept and value their anger as a sign of moral sensitivity rather than of moral insensitivity, and if they can identify when they feel a false sense of shame for being angry, then they will be freer to direct the energy from their anger into creative acts toward change.

New Testament scholar Tom Yoder Neufeld also points out that Matthew 18, the fourth of Matthew's five major discourses, a chapter that is often used to point out the importance of reconciling work in the church when there is offense, begins with "rage directed at those who exploit."[14] Matthew appeals to a tradition that both Mark and Luke also recall of "very harsh words": It would be better to cut off an offending limb (Matt 18:8) or "if a great millstone were fastened around your neck and you were drowned in the depth of the sea" than to cause "little ones" to stumble (Matt 18:6). Even if these words use hyperbole for effect, righteous anger directed at sin clearly can coexist with forgiveness of those who offend.[15]

Distinguishing between the concepts of forgiveness and reconciliation is also important. This distinction has grown in significance with the development of the idea that forgiveness is important for the sake of the injured person. Forgiveness is a moral act of the injured one that is independent of a restored relationship between the offender and injured person. In the words of a commentator on pastoral care, "Forgiveness is not the equivalent of reconciliation…; it is the means by which barriers to reconciliation (which may or may not follow) are removed."[16]

Christians might assume that if someone who has suffered from violence or violation has come to forgive a perpetrator, the injured one should be ready to be reconciled with the person who hurt them. However, emphasis on personal reconciliation may feel like a moral club to injured persons, pressing them to relate to an offender when they are not ready to do so.

In a Christian perspective, the ultimate hope *is* for reconciliation and communion—with God, other humans, and the earth.

However, such reconciliation is not always possible. Sometimes an offender refuses to acknowledge responsibility for the injury and continues hateful attitudes and actions. Sometimes the injured person does not know or loses contact with the injurer as may be the case in sexual assault or situations of genocide. Sometimes the offender kills himself as the man who shot the Amish children did. Sometimes an injured one is not ready to forgive until many years after the injury, by which time the offender has died. Sometimes the injured one chooses not to meet an offender because of the way it recalls trauma. But however impossible reconciliation may seem or be, forgiveness of offenders remains both possible and a Christian hope.

FORGIVENESS AS MORAL AND EMOTIONAL LETTING GO

What exactly does it mean to forgive someone who has injured you if it does not entail reconciliation? It is first a moral act rather than a feeling, though the two are related.

Consider for a moment the economic image of an owner and debtor, the image to which Jesus appealed in the Lord's Prayer. Someone who has access to wealth loans some of it to a poorer person. As so frequently happens in tenant systems, the debtor may become more and more dependent on the owner until he or she loses everything or falls deeply into a debt that can never be repaid. There is no way out, except either bankruptcy or forgiveness of the debt. The rather literal principle is simple: rather than exact justice, people who hold others in their power economically ought to forgive those who cannot pay their debts. This generous spirit reflects God's spirit in relation to us.

We can expand this principle to include not only material debts owed us but also moral debts owed us because others have trespassed against us. When another injures us, that person "owes" us at least an apology or perhaps restitution or reparations. If they consistently or deeply injure us, their moral debt to us may increase to the point where they cannot make restitution—as is the case in the Nickel Mines and Charleston situations. As far as we are concerned, the offenders are "morally bankrupt." There is no way out for them but to declare bankruptcy and for their debt to be forgiven. Jesus' principle continues to apply: rather than exact justice, powerful people ought to forgive weak ones who cannot pay their debts.

But does this apply to those who have been injured? They are not the "powerful ones" in the relationship, are they? They are the ones who have been robbed of those they loved and of their own physical or emotional well-being. However, even though it seems counterintuitive, the one who has been harmed in a relationship is more powerful than the offender in one significant way: morally. In his essay translated from Swedish, Christian ethicist Carl Brakenhielm has defined forgiveness as a "remotivating act" in a situation of moral conflict.[17] A moral injury, he wrote, robs people of rights that belong to them as human beings. The injurer has used personal power to rob another, to establish a relationship in which the injurer says, in effect, "I am up here and you are down there." However, from a moral perspective, it is the *injured* one who is "up" and the offender who is "down." When the Charleston church members confronted Dylann Roof in the courtroom and said they forgave him, they were "up" and he was "down" in this sense.

Forgiveness is a remotivating choice and process that changes the *moral character* of a relationship that has been injured by moral offense. Brakenhielm explained it this way: Someone who truly desires the forgiveness of another person seeks to affirm the human rights and personal worth of the injured person. The one who grants forgiveness affirms the offender's human worth, which the injury obscured.

Forgiveness entails *both* moral criticism—the source of anger and resentment—and the effort to affirm the recipient's worth as a human being and child of God. While the injured person lets go of the moral debt, he or she does not let go of the commitment to justice, which is the root of moral criticism. Forgiveness is not saying, "It's OK," as if there were no significant moral failure. If there were no serious wrongdoing, there would be no need for forgiveness. Forgiveness does not mean letting go of justice, but holding on to God's restorative and compassionate justice. In this perspective, "forgiveness is a way of pursuing justice, not the abandonment of justice."[18]

Forgiveness requires extravagant generosity of spirit because the injured one has to let go of the moral advantage she holds over the injurer. It may be the only thing the one who has been hurt can withhold from the offender to retain some power and self-respect in the relationship and to communicate the depth of the injury. When there is a strong community of support and there are adequate and sensitive resources for healing from injury, however, those who have been injured can and should nurture the disposition to forgive. A disposition to forgive arises from gratitude for God's forgiveness of our own injuries to God and others as well as from the joy and confidence of being accepted for who we are contrasted with the rejection we may face from others. As Brakenhielm has put it, "I cannot at one and the same time believe in God's forgiveness [and acceptance] and be hardened against other persons whose life is under the same grace that mine is.…Thankfulness for God's forgiveness [and acceptance] is not really thankfulness if it does not also come to expression in humans in turn forgiving other humans."[19] Focusing on gratitude to God for what is life-giving in ongoing daily life rather than focusing on injuries and their effects can become part of nurturing a disposition to forgive. It can be a spiritual antidote to the growth of resentment and bitterness.

When there is the intention to forgive in light of God's reconciling purposes, the injured or shamed person can take various steps. Joseph Liechty, who spent many years working and teaching in Ireland on themes related to reconciliation, has suggested that the first dimension of the process of forgiveness is *letting go of the right to vengeance*. This choice may coincide with intense anger and hatred,[20] but it is a foundational step for eventually overcoming them. While refusing to retaliate is not the whole of forgiveness, it is a profound step in the process.[21] Even when we feel hatred and pain, we can pray passionately for God's grace to break in and heal what is twisted and broken in us and in those who have injured us. We can pray that God will soften the hearts of offenders and that they will truly repent. We can pray that God remove our desire to retaliate. We can pray for our enemies.

Liechty described another aspect of the process of forgiveness as *offering love before it is deserved*, noting the biblical story of the prodigal son as an illustration.[22] This is expressed in the actions and attitudes of the injured ones in response to injury: they make clear that love, not vengeance, is the motivation that shapes them. These, too, are choices that can be made even when feelings of love are not present.

Part of this action, as Lewis Smedes describes it, involves revising our caricature of the person who injured us. When we taste resentment, our minds draw a caricature of the offender as a monster and "define his whole person" in terms of how he injured or shamed us. In the process of forgiveness, we change our picture of the offender back to the "weak and faulty human being he is (or was)."[23]

These actions can pave the way for the emotional dimension of healing. In time, sorrow can blend with anger, and compassion and sympathy can break through resentment. Transformed feelings on the part of injured ones can create openness on their part to possible reconciliation with those who have abused them. The practices of letting go of retaliation and offering love before it is deserved are spiritual dispositions and disciplines that undergird openness to both receiving and offering holy grace amid the tragedies of our lives.

Because forgiveness is an ongoing attitude and process, it is not neat and orderly, nor is it fully within our control. God's disposition to forgive us requires God to bear the burden of our offenses—past and present—in an ongoing way even during our transformation. So does our disposition to forgive others. Our intention to see an offender as other than a "monster" or to revise our feelings may be sincere but not strong enough to sustain the pain of injury at all times. Sometimes even the best intentions, moral choices, and "letting go" of pain do not seem to open the way to revised feelings toward those who injure. Developmental psychologist Evelyn Whitehead and her husband, James, a pastoral theologian, remind us that "forgiveness is more than a personal achievement. It is a gift and a grace that, spent by our anger, we must await in hope."[24]

CHEAP GRACE AND HONEST REPENTANCE

Those who have been deeply injured are wary of offering cheap grace and rightly so. The wariness comes from seeing all too clearly the possible misuses of forgiveness as a tool for power. For example, the demand for forgiveness or the exhortation to forgive can be used to gain or maintain control in a situation. Feigned repentance or false generosity of spirit while forgiving another can also become a way to gain personal advantage over the other. By forgiving too quickly, the offended one may reinforce a continuing, hurtful power relationship or a pattern of violence that might also endanger others. An offender might even adopt an understanding of God's forgiveness that allows him or her to go on sinning with a clear conscience.[25]

Injured ones who understand the misuse of forgiveness know that "grace cannot be dishonest without being cheap."[26] To respond to this problem, Liechty suggests that while the loving will to forgive may be unqualified and limitless, the acts of love may be calculated, strategic.[27] For example, the church can support "good punishment," as Christian ethicist James Logan put it,[28] and set clear behavioral boundaries and supervisory relationships for those who injure. The church should also expect and invite honest repentance.

Those who injure must wait in hope for forgiveness. In genuine repentance, an offender makes a serious plea: "I have done wrong. I have violated God's intention for me. I do not want to be separated from God and from you. I want you to trust me. And I promise from now on to be worthy of your trust." Repentance, or *metanoia*, means change or turning; it is more than saying one is sorry. Smedes has described repentance as "giant's work. Only a person who dares to look hard and deep into his potential for doing evil as well as good will have the courage to repent. And only a person who is willing to risk everything for the high stakes of honest reconciliation has the moral power."[29]

Based on the importance of repentance and forgiveness in Scripture, the postbiblical church developed doctrine and practices related to them. By 1439, the Roman Church held to a doctrine and sacrament of penance that consisted of contrition, confession, restitution, and absolution. Scholastic theology assumed that the first three were necessary to the fourth; popular belief held that they were also *sufficient* conditions for forgiveness.

Luther turned against this latter idea, arguing that works do not make us deserving of God's forgiveness—that forgiveness as well as repentance and faith are gracious gifts of God. Luther's point was that we can never demand forgiveness. We can only ask a favor.[30]

Anabaptist Mennonites saw the dangers of a broken link between God's gracious forgiveness and our moral lives—that is, of thinking that no matter what we do, God will forgive us. Although they affirmed with Luther the priority of grace, they emphasized the importance of following Christ in life. But in time this came to feel to some like one more condition for receiving God's acceptance and forgiving love.

A solution some have proposed is that while repentance is not a necessary condition for God to forgive an offender, repentance *is* necessary for a sinner to *experience* grace or forgiveness. In Brakenhielm's words, "One does not have to interpret prayer, repentance, and restitution as demands to be fulfilled in order to obtain forgiveness; one can simply consider them as presuppositions for experiencing God's forgiveness in a meaningful way." Understood in this way, the necessity of repentance "can very well be held together with the thought that God's forgiveness is unconditional and absolute."[31]

In the context of human relationships, this understanding can help mediate the problem of cheap grace. When an injured one offers forgiveness to an unrepentant offender, the offender cannot truly experience it. He cannot receive the grace offered him without honest repentance.

In fact, an unrepentant offender does not want forgiveness. Speaking in the aftermath of World War II, Christian poet, novelist, and historian Charles Williams recognized that "the deeper the injury, the less inclined the evildoer is to ask, even to desire, that the sin may be forgiven—perhaps the less able."[32] We cannot make another repent. If an offender refuses to repent, he will experience a community's attempts at restorative justice—which includes requiring him to bear responsibility for wrongdoing—as punishment rather than as one face of grace.

Honest repentance is clearly required for reconciliation, for in order for a relationship to be restored in some right form, both parties or groups must be willing to "experience the fellowship of sufferings."[33] That includes remembering and confessing pain, forgiving, and repenting—all difficult actions. Liechty names *absolution* as the final step in forgiveness: "the wronged party indicates an intention not to bear grudges."[34] The parallel final step in repentance might be appropriate acts of restitution or sharing resources that indicate the injured one's intrinsic value and the penitent's intention to empower the injured one for a better future.

In situations where offenders experience themselves as victims of others' actions or systemic abuse, they may also need to forgive those who hurt them. This may be so at least to set aside revenge in order to break out of a cycle of emotional and physical retaliation and move into a different future.

With honest completion of these final dimensions, a renewed relationship between injurer and injured becomes possible. It may be stronger than before the offense or it may be more distant, but the relationship will testify to the possibility that compassionate justice can prevail over violence and violation in relationships.[35]

CHRISTIAN COMPANIONSHIP: ACCOMPANY-ING VICTIMS AND OFFENDERS

In a fearful and greedy national climate, which fosters mass incarceration and an ideology of due punishment, Christian congregations and friends of Christ can model a strikingly different orientation toward forgiveness within the framework of restorative justice. The church can have a significant role in providing resources for healing from injury, promoting justice in relationships, and creating settings for the actual experience of repentance, forgiveness, and reconciliation. But it is hard work that requires spiritual labor, humility, and courage.

An immediate problem is that often among contemporary Protestants, including many believers' churches, the theology and practice of forgiveness are framed in individualistic terms. An individual sits or stands alone before God in public worship, receiving communion, privately confessing sin or pain, and seeking forgiveness or healing. Depending on the nature of the offense and its conspicuousness, a pastor may "need to get involved." In North America, where we imbibe cultural values that emphasize the desires and rights of the self—and privacy when it involves family, sex, or money—confessing specific sins or describing our wounds is not only uncomfortable, but also seems in bad taste. Room for the Christian community to address injury shrinks comparatively.

However, when we marginalize the role of the Christian community and its representatives in the mission of restorative justice, we not only let injured ones remain isolated in their pain and allow those who injure others to avoid facing the impact of their actions, but we also hinder both from having the eventual experience of forgiveness. In a Christian perspective, healing from injury and sin are spiritual realities. Spiritual healing takes place in the context of Christian worship, community life, and mission. For this to occur the church must both model and provide adequate spiritual space and practical structures that invite and support healing from injury; admonishment of sin; confession, repentance, and forgiving; and the celebration of movement toward reconciliation.

Accompanying the injured. As a companion of those who have been injured, the church can surround them with pastoral care as well as financial support for healing ministries outside the congregation or parish. Churches can recognize and understand victims' righteous anger and accept it as part of a process of restorative justice.

It is important also to remember that those who commit crimes injure not only the direct recipients of the actions. Those close to the recipients are injured as well.[36] When an offender kills himself and those around him, many people besides those killed or physically wounded also suffer profound injury and loss. In addition, families of people who commit crimes are often shamed and sometimes isolated. One of the remarkable aspects of the Nickel Mines situation was that members of the Amish community placed a "protective blanket" around Robert's wife and children. They showered the family with gifts, meals, and love after the shooting.[37]

Christians who walk alongside the injured should respect their psychological and spiritual healing process, exercising patience. Some who suffer injury may need many years to mourn and adjust to all they lost at the hands of those who did violence to them.[38] To assist in the process of mourning, the church can and must provide spiritual and emotional space for lament within the larger worshipping life of congregations. At the same time, we should recognize that psychological considerations can at times be used as an excuse by injured ones to avoid the necessary pain of the healing process or to rationalize "not forgiving." As companions of the injured, the Christian community also has a role in nurturing their disposition toward forgiveness.

Further, as Catholic religious social ethicist Christine Gudorf has pointed out, both victims and those who see themselves as potential victims often have trouble with trust and need to develop a sense of safety in relation to others. The church can have a strong role "in restoring the capacity of victims to trust" by being trustworthy itself.[39] This is a high calling and commitment.

Accompanying those who have injured others. The Christian community also has a responsibility to accompany sinners. On the one hand, this means confronting those who injure others, making clear the wrongness of their acts in relation to God's intentions for human life. This means specifically naming such acts, not simply speaking in abstractions. Theological ethicist Stanley Hauerwas has emphasized the importance of acknowledging sin before others: "We are seldom in a position to know the truth about our sin until we make our lives available to others in such a way that we may be taught the truth about ourselves."[40]

On the other hand, this means making space for repentant offenders to experience transformation through the renewing power of human and divine forgiveness and acceptance. If the ones they have injured cannot forgive them, are not ready to hear their genuine confession and observe their repentance, or are no longer living, other members of the church can receive their confession, thereby allowing the injurer to experience God's forgiveness through the congregation's or its representatives' own accepting love. In Christian perspective, it is not the case that only an injured one can forgive an offender.[41] The grace of God and God's church are not held hostage by the inability of injured ones to forgive repentant offenders.

The most "leprous" of criminal offenders in North America are sex offenders, and consequences are harsh. For a Christian congregation to work at restorative justice in such situations without endangering vulnerable adults and children is challenging. It is also a ministry that few public communities will be willing to tackle, banning these "strangers" to even greater isolation and need.[42]

In the act of acknowledging sin, offenders must also deal with shame. But theirs is an appropriate shame. The church is responsible

107

to help monitor the behaviors of abusers as well as to help reestablish relationships of trust with the Christian community that have been shamefully betrayed. Linking Christian discipline and forgiveness is assumed in the reconciling process outlined in Matthew 18. While church discipline has far too often been practiced in judgmental rather than forgiving ways, causing many who have experienced it this way to abandon church discipline altogether, there are also hope-filled accounts of Christian transformation through responsible admonishment, repentance, and forgiveness.

FORMATION AND WITNESS

Perhaps most important, the church has a *proactive* role in teaching and forming its members in living responsibly so that healing and forgiveness are less frequently necessary. Insofar as racism and privilege, poverty and greed—to name a few deeply destructive barriers to becoming a truly forgiving and reconciling community in Christ—we have work to do both within and outside the church.

The divine grace and human practice of offering restorative justice for both the injured and the injurers is an antidote to the fear and mistrust that pervade relationships and communities seared by moral injury.[43] Empowered by God, Christians can both listen to and tell friends and neighbors the truth of their lives, a precursor to saving work. As Stanley Hauerwas warned a group of graduates at a Christian college, unless we humans can tell one another the truth that can lead to repentance and forgiveness, "we are condemned to live in a world of violence and destruction."[44]

But even in that kind of world Christians can live with hope and joy, witnessing to another reality. We can do so because as a people we have been constituted by a reconciling God. We are not alone either in sin or grace, injury or offense; we are beloved of God and placed within a forgiven and forgiving Christian community. We are offered urgent, meaningful work—an ongoing ministry of reconciliation.[45] We are entrusted with formational practices of truth-telling, burden bearing, healing, honest repentance, and forgiveness, practices that prepare the soil for God's coming new creation. As Hauerwas proclaimed in his final words to the graduates, it is these practices that "make truth possible" within and beyond the church, "and with truth emerges the seed for peace among women and men on earth."[46] Such peace is holy fruit indeed.

Notes

1. Xolela Mangcu, "Should We Forgive the Charleston Killer?" *The Root*, posted June 21, 2015, accessed August 14, 2017, http://www .theroot.com/should-we-forgive-the-charleston-killer-1790860248. Mangcu is associate professor of sociology at the University of Capetown, South Africa.

Jamelle Bouie, in a June 22, 2015, Twitter conversation with Ta-Nehisi Coates from *The Atlantic*, warned that commentators may be looking for "cheap grace." Cited by Jack Jenkins, "Forgiveness, 'Cheap Grace,' and the Struggle for Justice in Charleston," *Think Progress*, June 23, 2015, accessed August 14, 2017, https://thinkprogress.org/forgiveness -cheap-grace-and-the-struggle-for-justice-in-charleston-702441885944/.

2. For a description of restorative justice and its theological basis, see the pioneering work of Howard Zehr, *Changing Lenses: A New Focus for Crime and Justice* (Scottdale, PA: Herald Press, 1990); and the biblical interpretation of Christopher D. Marshall, *Beyond Retribution: A New Testament Vision for Justice, Crime, and Punishment* (Grand Rapids, MI: Eerdmans, 2001), as well as his more recent *Compassionate Justice: An Interdisciplinary Dialogue with Two Gospel Parables on Law, Crime, and Restorative Justice* (Eugene, OR: Cascade Books, 2012).

3. Marshall, *Compassionate Justice*, 4, 6.

4. One example is Bill Pelke, founder of Journey of Hope, an organization that works against the death penalty and for the spiritually healing power of forgiveness. Pelke authored a book about his own transformation after four teenage girls in the small city where they lived murdered his beloved grandmother in her home. Paula Cooper, the girl who stabbed the elderly woman multiple times, was fifteen years old; she was placed on death row. Pelke eventually became convinced that his grandmother's Christian faith would have led her to have had compassion on the girl, and he prayed for that same compassion. In time, he began to campaign against her death sentence. Over the years, Pelke and Cooper exchanged hundreds of letters and he visited her fourteen times in prison. See Bill Pelke, *Journey of Hope: From Violence to Healing* (place of publication not identified: XLibris, 2003). After twenty-seven years in prison, Cooper was released and began to rebuild her life in positive ways. However, in May 2015, she took her own life. Sharon Cohen, "Death Row Inmate at 16, Later Freed, Can't Escape the Past,"

The Elkhart Truth, October 8, 2015, section C1-2. For more stories by victims of violence, see also The Forgiveness Project, accessed June 10, 2016, http://theforgivenessproject.com/stories/.

5. Portions of this essay were based on or revised from Gayle Gerber Koontz, "Seventy Times Seven: Abuse and the Frustratingly Extravagant Call to Forgive," *The Mennonite Quarterly Review* 89 (January 2015): 129–52. Used with permission.

6. Marshall, *Compassionate Justice*, 4, 6.

7. Thomas R. Yoder Neufeld, *Killing Enmity: Violence and the New Testament* (Grand Rapids, MI: Baker Academic, 2011), 94.

8. Donald B. Kraybill, Steven M. Nolt, and David Weaver-Zercher, *Amish Grace: How Forgiveness Transcended Tragedy* (San Francisco: Jossey-Bass, 2007), 90–98. Steven Nolt commented in a September 22, 2015, email to me that "in the Lancaster settlement, at least, it would not be uncommon for the Lord's Prayer to be used, silently, eight times each day—as a morning prayer, before and after breakfast, before and after lunch, before and after supper, and at bedtime."

9. Dawn M. Turner, "Emmanuel AME Church and the audacity to forgive," *Chicago Tribune*, September 28, 2015, http://www.chicagotribune.com/news/columnists/ct-emanuel-church-charleston-dawn-turner-20150928-column.html.

10. Walter Wink, *Engaging the Powers: Discernment and Resistance in a World of Domination* (Minneapolis: Fortress Press, 1992), 175–93.

11. Martin Savidge and Pat St. Claire, "Emmanuel AME Bible Study Reclaims Room: 'This Territory Belongs to God,'" CNN report, Wednesday, June 24, 2015, accessed September 12, 2015, http://www.cnn.com/2015/06/24/us/charleston-church-shooting-main/.

12. Ad Crable and Cindy Stauffer, "Nickel Mines, 5 Years Later: A Daily Walk for Amish on Path of Grief and Forgiveness, *Lancaster Online*, October 2, 2011, accessed September 18, 2015, http://lancasteronline.com/news/nickel-mines-years-later-a-daily-walk-for-amish-on/article_3e48d95b-61d4-52ba-bade-7bffc61a7961.html.

13. Beverly Wildung Harrison, *Making the Connections* (Boston: Beacon Press, 1985), 3–21.

14. Yoder Neufeld, *Killing Enmity*, 42.

15. Jesus' righteous anger at those who defiled the temple, making it a "den of thieves," also coexisted with his prayer on the cross, "Father, forgive them for they know not what they do."

16. B. H. Childs, "Forgiveness," in *Dictionary of Pastoral Care and Counseling*, ed. Rodney Hunter (Nashville: Abingdon, 1990), 438.

17. Carl Reinhold Brakenhielm, *Forgiveness*, trans. Thor Hall (Minneapolis: Augsburg/Fortress, 1993), 15.

18. Joseph Liechty, "Forgiveness," *Vision* (Spring 2007): 47. For a more extended discussion of the place of forgiveness in restorative justice, see Joseph Liechty, "Putting Forgiveness in Its Place: The Dynamics of Reconciliation," in *Explorations in Reconciliation: New Directions in Theology*, ed. David Tombs and Joseph Liechty (Aldershot, UK: Ashgate, 2006), 59–68.

19. Brakenhielm, *Forgiveness*, 91. I have added the words in the brackets.

20. William Neblett has noted that "to grant forgiveness when resentment still persists is not uncommon at all. In fact, many human relationships could not withstand the strain if it were otherwise, if the various purposes which forgiveness serves could not be fulfilled unless every last ounce of resentment were finally wiped away." Neblett, "Forgiveness and Ideals," *Mind* 83 (1974): 270.

21. Liechty, "Forgiveness," 46.

22. Most of the Old and New Testament materials seem to assume that conversion and repentance precede God's forgiveness, whether of a nation or of individuals. See Dorothy Jean Weaver, "On Imitating God and Outwitting Satan: Biblical Perspectives on Forgiveness and the Community of Faith," *Mennonite Quarterly Review* 68 (April 1994): esp. 156–61. However, Brakenhielm concluded that Jesus' view on the question is not clear. In the story of the prodigal son, for example, the son confesses after he is already in his father's arms (Brakenhielm, *Forgiveness*, 60). One could also argue that the fact that the son returned may have at least implied repentance on his part.

23. Lewis B. Smedes, *Shame and Grace: Healing the Shame We Don't Deserve* (San Francisco: Harper, 1993), 136–37. Miroslav Volf expands on the theme of remembering wrongs rightly, that is, in a way that heals wounded persons and their relationships with others, including their relation to the perpetrators. His own experience of being repeatedly interrogated and threatened by military personnel in communist Yugoslavia in 1983, followed by his attempts to reframe the memories of his main abuser, serve as the basis for his reflections. "God's Forgiveness and Ours: Memory of Interrogations, Interrogation of Memory," *Anglican Theological Review* 89 (Spring 2007): 213–55. He also draws on this experience in *The End of Memory: Remembering Rightly in a Violent World* (Grand Rapids, MI: Eerdmans, 2006).

24. Evelyn Whitehead and James Whitehead, *A Sense of Sexuality* (New York: Doubleday, 1989), 81.

25. Brakenhielm, *Forgiveness*, 5–7. Voltaire is reported to have said to the priest who assured him on his deathbed that God forgives all sin,

"Of course he will forgive me—that's his job!" (cited in Brakenhielm, *Forgiveness*, 11).

26. Lewis B. Smedes, "Forgiving People Who Do Not Care," *Reformed Journal* 33 (April 1983): 17.

27. Liechty cited Miroslav Volf, *Exclusion and Embrace*, for referring to this as strategic or calculating love, "Forgiveness," 51.

28. James Samuel Logan, *Good Punishment? Christian Moral Practice and U.S. Imprisonment* (Grand Rapids, MI: Eerdmans, 2008).

29. Smedes, "Forgiving People Who Do Not Care," 16.

30. One can meet Luther's objection and adopt a weaker version that penance is a necessary but not a sufficient condition for God's grace.

31. Brakenhielm, *Forgiveness*, 79. Theologians and biblical scholars debate whether God's forgiveness is "unconditional and absolute" or if it requires repentance.

32. Charles Williams, *The Forgiveness of Sins* (Grand Rapids, MI: Eerdmans [1942] 1984), 165.

33. Marshall, *Beyond Retribution*, 277.

34. Liechty, "Forgiveness," 52.

35. Marshall uses the term *compassionate justice* in the title of his second book on restorative justice.

36. Christopher Marshall makes a distinction between *primary victims* and *secondary victims*. He suggests that when injustice or bitterness created by an offense is still felt by later generations, there are also "*subsequent victims* of the offender, who may also need to find a place of release from their pain through forgiving the absent offender." *Beyond Retribution*, 265.

37. Daniel Burke, "From Grief to Grace: Wife of Amish Schoolhouse Shooter Breaks Her Silence," CNN, September 29, 2013, accessed September 5, 2015, http://religion.blogs.cnn.com/2013/09/29/from-grief-to-grace-widow-of-amish-schoolhouse-shooter-breaks-her-silence/.

38. Ronald Rolheiser, *The Holy Longing: The Search for a Christian Spirituality* (New York: Doubleday, 1999), 150–53, implies this in his description. In this chapter, he counsels patience in dealing with anger and loss, but also says that there is time for those who have experienced loss to move beyond the "forty days."

39. Christine E. Gudorf, *Victimization: Examining Christian Complicity* (Philadelphia: Trinity Press International, 1992), 93.

40. Stanley Hauerwas, "Why Truthfulness Requires Forgiveness: A Commencement Address for Graduates of a College of the Church of the Second Chance," 11 (unpublished manuscript of address given at Goshen College, Goshen, Indiana, April 1992, copy in the Mennonite Historical Library, Goshen).

41. Here I differ from those who assert that "only victims have the right to confer forgiveness on their abusers"—Christopher Marshall, *Beyond Retribution*, 264. I base this understanding partly on the image of the church as the Body of Christ on earth (the church has been given the responsibility to bind and loose, as representatives of God offering forgiveness—but not lightly—to the repentant) especially in cases where it is impossible for victims or survivors of abuse to offer it to the offender directly, as when the victim has not been able to take steps toward forgiveness or is now dead.

42. Some Canadian Mennonites have attempted creative thinking and practice that might assist other congregations in reaching out to sex offenders released from prison. See Mark Yantzi, *Sexual Offending and Restoration* (Scottdale, PA: Herald Press, 1998). See also Karen A. McClintock, *Preventing Sexual Abuse in Congregations* (Herndon, VA: Alban Institute, 2004), 1–15, 51–67, 83–102; and Dove's Nest: Faith Communities Keeping Children and Youth Safe, www.dovesnest.net.

43. In a Goshen College class held in the county jail, in a group made up of half incarcerated young men and half male and female college students, one prisoner said that this setting was the first time in his life he had felt safe enough to begin to reveal his feelings to others. A trustworthy cultural climate creates openings for restorative justice to begin to take root. Reported by Carolyn Schrock Shenk, sermon at Assembly Mennonite Church, Goshen, Indiana, March 1, 2015.

44. Hauerwas, "Why Truthfulness Requires Forgiveness," 20.

45. "All this is from God, who reconciled us to himself through Christ, and has given us the ministry of reconciliation; that is, in Christ God was reconciling the world to himself, not counting their trespasses against them, and entrusting the message of reconciliation to us. So we are ambassadors for Christ, since God is making his appeal through us" (2 Cor 5:18–20).

46. Hauerwas, "Why Truthfulness Requires Forgiveness," 20.

7

CONSIDERING ISSUES OF MASS INCARCERATION THROUGH THE LENS OF THE BEATITUDES

Shirley Paulson

Now is an opportune time for theologians to demonstrate the practicality of biblical teachings in the context of contemporary American issues related to mass incarceration. The early release of six thousand inmates in November 2015 due to changes in federal sentencing guidelines marked a turning point in public thought regarding the interrelated concerns with injustice, expense, and moral values. Politically, socially, and morally, Americans have arrived at a juncture where even conservatives and liberals are looking together for new solutions to mass incarceration. A theme running through our related problems with overpopulated prisons, immigration, and an unresolved Guantanamo detention camp has appeared: we are learning that throwing away people we do not like resolves nothing.

But theological reflection can provide a meaningful link between sacred texts and the contemporary situation. Since the articles in this collection comprise an ecumenical resource, I will note the distinctive gifts of my denomination, Christian Science, to the concerns of mass incarceration, especially in the biblical reflections. My experience with the Bible is that it often confronts thoughts, habits, and even worldviews that distort our perception of God's presence and love. It brings correction, comfort, and healing.

This essay begins with an analysis of the contemporary issues related to mass incarceration, and then presents a healing dialogue between biblical passages and the modern concerns with fear, lack, and insecurity. The dialogue allows for the biblical text to challenge modern notions of injustice and to be read through the eyes of contemporary experience. Healing is the expectation of lasting reform and genuine peace.

There are countless issues related to mass incarceration that ought to be addressed, a number of which might be summed up in two recent reports. John Malcolm, director of the Edwin Meese III Center for Legal and Judicial Studies at the conservative Foundation in Washington told *The Christian Science Monitor* in the summer of 2015,

> There are positives to locking people up, but there are negatives too, that we're beginning to address....The big question is, once someone has been incarcerated for two years, do they need to be there for five years? If prison is designed to send somebody a message, after you've sent them that message and have given them skills they need, and you determine that they're not going to pose a threat, perhaps it's time to free up a prison cell for someone who richly deserves it.[1]

Ta-Nehisi Coates argues in his examination of "The Black Family in the Age of Mass Incarceration," in the October 2015 issue of *The Atlantic*, that the concerns of sociologist and senator Daniel Patrick Moynihan, who fifty years ago predicted "the breakdown of the Negro family structure," would come home to roost, and they have. Coates claims,

> By 2000, more than 1 million black children had a father in jail or prison—and roughly half of those fathers were living in the same household as their kids when they were locked up. Paternal incarceration is associated with behavior problems and delinquency, especially among boys....The burden continues after the father returns home, because a criminal record tends to injure employment prospects. Through it all, the children suffer.[2]

A short list of the issues beneath the surface of these reports includes the following: criminal behavior and mentality, the strength or weakness of family, the right definition of crime, the appropriate form of punishment, the means of true correction, the obvious and not so obvious role of classism and racism, mental health, the philosophical meaning of sin and evil, the responsibility of society as a whole, the role of forgiveness and revenge, the rights of defendants as well as the rights of victims, and the bias of the press. No one person or human institution can take responsibility for the solutions to these serious concerns, but Jesus' teachings from his Sermon on the Mount do shed light on the path to progress for everyone.

The most glaring adjustment we would make if we were to structure our society on Jesus' model is that we would shift from discarding the people we dislike to loving them. Jesus affirms it is easy to love those who love you (Matt 5:46), but he teaches an entirely counterintuitive approach to those who have harmed or could possibly harm us—our "enemies": "You have heard that it was said, 'You shall love your neighbor and hate your enemy.' But I say to you, Love your enemies and pray for those who persecute you" (Matt 5:43–45). Contrary to a naïve willingness to turn a blind eye to crime, the kind of love he teaches is the most effective and yet demanding way to face up to the existence of crime in our society.

It is possible that one of the reasons for the rise in intensity about incarceration (and its related means of discarding unwanted people) is that America has embraced a new culture known as "victimhood." Conor Friedersdorf argues in an article in *The Atlantic*, "The Rise of Victimhood," that society's willingness to accommodate microaggressions[3] has led to an attitude of fear, where every slight is taken as an offense, another opportunity to emphasize oppression and social marginalization.[4] The lack of clear distinction between destructive crime and unintended or misinterpreted behavior drives up a fearful defensiveness, as we have witnessed in police overreaction and the increase in social microaggressions. It is no mere coincidence that the eruptions at the University of Missouri and Yale University[5] took place only weeks after the first early prison release, and the debates over political correctness and insensitivity are rising to the forefront of public thought. Harry Bruinius of *The Christian Science Monitor* summarizes the situation and the hope he sees through the smoke of battle:

Simmering racial insensitivity and ascendant political correctness have mixed to form an explosive atmosphere in which the line between bad taste and outright animus has at times been blurred. The result on one hand is an escalation of righteous and voluble umbrage on all sides. But beneath that very public race for the moral high ground is a place where the conversation is meaningful, probing how American Millennials are evolving society's sense of what is offensive and acceptable.[6]

Across the country, we are now looking for healing. Jesus' brief teachings in the Beatitudes provide clear guidance for getting at the root of victimhood thinking, microaggressions, and real criminal behavior. For decades, we have concerned ourselves more with blaming those who offend us rather than loving them. Are we ready to realize the power inherent in *loving* perpetrators of either minor or major offenses? Of course, it is risky; such a radical adjustment for society has only been attempted in small utopian communities. Victims of either serious crime or imagined crime[7] feel that the crime justifies revenge, not love! They feel empowered to take defensive action, and the most common reaction is to banish the nuisance, through public shame, litigation, incarceration, and capital punishment. But the alternative—continuing with the status quo—promises increased fear, victimization, and incarceration, none of which we can afford. The kind of love we find in the Beatitudes includes neither tolerance for evil nor tolerance for overreaction; the more powerful the love, the more peace and safety ensue.

Although the causes of victimization vary, fear of its power is equally acute on either side of the prison walls. The Beatitudes speak to both sides. Whatever heals the wounds of incarcerated individuals is the same principle that heals the victims of crime. Even members of a society in which the *fear* of victimhood is contagious and running rampant can benefit from these teachings. I will demonstrate the perspective of Christian Science on victimhood through reference to the writings of Mary Baker Eddy, the founder of the denomination, in dialogue with Jesus' Beatitudes.

BLESSED ARE THE POOR IN SPIRIT, FOR THEIRS IS THE KINGDOM OF HEAVEN. (MATT 5:3)

The foundational message in this first beatitude is that we recognize we need spiritual nourishment. Knowing that we *are* poor in spirit and in need of the kingdom of heaven, we are receptive to blessings from God. But the comfort and peace we seek will never be possible within the same framework of self-justification and reaction that escalated into a painful situation. The self-perpetuating cycle of insecurity and fear amplifies microaggressions, which in turn provoke greater fear and insecurity. As the world is learning through decades of attempts to cope with terrorism, we cannot overcome fear by discarding the people who threaten us; fear itself inevitably aggravates yet more violence and crime. Fear exacerbates any intense situation, and those who survive the violence are usually convinced they have been unjustly accused, unjustly punished, unjustly misunderstood, or at least unjustly deprived of opportunities.

Society needs an alternative—justice for those within and those outside the prison walls—and this beatitude that tells of the blessing for the poor in Spirit guides us to embrace God's rule. Eddy's explanation for the source of God's benevolence is thus:

> When the sick or the sinning awake to realize their need of what they have not, they will be receptive of divine Science [not referring to a denomination, but the law and order of God's realm], which gravitates towards Soul and away from material sense, removes thought from the body, and elevates even mortal mind to the contemplation of something better than disease or sin.[8]

God's rule is always going to contrast with the temptation of human fears, reactions, opinions, because God provides answers. God loves, God plays no favorites, and God's blessings are abundant. We can envision such a contrast through the game of musical chairs. In this simple game, children are taught to fight for survival in the world of "not-enough."[9] The game begins with a precondition of

118

lack, as the children are expected to move "through life" with happy music. When a crisis hits, and the music halts, everyone must immediately grab whatever chair is available to stay "alive" in the game. As the game proceeds, they continually "throw away" one child after another, until the "winner" is the only one remaining alive. The winner is also the one who fought the hardest against his neighbor, to secure his own supplies.

The game played in reverse offers some insight into God's realm as a reverse of the kingdom of "not-enough." I have performed this exercise with adults who witnessed in vivid terms the change that comes over our attitudes and actions when we believe we are living with abundance. We had just played "the game" the normal way, in which the "winner" achieves victory by "pushing" everyone else away. Then we reversed the procedure, beginning with one extra chair (abundance); then when the music stopped ("crisis" hit), the players naturally sit down without shoving others away because there is an assurance of abundance. That game continues with a welcome of one new neighbor at a time, each bringing one more chair. No one experienced concern for "not-enough," since there was always abundance. No one acted out aggression or competition, but it was natural to "love our neighbors as ourselves." These were the same people who, only moments before, had struggled with each other for their own survival.

This alternative way of life is no more a *game* in the kingdom of heaven than the desperate attempts to secure one's needs in the kingdom of "not-enough." God's order is radically different; yet it is accessible here and now, bringing the blessing of life without fear, blame, violence, and victimization. The practicality of such a radical shift is seen in human stories that ring true to us. A woman in Australia has given over $1,000 (Australian) to a children's charity because of her pledge to give one dollar every time she receives an attack about her religion on Twitter.[10] "Urban Warriors" offers an innovative antiviolence program in Chicago, building bonds between veterans and gang members.[11] The kingdom of heaven is not remote; it is seen right here and can be attained when we play the game of life by God's rules instead of by the fear of lack.

BLESSED ARE THOSE WHO MOURN, FOR THEY WILL BE COMFORTED. (MATT 5:4)

Mourning itself is not comforting, whether we mourn the loss of something or someone through criminal acts, or whether we mourn the experience of injustice inflicted by society. But the shift to a new view comforts even those who mourn the greatest losses. Jesus continues to contrast the old and new, implying that happiness comes through the new realization of God's kingdom. This is to come about, not in the afterlife, but in the present human experience. Eddy claims the salutary shift is tangible to those who move from human longings to spiritual ones:

> Who that has felt the loss of human peace has not gained stronger desires for spiritual joy? The aspiration after heavenly good comes even before we discover what belongs to wisdom and Love. The loss of earthly hopes and pleasures brightens the ascending path of many a heart. The pains of sense quickly inform us that the pleasures of sense are mortal and that joy is spiritual.[12]

But as long as society behaves as if it remains in the paradigm of "not-enough," its citizens reinforce their own conviction of not-enough by searching for the blame in their neighbors. Mistaking the real culprit—the *belief* of lack, or not-enough, which causes aggression—they turn the blame on someone else, who may well be a victim of another source. They blame the criminal without knowing the underlying cause of the crime. They blame society for arranging itself in dominant/subdominant relations.

Reversing the perspective to God's provision of more than enough brings comfort, because neighbors, or members of the community, are no longer enemies. God's abundance precludes the temptation to live in dominant/subdominant relationships, as the struggle over the same finite resources vanishes. The urge to blame yields to the realization that people are not naturally enemies. Even when some members of the community may struggle to move to the new view of God's abundance, and they still regard their neighbors as threats to their security, those who know the constancy of God's provisions can extend patience, forgiveness, and encouragement. Our mourning turns to a desire to lift others out of their own darkness.

BLESSED ARE THE MEEK, FOR THEY WILL INHERIT THE EARTH. (MATT 5:5)

Meekness is the most difficult assignment for victims, as they already feel their dignity and worth has been assaulted. These victims are those who feel that either criminals or society are working against them, perhaps validated by an individual who has assaulted or destroyed something of value. A call for meekness is just as difficult for those who have been physically and unjustly assaulted as for the arrogant, dominant personality. It can feel like a command to become weak or to give up hard-won public stature. But Jesus' promise for the inheritance of the *earth* precludes such loss, making clear the inheritance is not a collection of esoteric goods of a remote afterworld. The inheritance for the meek must mean the assurance of having all they need in the here and now. And it is only the meek who find such inheritance because only they can relinquish their pride of achievement and possession—the millstones weighing them down in the "not-enough" paradigm. Eddy reinforces the distinction between the "prince of this world" and the divine authority of meekness—another way of describing the opposite forms of musical chairs: "Meekness and charity have divine authority. Mortals think wickedly; consequently, they are wicked. They think sickly thoughts, and so become sick. If sin makes sinners, Truth and Love alone can unmake them."[13]

The beggar in one of Jesus' parables illustrates this principle (see Luke 16:19–31). Lazarus was not only a homeless beggar, but suffered from an intense disease. His rich neighbor offered him neither food nor comfort. When they both died, the accounts of their next-life experiences reveal the moral, or result, of their human attitudes. The rich man whose arrogance could fathom no meekness in his relationship with his lowly neighbor suffered unbearable, interminable anguish; but Lazarus, who had no earthly pride to cling to, was treated to the full array of Abraham's comforts.

Returning to the analogy with musical chairs, Lazarus easily relinquished the "not-enough" kingdom to welcome the "more-than-enough" of God's gifts, whereas the rich man's tenacious hold on his identity within the dominant/subdominant paradigm resulted in a loss of everything he treasured. Pride in his personal treasures had lured him into the "not-enough-for-his-neighbor" kingdom, and yet how easily the strength of meekness and charity would have reversed his own future. We all have what we need to support justice through the power of meekness.

BLESSED ARE THOSE WHO HUNGER AND THIRST FOR RIGHTEOUSNESS,[14] FOR THEY WILL BE FILLED. (MATT 5:6)

This beatitude is the key to God's compassion for humanity. Whoever feels victimized, whether by a criminal, an accident, society at large, or even paranoia, needs solace. There are holes in the fabric of life that need mending, and the beatific promise is that these holes are filled. Everyone agrees that a loved relative who was murdered will never be returned; rape will never be undone; destroyed treasures may never be replaced. But the promise of this beatitude differs from social, political, psychological, or economic attempts to create justice. The notion of being filled is the result of yearning for a relationship with the things that are right.

As of this date, all the men who participated in the "Planting Justice" program while incarcerated in San Quentin have returned home successfully. In a video discussion among four of them about their happiness and fulfillment, a common theme emerges.[15] They acknowledge they had been given an opportunity not only to learn gardening skills and a chance to get a job when they were released, but most importantly, they learned how to change within. They learned to tend both the "outer garden" and the "inner garden"—allowing them to bring to blossom all the things that were right. Righteousness came from the change within. Wilmer Osibin III said the program "gave me a great awareness to which I never knew was inside of me." And Anthony Forrest prayed for his change:

Every time I went to prison, I lost everything. I lost my father; I lost my mother; I lost my brother, my younger brother. So I wanted change, but I didn't think a program would do it. So what I did was, I got on my knees and I prayed. I asked God if this was real, to help me to change this time, because I don't want to come home the same way I came to prison. I was broken, losing everything. Didn't have nobody to really care for me or love me.[16]

As these men have learned, it requires great fortitude to admit that righteous thinking and living is fully satisfying. Such a claim may even enrage those who argue that internal change will never affect the needed outward changes. Virtuous struggles might never fill the starving bellies in homes stricken with poverty! But history teaches that broken hearts, broken homes, and broken wallets are rarely cured—or satisfied—by the gifts (or handouts) of others. Returning to the metaphor of the musical chairs game, if we consent to the idea of the amplitude of divine grace, where God gives us all the love, joy, peace, and kindness we need, there is a way to conceive deep satisfaction for all.

All of us—wealthy, poor, legislators, citizens, victims, and criminals—are invited to stand up for the righteous cause and face the foe of the "not-enough" paradigm. Legislators may conceive more equitable laws; wealthy citizens may find ways to share more justly; victims may feel the peace of forgiveness; criminals may be ready to repent; poor people may discover new resources at hand. Eddy maintains that the happiness of deep satisfaction is available to everyone, abundantly, because its source is in God. "Soul has infinite resources with which to bless mankind, and happiness would be more readily attained and would be more secure in our keeping, if sought in Soul. Higher enjoyments alone can satisfy the cravings of immortal man. We cannot circumscribe happiness within the limits of personal sense."[17] This beatitude comforts us with the assertion that justice starts with *God* as the solution to brokenness. There is no room for naïveté concerning the depth of hungering and thirsting required to break out of the worldly forms of injustice. But, according to the beatitude, yearning for righteousness feeds us and fills up the emptiness in our hearts and lives.

BLESSED ARE THE MERCIFUL, FOR THEY WILL RECEIVE MERCY. (MATT 5:7)

This next beatitude is a necessary corollary to the previous one. Mercy is granted to those who live justly and mercifully. But as Eddy notes, mercy is unavailable to those who commit crimes without reformation. "Do you ask wisdom to be merciful and not to punish sin? Then 'ye ask amiss.' Without punishment, sin would multiply. Jesus' prayer, 'Forgive us our debts,' specified also the terms of forgiveness. When forgiving the adulterous woman he said, 'Go, and sin no more.'"[18] The inevitable punishment of crime must not be confused with God's ever-present healing grace, however. God's unfailing grace, in Eddy's view, stems from God's original creation of good. As she claims, "Man is incapable of sin, sickness, and death. The real man cannot depart from holiness, nor can God, by whom man is evolved, engender the capacity or freedom to sin."[19] When sin occurs, therefore, it must be punished until reformation takes place, because sin is not the natural or permanent state of human kind.

The type of reformation implied in Jesus' beatitude requires the prevention of bad behavior and more. Receiving mercy is giving mercy; receiving the generosity of love for others is giving love generously. Returning to the main theme throughout all the beatitudes, that blessedness in some form appears when we make the shift from the earthly, mortal views of limitation to the realization of God's ever-present and bounteous love, we see how vengeance yields to mercy. On the one hand, revenge is a natural reaction to those who have no vision for God's bountiful love, but it not only fails to restore what is lost, it perpetuates the victim's misery. On the other hand, the reason mercy brings peace even to victims is that it draws on the availability of more than enough resources.

What could the beatitude of mercy look like in an era of mass incarceration? Wrong attitudes, beliefs, and behaviors must be and will be punished until the evildoer stops believing, accepting, and acting on them. But mercy is a better healer than revenge. In the paradigm of musical chairs, the one who cheats and steals the "chair" rightly claimed by another may be doing it because she fears she will not have enough to provide for her family. Or she may be angry that someone else stole from her. But if mercy allows her to make the adjustment to the viewpoint of more-than-enough, she would discover her native goodness and God-given security without threat of attack. Mercy is kind, precisely because it gives space for needed correction.

BLESSED ARE THE PURE IN HEART, FOR THEY WILL SEE GOD. (MATT 5:8)

The twin sons of Isaac—Jacob and Esau—exemplify the shift from the kingdom of lack to the awareness of God's provisions (see Gen 25—28, 32—33). Their troubles came to a head when Jacob stole the rightful inheritance from their father that was intended for his brother Esau. His desperation leading to the deceit and criminal act arose from his belief that he lacked something of importance that his brother possessed. Esau beat him to "the chair." Although Jacob may have thought he saved himself by running away, years later he still feared for his life when he was forced to return home. His prayer began with an acknowledgment that he was not worthy of the steadfast love and faithfulness God had extended to him. In an echo of the first beatitude's sentiment, Jacob knew he was "poor in spirit" and was willing to be transformed.

But he also begged for mercy, aware that he deserved the severest punishment. God's mercy came in the form of a man (or angel) who wrestled with him until the break of day and blessed him. Eddy's exegesis of this passage highlights Jacob's passage from his deceitful, greedy past to his pure heart. She wrote,

> Jacob was *alone*, wrestling with error,—struggling with a mortal sense of life, substance, and intelligence as existent in matter with its false pleasures and pains,—when an angel, a message from Truth and Love, appeared to him and smote the sinew, or strength, of his error, till he saw its unreality; and Truth, being thereby understood, gave him spiritual strength in this Peniel of divine Science.[20] Then said the spiritual evangel: "Let me go, for the day breaketh;" that is, the light of Truth and Love

dawns upon thee. But the patriarch, perceiving his error and his need of help, did not loosen his hold upon this glorious light until his nature was transformed.[21]

This purifying transformation shifted Jacob to the God-governed version of life ("musical chairs"), where Jacob proclaimed it to be a holy place. As he described it, "I have seen God face to face, and yet my life is preserved" (Gen 32:30). He saw not only God face to face, but he saw his brother in new light as well. "To see your face," Jacob said to Esau, "is like seeing the face of God" (Gen 33:10), and they embraced in tears of joy. Their first utterances were of generosity: in the language of the new (musical chairs) paradigm, "Brother, have the chair next to me; I have enough."

BLESSED ARE THE PEACEMAKERS, FOR THEY WILL BE CALLED CHILDREN OF GOD. (MATT 5:9)

This beatitude asks of society whether it is willing to bear the responsibility of the crimes of others. What is it about society's attitudes, decisions, and values that contributes to greed, violence, injustice, hopelessness, and poverty? Imagine what happens to perfectly good citizens when someone invades their rights, their possessions, their source of income, or their dignity. We see the same reaction in the children who are bumped off their chairs when there aren't enough for everyone. They do not intend to become violent for the sake of violence, nor do they become hopeless because they are weak people. Some people blame racism, misogyny, or classism, but such reactions to others' differences tend to surface when there is a need to bump someone off the only "chair" available. Defining the "other" becomes the tool with which society decides whom to eliminate.

But when such artificial categories of "others" are eliminated, humanity—perceived as God's children—is naturally concordant. Eddy draws an analogy between such concordant conditions and the inherent laws of harmony in music. "Harmony in man is as beautiful as in music," she writes, "and discord is unnatural, unreal....A discontented, discordant mortal is no more a *man* than discord is music."[22] Peacemakers, then, are those who live as children of God or within the realm of God's abundance of blessings for all. They are settled with and grateful for the gifts of God, and thus feel no need to establish dominance, provoke, steal, react, or seek revenge.

A good schoolteacher corrects his students with the conviction that the right answer is present; he guides their thought to be receptive of it. Peacemakers can participate in the correction of social ills by the same principle. As God's children, they seek the "answer," or solution to social unrest, in the natural harmony of *God's* order. On this basis, fairness is measured by God's abundant grace, justice is meted out by divine wisdom, and correction occurs through the authority of divine Love.

BLESSED ARE THOSE WHO ARE PERSECUTED FOR RIGHTEOUSNESS' SAKE, FOR THEIRS IS THE KINGDOM OF HEAVEN. (MATT 5:10)

According to this beatitude, the kingdom of heaven is present and available, even where human injustice appears to take the upper hand. Eddy affirms there is no such thing as perfect justice in human relations, but she trusts the divine authority in Jesus' admonition to love our *enemies*. She wrote,

> Love[23] metes not out human justice, but divine mercy....
> We must love our enemies in all the manifestations
> wherein and whereby we love our friends; must even
> try not to expose their faults, but to do them good when-
> ever opportunity occurs....Never return evil for evil;
> and, above all, do not fancy that you have been wronged
> when you have not been....Every man and woman
> should be to-day a law to himself, herself,—a law of
> loyalty to Jesus' Sermon on the Mount.[24]

Such an idea—doing good to those who have caused harm—would be naïve and foolish without Jesus' opening of thought to a different understanding of justice associated with the kingdom of heaven. Where lack incites fear, it feeds relentless colonialism and oppression, and fear distorts the truth in the press. The righteousness Jesus upholds is not a request to love such injustice itself, but to love those who are themselves victims of the "not-enough" system. The real need is to lift those who are mired in the world of fear and injustice to an awakened desire for God's law of mercy.

Therefore, loving those who would harm us, with patience, mercy, and forgiveness, offers the most expedient incentive for our so-called enemies to make their own shift to the kingdom of God. Whether or not they are receptive to the love we extend, they can no longer harm the consciousness of God's giving more than enough.

BLESSED ARE YOU WHEN PEOPLE REVILE YOU AND PERSECUTE YOU AND UTTER ALL KINDS OF EVIL AGAINST YOU FALSELY ON MY ACCOUNT. REJOICE AND BE GLAD, FOR YOUR REWARD IS GREAT IN HEAVEN, FOR IN THE SAME WAY THEY PERSECUTED THE PROPHETS WHO WERE BEFORE YOU. (MATT 5:11–12)

Because no one can claim greater injustice than Jesus Christ, he is uniquely situated to teach us how to rejoice and discern the blessing even when we endure persecution on his behalf. This final beatitude confirms the heavenly nature of the reward we seek. It promises that we can break the cycle of victimhood, from the fear of microaggressions to the most heinous of crimes. We are not confined to the rule of lack, where the survival of the fittest causes unnatural aggression. From the strength of knowing the greatness of our rewards in heaven, we are alert to criminality, whether it is overt or covert; we are tempted with neither the desire to rid ourselves of fellow human beings nor to exercise revenge; we can correct what is truly offensive to God; and we are eager to extend mercy from the generosity of God's mercy toward us. One by one, each of us can participate in halting the cycle of mass incarceration—or the endless game of musical chairs—because we are committed to the healing of social ills as well as our personal faults.

CONCLUSION

The existence of grossly overpopulated prisons is a symptom of an unhealthy society, and a healthy uproar is being heard in halls of government, hospitals, community centers, churches, and homes. Christians responding to the biblical admonition to visit those in prison (Matt 25:31–43) seek theological and practical means to accomplish these visits in person and metaphorically. In an ecumenical context, churches are striving to work together to heal the brokenness in society, in private homes, and in the hearts of victims and inmates, and in response, this paper turns to Jesus' Beatitudes for guidance. The children's game of musical chairs (and its reverse, played with abundance) illustrates the distinction Jesus makes between the blessedness of the kingdom of God and the suffering caused by lack. But the Beatitudes constitute neither platitudes nor childishness; rather, the love of God is powerful, inspiring repentance, unselfish love for others, and healing. They reverse the paradigm of living with lack to the possibilities of living with God's generosity.

Notes

1. Patrick Jonsson, "Early Release from Federal Prison," *The Christian Science Monitor* (October 7, 2015), http://www.csmonitor.com/USA/Justice/2015/1007/Early-release-for-6-000-federal-prisoners-A-risk-to-public-safety.

2. Ta-Nehisi Coates, "50 Years after the Moynihan Report, Examining the Black Family in the Age of Mass Incarceration," *The Atlantic* (October 2015), http://www.theatlantic.com/magazine/archive/2015/10/the-black-family-in-the-age-of-mass-incarceration/403246/.

3. Friedersdorf relies on a definition of "microaggressions" from Jonathan Haidt, a social psychologist at the NYU-Stern School of Business: "a form of social control in which the aggrieved collect and publicize accounts of intercollective offenses making the case that relatively minor slights are part of a larger pattern of injustice and that those who suffer them are socially marginalized and deserving of sympathy."

"Where Microagressions Really Come From: A Sociological Account," a blog by Jonathan Haidt, related to his book, *The Righteous Mind*, 2013, http://righteousmind.com/where-microaggressions-really-come-from/, topic 5, "The Social Structure of Microaggression."

4. Conor Friedersdorf, "Microaggressions and the Rise of Victim-hood Culture," *The Atlantic* (September 11, 2015), 7.

5. For a report on these events, where student protesters demanded greater diversity among the faculty and racial sensitivity on campus, see John Hasnas, "The Surprising Obstacle Mizzou and Yale Face in Increasing Diversity," *Fortune* (November 21, 2015), http://fortune.com/2015/11/21/the-surprising-obstacle-mizzou-and-yale-face-in-increasing-diversity/.

6. Harry Bruinius, "At Issue in Missouri Protests, How We 'Quit Intimidating Each Other,'" *The Christian Science Monitor* (November 11, 2015), http://www.csmonitor.com/USA/Education/2015/1111/At-issue-in-Missouri-protests-how-we-quit-intimidating-each-other.

7. "Imagined crime" could include a wide range of reactions, from unintended consequences of honest mistakes, the negative impact of natural forces, or imagined presuppositions of others' negative intentions.

8. Mary Baker Eddy, *Science and Health with Key to the Scriptures* (Boston: The Christian Science Publishing Society, 1896), 323. The gravitation "away from material sense" refers to the diminishing of the senses of self, whether they stem from the five physical senses, or more broadly, the perception of life based on empirical knowledge instead of the things of the heart.

9. While children's games are usually intended to provide merriment for children, a closer look at their cultural setting often reveals the accepted worldview of a community. Nursery rhymes, for example, are easy to repeat and become easy means by which we teach the next generation the values of the community. "Peter, Peter, pumpkin eater, had a wife and couldn't keep her. He put her in a pumpkin shell, and there he kept her, very well" is fun to say, but what does it teach about needing to "keep a wife"? Folk songs and games from European descent frequently teach children competition, to struggle to win or beat everyone else. By contrast, games for children of African descent tend to involve circles where the child in the center is embraced and protected by those encircling him or her; he/she becomes a leader to be copied. By using the example of musical chairs, I illustrate the worldview that requires competition to the defeat of everyone else.

10. Cathaleen Chen, "Muslim Woman Donates $1 to UNICEF Every Time She Gets Trolled on Twitter," *The Christian Science Monitor*

(November 12, 2015), http://www.csmonitor.com/World/Global-News/
2015/1112/Muslim-woman-donates-1-to-UNICEF-every-time-she-gets
-trolled-on-Twitter.

11. Brandis Friedman, "Urban Warriors," *WTTW Chicago Public Media*, March 18, 2015, 10:30 a.m., http://chicagotonight.wttw.com/2015/03/18/urban-warriors.

12. Eddy, *Science and Health*, 265.

13. Ibid., 270.

14. Some translations such as the New Living Translation and New Century Version use *justice* in place of *righteousness*: "Blessed are those who hunger and thirst for *justice*...."

15. Beth Waitkus is director of Insight Garden Program, founded in 2002, about a year after the 2001 attacks. Her motive was to "help [herself] regain her faith in humanity" after the 2001 attacks. She partners with Gavin Raiders, codirector of the Planting Justice Program in the prison, which nurtures an "outer garden" and "inner garden," where inmates learn gardening skills to take with them when they are released. Raiders reports all the men insist on the importance of the garden for their emotional and spiritual well-being, despite their concerns for how it would help when they transitioned to their communities. They are invited to work for the program at seventeen dollars and fifty-cents per hour when they are released.

16. David Fowley, "Incredible True Story of Men Released from Prison Who Defy the Return-to-Prison Statistics," *Light in Prison* (March 20, 2015), http://lightinprison.org/2015/03/20/incredible-true-story-of-men-released-from-prison-who-defy-the-return-to-prison-statistics/.

17. Eddy, *Science and Health*, 60–61.

18. Ibid., 10–11.

19. Ibid., 475.

20. According to the Word English Bible, the biblical term *Peniel* refers to "the face of God." And Eddy's use of the phrase "divine Science" is one of the ways she describes the laws of God.

21. Eddy, *Science and Health*, 308.

22. Ibid., 304, 305

23. Eddy uses *Love* or *divine Love* synonymously with God, so in this case, her meaning is a contrast between the power of divine Love (God) and human affections.

24. Mary Baker Eddy, *Miscellaneous Writings, 1883–1896* (Boston: The Christian Science Publishing Society, 1896), 11:14, 17–21; 12:8–10, 12–14.

8

HOW PAUL'S TRANSFORMATION ADDRESSES MASS INCARCERATION TODAY

Madelon Maupin

Christians naturally turn to the Bible for inspiration, guidance, and answers to challenging contemporary social issues, one of which is mass incarceration. As Christians wrestle with questions related to the need for and implementation of reform and justice for those impacted, turning to the Apostle Paul for insights is timely. While the reasons for his incarceration on several occasions differ from today's prisoners (for his faith versus a crime of passion, drug possession, etc.), his spiritual transformation does speak to those who today find themselves part of the prison population and seek both peace and justice.

What can be learned from this incomparable New Testament figure and his experiences of not just incarceration, but reformation and transformation? Can a review of Paul's life, letters, and those epistles attributed to him be relevant to one's own work on mass incarceration and the justice that is needed for those behind bars?

This chapter will attempt to answer such questions by looking at conditions of first century prisons and the general treatment of its prisoners to set a context for Paul's theology and his response to his own imprisonment as recorded in his New Testament letters. We will then narrow the focus to examine how Paul's theology of being a "prisoner in the Lord" (Eph 4:1) was more about his own fundamental spiritual renewal and change than where he was located—incarcerated or not. This will include seeing Paul's preaching of life in Christ as part of a larger divine mission. We will examine if Paul's experience of spiritual transformation through

Christ can become practical wisdom today, for both the incarcerated and those who work tirelessly on their behalf. The intention is to show that Paul's own profound change through Christ can provide a healing path for all parties concerned with this crucial social issue today.

Finally, as a Caucasian female who has never spent time in incarceration, my viewpoint is informed more by the way Paul's letters have transformed my life. I have, however, led Christian worship services in high-security U.S. penitentiaries and have some familiarity with inmates' fears as metal doors and gates clang shut on personal freedom. Thus, I share a commitment to find contemporary solutions to the very real needs of peace and justice, and hope that this discussion of Paul and his transformation and mission can help those incarcerated today.

CHARACTERISTICS AND USE OF PRISONS IN ANTIQUITY

To set the stage for examining how Paul's theology might speak to the issue of contemporary mass incarceration, it is helpful to examine how individuals in the first century Greco-Roman world were confined. Philosophically, prison was not thought of as a place where criminals could be rehabilitated and reformed into decent citizens. Rather, imprisonment was the way the individual "made good his offense by carrying out dull and heavy labor."[1] The Roman Empire needed cheap labor for its many building projects, and compounds or prisons were constructed to house political prisoners and other adversaries.[2] Such heavy labor occurred before their verdict was rendered. And while they would not be sentenced to more time in captivity, beating or even execution might certainly occur.[3]

Such practices go back into the ancient Near Eastern world, as shown in stories of prisoners from the Hebrew Scriptures, such as that of Samson. When the Philistines gouged out his eyes and forced Samson to grind in the mill at the prison (Judg 16:21), he was in such a place of forced labor. There, blinding was a common tactic to keep prisoners from escaping (see also 1 Sam 11:2).

When the ancient Israelites were exiled to Babylon, they too were sent to "workshops," or places of forced labor. The misery created in the incarcerated is described in Psalms, "Their hearts were bowed down with hard labor; / they fell down, with no one to help" (Ps 107:12).

Higher-ranking prisoners, such as kings or other popular figures, were often imprisoned rather than killed, and it is difficult to surmise if they, too, were subject to the same heavy labor as others. In such conditions, it was more common for the condemned to die in prison from malnutrition and disease. One example of a popular figure's confinement was Herod's initial imprisonment of John the Baptist (Matt 14:3–5). Jesus' cousin was held probably in Machaerus, at Herod's summer palace in today's Jordan. Archaeologists have identified a cave in the mountain beneath the hilltop fortress on the eastern side of the Dead Sea, 53 kilometers southwest of Amman, where John was probably detained before his beheading.[4] In the Book of Acts, Paul is temporarily confined awaiting clarification of his sentence (16:23–24) and later held at Herod's palace in Caesarea Maritima for two years (23:23—24:27).

Another widely accepted reason people were incarcerated was due to inability to repay creditors. This debt collection problem was widespread enough that in some locales, special debtor prisons were built to handle such cases. Evidence of this is recorded in the Gospel of Luke: "Thus, when you go with your accuser before a magistrate, on the way make an effort to settle the case,[5] or you may be dragged before the judge, and the judge hand you over to the officer, and the officer throw you in prison. I tell you, you will never get out until you have paid the very last penny" (Luke 12:58–59).

When Paul and Silas were imprisoned in Philippi, a single jailer placed them in the innermost cell, where their feet were fastened in stocks (Acts 16:24). Excavations at Philippi have uncovered a small crypt revered by early Christians as the prison, and adorned with frescoes depicting Paul and Silas. If this is indeed the prison, the crypt would likely have been within hearing distance of the guards, just as when Paul and Silas sang hymns, "'the prisoners were listening to them' (Acts 16:25). Perhaps the crypt, originally a cistern, served only as the 'innermost cell' (Acts 16:24) for maximum security or solitary confinement."[6]

Such harsh conditions in stocks were exceeded by prisoners forced to wear chains with feet shackled and hands manacled, including hands attached by chain to their neck, as the individual would be fastened to a post. Laws were eventually written to regulate the length of such chains, indicating it was a common enough practice that prisoners had to be given some protection against such inhumane behavior by their jailors.[7]

In addition to the horrific physical treatment, there was significant social shame that came from incarceration. The effects of prison on one's social status and the shame that occurred is captured in 2 Timothy 1:16. While written in Paul's name, but probably by a pseudonymous author, the point remains that shame was the inverse of the much-vaunted Roman value of honor: "May the Lord grant mercy to the household of Onesiphorus, because he often refreshed me and was not ashamed of my chain" (1:16). Because honor was such a predominant male virtue in the Roman world, one imagines how a prison sentence—like today—calls one's personal honor and integrity into question for the rest of the individual's life. Paul handles this public shame especially adroitly in his correspondence to the Philippian congregation when he tries to turn the humiliation from imprisonment to his advantage, if it results in Christ being exalted: "It is my eager expectation and hope that I will not be put to shame in any way, but that by my speaking with all boldness, Christ will be exalted now as always in my body, whether by life or by death" (Phil 1:20).

In sum, Roman prisons were brutal holding tanks for the execution of imperial justice to prisoners, whether there for political, financial, or religious reasons.[8] Such detention offered little opportunity for the kind of permanent reform that would send its citizenry back into productive lives throughout the empire.

SPIRITUAL TRANSFORMATION AND THE MISSION OF GOD

Before examining Paul's letters, it is useful to first see how the gospel worked its initial transforming power on him and his background. Paul's earlier commitment to the Pharisaical way of life, his attempt to maintain the purity of Judaism's teachings through its strict practices, all were challenged by the evangelistic fervor of Jesus' early followers preaching the gospel. Paul's resistance came to an astonishing halt when he experienced the voice of the resurrected Jesus on the road to Damascus (Acts 9). From that moment, through his sojourn in the desert to digest the life-changing path he was called to follow, across the thirty-year ministry throughout the Roman Empire to follow, Paul was on the road of spiritual renewal and transformation. He was unstoppable as he fulfilled his appointed mission to preach "the gospel of God" (Rom 1:1) to the Gentiles.

In addition to being Christianity's most successful missionary and evangelist, at the heart of Paul's transformation was a vision of what God was trying to do *to* and *for* the world. Michael Gorman explains, "Paul believed God had a mission in the world and, especially, that not only he and his colleagues, but also the churches he founded and/or 'pastored'" were part of it.[9]

This missional role, Gorman argues, is nothing less than *God's* divine mission (*missio Dei*) that finds its full participation in "a comprehensive transformation of conviction, character, and communal affiliation."[10] Such a divine commissioning included all receptive hearts and minds to the good news of salvation, including those at each rung of the socioeconomic ladder—high and low. Here is the gospel of Christ, the gospel of inclusion, the gospel for the outcast, the Gentile, the pagan, the spiritually ignorant, the prisoner, the runaway slave.

Before such transformation could fully take place, however, Paul would need to repent. What a perfect word to hint not only at the sorrow over past wrongdoing, but the profound rethinking required as the gospel of God takes over one's life. The Greek term for *repent, metanoia*, means "to change one's mind"—from *meta* + *noein*, "to think" (from *nous*, meaning *mind*). The meaning of the English word is transparent with its prefix "re-" (meaning "again") and the second syllable taken from the French infinitive, *penser*, "to think." *Repent* literally, then, is to "change one's mind."[11] In today's more secular language, it is the first step in "emotional intelligence," called *self-knowledge*.[12] One must rethink old patterns in order to establish new ones. For Paul, this action began with the transforming power of the Holy Spirit, not simply human effort.

One can only surmise how autobiographical is Paul's Letter to the Romans, declaring that repentance is the first necessary step to spiritual transformation. In Romans 2:1–4, Paul addresses people judging others, a challenge that those who are or have been incarcerated deal with endlessly: "Therefore you have no excuse, whoever you are, when you judge others; for in passing judgment on another you condemn yourself, because you, the judge, are doing the very same things....Do you imagine, whoever you are, that when you judge those who do such things and yet do them yourself, you will escape the judgment of God?...Do you not realize that God's kindness is meant to lead you to repentance?"

Here is the threefold intersection of the divine mission, repentance, and transformation, which Paul will develop throughout his letters, and which can provide a kind of spiritual roadmap for those incarcerated today.

JOY AS THE FUEL OF TRANSFORMATION

The irony of Paul's experience in the first century is that prisons were *not* set up to reform the individual as they are intended today.[13] And yet, from the time of his conversion, Paul was being re-formed, formed into a soldier for Christ, advancing the missional dimension of his evangelizing, a process that continued in his time in prison. While in confinement, Paul writes to his dear friends at Philippi that he is sustained by faith in the ever-present, eternal Christ. Paul goes on to offer counsel to those Philippians also experiencing persecution: "I know that I will remain and continue with all of you for your progress and joy in faith" (Phil 1:25).

More pointedly, Paul continues, "But even if I am being poured out as a libation over the sacrifice and the offering of your faith, I am glad and rejoice with all of you—and in the same way you also must be glad and rejoice with me" (Phil 2:17–18). What was the source of such joy, the inner quality independent of external circumstances, emerging from one's innermost convictions of faith and understanding? Paul was clear on the answer, and his Letter to the Philippians states it in multiple ways—Christ: "For to me, living is Christ," he would explain (1:21).

In fact, Christ was such a living, transforming presence for Paul that he welcomes the imprisonment as a way to spread the gospel of Christ. "I want you to know, beloved, that what has happened to me has actually helped to spread the gospel, so that it has become known throughout the whole imperial guard and to everyone else that my imprisonment is for Christ; and most of the brothers and sisters, having been made confident in the Lord by my imprisonment, dare to speak the word with greater boldness and without fear" (Phil 1:12–14).

Paul claimed each confinement as a potential victory for Christ in continuing the work of individual salvation and transformation, as seen with his fellow prisoner, Onesimus, in his Letter to Philemon (see v. 10).

NEW TESTAMENT PRISON LETTERS

During the periods when Paul was confined to jail, no longer able to travel throughout Asia Minor, Macedonia and Greece, Syria, and Palestine, he kept his ministry alive through letter writing. Four "Prison Letters"—Ephesians, Philippians, Colossians, and Philemon—have historically been attributed to the Apostle. An additional New Testament letter, 2 Timothy, is considered by some scholars to have been written by Paul from prison, and joins the other four in a group referred to as the "Captivity Letters." What do we learn about his imprisonment experiences by studying these Prison Letters? How can the theology of being a "prisoner in the Lord," as the author of the Book of Ephesians describes Paul (4:1), and Paul's description of his own transformation through Christ provide insight on issues of mass incarceration today?

To understand Paul's prison experience, we will focus our study initially on two of his Prison Letters, Philippians and Philemon, which most scholars would agree are two of the seven authenticated letters of Paul, including 1 Thessalonians, Romans, 1 and 2 Corinthians, and Galatians.

Philippians

Paul's Letter to the Philippians, addressed to his close and supportive friends, is written either from jail in Ephesus or Rome. Paul indicates he may soon be released (1:25; 2:24) or near execution (1:20;

2:17). While his intention appears to be to give hope and encouragement to the new church in Philippi, the stress of confinement comes through at key points: "It is right for me to think this way about all of you, because you hold me in your heart, for all of you share in God's grace with me, both in my imprisonment and in the defense and confirmation of the gospel" (1:7). Yet even in his imprisonment, Paul is aware of the opportunities for preaching the gospel, affirming that "it has become known throughout the whole imperial guard and to everyone else that my imprisonment is for Christ" (1:13).

Although written during his challenge of confinement while living in grim conditions, this Epistle to the Philippians is Paul's most joyous of his Prison Letters. He prays for the saints in Jesus Christ in Philippi (1:1), with joy in every one of his prayers (1:4). He proclaims Christ out of love (1:16); he strives to imitate Christ's humility (2:1–5); he asks his beloved friends to work out their salvation with fear and trembling (2:12) and to do all things without murmuring (2:14). He advises them (3:1–6), acknowledges their gifts (4:10–20), and exhorts them, "Finally, beloved, whatever is true, whatever is honorable, whatever is just, whatever is pure, whatever is pleasing, whatever is commendable…think about these things" (4:8).

In sum, Philippians is an unselfish and powerful message of encouragement, love, joy, faith, and hope to his treasured friends. But it is also a window into how Paul survived his confinement: by continuing his mission of spreading the good news, by focusing on how to support others, by loving through the misery surrounding him, by keeping Christ close to his heart. Might these be practical spiritual tools for those incarcerated today?

Philemon

Nowhere is a demand for reformation and transformation more evident than in Paul's one-chapter Letter to Philemon, yet it is reformation with a twist. As the only personal letter from Paul to an individual rather than a congregation, we see the logic and persuasion techniques Paul uses to challenge the economic engine of the Roman Empire—slavery. Having met a runaway slave, Onesimus, in prison, Paul writes his owner (Philemon) to ask for forgiveness for Onesimus. Appealing to the owner's love for Paul, the Apostle encourages Philemon to do a "good deed" (v. 14) and welcome his runaway slave, Onesimus, back. But Paul creates demanding criteria that stipulate reformation on the slave owner's part. Take him back "no longer as a slave but more than a slave, a beloved brother" (v. 16).

Philemon is important to the spiritual transformation discussion because it reveals how Paul encouraged it of those to whom prisoners were returning. How relevant today to family, business, and community members who need to undergo their own transformation of forgiveness and love in order to welcome those returning citizens back into society and the community. Such integration is a big part of the discussion of mass incarceration since a climate of shame and embarrassment can either linger or be erased by the welcome and loving embrace of those to whom the inmate returns.

The way Paul asks Philemon to take back a runaway slave and treat him no longer as a servant but as a fellow brother in Christ is exactly the kind of demand made on those each inmate returns to today. This is reformation, not just for prisoners, but also for the society that awaits their return.

How needed this is today when those who have checked off "incarceration" on a job application are almost always denied a fresh opportunity of earning income for themselves and their families. Efforts are underway to remove such a legal stipulation from job applications, giving former inmates a chance at fresh starts: "In recent months, a coalition from across the political spectrum has emerged in favor of moving away from 'tough on crime' rules that have bloated prisons with minor offenders over the last few decades, and made it difficult for them to get a job and return to society upon release."[14]

To recap, Paul's Letter to the Philippians counsels joy and courage in captivity, while his Letter to Philemon is Paul at his wily best, turning the tables from focus on the accused to the accuser, demanding spiritual transformation by both slave and master.

PAUL, THE PRISONER IN THE LORD

Given the number of days, months, and years Paul spent in forced confinement, we Christians marvel at his personal example of remaining faithful and even joy-filled. Of course, he was imprisoned for his faith, unlike today's inmates who are incarcerated for specific crimes. But even so, Paul serves as an example of hope because he understood that God was governing his life, part of the *missio Dei* referred to earlier. Whether in jail or on the street, we must all maintain this conviction in order to carry out God's missional work before us.

This section examines how Paul self-identified as a prisoner—not of Rome, but of Christ Jesus—and how this provided a kind of spiritual buoyancy otherwise incomprehensible. Paul refers to himself as the servant or slave of God, or "prisoner" of Christ. While the metaphor may be repugnant to modern ears, Paul is referring to the radical obedience to God's direction he came to rely on—whether it was changing travel plans to venture to Macedonia versus staying in Anatolia, or deciding to travel to Jerusalem by land versus the easier sea route. In both cases, and many more throughout Acts and Paul's letters, such radical obedience enabled him to fulfill his mission much more effectively. This did not exclude taking advantage of what legal justice there was, such as his own Roman citizenship and the rights that included, which Paul was quick to do on multiple occasions. Finally, by looking at both the 2 Corinthian correspondence and a key theological point in Romans, the case is put forward for the spiritual confidence Paul maintained, incarcerated or not.

Paul as Prisoner for Christ

In three of Paul's attributed "Captivity Letters," Ephesians, Philemon, and 2 Timothy, he refers to himself as a "prisoner for Christ Jesus" (Eph 3:1), "the prisoner in the Lord" (Eph 4:1), "Paul, a prisoner of Christ Jesus" (Phlm 1), and "[the Lord's] prisoner" (2 Tim 1:8). Whether written by the Apostle himself or by those who wrote in his name, nowhere does Paul see himself as a casualty of circumstance or Roman Imperial law, but rather fulfilling his master, Christ, and Christ's commands. While there are situations today where the innocent have been incorrectly jailed, casualties of circumstance,[15] Paul did not take this position for himself.

For example, in Ephesians, when Paul refers to himself as "a prisoner for Christ Jesus," it is "for the sake of you Gentiles—for surely you have already heard of the commission of God's grace that was given me for you, and how the mystery was made known to me by revelation" (Eph 3:1–3). His life's work and mission was to share the news of God's saving grace, and *where* that was to occur—imprisoned or free—was secondary to Paul being about that work. Nothing would stop him in this holy charge, as he shared with the church in Philippi when his jailers began to be converted (Phil 1:14).

Paul's evangelizing galvanized him to keep his eye always on the higher goal of his divine commissioning. He often used athletic metaphors of running a race, activities with which he would have been familiar, growing up in Tarsus, where two Roman legions were stationed and did such exercise. "It is by your holding fast to the word of life that I can boast on the day of Christ that I did not run in vain or labor in vain," he wrote to the Philippians (2:16). This single-minded focus, like an athlete pursuing the finish line, was part of what kept the Apostle feeling victorious as he watched new believers accept the gospel message. His self-identification as the "prisoner of Christ Jesus" could have been the way he was encouraging his fellow Christians also experiencing persecution, as is understood in the Philippians' community.

2 Corinthians

Further evidence of Paul's joy and spiritual freedom are rooted not in his relation to Rome but in his bond to God and Christ. This, above all, explains his unfailing sense of victory, despite external circumstance. For example, Paul explains to the Corinthians that "we do not proclaim ourselves; we proclaim Jesus Christ as Lord and ourselves as your slaves for Jesus' sake. For it is the God who said, 'Let light shine out of darkness,' who has shone in our hearts to give the light of the knowledge of the glory of God in the face of Jesus Christ" (4:5, 6).

When one reads the catalogue of hardships Paul describes to the Corinthians, this indomitable spirit emerges that is quick to acknowledge all the untoward circumstances, but never intimates they have conquered him. Just the opposite: "We are afflicted in every way, but not crushed; perplexed, but not driven to despair; persecuted, but not forsaken; struck down, but not destroyed;

always carrying in the body the death of Jesus, so that the life of Jesus may also be made visible in our bodies" (4:8–10). Is not this the same joy Jesus counseled his disciples to find in themselves when talking of his own coming departure: "So you have pain now; but I will see you again, and your hearts will rejoice, and no one will take your joy from you" (John 16:22)? And isn't this the same kind of spiritual resource that today's inmates must find in order to have some kind of peace in their confinement?

Romans

Paul's Letter to the Romans provides further theological foundation for the Apostle's missional behavior, as he writes to reconcile imperfect mortals with a perfect God. As a Jew, Paul had long been aware that the Law required perfection of men and women unable to live up to such a standard. Instead, Paul saw Christ as the great reconciler between God and man, closing the gap as one claims Jesus Christ as his or her savior. In that context, Christ reconciles man to God by Christ dying for man on the cross and forgiving man for those original sins based on Adam and Eve (Gen 3). One could argue that this is the ultimate prisoner reformation path.

But another way to read Romans is that Christ comes to teach and model the creation that is the image and likeness of God, as Genesis 1:26 explains. Such interpretation depends on whether one reads Romans as implying sin is inherent or *not* inherent in men and women—an outside power trying to gain entrance to the Human life,[16] thereby undermining the natural state as "image" and "likeness" (see Gen 1:26). While Paul certainly thought of sin as something substantial, lying far deeper in humanity than various sinful acts, or even than the impulse that prompts the act, one can read Romans as Paul not seeing sin as part of one's own true nature. Rather, his language indicates sin was both foreign and hostile to human nature:

> So I find it to be a law that when I want to do what is good, evil lies close at hand. For I delight in the law of God in my inmost self, but I see in my members another law at war with the law of my mind, making me captive

to the law of sin that dwells in my members. Wretched man that I am! Who will rescue me from this body of death? Thanks be to God through Jesus Christ our Lord! (Rom 7:21–25)

In Romans 8:31, Paul summarizes his conviction by declaring, "What then are we to say about these things? If God is for us, who is against us?" Origen, the second-century CE theologian from Alexandria, wrote a concise summary that captures well how so much of Paul's theology is bound up in the phrase "these things," when he noted, "It is because the Spirit of God dwells in us and because the Spirit of Christ, or Christ himself, is in us...because we act in the power of God's Spirit, because we have received the Spirit of adoption, because we are children of God, heirs and fellow heirs of Christ."[17]

CONCLUSION

To summarize, Paul's repentance and transformation were forged through his relation to God and Christ, tested under the most challenging of circumstances. And while he relied on his Roman citizenship to take full advantage of the current justice system, he never let his external circumstances dictate his joy or the dominion he found through communion with Christ.

My husband has been a chaplain in the jails of Orange County, California, for the past ten years, visiting inmates three times a week and talking with hundreds of men and women over the years. The pattern for those hungry for spiritual sustenance is consistent: what they never would have taken time for on the "outside," they have found in their desperation of hitting bottom on the "inside." While such men and women from every background (Caucasian, African American, Hispanic, Middle Eastern, Asian) do not welcome their confinement and fight hard to get out with the shortest sentence possible, those that seek a chaplain's visit recognize that the spiritual transformation that has occurred in them is life-changing. Because the chaplains are not allowed to reveal personal information or contact inmates after release, it is difficult to know how many of them have continued pursuing the gospel message of redemption and transformation.

From their experience, one could say that what Paul's theology might counsel the inmates of today is to find their joy through the spiritual resources available to them regardless of their physical environment: the gospel of good news, God's unfailing love for the human race lived so earnestly through the life of Jesus Christ. That someone like Paul, who never knew the historical Jesus, could be so thoroughly transformed by a revelation that would profoundly, permanently change him and the course of his life, can give hope to those incarcerated, their loved ones, and society at large.

This is the kind of inner transformation that provides the only lasting freedom for those incarcerated behind bars or the bars of regret and remorse, whether in the first century or the twenty-first. Christ is indeed our savior, wiping each one clean from sin, rescuing from the shame of past mistakes, regrets, and impulses. Paul's radical self-identification as "a prisoner of Christ Jesus" (Phlm 1) provides a healing insight to both those incarcerated and those working hard on their behalf in the name of both secular and theological justice today.

Notes

1. Karel Van der Toorn, "Prison," in *Anchor Yale Bible Dictionary*, ed. David N. Freedman (New York: Doubleday, 1992), 5:468.

2. The Latin term for prison is *ergastula*, a place of enforced labor (ibid.).

3. R. A. Wild and M. A. Powell, "Prison," in *HarperCollins Bible Dictionary*, rev. ed., ed. Mark Allen Powell (New York: HarperCollins, 2011), 831.

4. "St. John the Baptist," in *Oxford Dictionary of the Christian Church*, 3rd ed., ed. F. L. Cross and E. A. Livingstone (Oxford: Oxford University Press, 1997), 888.

5. The Greek phrase, ἀπηλλάχθαι ἀπ᾽ αὐτοῦ, can also be translated "settle with him," as indicated by the NRSV text note.

6. Daniel C. Browning Jr., "Prison, Prisoners," in *Holman Bible Dictionary*, ed. Trent C. Butler (Nashville, TN: Holman, 1991), 1139.

7. Van der Toorn, "Prison," 5:468–69.

8. For a link to pictures and an article on the Roman Mamertinum prison, which archeologists believe held famous prisoners, including the

apostle Peter, see http://www.ancient-origins.net/ancient-places-europe/infamous-mamertine-prison-and-supposed-incarceration-saint-peter-003447.

9. Michael J. Gorman, *Becoming the Gospel: Paul, Participation, and Mission* (Grand Rapids, MI: Eerdmans, 2015), 21.

10. Ibid., 23.

11. *The American College Dictionary*, ed. C. L. Barnhart (New York: Random House, 1962), 1027.

12. Daniel Goleman, *Emotional Intelligence* (New York: Bantam, 1995), 105.

13. Misty Kifer, Craig Hemmens, Mary K. Stohr, "The Goals of Corrections: Perspectives from the Line," *Criminal Justice Review* 28 (Spring 2003): 1–25.

14. Sarah Wheaton, "Obama Pushes for Reduced Prison Sentences," *Politico*, July 14, 2015, http://www.politico.com/story/2015/07/obama-mandatory-sentence-reform-120102#ixzz43Z5xpKdE.

15. Aidan Quigley, "How Davontae Sanford, wrongly imprisoned for murder, found justice," *Christian Science Monitor*, June 8, 2016, http://www.csmonitor.com/USA/Justice/2016/0608/How-Davontae-Sanford-wrongly-imprisoned-for-murder-found-justice.

16. By special capitalization of "Human," I refer specifically to the sinless image and likeness of God.

17. Quoted in Gerald L. Bray, ed., *Ancient Christian Commentary on Scripture*, New Testament, vol. 6, ed. Thomas C. Oden (Downers Grove, IL: InterVarsity, 2005), 237.

9

THE REVELATION TO JOHN, PRISONER ON THE ISLAND OF PATMOS

Don Thorsen

John—the author of the Book of Revelation—described himself as follows: "I, John, your brother who share with you in Jesus the persecution and the kingdom and the patient endurance, was on the island called Patmos because of the word of God and the testimony of Jesus" (Rev 1:9).[1] He was a prisoner of the Roman Empire, most likely during the latter reign of Domitian (81–96 CE). John seems to have been a political prisoner, due to being on the wrong side of sociocultural injustices toward those who, most certainly, had different beliefs, values, and practices, and may also have lacked Roman citizenship, tolerable race or ethnicity, or class privilege. If guilty of nothing else, John was a Christian, and so he wrote to fellow Christians about a revelation he received "in the spirit on the Lord's day" (1:10).

John's revelation left readers in a quandary. How was this revelation to be understood? What was its purpose? What was its practical relevance to their personal and collective experiences of life in general, and particularly of injustice, possibly including incarceration? After all, most everyone in the Mediterranean had been conquered, colonized, and exploited by the Roman Empire. Most people with whom John and his readers affiliated were militarily subject to sociopolitical marginalization, at best, and oppression and violent persecution at worst. Within this context of widespread as well as local domination, John recognized the momentousness of God's vision, and the benefit for others to hear its message. So today, how ought we to receive and promote the Book of Revelation?

Although the Book of Revelation touches upon a variety of Christian themes—past, present, and future—it castigates the kinds of injustice in the world that undeservedly imprison people for political and sociocultural reasons, rather than for justifiable reasons of criminality, and the book champions the overcoming of injustice, emphasizing the work of God as well as Christians and churches in promoting God's righteous reign. Let me begin by talking about the context of the Book of Revelation, discussing different ways that Christians interpret apocalyptic literature. In doing so, I will touch both upon God's role regarding implementing the revelation to John, and upon our role, both as individual Christians and as churches, in promoting in this day and age the righteous reign of God. Rather than promote passivity and unconcern about matters of justice, the Book of Revelation exhorts us to act responsibly and proactively on behalf of those who are treated unjustly for any reason, including those subject to mass incarceration.

BOOK OF REVELATION

How are we to interpret the apocalyptic writings in the Book of Revelation? There is no easy answer to this question, and there has been no consensus among Christians throughout church history. For this reason, Christians in the ancient church were hesitant to canonize it, making the Book of Revelation one of the last to be included in the New Testament. At the Council of Ephesus, in the year 431, Augustine's allegorical (or symbolic, figurative) interpretation of millennialism (also known as chiliasm) became the principal way of interpreting apocalyptic literature, but alternative interpretations were not precluded.

After the Protestant Reformation, an increasing number of Christians adopted more literal interpretations of the Bible, including its apocalyptic writings. This literalism flourished in the nineteenth century with premillennialist views as found in the Adventism of William Miller and Dispensationalism of John Darby. Literalistic interpretations of the Book of Revelation increased after Israel's capture of Jerusalem during the Six-Day War in 1967, as popularized by such writings as *The Late Great*

Planet Earth by Hal Lindsey and the *Left Behind* novels by Tim LaHaye and Jerry Jenkins.[2]

One's eschatology may impact how one lives in the world here and now. Let us compare, for example, three historic views: amillennialism, postmillennialism, and premillennialism. The three eschatological views pertain etymologically to how one interprets references to the thousand years (Lat., *millennium*), mentioned several times in Revelation 20. Of course, these three historic views have to do with more than the interpretation of Revelation 20; they pertain to how one generally interprets the whole of Revelation. Amillennialism suggests that there is no (a-) millennium, that is, no millennial kingdom expected, since the whole of the Book of Revelation ought to be interpreted symbolically, rather than historically predictive of future events. Although Jesus said he is coming again (see, for example, Matt 24:44, John 14:1–3, and Acts 1:10–11), the Book of Revelation should be interpreted allegorically, in line with Augustine. One does not know when Jesus will return, so one always ought to be ready for the end-time.

Postmillennialism argues that the end-time will occur after (post-) a millennial kingdom, of sorts, is established. Similar to amillennialism, references to the millennium are considered more allegorical (or symbolic, figurative) than literal. Postmillennialists tend to believe that Christians and churches are commanded to establish God's reign on earth before end-times arrive. Just as they are to proclaim the gospel of Jesus Christ, they are to establish the gospel on earth in every way, through word and deed. So postmillennialists are hopeful about the degree to which they, through the presence and power of God's Spirit at work in them, may contribute to establishing the kingdom of God.

Premillennialism tends to interpret the Book of Revelation more literally, believing that it speaks prophetically about future historical events. Premillennialists are vigilant in looking for "signs of the times," so to speak, by using Scripture to interpret current events. Since apocalyptic literature is thought to be predictive, then claims may be made about current events as substantiations of God's work (or of the devil's work). Some have noteworthily predicted the precise day and time of Jesus' second coming (for example, Miller and the Adventists). Of course, apocalyptic literature is still thought to exhibit allegorical meaning since discernment needs to be used, for example, in interpreting the meaning of the beast, mark of the beast, the number 666, and so on. For the most part, it is expected that Jesus will return and set up a thousand-year reign on earth—the millennial kingdom. Until then, Scripture suggests dire omens, involving wars, rumors of wars, famines, earthquakes, and so on (Matt 24:6–7). So premillennialists tend to be pessimistic about the future, expecting that only God can put the world right, and nothing we can do will help.

How one interprets apocalyptic literature in general, particularly the Book of Revelation, impacts how one lives in the world here and now. Although one's eschatology may not necessarily determine one's hopefulness (or hopelessness) about the future, it does have an impact. Postmillennialists tend to be more hopeful and proactive in being in the world; so do amillennialists, whose neutrality about the future tends to make them more proactive, if not necessarily hopeful. However, premillennialists tend to be less hopeful and proactive in being in the world. The latter tend to be Christians who place "not of this world" bumper stickers on their cars, even though Jesus said that he has sent Christians "into the world," engaging it constructively, rather than passively (see John 17:17–18). Some premillennialists may even experience *Schadenfreude* about wars, rumors of wars, famines, and earthquakes, since these occurrences represent signs that Jesus will soon return.[3]

INTERPRETING REVELATION

Despite the popular appeal of premillennialist views, which include sensational speculations about current events and predictions about future tribulation, most Catholic, Orthodox, Anglican, and other Protestant churches take a more neutral approach, following ancient allegorical interpretations of the Book of Revelation. I have always appreciated the four admonitions suggested by Shirley Guthrie about the Christian hope for the future. Let me summarize:

1. We must not want to know too much.
2. Biblical language about the future is symbolic.
3. There is no consistent biblical picture of the future, but a development in its thought.

4. The best insight we have into what God *will* do is found by looking at what he *has* done.[4]

Regarding the latter two points, Christians should take heed of the Book of Revelation, and not avoid reading and promoting it. Too often they stop at points one and two, and think there is nothing more that need be said or done about apocalyptic literature. But they fail to recognize the ongoing importance of beliefs, values, and practices found in the Book of Revelation, which are relevant for us today.

First, just as there is development in the biblical picture of the future, there is development in the proclamation of hope, salvation, and the ultimate reign of God. Christians ought to stay aware of these developments and integrate them into their own context today. Too often Christians (and non-Christians) lose hope about the future, feeling fearful or depressed about it. But the Bible is not hopeless; on the contrary, it contains vital reasons to hope for people's individual and collective well-being.

Second, if we want to know what God wants for the future, then we need to focus upon what God has done in the past. The past includes good news about justification by grace through faith, due to the atoning work of Jesus Christ. But the gospel message pertains to more than eternal life; it holistically integrates emphases that people (including Christians) too often dissociate and then disregard: justification and justice, spiritual and physical, individual and social, and so on.

One of the tangible emphases found in the Book of Revelation concerns justice: people suffering from injustice, God's resistance to injustice, and how the fight against injustice must continue throughout this life until all injustices cease. The Book of Revelation does not suggest sitting around and waiting; on the contrary, it begins with instructions to seven churches (Rev 2—3). In these instructions, churches are praised for what they were doing right, and chastised for what they were doing wrong. To the seven churches and to us, God commands Christians to be faithful, righteous, and just—the opposite of passively waiting around for God to do everything!

Just as John had been imprisoned and others, including Christians, suffered injustices by the Roman Empire, we today need to fight injustice—both individual and institutional—as part of our proclamation of the gospel in word *and* deed. The Book of Revelation gives us hope that our fight against injustice aligns with God's will as well as contributes to God's reign on earth. Hopefulness is a theme that can be found throughout Scripture, and not just because of all that God does for us. Christians are also hopeful because God empowers us; God strengthens us to do amazing things to bring about justice, restoration, and dignity, as well as salvation and eternal life. I have always liked the description Zechariah gave for the Israelites, who had been conquered and uprooted from their homeland of Israel. Rather than despair, Zechariah refers to the Israelites, held enslaved in a foreign country, as "prisoners of hope," since they never believed themselves to be without positive options for the future (Zech 9:12).

GOD'S ROLE AND OUR ROLE

In talking about God's reign on earth, let me begin by focusing upon what God *has* done. Christians believe that God sovereignly created the world, providentially cares for it, and gives both the law and grace to people for righteous, just living and for their salvation. God not only wants to save people spiritually, but also to empower them physically by grace through the presence and power of the Holy Spirit to live faithful, obedient lives.

Christian living is not determined by God alone, but by how God graciously enables people to respond in faith and obedience, which requires their synergistic cooperation with God's Spirit. Christians may disagree regarding the degree to which God's role is involved in people's lives, their salvation, and in their obedience to Christlike living vis-à-vis the role people play. But they all agree that both God and people indeed have genuine roles for Christlike living.

In the Bible, God performed many miraculous feats, and Jesus did as well through the presence and power of the Holy Spirit. But time after time, God permitted people sufficient freedom— enabled by divine aid, by divine grace—to choose to accept or reject God's will for their lives. Hence sin; hence also people choosing reconciliation, restoration, and love.

Regarding the Christian life and the life of churches, God expects believers to choose responsibly. By the grace of God, Christians are to emulate the teachings of God, of Jesus, of the Bible—God's revelation to all of humanity. God's revelation includes salvation; it also includes how we are to live lives of righteousness, justice, empathy, and compassion. In particular, God calls us to help those most in need—physically as well as spiritually, socially as well as individually. Just as Jesus holistically ministered to those around him, Christians and churches are to do the same, not neglecting "the least of these" (Matt 25:40, 45). Let me again focus upon the person and writings of John in the Book of Revelation. He talks about the importance of just living as well as spiritual waiting upon God. John relates how his vision pertains to the justice of God: "You are just, O Holy One, who are and were, / for you have judged these things" (Rev 16:5). Likewise, God's actions are described as just: "Yes, O Lord God, the Almighty, / your judgments are true and just!" (16:7; cf. 15:3, 19:2).

Since justice is a concern of God, as found in John's apocalyptic vision, then justice should be a concern of ours as well. Certainly John lived in a context familiar with injustice, with incarceration for reasons of conscience. Although the Book of Revelation does not state why he was imprisoned on Patmos, John clearly sees his imprisonment as part of the occasion for why God chose him for the revelatory experience amidst the varieties of injustices experienced by Christians.

If Christians (or "Christ followers") are to follow Christ, then they need to adopt the same values of Christ, of Christ's concern to overcome the injustices of sin as they affect people here and now—socially and individually—as well as how they affect people regarding life hereafter. Just as God calls Christians to proclaim the gospel in word and deed, they are to proclaim justice in word and deed. Justice as well as justification, after all, are at the heart of God's righteousness.

Let me note that the same word in Greek (*dikaiosuné*) may be translated either as *righteousness* or *justice*. Regrettably, some translations of the New Testament narrowly translate *dikaiosuné* as *righteousness* and never mention the word *justice*. But this omission is unfortunate since the word *dikaiosuné* refers primarily to God, who throughout the Old Testament was both concerned about matters of righteousness as well as of justice. So too ought Christians to be concerned about *both* righteousness *and* justice. Consider, for example, the poignancy of rereading Jesus' words in the Beatitudes when we translate him as saying, "Blessed are those who hunger and thirst for *justice* [*dikaiosuné*], for they will be filled" (Matt 5:6). If nothing else, New Testament references to *dikaiosuné* might better be translated by using both words: *righteousness and justice*.

COMPASSION AND ADVOCACY MINISTRIES

Christians throughout church history have shown compassion for those who are unjustly treated, including those who have been incarcerated, regardless of whether they were incarcerated justly or unjustly. Christians have administered compassion ministries, bestowing tangible acts of love and mercy on behalf of all those who are incarcerated.

A parallel to what has been called compassion (or mercy) ministries are advocacy ministries. If compassion ministries are concerned with caring for the *effects* (or symptoms) of injustice, then advocacy ministries are concerned with caring for the *causes* of injustice. If people are incarcerated justly, then advocacy ministries are concerned with making sure that prison conditions and the treatment of prisoners accord with civil laws and humanitarian needs. However, if people are incarcerated unjustly, then advocacy ministries are concerned with making sure that civil laws are implemented fairly, and without partiality (or discrimination). Impartiality applies to many reasons why people are discriminated against: race, ethnicity, gender, age, ability, class, language, nationality, religion, sexual orientation, and so on.

Let me just mention some of the ways that in the United States today groups of people are being unjustly mistreated regarding increased incarceration in prisons. The following examples are concerned with the mass incarceration particularly of blacks, as well as Hispanics. This is just one area of concern that Christians have about the exponential growth in U.S. prisons, but it should concern us nonetheless. Consider the following facts, which are concerned with mass incarceration in general, as well as about the incarceration of blacks and Hispanics:

- The number of inmates in state and federal prisons has increased nearly seven-fold from less than 200,000 in 1970 to 1,518,535 by midyear 2007. An additional 780,581 are held in local jails, for a total of 2.3 million.
- As of 2007, 1 of every 131 Americans was incarcerated in prison or jail.
- One in ten (10.4%) black males aged 25–29 was in prison or jail in 2007 as were 1 in 28 (3.6%) Hispanic males and 1 in 59 (1.7%) white males in the same age group.
- The 2007 United States' rate of incarceration of 762 inmates per 100,000 population is the highest reported rate in the world, well ahead of the Russian rate of 635 per 100,000.
- 40% of persons in prison or jail in 2006 were black and 20% were Hispanic.
- 82% of those sentenced to state prisons in 2004 were convicted of nonviolent crimes, including 34% for drug offenses, and 29% for property offenses.
- 1 in 4 jail inmates in 2002 was in jail for a drug offense, compared to 1 in 10 in 1983; drug offenders constituted 20% of state prison inmates and 55% of federal prison inmates in 2001.[5]

Of course, to the above facts, more could be added that describe inequities experienced by black and Hispanic people in the United States, especially among males. What are we to make of these seeming injustices of mass incarceration perpetrated against black and Hispanic people?

A widespread phrase we hear nowadays is "American exceptionalism." On the one hand, the United States is exceptional in many ways, and it is good to be patriotic in relationship to one's country. On the other hand, American exceptionalism can be used as an excuse to exempt us from honest and critical self-reflection upon beliefs, values, and practices of the government and peoples within the United States. As Socrates said, "The unexamined life is not worth living,"[6] and the intentional ignoring of real-life data about real-life people is as deadly for us collectively (for example, government, political parties, media, churches) as it is for individuals. And we in the United States need to reconsider publicly and as objectively as possible the causes that lead to the mass incarceration of blacks and Hispanics.

Christians sometimes point out how their earliest founders were persecuted and, indeed, martyred for their newfound religion. Although the persecution may not have occurred as often and widespread as Christians sometimes think, it was real nonetheless, and John was one of the victims. His vision—his revelation—came in response to his plight, and to the plight of other Christians. In it, God revealed that he had not abandoned John and other Christians. On the contrary, God remains in charge, even though for a time, persecution and tribulation occur. But that is not the end of the story!

Until the end-times occur, however one may conceive of them, Christians may have hope in the gracious aid of God, helping them confront both the spiritual and physical challenges they face in the world. Certainly the sins of people, individually and collectively, need to be confronted. In addition, problems with ignorance, misery, and various types of bondage need to be confronted. God will also aid in these confrontations, but Christians need to be responsible in ministering compassionately as well as advocating on behalf of those treated unjustly, unlovingly. To fulfill both the righteousness and justice of God, both compassion and advocacy need to be a part of the ministries of individual Christians and collectively of churches. And that includes compassion and advocacy ministries on behalf of those incarcerated, regardless of whether they have been justly or unjustly incarcerated. Christians and churches must become more vigilant in their ministries on behalf of all who are incarcerated.

CONCLUSION

In Luke 3:10, the crowds asked John the Baptist, in response to his preaching, "What then should we do?" A similar question needs to be asked by those of us who read the Book of Revelation, recorded by John. In addition, given the ongoing injustices in the world, for example, as exhibited by mass incarceration in the United States, in what kinds of compassion *and* advocacy ministries ought Christians and churches be engaged? Like the response of John the Baptist to the crowds, we should engage in more than words; we need to engage in words *and* deeds, addressing the causes as well as effects of sin—of injustice, oppression, and violence.

Just as John's vision in the Book of Revelation guaranteed that God will ultimately put all things right *and* just, we too ought to be "prisoners of hope" (Zech 9:12), knowing that God is graciously present and empowering us as we face the various challenges of life. With this hope, we act through deeds as well as words in working for the righteous and just world God wants reigning here and now, and not just for life hereafter. If anything, the Book of Revelation reminds us that God's reign is for the future *and* present, as much as it was for the past, and we today ought never to separate their interrelatedness as we faithfully pursue Christlike lives and ministries.

Notes

1. All Bible references come from *The New Oxford Annotated Bible*, 3rd ed., with the Apocryphal/Deuterocanonical Books, ed. Michael D. Coogan, New Revised Standard Version (New York: Oxford University Press, 2001).

2. See Hal Lindsey, *The Late Great Planet Earth* (Grand Rapids, MI: Zondervan, 1970); see also Tim LaHaye and Jerry B. Jenkins, the *Left Behind* Series of novels (Carol Stream, IL: Tyndale House, 1995–2007).

3. For more information about millennial views, see Robert G. Clouse, ed., *The Meaning of the Millennium: Four Views* (Downers Grove, IL: IVP Academic, 1977).

4. Shirley C. Guthrie, *Christian Doctrine: Teachings of the Christian Church* (Atlanta: John Knox Press, 1968), 384–88.

5. The Sentencing Project: Research and Advocacy for Reform, "Facts about Prisons and Prisoners," accessed August 15, 2017, http://www .ala.org/aboutala/sites/ala.org.aboutala/files/content/olos/prison_facts.pdf. Additional data is presented in other chapters in this anthology.

6. Socrates, quoted by Plato, *Apology*, in *Plato in Twelve Volumes*, vol. 1, trans. Harold North Fowler (Cambridge, MA: Harvard University Press, 1966), 38a.

III THEOLOGICAL EXPLORATIONS

10

LA NUEVA ENCOMIENDA
The Church's Response to Undocumented Migrants as Mass Incarcerated

Loida I. Martell

Over the past forty years, the laws of the United States have been slowly eroding the civil rights of a vast segment of our population. Under the guise of the "War on Crime," a staggering 2.2 million people, mostly people of color, are incarcerated primarily for non-violent crimes. Another five million are either under probation or on parole. Michelle Alexander's *The New Jim Crow: Mass Incarceration in the Age of Colorblindness* brought to national attention the racialized discourse that undergirded the so-called "drug wars," and its devastating effects on the African American community.[1] This erosion of civil rights has been most visible in the recent spate of public deaths by police officers of unarmed African Americans: the names of Michael Brown, Eric Garner, Walter Scott, Sandra Bland, Tamir Rice, Freddie Gray, and most recently, Laquan McDonald, are now seared in the public consciousness.[2] Yet these acts of violence against people of color are not new, but can simply be added to a roster of unwarranted deaths or mistreatment that include Anthony Báez, Amadou Diallo, Sean Bell, the beatings of Rodney King, the torture of Abner Louima, and the unjustified killing of José Antonio Elena Rodríguez by a border patrol officer. This erosion of rights has given rise to the Black Lives Matter movement, an outcry and protest to the seeming disregard for the human value and dignity of people of color.

In the aftermath of 9/11 and the various wars in the Middle East (Gulf War, Afghanistan, and Iraq), the newest tactic in law enforcement rhetoric is the use of encoded terminology such as "national security," and "War on Terrorism."[3] This has permitted a newly energized racialized attack on a longtime scapegoat: the migrant population. This rhetoric has now linked nativistic impulses with globalized forces, leading to a new social construct, that of the "illegal alien." Indeed, it is this link of globalization—which has mostly impacted the Global South and Africa—with racism, as it follows old colonial routes, that has led Howard Winant to claim that "globalization is the re-racialization of the world."[4] This classification of people has contributed to the growing number of incarcerated, particularly from the Latina/o population. Scholars have increasingly recognized that in this country, "illegal alien" is simply a racialized alias for "Latina/o."[5]

In this chapter, I argue that the status of "illegality" of migrants is a social construct that hinders freedom of movement and creates a class of people who are "incarcerated" *en masse* within a geographical space to create an exploitable source of cheap labor. This is done by coercion and threat, including the threat of deportation and, most recently, the threat of incarceration in "detention centers." This further incarceration in detention centers provides for additional profit-making in a globalized economy. As such, the status of undocumented people—whose movement and geographical allocation is thus controlled by a neocolonial power—has parallels to the colonial *encomienda* system instituted by the *conquistadores* in New Spain.

I then discuss the response of the church. I argue that in light of the biblical concepts of community and justice, the theological concept of the reign of God provides us with a new way of being, no longer based on *encomiendas* for profit but on communality through *vínculos*, perichoretic ties, created by the moving of the Spirit in our midst. I further argue that as a people of the reign, we are called to resist the hindrance of movement of people that leads to death by providing instead a vision of new ways of being "citizen" that is no longer based on exclusionary practices but on grace. The reign is where we do not exploit, but are hospitable, especially to the stranger. Finally, I argue that the entrance to the reign begins "outside the gate," where the *sobraja* and excluded—those marginalized at the borders, the transgressors of borders—reside, and where Jesus now stands and beckons the church to become a hospitable place where the *ger* and *nokrî* can join the dance of life.[6]

ENCOMIENDAS—FOR THE GOOD

During the colonization of the Americas, Spanish and Portuguese *conquistadores* used a system to subjugate the indigenous populations in the Americas that they inherited from the Roman Empire. Known as *encomiendas* (to entrust), it was used along with *repartimiento* (to distribute). Fundamentally, it was a system in which a tract of land was "entrusted" to a colonizer along with a given population of indigenous people that resided in that geographical area. The fundamental concept was that the *encomendero* was responsible for the well-being of the "souls" of those entrusted to his care. He was to evangelize and civilize them. They, in turn, were to work the land for monetary gain, whether it was working in the gold mines or in the fields for its crops. More recalcitrant or rebellious populations were "redistributed" (*repartidos*) to geographical areas far from lands familiar to them and subsequently placed under *encomenderos*. Lands appropriated and distributed in this manner often had a priest who accompanied the military person entrusted as overseer. Thus, the infamous slogan, *entre la espada y la cruz* (between the sword and the cross), was truly embodied: theology and conquest went hand in hand.

Very few *encomenderos* were concerned with the well-being of the indigenous people assigned to them. Instead, they cared more about the profits to be made from the labor of the conquered. The *encomienda* and *repartimiento* systems did accomplish several goals: First, they were excellent colonizing tools that effectively subjugated the indigenous population.[7] Second, they succeeded in doing so by breaking up the social organization of indigenous life. *Repartimiento* accomplished more than removing indigenes from their arable lands. At a more existential level, it also disrupted their fundamental ways of relating given the natives' understanding that the land and, indeed, all that inhabited it are "kin." Place is always "sacred space" that denotes a profound sense of relationality, communality, and spirituality. Thus, geographical ties served as intrinsic links (*vínculos*) that provided a deep sense of communal identity.[8]

To be forcibly removed from the land ruptured those communal ties in irreparable ways. The *conquistadores'* intentionally implemented systems did not simply restructure native societies, they destroyed them, replacing relationality with labor and production. *Encomiendas* and *repartimientos* reduced indigenes, if not quite to a status of slaves, certainly to feudal-like peonage. Third, these systems affirmed the hierarchical colonizing power of Spain, not only by enforcing massive migrations of whole populations, but also by reinforcing paternalistic notions of knowing and relating. That is, Western civilization and its production of knowledge, theology, and concept of society, indeed, its very notion of the *humanum*, were considered far superior to those of the people of the colonized lands. The indigenous culture, religions, and social ties were fully rejected as "pagan." Language, religious rituals, and religious sites were destroyed, indigenous populations were either forcibly "Christianized" or killed, and their ways of life and values were completely disregarded and marginalized. Ultimately, they became "silenced societies."[9]

The result of *encomiendas* and *repartimientos* was not simply profit-making on the part of the Spanish empire. They also led to the decimation of the indigenous populations in the Americas. In Mesoamerica, the population was reduced from approximately 25 million inhabitants to about 1.4 million within a century of the conquest. Elsewhere, entire tribes were wiped out. This genocidal loss can be partly attributed to the exploitation of the people for their labor and to the rupture of their social and economic structures in favor of the Iberian ones. The massive forced migrations and loss of the native peoples' ancestral homes certainly played a key role. The death and destruction of whole civilizations of people were the direct result of the forcible restrictions of movement exerted by those in power, that is, by the colonizing power exerted over them.[10]

TO MOVE OR NOT TO MOVE—THAT IS NO LONGER THE QUESTION

Migration has become a difficult issue to discuss in the United States because for too long it has been mired in demagoguery and impassioned rhetoric based on few facts and ignorance of the historical and global factors involved. It has become a political football, the plaything of pundits and politicians to score a few points in the polls or to pander to the fears of people in a globalized economy. It is, therefore, helpful to begin with some definitions and then proceed with a historical framework about migration, particularly about its historical trajectory in the United States.

Dictionaries often define migration or immigration as the movement of a person or persons to a geographical region not native to them, often with the purpose of establishing a new place of permanent residence, though sometimes for temporary residence—such as in the case of guest workers who work to harvest crops. The term *migration* is often limited to those who move within borders of nation-states where they have some legal residence, while *im/migration* often implies the transgression of political borders (that is, from one nation-state to another).[11] Nicholas De Genova has noted the problematic nature of such nomenclature and its inherent political and sociopolitical agenda. He prefers to use the term *migration* to note the movement of people in a global world.[12] Elsewhere, I have noted that such definitions do not consider that in a globalized world, it is not only persons or populations that "migrate" across borders; so too do corporations, military personnel, goods, and capital. Consequently, I used the term *im/migration* to refer to the movement of *people*, and *immigration* for corporate movements.[13] However, for this chapter, I defer to De Genova's usage of *migrant* or *migration* when referring to those persons who have moved geographical spaces in response to coercive globalized forces. I continue to apply the terminology of *immigrant* or *immigration* to the globalized or corporate bodies (such as transnational corporations) that transgress geographical, economic, and political borders in a bid for economic gain and political, military, or sociocultural power.[14]

Why Move at All?

Migration is rarely if ever a neutral, natural, or voluntary event. Rather, it is a disruptive one: it tears up communities and rends apart familial and communal ties. One becomes disconnected from human and social networks—what David T. Abalos refers to as the "vital connections"—that give rise to one's very identity.[15] Migration entails a journey fraught with danger. There is a risk of violence that potentially can leave one homeless. For those whose very identity is tied to the land as an integral part of the community, this *neo-repartimiento* implies becoming a "no-body."[16] Indeed,

> a migration always implies, in one direction, a separation from country of origin, homeland, roots, culture, home, memory or childhood; it is always emigration and the emigrant always runs the risk…of suffering a wound which will remain open, an exile without return.[17]

Those left behind are just as affected as those who are migrating. Communities are left bereft of emigrants' gifts, wisdom, crafts, and potential earnings. Families lose fathers, mothers, offspring, and relatives. Communities lose valued members of the tribe.

Given these realities, the question that arises is why move at all? There are several compelling reasons that motivate people to risk and disrupt their lives in this violent way: war, famine, and financial distress have been listed as causative factors.[18] Silvano M. Tomasi believes that a "widening income difference" is what lies at the "root of today's migrations."[19] This growing economic disparity is spurred by what has come to be known as "globalization."

Broadly speaking, globalization is related to an economic approach known as "neoliberalism," associated with the Chicago School of economic policies. Neoliberalism, in general, focuses on "free markets" and "free trade," decreased government regulations, privatization of government-based institutions, reduced government spending, and lowering of trade barriers. It is largely driven by transnational corporations that have been influential in policymaking, developing what are often known as "structural adjustment policies," and free trade agreements, such as the North American Free Trade Agreement (NAFTA) and the Central American-Dominican Republic Free Trade Agreement (CAFTA-DR). Structural adjustment policies (SAPs) are steps ostensibly enforced by the International Monetary Fund (IMF) and the World Bank to reduce debt in so-called Third World countries. Government programs are privatized, social services are curtailed, production is dedicated for export rather than local consumption, and spending is funneled toward repayment of high interest loans rather than for sustaining the vitality of the debtor nation. This subtly shifts the burden of national debt so that it is too often borne by the poor. Additionally, SAPs, in conjunction with free trade agreements, often bankrupt small businesses and farmers in affected nations, leading to economic crises and severe social distress.[20]

Globalization is thus a complex socioeconomic and political reality, "an emerging 'neo-liberal' democratic world order cemented by a new, dynamic, transnational, market capitalism" that has sociopolitical, religious, and even environmental consequences.[21] It is a system that is "associated with...extension of forms of production, rapid mobility of capital, information and goods, denationalization of culture, interpenetration of local communities by global media networks, and dispersal of socioeconomic power."[22] Wanda Deifelt considers it a "loose web of free economic, political, and cultural exchange" that is "guided by the interests of progress, capital gain, investment and profit" such that it often "repeats the pattern of social and political exploitation."[23] It is an ideology that sustains an economic philosophy and practices whose ultimate goal is the garnering of profits. *Profits* not *people* become the watchword; or in Nelly García Murillo's wonderful phrasing: in a globalized world, we have exchanged "well-being" for "well-having."[24]

Globalization is an economic and social tsunami that has entered geographical spaces, disrupting local economies, social structures, and whole communities by insisting on the free movement of *goods* and capital. In doing so, many are thus forced to migrate. In this sense, the movement of migration is that of a people moving away from the powers and principalities that have caused death in their communities, and thus it is a movement of people seeking life.

An Invitation to the Dance

Biologically, movement is a fundamental characteristic of living entities. All living organisms move. De Genova argues that freedom of movement is an ontological imperative and thus linked to our very "being-ness." It is related to "life in its barest essential condition"—that is to say, "life in its most apparently 'biological' and socially undifferentiated and unqualified (animal) sense"— and thus inseparable from human life.[25] Consequently, "the sovereign power to regulate or restrict human movement through space is thus never simply a matter of 'administration' or 'belonging.' It is the imposition of power over life itself."[26] While the United Nations has declared freedom of movement a "human right," De Genova argues that it is more basic than a right.[27] This is a crucial distinction since "human rights" have proved to be a slippery entity to grasp in a globalized world. History and political realities have demonstrated that when classes of people are declared "noncitizens" and are dislocated in liminal spaces of "not-belonging"— such as populations located in refugee camps, or deportees residing in detention centers, and even victims in concentration/internment camps—there is an inability or unwillingness to defend their rights. In effect, they become "right-less." They are people who reside not so much "at" the borders as in the liminal spaces within and in-between borders. There is no body politic that claims them, and therefore none to defend them.[28] They are the modern *anawim*, like those described in the biblical narrative of Exodus, a people not native to Egypt yet claimed by Egyptian political powers as property for oppressive labor, a people who can turn only to God and cry out for justice. The modern-day *anawim*, the "right-less ones," are treated as *sobrajas*—those whom society believes have no intrinsic value and thus can dispose of at will.[29]

While De Genova's argument about freedom of movement is a crucial insight, I believe that there is an additional theological argument—more so, a *theological imperative*—that undergirds such movement, one with biblical roots in our Christian tradition. The creation narratives in Genesis begin with movement. The *ruach* (Spirit) of God "moved" over the waters to bring forth life. God spoke and soon the face of the earth was filled with myriad forms of life and organisms moving in the "heavens" and on the earth, and God saw that it was "good." The First and Second Testaments are replete with narratives of pilgrimages.[30] Very often movement is initiated by invitation of God's Spirit. Spirit is "wind," "breath," movement, and life itself. In his encounter with Nicodemus, Jesus states, "The wind blows where it chooses, and you hear the sound of it, but you do not know where it comes from or where it goes. So it is with *everyone who is born of the Spirit*" (John 3:8, my emphasis). We go where Spirit takes us. We are *moved* by the Spirit. Spirit is the Third Person of the Triune God, the "wild child" who invites us to the dance.[31] Spirit is life itself and as loving, swirling, moving, inviting life, invites us to *perichoretic* (interpenetrating), loving *vínculos* (ties) with God and with each other. Life in God is defined by this joyous freedom of movement, this loving and adventurous invitation to the dance. The Second Testament, in particular the Book of Acts, is witness to the many who accepted this invitation: Peter moved to go to a Gentile centurion's home, thus initiating a new ministry with global implications beyond his ken; Philip moved to a desert to encounter an African eunuch, thus establishing the basis for a fruitful life; Paul felled by a call and moved to so many places, and in each planting seeds of gospel (*evanggelion*)—good news to the poor, the sick, the hopeless, the left out, and the leftovers—leaving behind hope and new life. Spirit is life and wherever Spirit moves there is life. Movement is foundational to life.

Thus, to impede movement is not only to hinder life but to hinder the very source of life itself. To force a "contra-movement" as in the case of deportation or the threat of deportation, by its very definition, impedes freedom and therefore the Spirit of movement. Such impediments are thus counter to the very beingness of who we are as a created people and as a community of God. It is sin because it causes stagnation, and stagnation leads to death.

ILLEGALITY, SPATIALITY, AND DETENTION: STOPPING THE DANCE FOR A PRICE

Mass incarceration, or as Löic Wacquant calls it, "hyperincarceration," is a relatively modern phenomenon. It came into full force in the 1970s with the initiation of the so-called "War on Drugs"—begun at a time in which crimes related to drugs were showing signs of waning.[32] The actual intent of this so-called war was a targeted attack on poor black and Latina/o communities. The prison population skyrocketed from approximately 300,000 in the 1970s to close to 2.2 million at present, including those detained in prisons, jails, and immigration detention centers. Of those incarcerated, nearly 40 percent are African American, even though they comprise only about 13 percent of the population. James Kilgore reported in 2011 that one in every eleven young African American males between the ages of twenty-five and twenty-nine is incarcerated, and that in 2010, the rate of incarceration for African Americans was six times that of those raced as white.[33] There are an additional 5.1 million people who are "virtually incarcerated" through "community correctional supervision," that is, probation or parole.[34] This has led Michelle Alexander to expand the notion of mass incarceration beyond actual imprisonment behind bars:

> Mass incarceration is a system that locks people not only behind actual bars in actual prisons, but also behind virtual bars and virtual walls…locking people of color into a permanent second-class citizenship. The term *mass incarceration* refers not only to the criminal justice system but also to the larger web of laws, rules, policies, and customs that control those labeled criminal both in and out of prison.[35]

This wider notion of incarceration is never more visible than when applied to migrants, particularly those from Latin America. The events of 9/11 allowed the government to widen its incarceration campaign against the Latina/o population not only by waging a War on Drugs, but also now by attacking "illegal aliens" in the War on Terrorism. Yet this construction of "illegality" is not new, and the true focus is not so much "national security" as that the media and pundits have wanted to frame the argument in this light. The history of migration, particularly from Mexico, Latin America, and the Spanish Caribbean, demonstrates that there is an economic impetus. Illegality is a social construct with financial goals in mind.

Illegality: The New *Encomienda*

This construction of illegality has two foundations. To begin with, there is a long history of racialization in this country that has allowed for the "othering" of nonwhite bodies, particularly populations associated with colonized lands. It is not surprising that the first laws against migration were passed to prevent people of color, specifically the Chinese, from settling in the United States and obtaining citizenship.[36] By and large, migration has been associated with people south of the border, and the "illegality" of their presence. As Alberto Ponce has rightly noted, illegality "allows for the 'legal' codification of inferiority and the maintenance of coloniality."[37] This process of "illegalization" is most striking when one considers the fact that living in the country without proper documentation is a *misdemeanor* and a civil matter; it is only in light of the 1965 reform bill that reentry after deportation is a felony.[38] Yet undocumented migrants are routinely treated as criminals: apprehended migrants are placed in detention centers, manacled, strapped with monitoring devices, and so forth. This treatment, in conjunction with the increasingly violent rhetoric and racialization associated with bodies of color, has added to the construction of "criminality" to migration. Thus, the so-called illegal alien is born in the popular imagination, and in political and social circles of power.

Second, this rhetoric of illegality has effectively hidden a long history of the use of Mexican and Latin American migrant labor from south of the border and the Caribbean, and the manipulation of the law regarding citizenship, to provide cheap labor to support the economic interests of the United States. I am always surprised at how few people who are so emotionally invested against "illegals" know about the Bracero Program or Operation Bootstrap—programs created to provide cheap labor from Mexico and Puerto Rico for U.S. agricultural and corporate interests and profits.[39] NAFTA and CAFTA-DR have also supported this push for cheap labor, as they favored the transmission of capital, goods, and corporate structures *into* Latin America and the Caribbean, and the purchase of resources at prices that primarily favored the United States. This, in turn, created a landless and jobless population, hired by U.S. corporate and agricultural interests at nonunion (that is, cheap) salaries, both within Mexico (in factories and industrial plants known as *maquiladores*) and Puerto Rico, or by encouraging their migration to the United States. Ponce rightly observes that "Mexican labor has been integral to the expansion of U.S.

capital production."[40] Nevertheless, I would add, not only Mexico; the same can be said of Puerto Rico, the Dominican Republic, and other colonized and neocolonized areas.

This history also includes the United States' military and economic invasion and colonization of Latin America and the Caribbean, of broken treaties and promises with their failed guarantees of cultural and economic sovereignty, the economic manipulation of trade, and imposition of corporate interests by the United States resulting in the loss of lands by native owners. This resulted in a push for those landless and unemployed farmers to migrate northward to serve North American economic interests, and consequently, in light of U.S. economic downturns, a simultaneous push to eject those same migrants out of the country they were initially invited to inhabit. This push-pull dimension often present in U.S. policies culminated in the immigration "reform" law of 1924 that approved the creation of the Border Patrol. This was followed by legislation in 1965 that first established quotas for migrants in the Western Hemisphere. These caps were applied in a highly racialized manner, disproportionately affecting Mexican nationals. Suddenly, almost overnight, the status of millions of Mexican agricultural migrants, who had been residing and working in the United States, changed when they were classified as "illegal" with the stroke of a pen. The Immigration Reform and Control Act of 1986 and subsequent legislation further exacerbated the problem, creating new categories of illegality, establishing sanctions against employers who hired undocumented migrants, and increasing "deportable offenses"—applicable even to legal residents although they might have been committed years prior to the passage of these bills.[41]

Thus, while a history of invasion, colonization, and neocolonization created a framework in which Latin America and the Caribbean provided the United States with a source of cheap migrant labor, it is the *legislative* tradition that has ensured that such a labor pool would remain within the confines of the U.S. border, albeit within the strictures of being classified as "illegals." Aviva Chomsky notes that the criminalization of migrants "justifies their location in the lowest ranks of the labor force."[42] She further asserts, "Illegality is a way to enforce a dual market and keep some labor cheap, in a postracial era. Illegality uses lack of citizenship...to make workers more exploitable."[43] This is achieved primarily through a threat of deportability, a mechanism complex enough to allow some to refer to it as a "deportation regime."[44]

The purpose of deportation is not to remove all undesirable migrants. Rather, the goal of the nation-state in establishing a deportability regime is so that the threat itself prevents whole groups of people from freedom of movement at all levels of life, thus creating "an unending and always disposable labor force for U.S. capital."[45] Aranda and Vargas have documented the fear and devastation that migrants feel under such a threat.[46] They fear driving and going to work. They fear going to hospitals or doctors when they are seriously ill, reporting violent crimes when they are victimized, even simply crossing a street, or going to a park. They are a people "hunkered down" and walled in. They are, for all intents and purposes, incarcerated, albeit without visible bars.

Nevertheless, while berated, insulted, marginalized, and made the objects of racial hatred by social commentators and political pundits, this very population is also essential for the economic success of various sectors. Chomsky and others have documented the financial gains that migrants bring to agriculture, manufacturing, construction, and other sectors. Despite the misinformation propagated, undocumented migrants pay for benefits in the form of social security and other taxes, though they will never be able to claim the benefits accrued to them.[47] They are supporting a system that benefits the citizens of this nation-state. Thus, through the cheap labor they provide as well as through the tax system, undocumented migrants are an incarcerated people who are an essential part of the financial fabric of this country. They are part of a colonized "new *encomienda*" system, purposely detained to be exploited for profit.

For-Profit Prisons: The New *Repartimiento*

The profit gained from undocumented (and in some instances, documented) migrants is not only derived directly through their labor, it is further derived through the industry that has arisen in light of their incarceration. The *legislative* arm has partnered in many ways with *corporate* interests, perhaps in analogous ways to those in which the "cross and the sword" partnered in the colonization of the Americas five hundred years ago. Until the late 1990s, most migrants that committed deportable offenses, or those found to be residing within the United States without proper authorization, were either forcibly returned to their countries of origin or could return voluntarily at their own behest. Since simply being in the country is not in itself a crime, but rather a civil violation, removal is not considered a punishment per se, though reentry after removal is considered a felony. Three significant changes took place after the late 1990s into the early years of the 2000s, and especially during the Obama presidency.

First, voluntary removals were reduced in favor of apprehension, detention, and deportations, which rose significantly from 50,000 in 1996 to 400,000 in 2008. Second, the Immigration and Naturalization Service (INS) was dismantled and the U.S. Immigration and Customs Enforcement (ICE) agency was created instead. Subsequently, oversight of immigration was transferred from the Department of Justice to Homeland Security, under the Homeland Security Act of 2002. Immigration was thus subtly and indirectly related to "national security" and "terrorism." Third, as a result of this shift to Homeland Security, specific legislation was passed, particularly in the southwest borderlands, which then became the model of how migrants, primarily Mexican and other Latin American migrants, were viewed and treated. The institution of Operation Gatekeeper in California and Operation Hold the Line in Texas militarized the border, and erection of actual walls or fences "created a humanitarian crisis" by denying migrants freedom of movement and aiming to "criminalize their presence within certain spaces."[48] These early legislative acts culminated and matured in Operation Streamline, enacted in 2005. Applied in the Tucson region, Streamline randomly chooses and shackles migrants slated for deportation, and imprisons them after they appear before a judge. As is often the case with other deportees, such migrants are often ignorant of the few rights afforded them. For example, they are often unaware that they can apply for asylum, or that they have a right to legal representation. Such deportees have no right to bail, and while they have a right to an attorney, this right is extended only if they can afford one. Chomsky describes the scene as follows:

174

Unlike most deportees, Streamlined migrants are charged with a criminal offense and imprisoned. The daily hearings fall somewhere between a kangaroo court and a slave auction. The migrants are shackled hand, foot, and waist, and sit in rows taking up half of the courtroom. The judge calls them in groups of ten or so, and their harassed lawyers, who represent four or five defendants a day, scramble to accompany them. Almost all of these migrants are captured in the desert, and are blistered, exhausted, disoriented, and dehydrated when they are placed in cells. They describe being stripped of their belongings and jackets and left to shiver in T-shirts under the air-conditioning, being placed seventy to eighty people deep in cells designed for four or five.[49]

It is no wonder that Galina Cornelisse describes detention of immigrants as a form of "state violence" that nonetheless remains "insulated against the usual forms of legal correction and political control."[50] In addition to Operation Streamline, under ICE, apprehensions have increased dramatically since 2006, and by 2010, some 363,000 migrants were incarcerated, primarily in for-profit prisons throughout the United States.

Serious questions have been raised about the degree to which the corporate interests of these privately held detention centers have been involved in the formulation of the legislation that has increased the detention of migrants; indeed, one must question why people with no criminal records or history of violence are being detained at all. In the words of Peutz and De Genova, they are not being detained for "what they have done but merely on account of what they are."[51] One must therefore conclude, along with Geiza Vargas-Vargas, that "detention is a new source of income for investors." He cites from the 2011 annual report of the Corrections Corporation of America (CCA), one of the largest publicly traded prison corporations in the United States:

The three primary federal government agencies with correctional and detention responsibilities, the BOP, ICE, and USMS, accounted for 43% of our total revenues for the fiscal year ended in December 31, 2011

($749.3 million)....We expect to continue to depend on the federal agencies and a relatively small group of other governmental customers for a significant percentage of our revenues.[52]

CCA is only one of three major private prison corporations. The GEO group (with 109 facilities) and the Management and Training Corporation (MTC, with 22 facilities) group along with CCA represent the top three companies with strong lobbies that provide significant campaign contributions to influence legislation that increases detainable offenses. Together, they belong to a "private think tank" known as the American Legislative Exchange Council (ALEC). This council is composed of state legislators and companies—who pay thousands of dollars to join. Vargas-Vargas cites the Center for Media and Democracy in describing this group:

> ALEC is not a lobby; it is not a front group. It is much more powerful than that. Through ALEC, behind closed doors, corporations hand state legislators the changes to the law that directly benefit their bottom line. Along with legislators, corporations have membership in ALEC. Corporations sit on all nine ALEC task forces and vote with legislators to approve "model" bills.... Corporations fund almost all of ALEC's operations.[53]

These bills are then presented to legislative bodies as authored by the legislators themselves. A good example of such legislative creation was the 2009 Arizona Senate Bill 1070, one of the most radical antimigrant bills passed to date, which became a model for legislation later passed in Georgia, Alabama, Indiana, South Carolina, and Utah, among other states. This was one of the first laws that allowed local law enforcement to perform the duties of ICE agents and detain "illegal aliens." It also led to much racial profiling since one was often detained simply because one "looked Hispanic." The intent behind these bills is to increase the prison population. "Prison corporations have a real interest in any and all legislation that increases the number of bodies that go through the detention or incarceration process," claims Vargas-Vargas, because "growth in the criminal population translates into returns for shareholders."[54] Indeed, Chomsky reports that CCA and GEO "doubled their revenues from the immigration detention business between 2005 and 2012."[55]

Prison corporations are not the only beneficiaries of the "detention" regime and prosecution of migrants. Kilgore reports how state-based union organizations such as the California Correctional and Parole Officers Association (CCPOA) and the New York Correctional Officers and Police Benevolent Association (NYSCOPBA) have supported mass incarceration, lobbied to promote harsher sentencing laws, and sought for greater benefits and wage packages for correctional officers.[56] Michelle Alexander, Aviva Chomsky, and others have documented how the militarization and privatization of these regimes have not only provided employment for the towns that house the detention centers/prisons, but also increase the tax base and infrastructure. Particularly during the recession years of the first decade of the twenty-first century, these budget surpluses proved to be a boon for many small towns that otherwise would have been devastated economically. In some cases, it has led some communities to consider prison populations as "a primary economic strategy."[57]

Ultimately, detention, deportability, and the propaganda of "illegality" serve to criminalize and obstruct freedom of movement. They are a means of regulating wealth and of obtaining profit.[58] They rob people of their humanity, hopes, and fundamental rights as human beings. Amid this *kairos*, that is, divinely appointed place and time, the Christian Church is called upon to respond and share with the world a gospel word, an *evanggelion*, a word of good news.

THE GOOD NEWS OF THE REIGN OF GOD: CREATING SACRED SPACES OF LIFE AND JUSTICE

For the church to discern what is its role and response in light of the sin of mass incarceration, and the injustice perpetrated upon migrant people—both documented and undocumented—it is imperative that we understand the theological foundation upon which we base that response. In the next section, I discuss the importance of Jesus' call to the Christian Church to be a sacrament of the reign of God (*basileia tou theou*), a concept that is both a reality of the end-time (what is often referred to as an "eschatological" moment, or God's fulfillment of God's salvific purpose of all creation) and a present unfolding of God's vision for the world.

The God of *Vínculos*

Many Christian communities confess belief in a triune God.[59] As such, God is above all a communal God, three Persons in one dynamic, perichoretic divine whole. *Perichoresis* is the theological term used, from its Greek roots, to denote both "mutual interpenetration" of the Persons as well as "active movement"— what Catherine Mowry LaCugna and others have referred to as a "divine dance." Elsewhere I have used the Spanish term *vínculos*— which literally means "the ties that bind"—to evoke this sense of intimate relations.[60]

This acknowledgment of God's triune nature underscores an important theological argument regarding the problem of the unjust treatment, detention, and exploitation of undocumented migrants: community is integral to the very being of God, and as such fundamental to the very fabric of creation. We are created to be in community, even as God is communal. Following the Orthodox insight of *theosis*—that salvation is defined by our final union with God so that we are "divinized," obtaining incorruptible natures and becoming like God—and those of Western theologians like Karl Barth, who posited that God created so that creation could be in union with God, one could say that God's ultimate vision and purpose (that is to say, the *eschatological vision*) is that all of creation will be in perichoretic ties (*vinculado*) with each other and with God.[61] "In the beginning," assert the Genesis narratives, God created a wonderfully diverse community, a world of difference of color, sound, beings, and species, and God saw that it was "very good" (Gen 1:1–31). John Zizioulas affirms that our very humanity is defined based on this being-in-community, of being a people in relationship with others and with God.[62]

From this perspective, sin can be understood as the rupture of these communal ties. Indeed, Gustavo Gutiérrez has often defined sin as a "breach" of friendship between God and humanity. It is this breach that subsequently causes a concomitant chasm amid the human community and between humanity and creation. This breach, avers Gutiérrez, is the root of injustice and suffering in the world.[63] As such, that which causes ruptures in community and in human relationships is sinful. Furthermore, following Zizioulas's insight, to be separated from our human ties, from our *vínculos*—as those who are detained, deported, isolated, or forced to reside in the liminal spaces of nonbeing between bordered spaces—is to be dehumanized not only at an ontological level, but in a way that opposes the theological vision and purpose for creation.

For church scholars as venerable as Irenaeus, and respected theologians from Karl Barth to Letty M. Russell, among others, God is concerned with this rupture of God's community. In Russell's words, "God is concerned with the mending of creation."[64] This soteriological concern is consistent with the divine purpose and goal (*telos*) for creation: God seeks to heal the ruptured *vínculos* amid creation to re-form the very creation God envisioned from "the beginning." Time and time again, we see God reaching out to the forgotten, the marginalized, the brokenhearted, and broken to extend a hand of healing and to restore them to community. God is identified in this way to such an extent in the First Testament that the Exodus becomes paradigmatic for the people of Israel: a people who were strangers in the land, considered *anawim* (rabble), were enslaved (a form of incarceration) and exploited for the enrichment and profit of those in power. Scripture tells us that God heard their cry and sent an advocate, demanding, "Let my people go!" (Exod 6:5–6; 8:1). There cannot be true community, true humanity, where a people are dehumanized, enslaved (*encomendados/as*), and not allowed the freedom to move as they please. God freed them and made of them a *pueblo*, a people, a covenantal community, a "light of the world" (Matt 5:14).[65] Later, when Israel oppresses and behaves unjustly to the "sojourner" (Hebr: *nokrî*) and to the stranger (Hebr: *ger*) in their midst, God sends prophets to remind them that they are to treat them justly because Israel was also once a stranger and sojourner (e.g, Exod 23:9).

The God Who Calls Us to Justice

The First Testament acknowledges that God is inherently a God of justice. In the same way that the Christian community claims that God is love (1 John 4:8), we also claim that God is the God of justice (ṣᵉdāqāh), mercy (raḥᵃmin), and faithfulness (ᵉmunāh). These four attributes are not simply things that God *does* but who God *is*. They are not simply four separate qualities, but are "virtually equated."[66] As such, God's call throughout Scriptures is that God's people are to do justice:

> [God] has told you, O mortal, what is good;
>   and what does the LORD require of you
> but to do justice, and to love kindness,
>   and to walk humbly with your God?
>
> (Mic 6:8)

The meaning of justice in the Bible is somewhat different than our understanding of the term in the secular world. Israel's understanding of *justice* was forged within the context of covenant, and therefore is always understood in a framework of relationship. It is why the Hebrew and Greek terms associated with justice in the Bible—ṣᵉdāqāh, mišpaṭ, dikaiosynē—are often translated as "righteousness" in English Bibles: to indicate a "right-wise" or righting of relationships. Justice is based on right relationships, first and foremost with God. Yet, a right relationship with God demands that there is a right relationship with the larger community, not only human but with all of creation. Justice implies intimate (perichoretic) *vínculos* from which *shalom*—God's bountiful blessings, grace, peace, and wholeness—flow. In Ephesians 4:11–16, this concept of "wholeness" is evoked by the word *perfeccionar* in Spanish and *equip* in English (NRSV). It is translated from the Greek, *katartismos*, which means to heal a fracture or mend a hole in a broken net.[67] Justice brings about peace because it implies making whole what was broken, divided, or rent asunder. Peace is not simply the absence of conflict but is the presence of God's bountifulness, and therefore implies wholeness for the community. "Let justice roll down like waters, / and righteousness like an ever-flowing stream" (Amos 5:24).

A secular notion of justice is equated with "fairness," and true justice is considered "blind"—that is to say, it is impartial and applied equally to everyone, such that it is fair and good for the largest majority of people amid competing and conflicting interests.[68] However, a biblical view of justice is intentionally biased in favor of "the least of these" in the community: the poor, the orphan and widow, the captive, the sojourner and "resident alien." In other words, justice is best exhibited when it defends the defenseless. In Israel, this was especially directed to the landless, the weak, and the marginalized. The purpose of justice is to "restore community when it has been threatened."[69] True justice protects life, nurtures it, and heals the fractures that threaten it. In this sense, hospitality is an expression of justice.[70]

Persons described as *bien educadas/os* in Puerto Rican society embody this biblical understanding of a "just person." In Spanish, the term *bien educado/a* does not translate as "well educated" in terms of academic achievement, but rather refers to the wise person in the community who treats people with respect and offers hospitality, particularly to the stranger. To be hospitable is to emulate God's grace, and to embody God's always welcoming Spirit. Elizabeth Conde-Frazier reminds us that hospitality entails creating spaces of respect by offering a mutual sharing of our lives. It means respecting the *imago Dei* of the other.[71] *Personas bien educadas*, those who are attentive to act justly, do not ask, "Who is my neighbor?" but rather ask, "To whom and *when* am I neighbor?" (see Luke 10:25–37).

To ask such questions is to comprehend the insistent Scriptural command to do justice to the "resident alien"/stranger (*ger*) or "sojourner" (*nokrî*). Like the widow, the poor, and other marginalized classes, they are the landless and often the powerless of society. They are without family ties, and therefore lack protection and privilege.[72] God is insistent that one is to do justice to the stranger and sojourner because Israel was a sojourner. Thus, in Exodus 22 and 23, there are injunctions to "not wrong the stranger," or oppress them. Deuteronomy 10:17–18 reminds Israel that God loves the *ger*, and therefore Israel is to feed them and clothe them. Those familiar with the story of Ruth will remember the injunction that the ears of grain that drop in the harvest are to be left so that the widow, the stranger, and the poor can take them for their own sustenance (Ruth 2; Lev 19:9–10). This spirit is brought to bear in Isaiah 58:7. The prophet challenges those who live a false piety while oppressing exploited workers. God calls upon such *encomenderos* to "share your bread with the hungry, / *and bring the homeless poor into your house*; / when you see the naked, to cover them, / and not to *hide yourself from your own kin*" (emphasis mine). One is to be more than neighbor; one is to be kin to the stranger and sojourner, to the homeless migrant, to the "right-less" ones who live in the in-between liminal spaces of not-belonging.

Reign of God: Embodied Justice

God's call to justice and to communal wholeness is not limited to the First Testament. In the Second Testament, we find that the central message of Jesus' proclamation was that God's reign, the *basileia tou theou*, was active and present amid Israel. *Basileia* is a verb noun that points not simply to a place but also to an action: it is God's active sovereignty over the "powers and principalities" of injustice and oppression. It is not an expression of abusive power; rather than a "power over," it is a "liberative power" that is imbued with grace, love, and justice.[73] The phrase is meant to be an eschatological and scriptural "shorthand" that affirms that God's purpose for creation is and will be done "on earth as it is in heaven" (Matt 6:10). It underscores and reminds us of God's initial vision for creation: that all humanity should live in community with God and all of creation. There was and is to be a space and place for all living creatures to thrive fully and in relation to each other. While there are scholars who insist that the reign does not refer to a place, using insights from indigenous theologies, I have argued elsewhere that the reign indeed is "place"—the encounter of divine and created spaces to establish a sacred space, particularly for those with no place to call "home."[74] Otherwise, why would Jesus say to a colonized, homeless, and poor people, "In my Father's house there are many dwelling places. If it were not so, would I have told you that I go to prepare a *place* for you?" (John 14:2, emphasis mine). Relations and community take *place* and the reign is the cross section of divine and created sacred space where communal *vínculos* are restored and nurtured.

It is not surprising then that Jesus' central message was that this reign was to be "good news" for the poor, a word of *release for the captives*, and a notification that the oppressed were to be set free (Luke 4:18–19). The reign is associated with feeding the hungry, healing the sick, and restoring to community the marginalized and expelled. In this sacred space, Jesus created a diverse community of people, and redefined the categories for "belonging." Citizenship in the reign is no longer based on blood, birth, gender, class, ethnicity, or race. It is based on God's unremitting grace and faithfulness. For Jesus, the proclamation of the reign also meant exposing the sins of empire: confronting the globalizing powers that pressed upon the powerless and the poor at the expense of their humanity; that in fact, the prevailing (imperial) justice of the time was "perverted justice"—one that violated God's call to protect the weak, the widow, the poor, and the stranger.[75] Jesus' opposition to such "powers" and his faithfulness to the "least" led to his crucifixion. Yet the last word in history was not to be death or oppression. The fundamental word of the reign is life. God's commitment to the reign and Jesus' ministry was embodied in Jesus' resurrection. Adopting Barthian language, the resurrection was God's resounding yes to the world's no.[76]

Orlando E. Costas argues that the scriptural claim that Jesus "suffered outside the city gate" (Heb 13:12) locates Jesus in the periphery, with the marginalized, among those who live daily beyond the gates of justice and power.[77] The same biblical passage goes on to state that Jesus remains there and beckons us. This implies two important theological principles: First, that the God of the First Testament, who is steadfastly faithful to the *ger* and *nokrî*, remains with them even today. God does not abandon those who live in the liminal spaces of "not-belonging" and "rightlessness." For us today, our "outside the gate" is precisely the liminal spaces of "between borders," outside borders, and in the spaces of "non-belonging," where millions are relegated and so many die in despair and hopelessness. Second, this biblical text is a theological reminder that God beckons those who claim fidelity and love to God, those who seek to follow Jesus, to join the Lord "outside the city gate": to be with the crucified, the exploited, and the "bent over" (Luke 13:10–17) ones who are powerless and voiceless. Thus, entrance to the reign begins "outside the city gate" in perichoretic *vínculo* with the least, the forgotten, the downtrodden, the marginalized, the *sobrajas*, and sojourners. Thus, the question remains:

To whom and when am I neighbor? According to Hebrews 13:12, I am neighbor to those outside the gate, where even today Jesus stands and beckons me to follow.

The Church as Sacrament of the Reign

The church must steadfastly continue to ponder this question: To whom and when am I neighbor? It is a question that must transcend nation-state fealties, ethnic pride, and racial categorizations. It is a question that must break with the increasing xenophobia and false nationalism that has gripped so many countries, allowing migrants and refugees to be the easy scapegoats of television personalities and political pundits. If the church is to be true neighbor, it must begin by allowing the Spirit to move it "outside the city gate" to stand alongside the poor, the orphan, the widow, the weak, the *ger* and the *nokrî*. In doing so, it must reclaim its role to be a sacrament of the reign of God. It is not the reign, but it is a sacrament of the reign. The term *sacrament* is a translation from the Greek *mysterion*, later translated into the Latin as *sacramentum*. Unlike our modern usage, the biblical meaning of *mystery* does not refer to something hidden, but rather to something hidden that is now revealed.[78] For the Apostle Paul, Jesus is God's *mysterion*, the good news revealed to the world. To say that the church is a sacrament of the reign is to say that when the world sees the church it should understand what is God's vision and purpose for us. We uncover something that was hidden: God's active presence in the liminal spaces "outside the city gate," amid the voiceless and right-less of the world. The world should see how we are to live as a people created for community, love, fidelity, hospitality, and justice. The church is called to model how we are to be neighbor in the world.

In light of the exploitation/*encomienda* of migrants, and their *repartimiento* to prisons for profit-making, the church should become a sacred space of life and humanization. It should be the divinely initiated *kairos* place where the *ger* and *nokrî* are no longer treated as "illegal," *sobrajas*, or where they are dehumanized. Rather, in this space, they are *familia* (family)/kin: brother, sister, friend. The church as sacrament of the reign can model for the world a space where people exist, not in liminal spaces of "not-belongingness" or "right-lessness," but rather as true citizens by

God's saving, welcoming, and loving grace. Such a place would not exploit, but rather nurture our gifts so that we can provide life-giving fruit of the Spirit that brings about *katartismos*, healing of the brokenness in our midst. As a sacrament of God's justice, the church must also protest a justice system that would incarcerate people *en masse* for profit-making. The church must resist a system that incarcerates people more because of who or what they are than any constructed rationale about what they might have done. The church cannot collude with unjust systems that deny people their right to a better life, and strip people of their humanity. We should join Rev. Benjamin Cantu's protest, who acknowledged that the church is not an immigration office but rather "*es casa de Dios y puerta del cielo*" (house of God and door to heaven).[79]

The church as sacrament of the reign is a divine space where the "Spirit blows." As a pneumatological sacred space, it becomes a sacrament of freedom of movement. It celebrates Pentecost daily. People of different nations and different tongues gather without fear as a community, invited to join in the "dance of the Spirit." It is a dance of joy, love, peace, and *koinonia* (fellowship). Community is formed. God's purpose and vision for all of creation is fulfilled. Justice and peace are experienced within this pneumatological space. In such a space, the church acknowledges the necessity of creating conditions conducive to living a quality of life to obviate the need to abandon one's homeland. As such, the church must speak out against the globalizing tendencies that have destroyed people's communities and livelihoods. We must protest economic systems that place profit above people. We must detain the economic tsunamis that have robbed people of their "daily bread," requiring them to move. Paradoxically, the pneumatological and prophetic impulses that move us to create conditions for people to remain in their geographical homes also require us to acknowledge that freedom of movement is a divine imperative, and not a legislative privilege. Subsequently, the church as sacrament of the reign should never serve as a blockade for migrating populations. We should never be the ones who stand at borders as human chains, yelling at children, "You shall not pass." Rather, as a people of the Spirit, we say, "Come Holy Spirit, blow and move us freely. Grant us the gift to join in your dance of life and joy." As a sacrament of the reign, we stand at the border with water, clothing, and open arms. We acknowledge the call in Matthew 25:35: "I was a stranger and you welcomed me." As sacrament, we are called to be home to the world's displaced homeless, a healing haven for the dehumanized, *casa de Dios y puerta del cielo*.

The church as a sacrament of the reign should be a sacred space on earth where God's *hesed* (abiding and faithful love), *s^edāqāh* (justice), and *rah^amin* (mercy) are lived out in faithful ways. We can embody for the world what true justice is, not only for the stranger and the sojourner, but for the voiceless, oppressed, rightless, and not-belonging ones. We can model for the world what it means to follow Jesus as we stand with the *sobrajas* of the world outside the gate. There we can form living perichoretic *vínculos* of love that serve as a healing sacrament to a world torn asunder by intolerance, xenophobic hate, racism, and homophobia. The blood of our sisters and brothers calls out from a bleeding earth. The church as sacrament of the reign is called to be a light unto the world. Hear then the call of the Lord to be a citizen of the reign:

> The Spirit of the Lord is upon me,
>> because he has anointed me to bring good news to
>> the poor.
> [He has sent me to heal the brokenhearted].[80]
> He has sent me to proclaim release to the captives
>> and recovery of sight to the blind, to let the
>> oppressed go free,
> to proclaim the year of the Lord's favor.
>
> (Luke 4:18–19)

Notes

1. Michelle Alexander, *The New Jim Crow: Mass Incarceration in the Age of Colorblindness*, 2nd ed. (New York: The New Press, 2011). "Jim Crow" refers to the series of laws and culture that prevailed in the post-Reconstruction South (approximately from 1877 through the civil rights era in the 1960s) that legalized segregation, reduced many African Americans to positions of employment that often amounted to servitude, and created a reign of terror through violence and lynchings. Alexander is not the first or only person to make a parallel from the incarceration of African Americans to Jim Crow. See Joan Martin, *More than Chains and Toil* (Louisville, KY: Westminster John Knox Press, 2000), 148; and Löic

Wacquant, "Class, Race, and Hyperincarceration in Revanchist America," *Daedalus* 140, no. 3 (Summer 2010): 74–90.

2. Even in the midst of writing this, new cases continue to appear in the news, such as that of Gregory Gunn, a fifty-eight-year-old African American shot and killed by a white police officer in Montgomery, Alabama; Alton Sterling who was shot by two police officers in Baton Rouge, Louisiana, while on the ground handcuffed; and Philando Castile who was shot and killed while reaching for his license and registration during a routine traffic stop for a broken tail light in St. Anthony, Minnesota. His fiancée and her young daughter were in the car and witnessed the shooting.

3. For more on codification of language, see Ian Haney López, *Dog Whistle Politics: How Coded Racial Appeals Have Reinvented Racism and Wrecked the Middle Class* (New York: Oxford University Press, 2013).

4. Howard Winant, "The New Imperialism, Globalization, and Racism," in *The New Politics of Race: Globalism, Difference, Justice* (Minneapolis: University of Minneapolis Press, 2004), 131.

5. See, for example, Alberto Ponce, "Racialization, Resistance, and the Migrant Rights Movement: A Historical Analysis," *Critical Sociology* 40, no. 1 (January 2014): 10–11. See also Elizabeth Aranda and Elizabeth Vaquera, "Racism, the Immigration Enforcement Regime, and the Implications for Racial Inequality in the Lives of Undocumented Young Adults," *Sociology of Race and Ethnicity* 1, no. 1 (January 2015): 88–104.

6. As I explain later in this chapter, *ger* and *nokrî* are the Hebrew terms for *resident alien* and *sojourner*, respectively. See the remainder of the chapter for further definitions of other unfamiliar terms.

7. Jorge Isauro Rionda Ramírez, "Ordenamiento y organización territorial en la Nueva España (siglo XVI)," *Revista de la Historia de América* 146 (Enero–Junio 2012): 102.

8. For more, see Vine DeLoria Jr., *God Is Red: A Native View of Religion*, 3rd ed. (Golden, CO: Fulcrum Publishing, 2003), 64–67; George E. "Tink" Tinker, *American Indian Liberation: A Theology of Sovereignty* (Maryknoll, NY: Orbis Books, 2008), passim; Loida I. Martell-Otero, "My GPS Does Not Work in Puerto Rico: An *Evangélica* Spirituality," *American Baptist Quarterly* 30, nos. 3 and 4 (Fall/Winter 2011): 256–75.

9. I obtain this insightful concept and phrasing from Abelkabir Khatibi, as cited in Walter D. Mignolo, *Local Histories/Global Designs: Coloniality, Subaltern Knowledges, and Border Thinking*, Princeton Studies in Culture (Princeton, NJ: Princeton University Press, 2000), 71.

10. While disease certainly played a role, it was often a consequent of the colonizing forces that introduced heretofore unknown infectious

agents, coupled with the dire conditions under which the native populations lived because of the *encomienda* and *repartimiento* systems.

11. *Webster's New Collegiate Dictionary* (1977), s.v. "immigration,"
and "migration." Cf. *Shorter Oxford English Dictionary*, vol. 1, *A–M*
(2007), s.v. "immigration," and "migrant."

12. Nicholas P. De Genova, "Migrant 'Illegality' and Deportability
in Everyday Life," *Annual Review of Anthropology* 31 (2002): 420–21.

13. See Loida I. Martell-Otero, "Creating a Sacred Space: An
Iglesia Evangélica Response to Global Homelessness," *Dialog* 49, no. 1
(March 2010): 10–11.

14. Manuel Maldonado-Dennis preferred to use the term *emigration* to convey this sense of coercive forces acting upon and leading to the
abandonment of populations of their homelands to other nation-states.
One then becomes an "exile." See his *The Emigration Dialectic: Puerto
Rico and the USA* (New York: International Publishers, 1980), 24.

15. David T. Abalos, *Latinos in the United States: The Sacred and the
Political* (Notre Dame, IN: University of Notre Dame Press, 1986), 91.

16. For more, see Martell-Otero, "Creating a Sacred Space," 9–18.

17. Denis Müller, "A Homeland for Transients: Towards an Ethics
of Migrations," trans. John Bowden, in *Migrants and Refugees*, ed. Diet-
mar Mieth and Lisa Sowle Cahill, *Concilium* (London: SCM, 1993/4),
131.

18. Hal Kane, in *The Hour of Departure: Forces That Create Refugees and Migrants* (Washington, DC: Worldwatch Institute, 1995), lists
persecution, warfare, lack of jobs, environmental degradation, redraw-
ing of borders, forced settlement, poverty, and political disempowerment
but fails to draw the connections between many of these and the concomitant social structures, including corporate migration, that cause them.
He fails to note the religious persecution that underlies much of gender/
heterosexist oppressions; nor does he recognize the growing tragedy of
slavery and the sex trade.

19. Silvano M. Tomasi, "The World-Wide Context of Migration:
The Example of Asia," in *Migrants and Refugees*, 6.

20. For a fuller discussion, see John Sniegocki, "Neoliberal Globalization: Critiques and Alternatives," *Theological Studies* 69, no. 2 (June
2008): 321–39; and Jorge Nef and Wilder Robles, "Globalization, Neoliberalism and the State of Underdevelopment in the New Periphery,"
Journal of Developing Societies 16, no. 1 (April 2000): 27–49.

21. Carl Raschke, "Globalization and Theology," *Religion Compass*
5, no. 11 (November 2011): 638.

22. Gemma Tulud Cruz, "Between Identity and Security: Theological Implications of Migration in the Context of Globalization," *Theological Studies* 2 (June 2008): 357–58.

23. Wanda Deiftelt, "Globalization, Religion, and Embodiment: Latin American Feminist Perspectives," in *Shaping a Global Theological Mind*, ed. Darren C. Marks (Hampshire: Ashgate Publishing, 2008), 41.

24. Nelly García Murillo, "Christian Higher Education in a Global Context: Implications for Curriculum, Pedagogy, and Administration," *Evangelical Review of Theology* 36, no. 1 (January 2012): 5. See also Arthur Schmidt, "Globalization, Neoliberal Ideology, and National Identity: The Historical Uncertainties of NAFTA," *Caribbean Studies* 29, no. 1 (January–June 1996): 72.

25. Nicholas De Genova, "The Deportation Regime: Sovereignty, Space, and the Freedom of Movement," in *The Deportation Regime: Sovereignty, Space, and the Freedom of Movement*, ed. Nicholas De Genova and Nathalie Peutz (Durham, NC: Duke University Press, 2010), 39. Ontology is defined as the study of our "being-ness" and the nature of existence.

26. Nathalie Peutz and Nicholas De Genova, "Introduction," in *The Deportation Regime*, 12–13.

27. See United Nations, *International Bill of Human Rights*, "The Universal Declaration of Human Rights," Article 13, General Assembly Resolution 217, adopted December 10, 1948 (Paris), http://www.un.org/en/universal-declaration-human-rights/. De Genova, "The Deportation Regime," 39.

28. See Galina Cornelisse, "Immigration Detention and Universal Rights," in *The Deportation Regime*, 119.

29. *Anawim* are "the multitudes," or "rabble"; the equivalent of our modern "street people." They are the impoverished, those who depend on God for justice and to fulfill their needs. They are those in society for whom others have no care or concern. *Sobraja* is Spanish for *leftovers*, things that we scrape off our plates and discard without a second thought. Ada María Isasi-Díaz uses the term "surplus people" to convey a similar concept; see "Un poquito de justicia—A Little Bit of Justice: A *Mujerista* Account of Justice," in *Hispanic/Latino Theology: Challenge and Promise*, ed. Ada María Isasi-Díaz and Fernando F. Segovia (Minneapolis: Fortress Press, 1996), 329.

30. See United States Conference of Catholic Bishops, *One Family under God: A Statement of the U.S. Bishops' Committee on Migration*, rev. ed. (Washington, DC: United States Conference of Catholic Bishops, 2001), 2. (Author's note: I use the terminology of First and Second Testaments as

more inclusive than the more commonly used Old and New Testaments, or Hebrew and Greek Bibles.)

31. Zaida Maldonado Pérez, Loida I. Martell-Otero, and Elizabeth Conde-Frazier, "Dancing with the Wild Child: *Evangélicas* and the Holy Spirit," in *Latina Evangélicas: A Theological Survey from the Margins,* by Loida I. Martell-Otero, Zaida Maldonado Pérez, and Elizabeth Conde-Frazier (Eugene, OR: Cascade Books, 2013), 14–15. See also Molly T. Marshall, *Joining the Dance: A Theology of the Holy Spirit* (Valley Forge, PA: Judson Press, 2003).

32. Wacquant, "Class, Race, and Hyperincarceration," 78–79.

33. See James Kilgore, "Mass Incarceration and Working Class Interests: Which Side Are the Unions On?" *Labor Studies Journal* 37, no. 4 (December 2012): 359.

34. Alexander, *The New Jim Crow,* 94.

35. Ibid., 12–13.

36. For more on this historical overview, see Ronald Takaki, *A Different Mirror: A History of Multicultural America* (New York: Little, Brown and Company, 1993). For a history of racialization, see Michael Omi and Howard Winant, *Racial Formation in the United States: From the 1960s to the 1990s,* 2nd ed. (New York: Routledge, 1994).

37. Ponce, "Racialization, Resistance, and the Migrant Rights Movement," 10.

38. Aranda and Vaquera, "Racism, the Immigration Enforcement Regime," 89.

39. For more on these programs, see Aviva Chomsky, *"They Take Our Jobs!" And 20 Other Myths about Immigration* (Boston: Beacon Press, 2007), 19–22; Aviva Chomsky, *Undocumented: How Immigration Became Illegal* (Boston: Beacon Press, 2014), 55–60. See also Martell-Otero, "Creating a Sacred Space," 12–13.

40. Ponce, "Racialization, Resistance, and the Migrant Rights Movement," 15.

41. For a summative timeline of legislative decisions, see Chomsky, *They Take Our Jobs!* 199–209. For a broader framework about how the United States has treated different groups legislatively and socially throughout its history, see Takaki, *A Different Mirror,* passim.

42. Chomsky, *Undocumented,* 18.

43. Ibid., 39.

44. See, for example, Aranda and Vargas, "Racism, the Immigration Enforcement Regime," 90; also De Genova, "The Deportation Regime," 34.

45. Ponce, "Racialization, Resistance, and Migrant Rights Movement," 17.

46. Aranda and Vargas, "Racism, the Immigration Enforcement Regime," 96–98.

47. Chomsky, *Undocumented*, 118–24. See also Chomsky, *They Take Our Jobs!* 36; Patricia Fernández Kelly, "To Welcome the Stranger: The Myths and Realities of Illegal Immigration," *Perspectivas* 10 (Fall 2006): 16–19.

48. Miguel de la Torre, *Trails of Hope and Terror: Testimonies on Immigration* (Maryknoll, NY: Orbis Books, 2009), 15. Andrew Burridge, "Differential Criminalization under Operation Streamline: Challenges to Freedom of Movement and Humanitarian Aid Provision in the Mexican-US Borderlands," *Refuge* 26, no. 2 (Fall 2009): 78.

49. Chomsky, *Undocumented*, 6–7.

50. Cornelisse, "Immigration Detention," 105.

51. Peutz and De Genova, "Introduction," 12.

52. Geiza Vargas-Vargas, "The Investment Opportunity in Mass Incarceration: A Black (Corrections) or Brown (Immigration) Play?" *California Western Law Review* 48, no. 2 (Spring 2012): 355–56.

53. Ibid., 363.

54. Ibid., 357.

55. Chomsky, *Undocumented*, 111.

56. Kilgore, "Mass Incarceration and Working Class Interests," 367.

57. As cited in Chomsky, *Undocumented*, 112. See also Alexander, *The New Jim Crow*, 77–80.

58. Cornelisse, "Immigration Detention and the Territoriality of Universal Rights," 114.

59. I respectfully acknowledge those communities that do not confess a trinitarian tradition. I would hope that there are, nevertheless, aspects of my argument in the paragraphs that follow that would resonate with nontrinitarian Christian communities as well as those who confess God as triune.

60. Catherine Mowry LaCugna, *God for Us: The Trinity and Christian Life* (New York: HarperCollins, 1991), 271–72. Martell-Otero, "My GPS Does Not Work in Puerto Rico," 259, 267. Maldonado Pérez, Martell-Otero, and Conde-Frazier, "Dancing with the Wild Child," 20–21.

61. Karl Barth, *Church Dogmatics*, III.1, *The Doctrine of Creation*, trans. J. W. Edwards, O. Bussey, and H. Knight, ed. G. W. Bromiley and T. F. Torrance, rev. ed. (Peabody, MA: Hendrickson, 2010). See especially sections 2 and 3, where he formulates his fundamental thesis that creation is "the external basis of the covenant" and the covenant is "the internal basis of creation." See also Vladimir Kharlamov, ed., *Theosis:*

Deification in Christian Theology, vol. 2 (Eugene, OR: Pickwick Publications, 2011).

62. John D. Zizioulas, *Communion and Otherness: Further Studies in Personhood and the Church* (New York: T&T Clark, 2006), 99–112, 155–70.

63. Gustavo Gutiérrez, *A Theology of Liberation: History, Politics, and Salvation*, trans. and ed. Caridad Inda and John Eagleson, rev. ed. (Maryknoll, NY: Orbis Books, 1988), xxxviii.

64. Letty M. Russell, *Household of Freedom: Authority in Feminist Theology*, The 1986 Annie Kinkead Warfield Lectures (Philadelphia: Westminster Press, 1987), 71.

65. Cf. Deuteronomy 7:6–9. The Jewish concept of chosenness is closely linked to the concept of being a witness of God's presence and justice in the world. For more, see Donniel Hartman, *Putting God Second: How to Save Religion from Itself* (Boston: Beacon Press, 2016).

66. John R. Donohue, "Biblical Perspectives on Justice," in *The Faith That Does Justice: Examining the Christian Sources for Social Change*, ed. John E. Haughey (New York: Paulist Press, 1977), 69. I appreciate the insight about the interrelatedness of God's steadfast love (*hesed*), mercy, and faithfulness with justice that Donohue provides.

67. See Markus Barth, *Anchor Bible Commentary*, vol. 34A, *Ephesians 4–6* (Garden City, NY: Doubleday, 1974), 439.

68. See, for example, John Rawls, *A Theory of Justice* (Cambridge: The Belknap Press of Harvard University Press, 1971), chap. 1, particularly pp. 3–7.

69. Donohue, "Biblical Perspectives on Justice," 69. Cf. José Míguez Bonino, "The Biblical Roots of Justice," *Word and World* 7, no. 1 (Winter 1987): 15.

70. See, for example, Letty M. Russell, *Just Hospitality: God's Welcome in a World of Difference*, ed. J. Shannon Clarkson and Kate M. Ott (Louisville, KY: Westminster John Knox, 2009).

71. Elizabeth Conde-Frazier, "From Hospitality to Shalom," in *A Many Colored Kingdom: Multicultural Dynamics for Spiritual Formation*, ed. Elizabeth Conde-Frazier, S. Steve Kang, and Gary A. Parrett (Grand Rapids, MI: Baker Academic, 2004), 171. For more on *buena educación*, see Loida I. Martell-Otero, "From Foreign Bodies in Teacher Space to Embodied Spirit in *Personas Educadas*: or, How to Prevent 'Tourists of Diversity' in Education," in *Teaching for a Culturally Diverse and Racially Just World*, ed. Eleazar S. Fernandez (Eugene, OR: Cascade Books, 2014), 63–68.

72. For more, Diether Kellerman, s.v. "gûr," in *Theological Dictionary of the Old Testament*, vol. 2, *bdl–gālah*, ed. Johannes Botterweck

and Helmer Ringgren, trans. John T. Wills, rev. ed. (Grand Rapids, MI: Eerdmans, 1977), 443. Also, B. Lang, s.v. "nokrî," in *Theological Dictionary of the Old Testament*, vol. 9, *mārad–nāqā*, ed. Johannes Botterweck, Helmer Ringgren, and Heinz-Josef Fabry, trans. David E. Green (Grand Rapids, MI: Eerdmans, 1998), 425. See also Frank Crüsemann, "'You Know the Heart of a Stranger' (Exodus 23:9): A Recollection of the Torah in the Face of New Nationalism and Xenophobia," trans. John Bowden, in *Migrants and Refugees*, 99.

73. Joan M. Martin, "A Sacred Hope and Social Goal: Womanist Eschatology," in *Liberating Eschatology: Essays in Honor of Letty M. Russell*, ed. Margaret A. Farley and Serene Jones (Louisville, KY: Westminster John Knox, 1999), 210.

74. Loida I. Martell-Otero, "Neither 'Left Behind' nor Deciphering Secret Codes: An *Evangélica* Understanding of Eschatology," in *Latina Evangélicas*, 112–15. Cf. Donohue, "Biblical Perspectives on Justice," 86.

75. José Míguez Bonino, "The Biblical Roots of Justice," 15–16. In the First Testament, such "perverted justice" demanded swift prophetic denunciation.

76. Karl Barth, *Church Dogmatics*, III.2, *The Doctrine of Creation*, trans. H. Knight, G. W. Bromiley, J. K. S. Reid, and R. H. Fuller, ed. G. W. Bromiley and T. F. Torrance (Edinburgh: T&T Clark, 1960), 143.

77. Orlando E. Costas, *Christ outside the Gate: Mission beyond Christendom* (Maryknoll, NY: Orbis Books, 1982), 188–94. See also Loida I. Martell-Otero, "Liberating News: An Emerging U.S. Hispanic/Latina Soteriology of the Crossroads," (PhD diss., Fordham University, 2005), 265–66, 310–12.

78. James D. G. Dunn, "Mystery," in *The New Interpreter's Dictionary of the Bible*, vol. 4, *Me–R*, ed. Katherine Doob Sakenfeld et al. (Nashville: Abingdon, 2009), 185. Cf. Christine Mohrmann, "Sacramentum Dans Les Plus Anciens Textes Chrètiens," *Harvard Theological Review*, 47, no. 3 (July 1954): 141–52.

79. As cited in Daniel Ramírez, "Borderland Praxis: The Immigrant Experience in Latino Pentecostal Churches," *Journal of the American Academy of Religion* 67, no. 3 (Summer 1999): 588 (my translation).

80. Included in the New King James and the Spanish Reina Valera versions.

11

A BEGINNING UNDERSTANDING OF THE NATURE OF GOD'S JUSTICE AND THE U.S. JUSTICE SYSTEM

W. Scott Axford

When the People of God who are the church of Jesus Christ consider the wider world in which we live, and think about humanity and the human societal arrangements that have necessarily been constructed, we need first to begin by reminding ourselves of the particular truth by which we live and the witness with which we are specially charged. This worldview is our starting point as the church when we consider daily issues, whether it be mass incarceration or any other cultural or political questions.

We begin as *theologians*: pastoral, academic, lay—and not (as many do) primarily as social scientists, credentialed or not, political or otherwise. We begin as followers of Jesus Christ, crucified, risen, and ascended, the head of the church through whom we know and confess the Father, Son, and Holy Spirit, into whose name we all are baptized. We begin with the nature and being of the deepest reality there is. We begin with God.

Beginning there as the church, we can indeed offer a word in season (Isa 50:4) to the larger culture and its public square. If we are to have due concern for the issue of mass incarceration, and for the questions increasingly asked about the rightness and functionality of the justice system in the United States of America, then we begin with the very nature of what we represent: the nature of the triune God, and this nature's implications for our understanding of the justice and righteousness of God. As noted below, in Biblical usage, "righteousness" is based in relationship—in humanity's relationship to God. We often hear of striving to "be in right relation" to God: this has a deep resonance with Christian belief and understanding, because the God we relate to is himself a communion (of relationships) of Persons—Father, Son, Holy Spirit. We try to have an acceptable relationship to a God, who is in his nature three divine Persons in mutual relations. This is our source as God's created human beings who are also United States citizens in relationship with one another (and indeed all other human beings in the world)—our guide for a more perfect ordering of our country's life and affairs, and for pursuing the liberty and justice for all to which we have long pledged our allegiance.

The church is best able to contribute to this more perfect ordering when it remembers the Reverend Professor Karl Barth's memorable comment in his 1932 *Church Dogmatics*: "Talk about God has true content when it conforms to the being of the Church, that is, when it conforms to Jesus Christ...'let him prophecy in accordance with faith' (Romans 12:6)."[1] In other words, conforming truly to Jesus Christ, the church helps to build true community in society.

Justice is defined as "the standard by which the benefits and penalties of living in society are distributed."[2] For Christians, this justice is related to love and grace, which are *not* contrasting principles to judgment and justice. A 1980 U.S. Roman Catholic-Reformed dialogue on human rights[3] emphasized this point. In common usage, strict justice is thought to be opposed to love and forgiveness. That is, we think of serving justice—what is right in the face of what is wrong, what is proper remedy or redress for a crime or transgression—as being on one side, and our response of forbearance or compassion for the guilty as being on the other side. The Roman Catholic representatives commented that Christian love is at root the form and basis of other virtues, and that love, therefore, goes far beyond concepts of justice and right—because justice and right first derive *from* Christian love. They have a common source, not opposing ones. "Christian love" means regarding the being and reality of the actual other person with utter ontological seriousness. The person we see before us is also a child of God endowed by its Creator with its own full being, one who is therefore an actual and real human being. As the Reverend Ralph Waldo Emerson wrote a century and a half ago, "Let us treat the men and women well: treat them as if they are real: perhaps they are."[4] Justice can also have the more objective (and less directly relational) sense of reference to explicit written law (divine or civil), whether at the Judgment Seat or civil courtroom. Such justice carries with it a distinct context, and has its own objective content. Justice is rooted in love when it applies these more objective principles to particular persons and situations for the purpose of effecting what is best for those persons and the persons (the community) around them.

The human rights dialogue also noted that, despite common use of the two terms interchangeably, the Reformed Churches tend to refer more to *righteousness* than to *justice*. This derives in part from their longstanding emphasis on biblical passages and how they are translated into English, starting from the Reformation's vernacular translations, which is somewhat different than the Roman Catholic Church and its continuity in Latin. For example, the Hebrew word *sdq* (used five hundred times in the Old Testament) is translated as *dikaio* in Greek (225 New Testament appearances), and then as *justitia* in Latin—and then as *righteousness* in English, via Anglo-Saxon *rightwise*. This nuanced meaning of the word *righteousness*—"the state of being in the right, or being vindicated"[5]—points less to an *objective* set of standards, as just noted above, and more toward an understanding of righteousness based on a *relation* to God. When Israel's King David confesses that it is "against you, you alone, have I sinned" (Ps 51:4), he acknowledges not only that he broke some objective written rules (which he did), but that his sin is against God, in the context of his *relationship* with God (and God's relationship with him).

Put another way, it is said that a person cannot be good without God; that is, we cannot abstract out certain principles apart from our ongoing, living relationship with our Divine Creator. If we think of law as righteousness, then such matters are understood as the pattern by which the life of the community is expressed, a community (many persons in many relations) who, as the people *of God*, are formed and defined by their relationship *to God*. This emphasis renders law as something less explicitly printed or codified, and as something more based in relations—as when the prophet Jeremiah describes God's Law as one written on his people's hearts (Jer 31:33). Thus when we bring a righteousness-translated nuance to justice, we employ a *transitive* understanding.

196

The distinction is in the grammar: a transitive verb has an object ("He baked pies"), while an intransitive verb ("She ran") does not.[6] A transitive use of *justice* means that it has an intrinsic object or *relation*. It is deeply trinitarian: the Trinity's *hypostases* (in Greek, rendered as *persons* in English) are inherently, by *being*, persons in *relation*, and not separate, outside, added on entities, however mutual or solid. They are all of one piece. Justice, in this transitive and relational understanding, does not exist on its own or as an abstract concept or idea. Rather, there is an object and a context for this justice, based on the relational and personal nature of the triune God, and on this God's relation to us human persons whom God created in God's divine image (Gen 1:27). Justice is not a system out there on its own (as may be said of many all-too-human constructions); it exists in the context of these triune relations, and in the human relations that the Father, Son, and Holy Spirit create, restore, and maintain. That is why trinitarian understanding—so basic to Christianity—is so important to our understanding of justice.

And then, we have Saint Paul's understanding of righteousness as linked to *salvation*. (Heb 11:1ff. and elsewhere). This was the subject of an earlier National Council of Churches Faith and Order project, "Justice and Salvation" (2004–12).[7] Some Christian traditions place more emphasis on the necessity of God's vindictive (and vindicating) judgment, defending as well as punitive, faithful to the divine Law, upholding and rewarding those who do his will as revealed in Jesus Christ. Other traditions question prioritizing divine threat of punishment, emphasizing the gospel's hope and purpose for humanity as God's conquering love in Christ (Rev 17:14), one that justifies rather than condemns sinners and that is meant to restore this created-and-fallen-away humanity to the kingdom of God.[8] Justice and righteousness involve divine (and human) judgment and salvation, tying the two together. And just like the Trinity, it is based on relationships.

When the National Council of Churches' Convening Table on Theological Dialogue and Matters of Faith and Order gathered in 2015 through 2016 to discuss mass incarceration and the United States' criminal justice system, it soon realized that more is involved for Christians than a too quick conflation of what we see on earth with what God has revealed and mandated. The Faith and Order table resisted assuming an automatic, implicit congruence between the divine justice we strive to understand and the precepts and practice of today's secular American system. Are the two currently of a common worldview throughout? Said the table as a theological rebeginning, "We think not."

With this understanding of what the church means by God's justice and our righteousness before God—and approaching the issue of the righteousness of the United States' justice system and present-day concerns about mass incarceration from a more theologically informed perspective—Christians (and all Americans) might ask different and deeper questions. In conclusion, or better yet as a start, we might consider these:

- Does God's justice require "paying a debt to society" more than a restorative "time out" for a damaged soul?
- Does God's justice require that defenseless (nontransgressing) citizens be protected? Avenged? Vindicated?
- Does incarceration of bodies relate to cure of souls?
- What role has restoration of God-given relations between persons to play in structuring civil society?
- Is the United States' criminal justice system and its structuring of society informed primarily by our relation to God (and thus to each other), or more by secular, abstract ideas?
- Is God truly no respecter of persons, and thus of racial preferences (et al.) in our common God-given humanity (Acts 10:34; Gen 1:27)?

Notes

1. Karl Barth, *Church Dogmatics*, I.1: *The Doctrine of the Word of God*, 2nd ed., trans. Geoffrey.W. Bromiley, ed. Geoffrey W. Bromiley and Thomas F. Torrance (Edinburgh: T&T Clark, 1975), 12.

2. Steven C. Mott, "Justice," in *Harper's Bible Dictionary*, ed. Paul J. Achtemeier (San Francisco: Harper & Row, 1985), 519.

3. *Ethics and the Search for Christian Unity: A Roman Catholic/Presbyterian-Reformed Consultation* (Washington-Princeton: U.S. Catholic Conference, 1981).

4. Ralph Waldo Emerson, *Essays and Lectures* (New York: Library of America, 1982), 479; see also Ralph Waldo Emerson, "Experience," Essays Second Series (1844), n.d., accessed August 15, 2017, http://archive.fo/qd7cW.

5. John Reumann, "Righteousness," in Achtemeier, ed., *Harper's Bible Dictionary*, 871.

6. This point, as for so many insights on trinitarian theology, comes from Catherine Mowry LaCugna, *God for Us: The Trinity and Christian Life* (San Francisco: Harper San Francisco, 1991), esp. 66.

7. Faith and Order Commission of the National Council of Churches, "A Journey to Open Up Other Journeys: Justice and Salvation," *Ecumenical Trends* 41, nos. 9–11 (October, November, and December 2012).

8. ...and not because we in strict justice deserve it!

12

CRYING OUT IN THE WILDERNESS
Proclamation, Empowerment, and Justice

Felicia Y. Thomas

The proclamation of justice and empowerment amid oppression is an imperative of faith. Mass incarceration is a form of oppression. As people of faith we cannot remain silent while our nation holds the "disturbing distinction of being the world's leading jailer."[1] We must proclaim a message that releases captives and liberates the oppressed. This is truly good news. I want to begin with the intellectual and spiritual context for my reflection on how to respond to injustices like mass incarceration. For me, context is deeply intertwined with biography, so I begin with a bit of personal history. I am an ordained Protestant minister—an American Baptist to be more precise—so proclamation, or the preaching of good news, lies at the heart of my faith and vocation. I am also a historian. Thus, I am always inclined to explore and grapple with interpretations, events, movements, and characters from the past because I am convinced that who and what came before shapes our present and our future. And I am an African American woman—not either/or but both/and. I cannot, do not, and will not choose to deny or ignore my blackness or my femaleness. I am always black and always female. I am always female and always black. As an African American clergywoman and scholar, I stand within a long, rich heritage of black female champions of justice, faith, and empowerment for all people.

An earlier version of this chapter was first delivered on April 15, 2016, as a speech at the Ecumenical Advocacy Days in Washington, DC.

One example is Phillis Wheatley (1753–84), whose love of freedom could not be suppressed despite her slave status. Wheatley, an enslaved woman, embodied the spirit of the American Revolution. She boldly proclaimed liberty with this assertion: "In every human Breast, God has implanted a Principle, which we call Love of Freedom; it is impatient of oppression, and pants for Deliverance."[2] Wheatley believed that the passion for liberty, justice, and equality, an innate human quality, was a gift from God. Maria W. Stewart (1803–79), a free black woman, challenged antebellum conventions as the first woman in America to speak publicly before a "promiscuous" audience of men and women. She declared, "It was contempt for my moral and religious opinions in private that drove me thus before a public."[3] Stewart could not remain demure in the face of multiple oppressions. Stewart mounted lecterns to speak out against racism, sexism, and class oppression. Likewise, Amanda Berry Smith (1837–1915), a powerful African American evangelist, challenged societal limitations based on race, class, and gender. Faith empowered Smith to be courageous in her proclamation against injustice: "The Lord gave me great liberty in speaking. After I had talked a little while the cold chills stopped, my heart began to beat naturally and all fear was gone, and I seemed to lose sight of everybody and everything but my responsibility to God and my duty to the people."[4] Phillis Wheatley, Maria W. Stewart, and Amanda Berry Smith spoke out against oppression and proclaimed messages of empowerment and justice on behalf of the voiceless in their times.

I am also preoccupied with bringing theological insight and biblical understanding to contemporary activism. I do so from a womanist perspective, which emphasizes themes of incarnation, suffering, resistance, transformation, and liberation. I am concerned with womanist theory and practice as resources challenging the ways that oppression is localized in "colored" (nonwhite) bodies, female bodies, poor bodies, disabled bodies, and queer bodies. Furthermore, the struggle for equality, justice, and peace for all humanity is the foundation upon which womanist thought and action is built.

The core of womanist proclamation, then, is best expressed in a set of radical equations: silence equals death and truth telling equals life. Such proclamation undermines the death-dealing power of silence by speaking truth to power. This is good news.

Faithful proclamation of this good news signals our hope for the empowerment of all oppressed and marginalized bodies. At its core this gospel calls us to work toward the radical goal of peace with justice, rather than peace and security for "just us."[5]

A biblical and ethical framework for such proclamation is the Great Commandment:

> One of the scribes came near and heard them disputing with one another, and seeing that he answered them well, he asked him, "Which commandment is the first of all?" Jesus answered, "The first is, 'Hear, O Israel: the Lord our God, the Lord is one; you shall love the Lord your God with all your heart, and with all your soul, and with all your mind, and with all your strength.' The second is this, 'You shall love your neighbor as yourself.' There is no other commandment greater than these." (Mark 12:28–32)

Here Jesus clarifies the dual imperatives of faithful religious practice: piety and activism. As Christians, we must love God completely and love others deeply. We, no less than the scribes of Jesus' time, must struggle with the inherent tension of these sometimes competing priorities. Some gravitate more easily and naturally toward the practice of piety, in which love for God is manifest in abiding commitments to prayer, devotion, study, and worship. Others are more drawn to activism—convening, working, agitating, and protesting. Balancing the requirements of loving God and loving neighbors is tough to achieve and nearly impossible to maintain. Still we are called to make every effort to love God and others in faithful response to our experience of God's enduring love and unfailing grace toward us.

An earlier passage from Mark, quoting the Prophet Isaiah, undergirds our efforts, and our hope:

> See, I am sending my messenger ahead of you,
>   who will prepare your way;
> the voice of one crying out in the wilderness:
>   "Prepare the way of the Lord,
>   make [God's] paths straight."
>
> (1:2b–3)

The first chapter of Mark paints a vivid word portrait. If we read deeply enough, our audible imagination is engaged and it is possible to *hear* John crying in the wilderness. This John is more witness and prophet than baptizer. This John proclaims, "The one who is more powerful than I is coming after me" (Mark 1:7). This John speaks truth. This John reminds us that bearing prophetic Christian witness means telling truth to power, whatever our location. Whether relegated to the margin of public opinion or driven into a wilderness by callousness and incivility, we must cry out. Truth-telling may be an essential job but it is rarely popular. Our role as prophetic witness does not inoculate us against the pain of the truth we must tell: "The truth will make you free but first it will really piss you off."[6] To tell the truth is to risk being ignored, ridiculed, or ostracized: "When we speak we are afraid our words will not be heard or welcomed. But when we are silent, we are still afraid. So it is better to speak."[7] As people of faith, we must resist the temptation to maintain silence because we are afraid. Telling the truth can lead us to more fully embody our faith by becoming the truth we proclaim. Thus, we can cry out that all tolerance for inequity is *sin*.

So we tell our truths. We cry out in the wilderness and in so doing, we prepare the way of the Lord. Every day I am reminded that preparing the way of the Lord involves interpreting the past and analyzing the present as I move forward in hopes of a brighter future. So I teach history, preach sermons, and organize in my community, as I pray, study, and worship, always mindful that piety and activism go hand and hand. Each empowers the other. Each empowers me. Each brings glory to God. Crying out in the wilderness is one dimension of faithful witness. Hearing good news in the cries and groans of the least, the last, and the lost is another. And bringing that good news from the middle of nowhere to the center of power is yet another dimension of our witness.

Let us continue to hold piety (loving God) and activism (loving neighbors) in dynamic tension as we lift our voices in solidarity with those who have been forced to the margins of our increasingly global society by systems of mass incarceration, racism, classism, sexism, heterosexism, ageism, and all the other "isms" that deny certain individuals and groups full human(e) rights. We gather here, now with all sincerity and humility, to prepare the way of the Lord and make God's paths straight! We, like John, are called to be voices crying out in the wilderness. Let us cry loud and spare not!

Notes

1. American Civil Liberties Union, "Mass Incarceration," accessed December 5, 2016, http://aclu.org/issues/mass-incarceration.

2. Phillis Wheatley, "Letter to Rev. Samson Occum," February 11, 1774, reprinted in William H. Robinson, *Phillis Wheatley and Her Writings* (New York: Garland Publishing, 1984), 327.

3. Maria W. Stewart, "Mrs. Stewart's Farewell Address to Her Friends in the City of Boston" (1833), in Maria W. Stewart and Marilyn Richardson, *Maria W. Stewart, America's First Black Woman Political Writer: Essays and Speeches* (Bloomington, IN: Indiana University Press, 1987), 70.

4. Amanda Berry Smith, *An Autobiography: The Story of the Lord's Dealings with Mrs. Amanda Berry Smith, the Colored Evangelist* (New York: Oxford University Press, 1988), 157.

5. See Guy Nave, "Justice…Not 'Just Us'," *Sojourners*, November 14, 2014, http://sojo.net/articles/justice-not-just-us.

6. Joe Klass, *Twelve Steps to Happiness* (New York: Ballantine Books, 1990), 15. These words are often attributed to Gloria Steinem, who also used them in speeches.

7. Audre Lorde, "A Litany for Survival," *The Collected Poems of Audre Lorde* (New York: Norton, 2000), 255.

13

MASS INCARCERATION, CAPITAL PUNISHMENT, AND PENAL ATONEMENT THEORIES
Correlation, or Something More?

Greg Carey

This paper explores an affinity between penal atonement theories and "tough on crime" stances such as support for capital punishment and support of relatively tough sentencing standards. Penal atonement theories correlate with our mass incarceration problem, potentially legitimating more frequent and lengthy incarceration as well as capital punishment. Admittedly, few individuals explicitly infer their criminal justice opinions from their theologies. This affinity eludes conclusive empirical proof, but it (1) makes intuitive theological and cultural sense and (2) reflects correlations in doctrinal standards, official statements by church bodies, and public opinion polls.

THEOLOGICAL AND CULTURAL INTUITION

The Christian question of atonement asks how the event of Jesus—his life, death, and resurrection—brings about the benefits of salvation by rectifying sin and reconciling human beings with God. In answering this question, Christian theology has tended to emphasize Jesus' death above his life and, to a lesser degree, his resurrection. The Apostles' Creed and the Nicene Creed refer to Jesus' earthly career only in terms of his birth and death, a result of doctrinal disputes that have heavily influenced the theological tradition. The New Testament itself contains manifold metaphors

for the saving significance of Jesus' death, including ransom, sacrifice, and atonement, but no New Testament document sets forth
a discursive atonement theory, much less a monolithic one.[1] The
more recent trend among ecumenical theologians has been to discuss models of the atonement, observing both their promise and
their limitations, and attending to the ways in which our atonement models reflect cultural moments and values.[2]

Penal atonement models set themselves apart with the notion
that human sin requires a penalty. All atonement models confess
that Jesus somehow died "for us and for our salvation," as the Nicene
Creed puts it. Substitutionary models propose that Jesus died "in
the place of" sinful humanity, not simply "on our behalf." As a sub-
set of substitutionary models, penal atonement theories teach that
Jesus specifically suffered a penalty that humans deserve, absolving
humans from the need to undergo that penalty. That penalty may
be construed in various ways: Do we emphasize simply that Jesus
died, or is it also important that he submitted to spiritual suffering
and physical pain? A decade has passed since Mel Gibson's film *The
Passion of the Christ*, but that film expresses a piety that meditates
upon the intensity of Jesus' suffering. During his flogging, Gibson's
Jesus voluntarily offers himself to additional torture, as if the *degree*
of his suffering were essential to the salvific process.

Penal atonement models, then, rely upon a *retributive* model
of justice. All Christian theologies celebrate God's love for humanity and desire to redeem it. Penal models distinguish themselves by
insisting that divine justice also requires punishment for sin. Even
God's love cannot obviate the need for a sentence to be carried
out.[3] As Charles Hodge insisted, divine love must be carried out in
accord with justice—and "there can be no remission without such
punishment."[4] In the mysteries of grace, divine justice is somehow
satisfied when Jesus, an innocent victim but a voluntary one with a
divine identity, suffers that punishment in place of and instead of
those who deserve it. Applied to crime, we might capture retributive justice in the phrase "punishment that fits the crime." We also
blur the language of retributive justice with financial metaphors by
using language such as "paying a penalty" together with "paying
one's debt to society." When society convicts a person of a crime,
retributive justice establishes punishments in terms of restrictions

of liberty, service, money, or incarceration that correspond to the perceived severity of the crime.

Clearly, not all Christians build a connection between penal atonement theories and retributive justice. But penal substitutionary models share a deep structure with retributive justice. J. Denny Weaver has argued that satisfaction models of the atonement, which include penal atonement, lack meaningful implications for ethics.[5] That is not quite true. Satisfaction models presuppose retributive ethics, hardly an adequate framework for discipleship but surely bearing ethical implications. As S. Mark Heim puts it,

> The idea that Christ's death provided an infinite satisfaction to offset humanity's infinite offense is taken to empower those who regard themselves as the custodians of that merit with the right to conquer and condemn others.[6]

Might not one reasonably intuit that people committed to an atonement theory that presupposes retributive justice might also be inclined to support penalties, especially mandatory and lengthy incarceration and capital punishment, for criminal offenses? The logic works from the greater to the lesser: If God requires suffering as punishment for human sin, even suffering on the part of an innocent Jesus, would not human crimes also call out for punishment?

ECCLESIAL COMMITMENTS AND PUBLIC OPINION

Among white Protestant churches that speak to the issue, ecumenical bodies tend to reject capital punishment, while Evangelical churches have a history of endorsing it. African American Protestants, keenly aware of inequity in the criminal justice system, not to mention the heritage of lynching, have typically critiqued both capital punishment and harsh sentencing practices; meanwhile, many African American churches and preachers promote a theology in which Jesus' death—often his blood—accomplishes salvation. From a longer historical view, Catholic social teaching has traditionally affirmed retributive justice and capital punishment, but since 1980, the United States Conference of Catholic Bishops has consistently identified capital punishment as contrary to a culture of life. Since 2014, the USCCB has also taken on mass incarceration as a moral problem. In 2000, the U.S. bishops explicitly denied the adequacy of penal retribution as a criminal justice model:

> Just as God never abandons us, so too we must be in covenant with one another. We are all sinners, and our response to sin and failure should not be abandonment and despair, but rather justice, contrition, reparation, and return or re-integration of all into the community.[7]

Citing Thomas Aquinas, the bishops acknowledge that punishment has a purpose, but only when it aims toward restoration.

On October 9, 2015, the National Association of Evangelicals (NAE) revised its public stance on capital punishment. Resolutions from 1972 and 1973 endorsed capital punishment for some crimes, with a qualification that legislation should "include safeguards to eliminate any inequities."[8] The logic of the 1973 resolution relied upon one explicit and one implicit assumption. Explicitly, the resolution maintained that "the attitude of criminals," their willingness to commit certain crimes, is affected by capital punishment's deterrent effect. Implicitly, that resolution held that some crimes *deserve* capital punishment, while others do not. "If no crime is serious enough to warrant capital punishment," the resolution asserted, "then the gravity of the most atrocious crime is diminished accordingly."[9]

The NAE's 2015 resolution, however, acknowledges that Christians may legitimately disagree concerning capital punishment. Some support the death penalty "as the best way to render justice," among other considerations.[10] Others reject capital punishment on the grounds of inequities in the criminal justice system (an implicit acknowledgment of capital punishment's moral legitimacy) or because of "the sacredness of all life." The NAE's 2015 resolution leaves room for diversity of opinion, but by no means does it reject "punishment fits the crime" logic.

Is it coincidental that a Christian group that affirms that some crimes "warrant" capital punishment would also commit itself to a penal model of atonement? The NAE's statement of faith affirms belief in Christ's "vicarious and atoning death through His shed blood."[11] In this clause I perceive two basic metaphors for the atonement, perhaps standing in tension with one another. "Through His shed blood" often indicates priestly or sacrificial models of atonement that have roots in Judaism's Day of Atonement ritual. The sacrificial animal's blood atones for sins by cleansing or purifying the beneficiaries. On the Day of Atonement, the issue is not that the animal suffers and dies on behalf of sinful people; the key feature is the power of blood to cover or "atone" for sins. As Leviticus 17:11 sets forth,

> For the life of the flesh is in the blood; and I have given it
> to you for making atonement for your lives on the altar;
> for, as life, it is the blood that makes atonement.

Revivalist hymnody acknowledges this basic atonement model by asking, "Are you washed in the blood of the Lamb?" and by affirming, "There is power in the blood." Properly speaking, blood imagery relates to cleansing or purifying, not punishment or suffering.[12] The term *vicarious*, however, evokes the notion of substitution, that Jesus somehow died in the place of mortals. Many, many Christians understand *vicarious* to mean that Jesus suffered and died to pay the penalty for human sin by dying, "through his shed blood."

In short, the NAE's Statement of Faith seems to affirm a penal notion of the atonement. Likewise, the Southern Baptist Convention's Baptist Faith and Message confesses Jesus' "substitutionary death on the cross."[13] Substitutionary atonement models do not necessarily entail penal substitution, but they do include penal theories. We note that "substitutionary" in this current confession represents an insertion into the text of the less specific Baptist Faith and Message of 1963—hardly an accident. We might also note that the "new" Baptist Faith and Message appeared in the year 2000, the same year in which that denomination affirmed a resolution, "On Capital Punishment," expressing "support for the fair and equitable use of capital punishment by civil magistrates."[14]

Other Christian bodies explicitly confess a penal atonement model while commending capital punishment. The Lutheran Church—Missouri Synod's 1932 doctrinal statement speaks of

Jesus' "suffering and dying in the place of mankind."[15] In 1980, the LCMS backtracked a bit from its 1967 endorsement of capital punishment's legitimacy, affirming government's right to impose capital punishment without explicitly granting the church's approval.[16] In contrast, the National Council of Churches has rejected capital punishment since 1968, following the lead of most mainline churches. The Evangelical Lutheran Church in America has not taken a public position on the issue.

In fairness, we should not overstate the link between conservative Evangelicals and support for the death penalty. For one thing, prominent Evangelicals like Ron Sider and the Sojourners movement have long resisted the death penalty, not to mention the nonviolent commitment of Anabaptists and others.[17] Moreover, race correlates far more strongly with support for capital punishment than does religious affiliation. White Evangelicals, white mainliners, and white Catholics represent the death penalty's most reliable advocates, while most black Protestants and "nones" (that is, persons claiming no religious affiliation) reject capital punishment. Indeed, the gap among white Evangelicals and mainliners is quite small: 71 percent of white Evangelicals support the death penalty, while 66 percent of mainliners do.[18] I suspect we may trace this small gap among white Protestants to two factors. First, white people are simply more likely to support capital punishment than are nonwhites. Second, though I have no empirical data to support this hunch, I suspect that penal atonement models function as a subconscious default in white American religion. In any event, it remains the case that significant Evangelical bodies explicitly endorse both penal atonement theories and the application of the death penalty, while ecumenical denominations do not. While religious identification lies far behind race as a predictor of attitudes toward capital punishment, the difference of opinion between Evangelical and mainline Protestants is significant.

The link between penal atonement models and "tough on crime" opinions holds among white Christians but not among African Americans and Hispanics. Historically, African American churches may or may not affirm substitutionary or, more specifically, penal atonement models, but relatively few African Americans endorse capital punishment and many resist mass incarceration.[19] The African Methodist Episcopal Church's "Articles of Our Faith," for example, confesses that Jesus "suffered, was crucified, dead and buried, to reconcile his Father to us, and to be a sacrifice, not only for original guilt, but also for actual sins of men."[20] Yet the AME Church recently held a press conference calling for criminal justice reform.[21] The National Baptist Convention's "Articles of Faith" provides latitude for many atonement models, maintaining that Jesus' death "made a full atonement for our sins" and affirming justification as bestowed "only through faith in the Redeemer's blood."[22] The NBC also has a Criminal Justice Commission charged not with legislative advocacy but with addressing the causes of crime and ministering to individuals and families.[23] Due to disproportionate rates of incarceration and capital punishment, race apparently plays a far greater role than doctrine in shaping attitudes toward criminal justice issues.

Among whites, Christian groups that favor penal atonement theories, often to the exclusion of other models, also are more likely to favor "tough on crime" approaches to criminal justice issues. To be clear, American attitudes on criminal justice are notoriously "mushy," blending retributive and reformist tendencies without a high degree of self-reflection.[24] Empirical data on attitudes toward incarceration and sentencing prove more elusive than those concerning capital punishment, but multiple studies have established a link between conservative Christianity and relatively punitive criminal justice attitudes.[25] It seems that white Evangelicals have had a historical affinity for what are called tougher law and order positions. This should not be surprising, given the affinity of white Evangelicals for conservative politics in general. Again, however, attitudes toward criminal justice often reflect perceptions of race.[26] For example, a Public Religion Research Institute poll shows that white Evangelicals are significantly more likely than other groups to believe that "Police officers generally treat blacks and other minorities the same as whites." The opinion gap between white Evangelicals and mainliners on this question is 15 percent—at 62 percent to 47 percent.[27] The same Institute's 2014 American Values Survey revealed that, although a large minority of Americans (45 percent) believe that discrimination against whites has become just as great a problem as discrimination against blacks and other minorities, 63 percent of white Evangelicals (and 49 percent of white mainliners) think so.[28]

Data do suggest a link between conservative religious values and punitive attitudes toward criminal justice, though race plays a far more important role. This conclusion falls a bit short of establishing a link between adherence to penal atonement models and support for punitive criminal justice policies, including ones that contribute to mass incarceration and capital punishment. However, other considerations strengthen the argument for such a link. Christian groups that explicitly affirm penal atonement theologies tend to endorse capital punishment, while other churches do not. White Evangelicals belong to churches that tend to endorse penal atonement models, and white Evangelicals also tend to hold more punitive approaches to capital punishment than do other religious groups. We cannot establish a causal link between penal atonement theories and attitudes toward punishment, but it is quite reasonable to note their correlation. We should also acknowledge factors that complicate this association such as the broader affinity of white Evangelicals for conservative politics and the historical interstices among race, politics, and religion in the United States. It makes intuitive theological sense to posit that penal atonement theologies reinforce punitive attitudes toward incarceration, which contribute to the problem of mass incarceration. Some data lend themselves to this hypothesis. But the picture remains somewhat cloudy.

INTERVENTION

Penal models of the atonement are compatible with incarceration- and sentencing-based responses to criminal justice. Although incarceration may be understood to serve multiple functions, including deterrence, rehabilitation, and restoration, the correlation between the perceived seriousness of an offense and the length of a prison sentence suggests that retribution fundamentally underlies incarceration. In a recent unpublished paper, Erin Runions observes that even faith-based prison rehabilitation programs frequently rely on a penal atonement model, according to which Christ's "payment" for the debt of sin allows inmates to "pay their debt to society."[29] Penal atonement theories and retributive justice alike render suffering as a good thing in that suffering fulfills the requirements of justice.

For a very long time, black and womanist theologians, among others, have challenged the notion of "good" suffering. No one would deny that suffering can lead to positive outcomes, but theologians like Dolores Williams, James Cone, Shawn Copeland, and others outright reject suffering as a good in itself. As the title of Cone's recent *The Cross and the Lynching Tree* suggests, the cross unites Jesus with the suffering of innocent victims. What is redemptive, Cone argues, is not Jesus' suffering on the cross but "the faith that God snatches victory out of defeat, life out of death, and hope out of despair, as revealed in the biblical and black proclamation of Jesus' resurrection."[30]

The gospel we proclaim bears with it doctrinal and metaphorical connotations. Penal atonement theories surely hold a long-standing and widely held place in the history of Christian theology. At the same time, faithful theological discourse requires introspection regarding its relationship to cultural moments. If we accept that mass incarceration in the United States represents a societal failure, one that intersects with issues like race, class, and gender in important ways, theological models that legitimate and may contribute to that problem cry out for closer scrutiny in contexts ecumenical and denominational, academic and pastoral. Preachers and educators, who perhaps rarely wander into the weeds of doctrine, may prove especially relevant in this cultural moment.

Notes

1. See Arland Hultgren, *Christ and His Benefits* (Philadelphia: Fortress, 1987); Mark D. Baker and Joel B. Green, *Recovering the Scandal of the Cross: Atonement in New Testament and Contemporary Contexts* (Downers Grove, IL: InterVarsity, 2011).

2. Peter Schmiechen, *Saving Power: Theories of Atonement and Forms of the Church* (Grand Rapids, MI: Eerdmans, 2005); Scot McKnight, *A Community Called Atonement*, Living Theology (Nashville, TN: Abingdon, 2007).

3. Sharon L. Baker, *Executing God: Rethinking Everything You've Been Taught about Salvation and the Cross* (Louisville, KY: Westminster John Knox, 2013), esp. 66–70, 83–99; J. Denny Weaver, *The Nonviolent*

Atonement (Grand Rapids, MI: Eerdmans, 2001), 71–72; Schmiechen, *Saving Power*, 116.

4. Charles Hodge, *Systematic Theology* (New York: Scribner, Armstrong, and Co., 1871), 2:478; cited in Schmiechen, *Saving Power*, 107.

5. Weaver, *Nonviolent Atonement*, 79.

6. Heim, *Saved from Sacrifice: A Theology of the Cross* (Grand Rapids, MI: Eerdmans, 2006), 252.

7. United States Conference of Catholic Bishops, *Responsibility, Rehabilitation, and Restoration: A Catholic Perspective on Crime and Criminal Justice*, November 15, 2000, http://www.usccb.org/issues-and-action/human-life-and-dignity/criminal-justice-restorative-justice/crime-and-criminal-justice.cfm.

8. Every denominational statement I have encountered on capital punishment cautions against inequities in the administration of criminal justice.

9. National Association of Evangelicals, 1973 Resolution, "Capital Punishment," accessed December 15, 2016, http://nae.net/capital-punishment-1973/.

10. National Association of Evangelicals, 2015 Resolution, "Capital Punishment," accessed December 15, 2016, http://nae.net/capital-punishment-2/.

11. National Association of Evangelicals, "Statement of Faith" accessed December 15, 2016, http://nae.net/statement-of-faith/.

12. Schmiechen, *Saving Power*, 22–23. See Christian A. Eberhart, "Conclusion," in *Ritual and Metaphor: Sacrifice in the Bible*, ed. Christian A. Eberhart, Society of Biblical Literature Resources for Biblical Study 68 (Atlanta: Society of Biblical Literature, 2011), 153–56; and Jeffrey S. Siker, "Yom Kippuring Passover: Recombinant Sacrifice in Early Christianity," in Eberhart, ed., *Ritual and Metaphor*, 65–82.

13. Southern Baptist Convention, "The Baptist Faith and Message: The 2000 Baptist Faith and Message," accessed December 15, 2016, http://www.sbc.net/bfm2000/bfm2000.asp.

14. Southern Baptist Convention, "On Capital Punishment: Orlando, Florida, 2000," accessed December 15, 2016, http://www.sbc.net/resolutions/299.

15. The Lutheran Church—Missouri Synod, "A Brief Statement of the Doctrinal Position of the Missouri Synod," accessed December 15, 2016, http://www.lcms.org/doctrine/doctrinalposition#redemption.

16. The Lutheran Church—Missouri Synod, "Report on Capital Punishment," accessed December 15, 2016, https://www.lcms.org/Document.fdoc?src=lcm&id=1054.

17. Ron Sider, *Completely Pro-Life: Building a Consistent Stance* (Downers Grove, IL: InterVarsity, 1987).

18. Pew Research Center, "Less Support for the Death Penalty, Especially among Democrats," April 16, 2015, http://www.people-press.org/2015/04/16/less-support-for-death-penalty-especially-among-democrats.

19. According to the Pew Center's March 2015 poll, only 37 percent of black Protestants support the death penalty. I notice, however, that blacks in general voice slightly lower support (34 percent) than do black Protestants. Pollsters do not yet sort out Hispanic Christians, but Hispanic support for the death penalty stands at 45 percent, with whites at 63 percent.

20. African Methodist Episcopal Church, "Articles of Our Faith," accessed December 15, 2016, http://ame-church.com/our-church/our-beliefs/.

21. "The National African Methodist Episcopal Church to Hold 'Liberty for All' Press Conference Tomorrow, Wednesday, September 2, 2015, at 10 AM EST," accessed December 15, 2016, http://www.prnewswire.com/news-releases/the-national-african-methodist-episcopal-church-to-hold-liberty-and-justice-for-all-press-conference-tomorrow-wednesday-september-2-2015-at-10-am-et-300136196.html.

22. The National Baptist Convention, USA, "What We Believe," accessed December 15, 2016, http://www.nationalbaptist.com/about-us/what-we-believe.html.

23. The National Baptist Convention, USA, "National Baptist Criminal Justice Commission Guidance Statements," accessed December 15, 2016, http://www.nationalbaptist.com/departments/criminal-justice-commission/guidance-statements.html.

24. Francis T. Cullen, Bonnie S. Fisher, and Brandon K. Applegate, "Public Opinion about Punishment and Corrections," *Crime and Justice* 27 (2000): 1–79.

25. Harold J. Grasmick and Anne L. McGill, "Religion, Attribution Style, and Punitiveness toward Juvenile Offenders," *Criminology* 32 (1994): 23–46; Brandon K. Applegate, Francis T. Cullen, Bonnie S. Fisher, and Thomas Vander Ven, "Forgiveness and Fundamentalism: Reconsidering the Relationship between Correctional Attitudes and Religion," *Criminology* 38 (2000): 719–54; Christopher D. Bader, Scott A. Desmond, F. Carson Mencken, and Byron R. Johnson, "Divine Justice: The Relationship between Images of God and Attitudes toward Criminal Punishment," *Criminal Justice Review* 35 (2010): 90–106. See Grasmick, "Crime and Criminal Justice," in *The Encyclopedia of Politics and Religion*, ed. Robert Wuthnow (New York: Routledge, 2013), 1:199–202.

26. I hesitate to speculate on the role racism may play in this phenomenon. The disproportionate share of white Evangelicals in the Jim Crow South may be a factor. Southern Baptists and the Presbyterian Church in America have both acknowledged their historical links to racialized oppression and have worked toward reconciliation.

27. Public Religion Research Institute, "Survey: Deep Divide between White and Black Americans on Criminal Justice System's Racial Equality," May 7, 2015, http://publicreligion.org/research/2015/05/divide-white-black-americans-criminal-justice-system/.

28. Robert P. Jones, Daniel Cox, and Juhem Navarro-Rivera, *Economic Insecurity, Rising Inequality, and Doubts about the Future: Findings from the 2014 American Values Survey* (Washington: Public Religion Research Institute, 2014), 40 (available online at http://publicreligion.org/site/wp-content/uploads/2014/11/PRRI-AVS-with-Transparancy-Edits.pdf).

29. Erin Runions, "In Whose Interest: Biblical Christianity and the Prison Industrial Complex," unpublished paper, cited with author's permission. Runions engages Winnifred Fallers Sullivan, who records prisoner testimonies regarding the sense of being compelled to convert to Christianity (*Prison Religion: Faith-Based Reform and the Constitution* [Princeton: Princeton University Press, 2011], 201–2). Hollis Phelps argues for a correlation between the debt imagery in Anselm's exposition of the atonement and the function of debt in neoliberal economics ("Overcoming Redemption: Neoliberalism, Atonement, and the Logic of Debt," *Political Theology* 17 [2016]: 264–82).

30. James Cone, *The Cross and the Lynching Tree* (Maryknoll, NY: Orbis, 2011), 150. Cone cites among other works Dolores S. Williams, "Black Women's Surrogacy Experience and the Christian Notion of Redemption," in *After Patriarchy: Feminist Transformations of the World Religions*, ed. Paula M. Cooey, William R. Eakin, and Jay B. McDaniel, Faith Meets Faith (Maryknoll, NY: Orbis, 1991), 1–14; Jacquelyn Grant, *White Women's Christ and Black Women's Jesus: Feminist Christology and Womanist Response* (Atlanta: Scholars Press, 1989); and Shawn Copeland, "'Wading through Many Sorrows': Toward a Theology of Suffering in Womanist Perspective," in *A Troubling in My Soul: Womanist Perspectives on Evil and Suffering*, ed. Emilie Townes, Bishop Henry McNeal Turner Series in Black Religion (Maryknoll, NY: Orbis, 1993), 109–29. See Kelly Brown Douglas, *Stand Your Ground: Black Bodies and the Justice of God* (Maryknoll, NY: Orbis, 2015), 171–203.

14

THE PROPHETIC CRY FOR JUSTICE
A Pentecostal Response to the Racism of Mass Incarceration

Peter Althouse

Two Pentecostal leaders urged their congregations to observe Black Lives Matter on December 14, 2015, in response to the grand jury decisions not to indict police officers in the unwarranted killing of unarmed black men in Ferguson and Staten Island. Bishop Charles E. Black Sr. of the Church of God in Christ and George O. Wood, General Superintendent of the Assemblies of God, admonished their churches to stand in solidarity with their brothers and sisters to affirm the value of black lives. The release declares, "If Spirit-filled Christians cannot find a way to work together to heal their divisions, what hope is there for the rest of the country?" Wood called for prayer for all law enforcement and judicial officers "that they would be servants of justice, reconciliation, and peace in the communities they serve."[1]

Many people are uneasy about the failure of the criminal justice system to protect black Americans and the legitimization of excessive use of police force in subjugating African American communities. However, the events in Ferguson and Staten Island as well as a litany of unarmed black men and women dying at the hands of the police, are only the tip of the iceberg. Over the past forty years the prison population has exploded from 300,000 to more than 2.3 million, with most of the increase targeting drug crimes committed by blacks and Hispanics, despite the evidence that whites use drugs at about the same rate. In some states, black

This essay was originally published in *Ecumenical Trends* 45, no.7 (July/August 2016). It is copyrighted by *Ecumenical Trends* and is reprinted with permission.

men are incarcerated for drug crimes at a rate twenty to fifty times greater than white men.[2] Moreover, the United States has the highest rate of incarceration in the world, excessively more than other developed countries and surpassing repressive regimes.[3] U.S. policies and practices regarding mass incarceration legitimize racial discrimination through interlinking social systems that subjugate "people of color" in legal systems that label, imprison, segregate, and subsequently deny access to meaningful employment, housing, and public benefits.

What is the church's response? How might denominational leaders respond to mass incarceration when congregants are mostly unaware, or even supportive of "tough on crime" ideology? I propose that the church's response can and should draw on the prophetic tradition that calls for justice and human dignity as found in Scripture. More specifically, the high value of the prophetic found in the charismatic ethos of Pentecostal churches can provide a basis for unified response calling the United States to equal and transparent justice. However, I do not view the prophetic here as an abstract principle of social justice. Rather, the prophetic is the upwelling of the Spirit of God in believers that empowers the people of God to discern injustices in the world that contradict the justice of the reign of God. This view is consistent, I would suggest, with how Pentecostals discern the world through the lens of the Spirit's call. Stated differently, the voice of the prophetic is the voice of the Spirit of God calling the world to righteousness.

To lay out my arguments I will first briefly outline the realities and extent of mass incarceration in the United States, how the systems are linked together in what is identified as the "prison industrial complex,"[4] and the way that imprisonment and the criminal label marginalize, dominate, and segregate minorities, especially poor African Americans and Hispanics. The effects not only have implications for the felon who must suffer the degradation of lengthy terms in overcrowded and substandard prisons, but affects the spouses, children, extended families, and communities through government policies that deny gainful employment and social services. The police force and prosecutors are implicit links in the racist outcomes of the mass incarceration system in that they selectively target, arrest, and charge minorities in poor black and Hispanic communities especially. I will then offer a theological response to the crisis of mass incarceration through the lens of Pentecostal theology. Specifically, the prophetic cry against the injustices perpetuated by the powerful is needed to restore dignity to those who have been stripped of their humanity in the systems of mass incarceration.

MASS INCARCERATION

Marc Mauer, the director of The Sentencing Project, uses the term *mass incarceration* to describe the crisis of the contemporary American prison system.[5] Mass incarceration is a penal system that links together multiple systems that not only imprison people behind bars, but in a more devastating way, label people as criminals even if they are not physically imprisoned. Once labeled criminals, they are relegated to an underclass deprived of the social resources and social rights that have become the backbone of the social safety net. Being deprived of these services relegates felons as well as their families to an impoverished existence with only faint hope of ever making a better life. Mass incarceration not only affects the person that has been labeled a felon, but has collateral damage on their spouses, children, and even communities.[6] It affects the felon's personal finances as states are aggressively trying to recoup the high cost of mass incarceration through a myriad of fines. This makes it difficult for the incarcerated and family to ever gain financial stability, but it also restricts the felon in employment opportunities and workplace licenses, and bars them from low-income housing and welfare subsidies, such as food stamps. Such restrictions create insurmountable barriers to community reintegration and contribute to recidivism. At its most extreme, mass incarceration imprisons people in overcrowded, supermax prisons with the goal of incapacitation in tactics and methods that the California Supreme Court considers to be cruelty through deliberate indifference in blatant disregard for mental health treatment and substandard health care.[7]

Moreover, a disproportionate number of poor African Americans, Hispanics, and ethnic immigrants are overrepresented, or suffer the consequences of labeling, even though whites are just as likely to engage in criminal activity at the same rate as blacks or Hispanics. The rhetoric of the "war on drugs" or "get tough on crime" is thinly veiled, racist code for the "war on blacks" and "get tough on blacks."[8] Although the interlinked systems of incarceration that include policing, judicial process, incarceration, and post-incarceration such as parole or community service are treated as colorblind, they reveal a disturbing trend of institutionalizing racial practices that are structural in nature.

To make matters worse, mass incarceration has become big business that has victimized the incarcerated, their families, and communities. On the one hand, mass incarceration is costly to taxpayers, not only in terms of the high monetary costs of the expansion of the penal system in the longer terms and greater number of prisoners, but in that tax revenue has been diverted from other institutions and programs such as medical intervention, education, and community programs that have more success in diverting individuals from entering the penal system and helping to prevent recidivism. To offset these costs, various states have sought ways to privatize prisons under the unproven assumption that private corporations are better able to provide these services at lower costs than the government. These no-frill prisons have adopted policies of incapacitation that degrade the humanity of prisoners. Private prisons have also contributed to the increase of mass incarceration because the states guarantee full capacity. Some of these costs are offset by charging prisoners and their families for their incarceration and use of facilities such as telephone communication.[9]

On the other hand, prisoners are seen as cheap labor for industrial and commercial production. As industrial and manufacturing jobs have largely been transported overseas in the search for cheaper labor, prisons have become a resource for cheap labor. Prisoners earn as low as thirty cents an hour and produce substantial profits for American corporations. Prisoners are denied many of the most basic human and civil rights: workplace regulations such as minimum wage, safe work environments, and unionization. The use of prisoners for cheap labor further devastates the black communities most in need of these jobs. Educated and skilled middle-class African Americans have moved into the suburbs, leaving unskilled and semiskilled blacks without the means to provide for their families, thereby exacerbating the flow of individuals into the penal system. In other words, the incarcerated suffer financial hardship while businesses rake in huge profits, and the black communities that used to fill these working positions come under financial hardship because manufacturing jobs have either gone off shore or been forced onto prisoners at excessively substandard labor value.[10]

For mass incarceration to function effectively it must draw together numerous judicial and social systems. They range from mass media as the space for cultural rhetoric to gain popular credibility;[11] political institutions, enforcement, and prosecutor decision-making as to who will or will not be charged and imprisoned; the extent of the charges; federal, state, and local governments that enact policies to maintain incarceration; and the effects long past physical imprisonment; the judiciary that justifies its continuation; and prison systems. Mass incarceration is increasingly seen as a means for incapacitation as punitive, retributive, and deterrence, rather than restorative, rehabilitative, and reconciling. These systemic links work together to maintain the racist practices of mass incarceration, and conversely may begin to unravel if they were decoupled.

More could be said, and has been said, about race and mass incarceration. My purpose is to offer a brief outline to show how it has become an issue of social justice in need of a theological response from all churches. In the following section, I will suggest a response developed from within the Pentecostal theological tradition that I hope will offer venues for all Pentecostals in partnership with other churches to end this injustice.

THEOLOGICAL RESPONSES FROM A PENTECOSTAL PERSPECTIVE

The question I would like to take up is: What might a Pentecostal response to mass incarceration look like? In *Spirit of the Last Days*,[12] I proposed that a Pentecostal prophetic critique rooted in the already–not yet of the coming kingdom of God was a way for Pentecostals to engage issues of social justice, human rights and dignity, political theology, and environmental concerns. Other Pentecostal theologian-ethicists have taken up the concerns of social justice and developed the theological concept of prophecy as a means to offer a Pentecostal response. They have retrieved the ancient prophetic tradition that challenges the social evils of society and applied the biblical notions of dignity and liberative hope to combat social sin. Four of these theologians will be taken up here with the effort to apply their theologies to the problem of mass incarceration. They include Eldin Villafañe, Murray Dempster, Cheryl Sanders, and Leonard Lovett.

Eldin Villafañe is a Hispanic/Latino Assemblies of God minister and professor of social ethics at Gordon-Conwell Theological Seminary, who argues that in order for the Pentecostal Church to be true to the Gospel's prophetic voice so that it can continue to minister with and to the poor and oppressed, it must construct a social ethic that affirms Latina/o cultural heritage from its status as a sectarian church.[13] Villafañe highlights the social role of the Hispanic church as a "prophetic indictment" that challenges racism, political oppression, economic exploitation, and social-cultural marginalization.[14] The Hispanic storefront churches (*barrios*), with their dynamic *cultos* found in urban city centers, are disenfranchised, oppressed, and marginalized in relationship to the political and economic powers of the city's wealthy. The prophetic witness of the Hispanic church must unmask and challenge the institutional and dehumanizing "powers and principalities" as a church called to bring hope, forgiveness, and community (*koinonia*) to the world.[15] The prophetic counterculture denounces personal and social factors that are destructive to human life through its call to repentance, righteousness, and justice.[16] The prophetic voices that challenge sinful social structures and long for social justice have been missing in the emphasis on the Spirit's charismatic empowerment. The Hispanic Pentecostal Church offers a distinctive spirituality that sees charismatic empowerment found in the baptism in the Spirit as valid "signs and wonders" of, and prophetic witness to, the reign of God.[17] The implication of the prophetic witness of the Hispanic Pentecostal community is that the *koinonia*, *leitourgia*, *kerygma*, and *diakonia* of the church must demonstrate to the world the faithful, loving, and just structures of social relationships that reflect the gospel, while denouncing the influence of individualism, materialism, classism, racism, and sexism as the dominant idols of American culture.[18]

Murray Dempster is a white Assemblies of God minister and

distinguished professor of social ethics, emeritus, at Southeastern University. In different publications, Dempster has teased out the implications of Pentecostal ministry for social justice. In practice, Pentecostal churches implement social programs that care for the poor and oppressed, but the desire to change unjust social conditions is becoming the hallmark of Pentecostal ministry.[19] However, Dempster purposefully links social justice to the prophetic tradition in Scripture to develop a social ethic. The Old Testament prophets nurture both the individual and corporate ramifications of social concern by insisting that it exists, and is kept alive, in the Law and covenant, but most especially in the pursuit of social justice as a visible expression of God's ethical character. The quality of social concern in the believing community reflects the community's view of God.[20] Grounding social justice in Yahweh gave the prophets' message against injustices within and without the covenant community moral conviction. They gained insight into the political, economic, and social institutions that perpetuated social injustices, and thereby induced God's people to look to God's moral character with fresh insight.[21] Dempster then turns to Amos as an exemplar of the latter prophets who employed "prophetic criticism" as an indictment of individuals and groups who insisted on exploiting the poor, for example, profiteering on the urban poor, driving farmers into debt in order to foreclose and take their land, as well as social systems that maintained injustice. Amos called for reform of the sinful social conditions that perpetuated social injustices by reflecting on God's moral character as the basis for pursuing social justice.[22]

The prophetic tradition is the basis on which a Pentecostal social consciousness can be developed. Jesus the prophet proclaimed the Year of Jubilee when the prisoner is set free and the debt-ridden farmer is forgiven his debts so that he may keep his covenantal inheritance.[23] Jesus' ministry is the continuation of the prophetic tradition, and the outpouring of the Spirit at Pentecost is the continuation of Jesus' prophetic ministry in the charismatic community through the inauguration of the eschatological kingdom of God. In the charismatic community, injustices related to race, ethnicity, wealth, and sex are overcome by the Spirit as typified in the equalizing phenomenon of glossolalia, and this portrait becomes the basis for a Pentecostal position on social justice.[24]

Cheryl Sanders is a Church of God (Anderson, Indiana) minister and professor of Christian ethics at Howard University who has an interest in the intersection of black theology, personal and social ethics, and the standards of worship in the "sanctified" church, that is, the Holiness, Pentecostal, and Apostolic churches. The common thread in the sanctified churches is that they all emphasize the experience of Spirit baptism though with disagreement over whether or not the experience is validated by glossolalia.[25] The underlying framework in *Saints in Exile* is the double rejection experienced by the sanctified black church in which the world with its sinful, oppressive, and discriminatory practices rejects the saints, and the saints reject the world by purging themselves of the world's secularizing influence through their own cultural authenticity and biblical understanding. To put it in theological language, they are "in this world but not of it" (John 17:16). The emphasis on cultural resistance in liturgies and structures rejects patterns of oppression and racism.[26]

Sanders uses "prophetic" as an adjective to nouns such as *ministry, mandate, task, initiative*, etcetera, throughout her writing to highlight the work of resistance to oppression, social justice, and empowerment ethics of the African American churches that continue to experience racism.[27] In "Pentecostal Ethics and the Prosperity Gospel," Sanders adopts the language of prophetic action to highlight the need for African American preachers to struggle against white racism. Her concern is that African American preachers who promote the prosperity gospel must also embrace the social ethics role of the biblical prophets who spoke against oppression and poverty. Faith-based government funding that has strings attached and conservative political discourses on family values have been developed to lure white Evangelicals, and prosperity preachers too are being lured. Sanders asks, however, "Are there any signs of a resurgence of prophetic activism among those who are willing to call forth the fires of Pentecost as the souls of black folk rages on?"[28] There are Pentecostal preachers who refuse to serve materialism and wealth accumulation, instead choosing to be prophetic and an activist in regard to social concerns.[29] Sanders concludes the chapter with an important call to the black Pentecostal Church: "The most important task of black preaching and activism is to build prophetic community, that is, to exercise one's individual gifts of ministry and leadership toward the end of empowering congregations to hear the voice of God in conversation with the deepest concerns of the people and communities one is called to serve."[30] The hope, for Sanders, is the possibility of social reconciliation between the poor and affluent, but she cautions that in order for reconciliation to be genuine, African American Pentecostal leaders must acknowledge the negative impact of race, sex, and class on their congregations that will require prophetic engagement that challenges the idols of consumerism, conservativism, and shallow discourses regarding multiculturalism.[31]

Leonard Lovett is a Church of God in Christ minister who at the time of writing has served as the denomination's ecumenical officer since 2004. Lovett has worked to bring to light the problems of racism for black Pentecostals and announced a prophetic call to white Pentecostals to engage in serious work to overcome racism. In *Kingdom beyond Color*, Lovett defines his role as a Pentecostal minister and scholar as both priestly and prophetic. He is priestly in that he works to bind up and heal the wounds of the injured, but he is prophetic in that he is called to "challenge the status quo" and "speak truth to power." His work is "prophetic protest writing" that challenges the evils of racism and injustice.[32] His method of discourse is a mode of autobiography that he views as fruitful for theology and "prophetic ethics."[33] In "Ethics in a Prophetic Mode," Lovett follows James McClendon and uses polemic and testimony to attest to the power of grace, healing, and transformation as an illustration of the ancient prophets' challenge to the status quo of institutional and systemic racism in the world and even in Pentecostalism itself.[34]

One chapter in *Kingdom of Color* is devoted specifically to the problem of racism in the criminal justice system, especially the role of some police and the way they target young people of color, charge them with questionable crime violations, and process them into a system that defines the rest of their lives as criminal.[35] He is concerned that some police employ a practice of a "long ride to the station" over any perceived resistance to their authority as a way to intimidate potential violators in the future.[36] (This is precisely what happened in Baltimore in the case of Freddie Gray Jr., a twenty-five-year-old black man who was arrested for the alleged possession of a switch blade, placed in police transport without being secured, and driven by police in such a way as to cause spinal injury and death.) Lovett is critical of how the criminal justice system favors white privilege and treats African Americans harshly. Lovett argues that the way to deal with police brutality and the racism of the criminal justice system is through prophetic protest—to speak in the name of the Lord without fear.[37] However, he is careful not to condemn the police as a whole and has worked with a number of police forces to various ends, but he denounces racist police, the methods they use to oppress, and the brutality of their intimidation.[38]

Lovett is critical as well of the Euro-American church that failed to take advantage of the opportunity to "collectively and prophetically" indict racism during the civil rights era. Lovett cites Martin Luther King as God's gift in a troubled time, who spoke as "vocal social prophet." On the eve of his assassination, King delivered his final speech at Charles H. Mason's Church of God in Christ temple, one of the oldest Pentecostal churches in the United States. King's nonviolent resistance against racism and segregation ultimately cost him his life. Lovett sees a parallel to Seymour's revival at Azusa Street in 1906, where eyewitness biographer Frank Bartleman said, "The color line was washed away." However, Lovett bemoans the racial and ethnic fractions that later divided the fledgling movement. And yet where the power of the Spirit is supreme, argues Lovett, race can no longer act as a barrier to fellowship where love reigns.[39] Lovett contends that liberation is the consequence of genuine renewal and presence of the Spirit. He declares, "I dream of a movement of Pentecostal-charismatic Christians so sensitive to the guidance of the Spirit and God's initiative and liberating activity that they will know when to tear down oppressive structures, and when to build new structures or they will receive wisdom to work within existing institutional structures as change agents."[40]

FINAL REFLECTIONS

I have argued that the prophetic cry against injustice is the basis for a Pentecostal response to mass incarceration as a method for racial oppression. All people have inherent dignity under God, but the systematic incarceration of blacks and Latinos in the criminal justice system perpetuates an evil that must come under God's judgment and must be actively resisted by the whole church. Pentecostals must participate in this resistance. As the ancient prophets of old, I believe that Pentecostals have within their theological ethos a means whereby they can and should condemn the oppression of racism in the incarceration system. The prophetic voice that springs from the upwelling of the Spirit calling into existence the coming kingdom is the voice of hope against the injustice of mass incarceration. The missive published by Bishop Charles E. Black Sr. and General Superintendent George Wood to proclaim that Black Lives Matter and stand together with the oppressed is a good first step. Unfortunately, Wood was criticized by some of his ministers for taking this stand.[41] Obviously, more work needs to be done. The racist actions of some police are cogs in a whole complex system of mass incarceration that needs to be challenged and transformed into a more just reality.

Notes

1. George O. Wood, "Call for AG Churches to Observe 'Black Lives Matter Sunday' in Coordination with Church of God in Christ," December 11, 2014, http://rss.ag.org/articles/detail.cfm?RSS_RSSContentID=28902&RSS_OriginatingRSSFeedID=3359.

2. See http://www.pewtrusts.org/en/research-and-analysis/reports/2012/06/06/time-served-the-high-cost-low-return-of-longer-prison-terms, accessed January 28, 2015.

3. Michelle Alexander, *The New Jim Crow: Mass Incarceration in the Age of Colorblindness* (New York: The New Press, 2010), 7.

4. The term "prison industrial complex" was first coined by Mike Davis, "Hell Factory in the Field: A Prison Industrial Complex," *The Nation* (February 20, 1995): 229; and Angela Davis, *The Prison Industrial Complex*, audio CD (Oakland, CA: AK Press, 2001).

5. Marc Mauer, *Race to Incarcerate* (New York: The New Press, 1999).

6. See Sara Wakefield and Christopher Wildeman, *Children of the Prison Boom: Mass Incarceration and the Future of American Inequality* (Oxford: Oxford University Press, 2014).

7. Jonathan Simon, *Mass Incarceration on Trial: A Remarkable Court Decision and the Future about Prisons in America* (New York: The New Press, 2014).

8. Alexander, *New Jim Crow*, 53, 59.

9. Kristen D. Levingston, "Making the 'Bad Guy' Pay: Growing Use of Cost Shifting as an Economic Sanction," in *Prison Profiteers: Who Makes Money from Mass Incarceration*, ed. Tara Herivel and Paul Wright (New York: The New Press, 2007), 52–79.

10. Mauer, *Race to Incarcerate*, 12–13; see the collection of essays in Tara Herive and Paul Wright, eds., *Prison Profiteers: Who Makes Money from Mass Incarceration* (New York: The New Press, 2007).

11. See for instance, "Television, Public Space and Prison Population: A Commentary on Mauer and Simon," in *Mass Imprisonment: Social Causes and Consequences*, ed. David Garland (Thousand Oaks, CA: Sage, 2001), 28–34; Paul Y. Sussman, "Media on Prisons: Censorship and Stereotypes," in *Invisible Punishment: The Collateral Consequences of Mass Incarceration*, ed. Marc Mauer and Meda Chesney-Lind (New York: The New Press, 2002), 258–78.

12. Peter Althouse, *Spirit of the Last Days: Pentecostal Eschatology in Conversation with Jürgen Moltmann* (London: T & T Clark International, 2003).

13. Eldin Villafañe, *The Liberating Spirit: Toward an Hispanic American Pentecostal Social Ethic* (Grand Rapids, MI: Eerdmans, 1993), xi.

14. Ibid., 103.

15. Ibid., 126–27.

16. Ibid., 156.

17. Ibid., 204.

18. Ibid., 216–17.

19. Murray W. Dempster, "Evangelism, Social Concern, and the Kingdom of God," in *Called and Empowered: Global Mission in Pentecostal Perspective*, ed. Murray W. Dempster, Byron D. Klaus, and Douglas Petersen (Peabody, MA: Hendrickson, 1991), 22.

20. Murray Dempster, "Pentecostal Social Concern and the Biblical Mandate of Social Justice," *Pneuma: The Journal of the Society for Pentecostal Studies* 9, no. 2 (Fall 1987): 129, 131.

21. Ibid., 138.

22. Ibid., 142.

23. Ibid.

24. Ibid., 148–49.

25. Cheryl J. Sanders, *Saints in Exile: The Holiness–Pentecostal Experience in African American Religion and Culture* (Oxford: Oxford University Press, 1996), 5.

26. Ibid., 63–64.

27. See, for instance, Cheryl J. Sanders, *Ministry at the Margins: The Prophetic Mission of Women, Youth & the Poor* (Downers Grove, IL:

InterVarsity Press, 1997); Cheryl J. Sanders, *Empowerment Ethics for a Liberated People: A Path to African American Social Transformation* (Minneapolis, MN: Fortress Press, 1995).

28. Cheryl J. Sanders, "Pentecostal Ethics and the Prosperity Gospel: Is There a Prophet in the House?" in *Afro-Pentecostalism: Black Pentecostal and Charismatic Christianity in History and Culture*, ed. Amos Yong and Estrelda Y. Alexander (New York: New York University Press, 2011), 141.

29. Ibid.

30. Ibid., 150.

31. Ibid., 151.

32. Leonard Lovett, *Kingdom beyond Color: Re-Examining the Phenomenon of Racism* (np: Leonard Lovett, Xlibris Corporation, 2006), 16.

33. Leonard Lovett, "Ethics in a Prophetic Mode: Reflections of an Afro-American Radical," in *Afro-Pentecostalism: Black Pentecostal and Charismatic Christianity in History and Culture*, ed. Amos Yong and Estrelda Y. Alexander (New York: New York University Press, 2011), 163n2.

34. Ibid., 152, 160.

35. Lovett, *Kingdom beyond Color*, 51.

36. Ibid., 59.

37. Ibid., 55.

38. Ibid., 57.

39. Ibid., 98–99.

40. Ibid., 135; also Leonard Lovett, "Liberation: A Dual Edged Sword," *Pneuma: The Journal of the Society for Pentecostal Studies* 9, no. 2 (Fall 1987): 155–71, quotation at 168. Reminiscent of Martin Luther King, Lovett concludes the article with "I dream" statements.

41. For George Wood's justification and clarification of his decision regarding Black Lives Matter, see George O. Wood, "Which Lives Matter?" *Influence Magazine* 9 (December 2016–January 2017): 32–43.

15

"GET ON THE CART!"
Wesleyan Discipleship in an Age of Endemic Incarceration

Benjamin Hartley; Glen Alton Messer, II; and Kirsten Sonkyo Oh

Fyodor Dostoyevsky once said that the soul of society "can be measured by its prisons."[1] If that is true, then the soul of society in the United States is sick. The statistics on mass incarceration provided elsewhere in this volume illustrate the endemic nature of the problem much like epidemiological data shows the occurrence of a disease, but the stories from prisoners and their families—which the three of us have heard and told—show even more poignantly the depth of the wounds caused by the tragedy of incarceration that defies Christian virtues in this country. We pray this chapter will be one of many applications of healing balm to address this societal disease.

The task of ending our society's addiction to locking people up is too great a task for any one Christian tradition. For a disease as endemic as this one, we need deep resources for theological healing as well as countless deeds of pastoral care and political action to address the problem. Our church families and denominations must work together and learn from one another about how we can continue to "remember those who are in prison" (Heb 13:3) and "proclaim release to the captives" (Luke 4:18) in ways that express the fullness of who we are as Christians united and as members of particular families within the Christian movement.

Our Christian tradition is Wesleyan, our group in that tradition is the United Methodist Church (UMC), and our argument in this paper is just as bold as Dostoyevsky's. We believe that the health of the whole Christian community is measured by its love of prisoners; loving the prisoner was and is constitutive of Wesleyan discipleship. Visiting prisoners was a key activity very early in the first rise of Methodism in Oxford.[2] It did not stop there as a youthful exercise of discipleship either. In one nine-month stretch, John Wesley preached as many as sixty-seven times in various prisons and jails.[3] His attentiveness to prisoners was less at other times, but Wesley continued to visit prisons on dozens of occasions throughout his life.[4]

Visiting and helping prisoners also became a key marker of discipleship in the *General Rules* early Methodists sought to live by. The second section of the *Rules* stressed discipleship of care "by doing good" to everyone and "by visiting or helping them that are sick or in prison."[5] No dimension of "doing good" in the *General Rules* was more behavior specific than the expectation that a Methodist visits those who are in prison. The sick could be found in many different places, those suffering from lack of clothing could be anywhere, but those who were in prison were found only there. This dimension of the *General Rules* found further institutional expression at the 1788 Methodist Conference in Britain, which called for all preachers to visit those who were in prison.[6]

The Wesley brothers and their friends even accompanied condemned prisoners on the wooden cart as prison officials drove them to the gallows. They hugged them, spoke with them, prayed with them, read Scripture with them, sang with them, and otherwise comforted them—often amid jeers and refuse thrown from the crowds.[7] Early Methodists were bold enough to get on the cart. The way we today choose to address the problem of incarceration will involve a similar boldness, even though our "cart" may take many different forms.

Not everyone will be able to focus as much as the Wesley brothers did on prison ministry, but if one is not seeking out ways to love those who are imprisoned—directly or indirectly even in small ways—or is not active in encouraging those who do so, then we must at least ask if we are taking the demands of Christian discipleship seriously. We readily acknowledge that most of us fall short of the mark; it is easy to point out all the ways we are *not* loving prisoners very well. Our confession of failure is not for self-flagellation but rather to point us toward God's grace in Christ, who was both imprisoned and executed by a powerful Roman empire.

In the church today, many people in the United States and elsewhere continue to minister to prisoners as well as "returned citizens" released from prison. This is encouraging! Our current context in United States society, with its massive prison population, calls for an equally massive ministry to prisoners. As we will discuss below, our own context is not so very different from eighteenth-century Britain regarding our society's focus on retribution instead of restorative justice.[8] The United Methodist social principle on restorative justice staunchly states the biblical mandate for restorative justice that seeks to heal rather than punish (see Ezek 33:11):

> Restorative justice grows out of biblical authority, which emphasizes a right relationship with God, self, and community....
> Most criminal justice systems around the world are retributive. These retributive justice systems profess to hold the offender accountable to the state and use punishment as the equalizing tool for accountability. In contrast, restorative justice seeks to hold the offender accountable to the victimized person, and to the disrupted community. Through God's transforming power, restorative justice seeks to repair the damage, right the wrong, and bring healing to all involved, including the victim, the offender, the families, and the community.[9]

Declarations about restorative justice are critical contributions, but United Methodists around the country also back up these words with Christian discipleship in action. Along with our ecumenical partners, United Methodists today are engaged in practical ministry with incarcerated persons in many ways:

- As of 2007, there were forty-seven United Methodist prison chaplains employed at state and federal prison facilities.
- Together with many other churches and denominations, United Methodists participate in a network of "Healing Communities," where congregations are

trained and committed to being hospitable places for returned citizens and their families. Over fifty UMC congregations are a part of this expanding ministry.[10]

- At the beginning of 2012, the United Methodist Board of Pensions, the investment arm of the UMC, decided to divest from all companies that profit from the prison systems, such as Corrections Corporation of America, when they realized this misappropriation of investments.
- Prison PATCH (Parents and Their Children) and Prison MATCH (Mothers and Their Children) are ministries in Missouri and North Carolina, respectively, with significant UMC participation to help build closer relationships between incarcerated women and their children.[11]
- For decades, the United Methodist Church's Social Principles have opposed the death penalty together with the National Council of Churches, and we are beginning to see its demise in a growing number of states in the United States.
- The National Black Methodists for Church Renewal meeting in March 2014 named mass incarceration as one of their main advocacy issues and one that is strongly tied to the wider sin of racism in our nation.[12]

The people who engage in the above activities do so for a variety of reasons. Their work is to be celebrated! We further believe that their ministry can be enhanced and others inspired to follow their example if those others recognize how this work can deepen their relationship with Jesus and the Way he calls us to follow as his disciples.

Our purpose in this chapter, then, is to demonstrate how "getting on the cart" by ministering to and advocating for prisoners, their families, and victims of crime is integral to Christian discipleship. We are going to do that by drawing from the experience of early Methodist work among prisoners as our starting point. Our historical "case studies" are arranged to correspond to what Wesleyans call the "order of salvation" expressed in the prevenient, justifying, and sanctifying nature of God's grace. We introduce our historical vignettes by providing the reader with a sense of the context and then offer our theological reflections about the meaning they had for early Methodists and can now have for our own discipleship.

Our reflections will often come in the form of questions rather than prescriptions about how we might want to change. We think the Holy Spirit inspires change. This chapter, then, is an exercise in imaginative reflection on historical events to provide theological insight about how we can grow today as disciples, learning from Jesus and early Methodists "on the cart." We hope Christians from other denominations can be inspired by these stories as well.

Before discussing our historical case studies and how they align with Wesley's order of salvation—God's prevenient, justifying, and sanctifying grace—it is important to first explain in a bit more detail what we mean by these aspects of grace in Wesleyan theology. Wesleyan theology starts with God, who created humankind in God's own image; upon Adam and Eve, God bestowed a caretaking role over all the creatures. The story of Adam and Eve, however, is a story of the corruption of God's good creation and of humanity's continued bent to sinning. The entirety of the Christian life is thus a process of growth and healing by grace. By prevenient grace, we speak of God's grace spread abroad over all of creation and a grace where God initiates and engages the human will to invite a response (see John 6:44; see also Jer 31:3; 1 John 4:10). By justifying grace, we are reconciled to God when a person realizes his/her own sinful state, repents, and accepts by faith the way of Jesus Christ. Through sanctifying grace, God provides both the desire and the power to grow toward holiness or wholeness. We begin, therefore, with prevenient grace and discuss, in turn, justifying grace and sanctifying grace as these aspects of Wesley's theology are seen in the prison ministry of early Methodists.

Some of these historical case studies can be a challenge to our discipleship as we are forced to confront aspects of early Methodist practice with prisoners with which we may disagree or even find offensive. In these cases, we invite the reader to reflect on the reasons why the story may be disturbing. Is it because our understanding of discipleship has become warped by our cultural and historical context? Was there something about the experience of early Methodists that we ought to critique or even condemn?

Finally, the vignettes we have chosen are not just from the ministry of the Wesley brothers. Other scholars have discussed the Wesley brothers' involvement with prisoners extensively. By highlighting the work of other Methodists, both leaders and laypersons, in addition to John and Charles Wesley, our intent is to bring to mind all the people in our own day who labor with and love prisoners without recognition. Prison ministry is something into which all disciples of Jesus are invited.

PREVENIENT GRACE AND PRISON REFORM

In Wesley's sermon "The Scripture Way of Salvation," he describes "prevenient grace" as "all that light wherewith the Son of God 'enlighteneth every one that cometh into the world'; showing every man 'to do justly, to love mercy, and to walk humbly with his God.'"[13] We confess that even a brief look at the way prisoners are treated in the United States challenges Methodists to recognize that our flawed human response to crime does little to cooperate with the prevenient nature of God's grace. We, as a society, have chosen to make it easier to see the sins committed by prisoners rather than see them as beloved children of God whose souls are in peril because of sin sickness. We, like John Wesley, need to open our hearts and our eyes to see prisoners as they are seen by God, as persons in need of healing and redemption. This change is necessary in us and as an example to the society around us, in order that we may stop standing in the way of God's prevenient grace. Through faithful discipleship that helps align us with our fallen sisters and brothers, we believe the light of God's prevenient grace can shine more brightly in our world for prisoners, returned citizens, their families, and those who have been harmed and with whom healing needs to be about restoration, rather than amputation, of relationships.

Wesley too trusted in the prevenient nature of God's grace and sought to reform a prison system in England to be more consistent with that grace. One had to strain one's eyes and ears to see and hear grace in the eighteenth-century prisons of England. Children as young as fourteen were condemned to death. Even the most minor of crimes—theft of six pence, forgery, snatching of a woman's handkerchief—could be punishable by death.[14] At least 160 different felonies in the eighteenth century could result in capital punishment.[15] The conditions in prisons were so bad that the stench was something neighbors living close to prisons complained about and was reason enough for many to avoid the neighborhoods where prisons existed—to say nothing of going inside them.

The journal of John Wesley contains several examples where he sought to improve the conditions of prisons. In one instance, Wesley celebrated an exception to the dire conditions of prisoners throughout Britain. In a January 1761 letter to the editor of the *London Chronicle*, he noted the improvement of prison conditions at the Newgate prison in Bristol, which he witnessed a few months earlier in October. He carefully enumerated all the ways the prison had improved since his visit a few years earlier. He specifically praised the jail keeper of the prison and ended his letter with a probing question: "And does not the keeper of Newgate deserve to be remembered full as well as the Man of Ross [a famous philanthropist at the time]? May the Lord remember him in that day! Meantime, will no one follow his example?"[16]

Although he did not mention his name specifically in the letter to the *London Chronicle*, Wesley knew the jailer at Newgate prison in Bristol. He was a Methodist. Abel Dagge was converted to Christianity under the influence of George Whitefield in 1737. He deserves to be remembered by persons engaged in prison ministry today as the first Methodist employee of a prison system. Even from within "the system," he made a profoundly positive impact on the lives of hundreds of prisoners.

Wesley's letter to the editor concerning prison conditions is also noteworthy for having been written over a decade before prison reform initiatives started to gain traction in England with the passage of legislation in 1773 that permitted justices to appoint clergy to county jails and pay them a small salary. Further legislation to improve the situation for prisoners passed in subsequent years through the influence of John Howard's political activism.[17] John Wesley admired John Howard, a Calvinist Evangelical: "I had the pleasure of a conversation with Mr. Howard, I think one of the greatest men in Europe. Nothing but the mighty power of God can enable him to go through his difficult and dangerous employments. But what can hurt us, if God is on our side?"[18] The praise Wesley lavished on Howard was reciprocated: "I saw in him [Wesley] how much a single man might achieve by zeal and perseverance, and I thought, why may I not do as much in my way as Mr. Wesley has done in his, if I am only as assiduous and persevering. And I am determined I would pursue my work with more alacrity than ever."[19] Here is a striking example of ecumenical friendship from the eighteenth-century Evangelical movement, of which both Wesley and Howard were a part. Christians seeking to enact the love of Christ in the lives of those whom society counts worthless encouraged each to work all the harder to make good on the teachings of Jesus.

Another friend of the Wesley brothers, Methodist preacher Silas Told (1711–79), advocated for reform in the English prison system in a different way than Wesley. In Wesley's journals, one searches in vain for an example of Wesley questioning the justice of the death penalty for any of the persons to whom he ministered "on the cart" or in prison cells. (Wesley did, however, implicitly question the value of holding debtors in prison for small sums and, together with other early Oxford Methodists, sometimes paid what debtors owed.) In contrast to Wesley, Silas Told questioned the justice of the death penalty on several occasions. That he did so may have been the reason why his autobiography was only published in 1806, twenty-seven years after his death.

In the early nineteenth century, as Evangelicals were gaining traction in their fight against the slave trade, it became common for Evangelicals in Britain to call for reform in capital punishment as well. Methodists joined the Capital Punishment Society to that end.[20] Silas Told called for leniency for persons who committed crimes when they were intoxicated, wrote letters to the king advocating that particular prisoners not be executed, and decried the injustice of the death penalty when he believed its victim was innocent. The following is just one of several examples of Silas's condemnation of capital punishment:

> I return now to Mary Edmonson, who, as before observed, was tried by judge Dennison upon mere circumstances, as no positive evidence against her could be produced. However, I understood that the prisoner suffered very severe and rigorous treatment from the

judge, because she insisted upon her innocence and integrity, the judge still laying the murder to her charge, calling her a notorious vile wretch, assuring her that she would be d___d if she denied the fact, as matters were so evident, particularly seeing that her apron and cap were found covered with blood in the copper-hole; yet, as she was condemned on circumstances only, and as I attended her to the place of execution, I have every reason to believe she was condemned innocent of the charge.[21]

It is important to stress that one of the most brutal depictions of punishment in Silas Told's autobiography was not of a prisoner like Mary Edmonson in an English jail, but of a Jamaican slave whom Told had watched suffer a brutal beating during his years as a British sailor aboard a slave ship.[22] In relating this story, it would not have been difficult for readers to see the relationship between the injustice of the slave trade and the injustice of the British penal system in a way analogous to how Michelle Alexander in our own day has sought to compare Jim Crow laws of the early twentieth century with incarceration today. The injustice in the criminal justice system is a racist injustice, which disproportionately affects African Americans and Native Americans in the United States.[23]

Whether it was in advocating for better prison conditions, recording the stories of those who were executed unjustly, or writing letters requesting more lenient sentences, these early examples of Methodist advocacy for prisoners can serve as inspiration today to continue the work begun so many years ago. God's grace can indeed "enlighteneth every one that cometh into the world" and can even enlighten a prison system too often seen as a place only where sin runs rampant rather than a place where God's grace still stubbornly resides.

As you consider your local jail or nearby prison, are there examples of goodness and grace promoted by employees at those facilities—correctional officers, wardens, defense attorneys—whom you could encourage much like Wesley sought to encourage Abel Dagge? There are often people in local communities who would like to volunteer to spend time with prisoners. Might there be a role for people from your church to participate in this ministry—or to befriend correctional officers and to assist them in their discipleship? In reflecting on the story of Mary Edmonson in Silas Told's book, are there similar stories you could tell of prisoners or "returned citizens" that could help people in your congregation and community see them as God sees them rather than as problems to be solved or people to be feared? Can you use those stories to help people see political advocacy for prison reform today as integral to discipleship and not mere out-of-touch idealism?

JUSTIFYING GRACE AND PRISONER EVANGELISM

Let's be honest. For many readers of this book who belong to denominations affiliated with the National Council of Churches of Christ, evangelism is not an easy subject to talk about. While some forms of evangelism are practiced in harsh and manipulative ways, often our mental picture of evangelism is based on caricatures of some of our more conservative sisters and brothers in Christ, which is neither fair to them nor helpful for our own growth in grace. We believe Pope Francis of the Roman Catholic Church got it right when he stressed, in his first encyclical, the *joy* of the Gospel as integral to evangelism. He was right too in diagnosing the problem of many pastors regarding evangelism. He wrote,

> At times our media culture and some intellectual circles convey a marked skepticism with regard to the Church's message, along with a certain cynicism. As a consequence, many pastoral workers, although they pray, develop a sort of inferiority complex which leads them to relativize or conceal their Christian identity and convictions. This produces a vicious circle. They end up being unhappy with who they are and what they do; they do not identify with their mission of evangelization and this weakens their commitment. They end up stifling the joy of mission with a kind of obsession about being like everyone else and possessing what everyone else possesses. Their work of evangelization thus becomes

forced, and they devote little energy and very limited time to it. (*Evangelii Gaudium* 79)[24]

Similarly, it is important in ministry with prisoners that evangelism not be forced or fake but emerge from a deep life of discipleship, which desires that others also come to know and love Jesus. We believe early Methodists had that kind of depth and sincerity in evangelistic practice. It is a habit of heart and mind that needs to be restored by many people who identify with mainline Protestant denominations.

In addition to trying to promote prison reform—a task that bore little fruit in his lifetime—Silas Told was probably the most effective evangelist with prisoners in early Methodism. After hearing Wesley preach on Matthew 25:31–46, Silas was cut to the heart and resolved to do precisely what was said—to visit those who were in prison. Sarah Peters, doubtless a courageous woman, was responsible for taking him on his first visit to a prison.[25] Silas Told spent the next twenty-five years of his life trying to live out what he read in Matthew 25 and what Sarah Peters had revealed to him. John Wesley spoke at Silas's funeral and gave him effusive praise:

> For many years he attended the malefactors in Newgate without fee or reward; and I suppose no man for this hundred years has been so successful in that melancholy office. God had given him peculiar talents for it, and he had amazing success therein. The greatest part of those whom he attended died in peace, and many of them in the triumph of faith.[26]

Notice how, in this quotation, Wesley's praise of Told is specifically focused on how he helped "death row" prisoners receive justifying grace and the gift of assurance. Indeed, for Wesley and the whole Methodist movement, it was vitally important to have a good death.

Helping people to receive assurance of their salvation was Wesley's own primary motive for engaging in prison ministry, as "A Word to a Condemned Malefactor" makes clear.[27] In this sermon, Wesley does not shrink from emphasizing the gravity of sin or the gratuitous nature of grace:

> Know yourself; see and feel what a sinner you are....
> How is your whole soul prone to evil, void of good, cor-
> rupt, full of all abominations! You cannot atone for the
> sins that are past....Nay, if you could live like an angel
> for a thousand years, that would not atone for one sin....
> One thing is needful: "Believe in the Lord Jesus Christ
> and thou shalt be saved!"[28]

Wesley's message, of course, is a simple one. Few sermons of
Wesley's are as pointed as this one in diagnosing both the depth of
the problem and describing the riches of God's justifying grace for
the sinner. To the eyes of some today, the contrast Wesley makes
between the sinner and the salvation offered might seem overly
extreme. But remember that the hearers of these sermons were
living their final minutes before death on the scaffold. There was
little time to make subtler points. Eternal salvation was at stake.

We may very well choose different words from Wesley in
sharing the good news of Jesus and we may do it differently, but
it is still important to invite people to follow in Jesus' way. How
would we witness both to the truth of sin and the hope of salvation with people from our communities today? It is not simply
about plastering over past bad deeds. The crime and the suffering
brought about by the actions of prisoners are real. To find places
in communities upon their return, one must have clear-eyed honesty. Prisoners need to move toward repentance and restoration to
right relationship with their neighbors. How do we offer love and
forgiveness, the salvation of Christ and the acceptance of Christian
community, and tangible freedom from the sin that damaged lives
beforehand? Here is where Christian discipleship becomes a challenge for those on the "outside" as well as those on the "inside."

There is a necessity of remembering the worth of the individual as a beloved child of God by receiving and embracing those on
the "outside" by the cleaning and clothing of the one who returns
(see Luke 8:39). Where the imprisoned and the returned citizens
are harmed for life with a criminal record that may prevent possible employment and present housing issues, the victims of crime,
along with families of the offenders and victims, may be stigma-
tized and ostracized by yet another label. God's justifying grace

241

compels us to bring the liberative and redeeming power of the good news of Christ's life, death, and resurrection to these persons.

It is important to remember that evangelism is not—in the eighteenth century or today—only an evangelistic sermon or an intense one-on-one conversation where one is invited to "pray the prayer." It would be a caricature of Silas Told's and Wesley's ministry with prisoners if we thought it consisted only in this. Told's autobiography relates how he established religious societies in prison, which met together to hear him preach and held one another accountable using the *General Rules* of the Methodists.[29] It is likely that in the context of these gathered communities, hearts were changed and new habits formed, which was and is the intent of Wesleyan discipleship in groups.

As we consider Silas Told's and John Wesley's evangelistic work with prisoners, we wonder how Wesley's preaching to prisoners affected his own discipleship. When prisoners received justifying grace and the gift of assurance, which was so important to Wesley, did these conversations themselves become a means of grace for Wesley to receive the assurance he had so struggled to attain earlier in his life and likely was something with which he continued to struggle? We cannot say for sure, but it is likely.[30] Throughout the ministry of John Wesley, and in the ministries of many who followed him, the model of ministry was not one of mere condescension; he did not understand things in such a way that he was going to others to save them. Rather, he believed that we are saved *together* by the grace of God. Ministry to others is always ministry *with* others. Since Jesus himself instructed his disciples to visit prisoners, Wesley undoubtedly understood this ministry as not only a means of grace for them, but also for those who went to the prison to be present with them.

We invite you to consider for yourself and to ask others with whom you minister—even prisoners or "returned citizens" themselves—what excellent evangelism would look like in a prison context or with persons who are recently released from prison. Perhaps, like the early Wesleyan movement, an invitation to evangelism ought best to happen in the context of what early Methodists called "class meetings" or "band meetings"—forms of small group ministry. A good example of a ministry to prisoners trying to do this today is Kairos Prison Ministry International, a ministry with significant United Methodist and wider ecumenical participation. Weekend retreats are offered both inside and outside prisons for prisoners and their families to build a stronger sense of Christian community.[31] Being involved with such a ministry ought to be something that Methodists, if not all Wesleyans and all disciples of Christ, do quite naturally!

SANCTIFYING GRACE: PRISON MINISTRY AND FAMILIES

Our growth in holiness as Christians can be either greatly helped or hindered by the people who are closest to us. For most of us, those persons are members of our families—parents, grandparents, spouses, brothers, sisters, and children. Families and friends of prisoners are often just as deeply impacted by the incarceration of their loved ones as prisoners themselves. According to Kairos Prison Ministry, "Spouses, parents and relatives of those in prison often 'do time' right along with their loved ones."[32] Accompanying both friends and family members of prisoners through their challenges is also a critical ministry. Similarly, friendships can be very important for those prisoners who are estranged from family members. The healing of relationships between prisoners on the "inside" and the rest of us on the "outside" moves us beyond justifying grace into what Wesley understood as sanctifying grace.

The historical vignettes we share in this section are reminders that *our* growth in Christian sanctification is intimately connected to the "works of mercy" that we are privileged to show toward others. In Wesley's sermon "On Zeal," such works of mercy were identified as even more important for our growth in holiness than the more typical acts of personal devotion (Bible reading, prayer, etcetera)

> In a Christian believer *love* sits upon the throne,...namely, love of God and man [sic]....In a circle near the throne are all *holy tempers*; long-suffering, gentleness, meekness.... In an exterior circle are all the *works of mercy*, whether to the souls or bodies of men [sic]. By these we exercise all holy tempers; by these we continually improve them,

so that all these are real *means of grace*, although this is not commonly adverted to. Next to these are those that are usually termed *works of piety*: reading and hearing the Word; public, family, private prayer, receiving the Lord's Supper; fasting or abstinence. Lastly, that his followers may the more effectually provoke one another to love, holy tempers, and good works, our blessed Lord has united them together in one—*the church*.[33]

As this sermon excerpt illustrates, our work with prisoners can—and often does—result in further growth for ourselves as much as it helps those whom we serve.

One example of this happening in the life of Silas Told—and one of his most heartrending stories—involved his ministry with the Anderson family. Mr. Anderson was condemned to death for stealing sixpence when he was out desperately searching for work or food. Told was moved by the love Mr. and Mrs. Anderson shared with one another when he saw them at his preaching services in the prison. He accompanied Mr. Anderson to the gallows and, while preaching to his own congregation outside the prison, expressed his anger about "the unfortunate case of Mr. Anderson, who died for six-pence, being the first crime, if criminal, which I think not, were circumstances considered." Told spent three days searching for Mrs. Anderson after her husband's execution and eventually found her in a small, dirty room that he described as "more nauseous than the cells of Newgate."[34] Silas Told and his wife gave Mrs. Anderson a place to stay, helped her safely give birth to a baby daughter, and saw that she gained employment as a housekeeper.[35]

Silas Told relates that his experience with Mr. and Mrs. Anderson caused him to preach about it to a congregation beyond the prison walls. He did this to encourage his congregation's growth in holiness. Silas's experience of anger amid injustice can be understood as a "holy anger," which he desired his congregation to embrace as well. Too many Christians in the United States today are not angry enough about the many injustices of the criminal justice system. Methodists and other Christians would do well to see growth in holy anger as just as important an example of growth in holiness as spiritual consolations through prayer.

John Wesley had a similar experience to Silas Told, one that similarly allowed him to relate the story to others and so to encourage their growth in holiness. In this case, it was a growth in a kind of "holy generosity" rather than "holy anger." In 1759, shortly after the British invasion of French Canada, Wesley ministered to soldiers of his nation's enemy. Eleven hundred French prisoners of war were imprisoned near Bristol where Wesley was staying while finishing up a book project, the fourth volume of "Discourses." He walked a mile outside of town and was appalled by what he saw.

> [They] were confined in that little place, without anything to lie on but a little dirty straw, or anything to cover them but a few foul thin rags, either by day or night, so that they died like rotten sheep. I was much affected and preached in the evening on (Exodus 23:9), "Thou shalt not oppress a stranger: for ye know the heart of a stranger, seeing ye were strangers in the land of Egypt." Eighteen pounds were contributed immediately, which were made up four and twenty the next day. With this we bought linen and woolen cloth, which were made up into shirts, waistcoats, and breeches. Some dozen of stockings were added; all of which were carefully distributed where there was the greatest want. Soon after, the Corporation of Bristol sent a large quantity of mattresses and blankets. And it was not long before contributions were set on foot at London and in various parts of the kingdom; so that I believe from this time they were pretty well provided with all the necessaries of life.[36]

Wesley's journal here recounts both how his stirring encounter with French prisoners influenced his preaching to the people of Bristol as well as how these events resulted in the mobilization of Methodists and doubtless other sympathetic Christians to meet the needs of French prisoners. The French prisoners were not only strangers but also enemies of the British state.

Reflecting upon this event, one is struck by the fact that Wesley's action on behalf of the French prisoners was something of an accident. He was not in Bristol to visit them. His walk a mile outside of town appears more like a "study break" than an intentional foray into a new ministry. It is a reminder of similar chance encounters we have with strangers in our land and also of how we too often fail to respond to the promptings of the Holy Spirit to act like Wesley did. Wesley does not tell us what happened to the French prisoners he visited, and we do not even know if he could engage them in conversation. They were strangers and enemies, however, and he sought to love them in simple, practical ways.

Few people in the United States realize that there are approximately 74,000 noncitizens of the United States who are in federal and state prisons. This is about 5 percent of the total state and federal prison population.[37] This number does not include the 400,000 persons who are held each year in detention centers around the country operated under the auspices of the Department of Homeland Security.[38] Persons imprisoned by the U.S. military are also not included in either of these sets of statistics.

Wesley's encounter with French prisoners of war is a reminder of how so often ministry with prisoners is resisted by Christians because we allow our hearts to be shaped more by a vindictiveness toward our enemies (sex offenders, terrorists, etcetera) that demands punitive recompense than by Jesus' love for them that we are called to emulate. One of the most beautiful examples of Christians ministering to strangers occurred in a detention center in Seattle, Washington, in 2006. Twenty-two undocumented Chinese migrants were detained when they were discovered as stowaways on a container ship.[39] Chinese congregations in the Seattle area were at first embarrassed by their fellow countrymen for having immigrated illegally in this way, but they soon began leading a multicongregational effort to minister to their needs, both spiritual and material.[40] A number of these immigrants became Christians and some returned to China and other countries and even started new churches in their homelands as a natural outgrowth of the gospel they received.

JABEZ BUNTING AND THE FAILURE TO LIVE OUT THE TEACHINGS OF CHRIST

The examples we have reflected upon so far in this chapter have all illustrated mostly positive dimensions of ministry with prisoners. It is important, however, to also mention how, a few years after Wesley's death, the Methodist movement could also be mean-spirited toward prisoners. It is a reminder to us that sanctifying grace is also received when we confess our failures to love as Jesus loves and to live as Jesus lives. A story about Jabez Bunting illustrates this better than anything else we have read and serves as a call to confession for us when we feel or even act similarly out of a sense of fear or vindictiveness in our own day in a culture that sometimes seems to revel in the endemic disease of incarceration.

Jabez Bunting was the most influential leader in British Methodism during the generation after Wesley's death in 1793. In 1820, Bunting became president of the Methodist Conference in Britain at the age of forty-one.[41] He was, in many respects, a bureaucrat's bureaucrat, assiduous in his attention to detail and denominational finances, and precise in his preaching. Bunting was no friend of radical labor leaders, however. He was filled with dismay when he learned that six of the seventeen persons hanged for the Luddite uprising were sons of Methodist preachers and saw this as sure evidence that the spread of Methodism in Yorkshire had been superficial at best.[42] In the wake of the Peterloo Massacre of protesting workers in 1819, Bunting encountered a prisoner, Samuel Bamford, in the Lincoln jail who was facing charges of high treason for his leadership role in the Peterloo protest. Bamford and Bunting apparently had a brief exchange whereby Bamford informed the prestigious Bunting that Bamford's grandfather had helped introduce Methodism to the Middleton area. Dismayed by Bunting's cold response, Bamford wrote, "The reverend gentleman went away with his company without vouchsafing a blessing or a word of advice to me—not that I cared much about it—but I thought old John Gaulter, or little Jonathan Barker [earlier Methodist leaders], would not have done so."[43]

The difference in character—and understandings of the demands of Christian discipleship—between John Wesley and Jabez Bunting is striking. Both men faced people in prison who were despised because of their conflict with the British monarch and government. In Wesley's case, they were French (mostly Roman Catholic) prisoners during a war that was not yet safely distant from the previous century's struggles over whether Britain would be Protestant or Catholic in the religious divide of the day.

Bunting found himself close to labor strife that had him in dangerous proximity to those struggling for reforms against the laws and
policies of the crown and government. Both men were challenged
with the question of how to minister to prisoners who are despised
by those with power—and how to do so when such ministry could
call into question one's own safety. Wesley placed the demands of
Christ's teachings above all else. Bunting ran the other way, siding
with the powers that be and letting the gospel fend for itself.

CONCLUSION

In the eighteenth century, the idea that work with prisoners was a constituent dimension of Wesleyan discipleship was
not really a debatable point. John and Charles Wesley followed
the example of one of their fellow Methodists and began visiting
the Oxford prisons when the Methodist movement was still in its
infancy. Ministry with prisoners was something that the Wesley
brothers did throughout their lives. It was not limited to them
either. George Whitefield, Silas Told, Sarah Peters, and many others were also engaged in ministry with the imprisoned. Such an
"all hands on deck" call for work with prisoners was just as appropriate for the eighteenth century as it is today. The prison population skyrocketed in the eighteenth and early nineteenth century in
a way not that dissimilar to what has occurred in the U.S. prison
population since the 1970s.[44]

No time is unique in terms of the threats and terrors faced
from within and without. A passing familiarity with history shows
that the only thing "exceptional" about a given time is whether
we live in it. The gospel of Christ Jesus lays a perennial challenge
before Christians in every age: Will we see prisoners, victims,
and their families as sacred to God or as castaways from civilization? Will we seek justice to restore individuals and communities
rather than to punish for vengeance's sake? Just as the prisoner is
challenged to turn away from the sin of crimes committed that
transgress against God's children, we are challenged to turn away
from the sins of hatred and indifference that we use to justify our
standing in judgment of others rather than seeking their care, consolation, and salvation. Jesus says "do not judge." He also teaches

his disciples to "visit those who are in prison" (to care for their well-being). We get to decide whether we will stand with those like Jabez Bunting, who failed in this central aspect of discipleship, or whether we will stand with those like John Wesley and Silas Told, who took Jesus at his word. The place for our creativity lies in how we choose to enact the teachings of Christ—if we choose to engage that creativity at all. Love of enemies and care for prisoners is not an optional part of discipleship. It is a measure by which Jesus counts each of us as sheep or goats. Which will you strive to become?

Notes

1. Cited in T. Richard Snyder, *The Protestant Ethic and the Spirit of Punishment* (Grand Rapids, MI: Eerdmans, 2001), 2.

2. Kenneth L. Carder, "Castle Prison and Aldersgate Street: Converging Paths on the Methodist Way" (unpublished address, February 5, 2009), pdf file; Richard P. Heitzenrater, "Prison Ministry in the Wesleyan Tradition," in *I Was in Prison: United Methodist Perspectives on Prison Ministry*, ed. James M. Shopshire et al. (Nashville: General Board of Higher Education and Ministry, The United Methodist Church, 2008); Charles Yrigoyen Jr., "'I Was in Prison and You Visited Me': The Prison Ministry of John and Charles Wesley and the Early Methodists," *Evangelical Journal* 29, no. 1 (2011): 11–23.

3. Harmon L. Wray, Peggy Hutchison, and Brenda Connelly, *Restorative Justice: Moving beyond Punishment* (New York: General Board of Global Ministries, 2002), 29.

4. Yrigoyen, "'I Was in Prison,'" 14.

5. *Book of Discipline of the United Methodist Church, 2012* (Nashville: United Methodist Publishing House, 2012), 77.

6. See "Mission Plan for Restorative Justice Ministries," in *Book of Resolutions, 2012* (Nashville: United Methodist Publishing House, 2012), 651–62; online version of text accessed October 3, 2017, http://main.umc -gbcs.org/resolutions/mission-plan-for-restorative-justice-ministries -5034-2008-bor.

7. Charles Wesley composed several hymns for "condemned malefactors." For an analysis of these hymns, see Joanna Cruickshank, "Singing at the Scaffold: Charles Wesley's Hymns for Condemned Malefactors," *Proceedings of the Wesley Historical Society* 56 (2007): 129–45.

8. Nearly fifteen years ago, the United Methodist Women focused on this theme of restorative justice in their Mission study for 2002. See Wray, Hutchison, Connelly, *Restorative Justice*.

9. "Criminal and Restorative Justice," in *The Book of Discipline*, 137.

10. The UMC General Board of Church and Society has had a partnership with Healing Communities for a number of years. See "Social-Justice Agency Forms Partnership with Healing Communities," accessed August 16, 2016, https://www.umcsc.org/home/social-justice-agency-forms-partnership-healing-communities/. For more information about Healing Communities, see http://www.healingcommunitiesusa.com/.

11. The founding of Prison PATCH is told in Wray, Hutchison, and Connelly, *Restorative Justice*.

12. National Black Methodists for Church Renewal began in 1968 to advocate for the interests and inclusivity of blacks in the UMC as well as to serve as the spiritual agitating conscience of the whole church. See Heather Hahn, "Black Caucus Commits to Increase Advocacy," accessed December 9, 2016, http://www.umc.org/news-and-media/black-caucus-commits-to-increase-advocacy.

13. John Wesley, "The Scripture Way of Salvation," accessed December 9, 2016, http://www.umcmission.org/Find-Resources/John-Wesley-Sermons/Sermon-43-The-Scripture-Way-of-Salvation.

14. Robert F. Wearmouth, *Methodism and the Common People of the Eighteenth Century* (London: Epworth, 1945), 77–113.

15. Sean McConville, *A History of English Prison Administration, vol. 1, 1750–1877* (London: Routledge & Kegan Paul, 1981), 58.

16. *The Works of John Wesley, vol. 21, Journals and Diaries IV (1755–65)*, ed. W. Reginald Ward and Richard P. Heitzenrater (Nashville: Abingdon, 1992), 296.

17. McConville, *History of English Prison Administration*, 127.

18. Cited in ibid., 79.

19. Ibid.

20. Cruickshank, "Singing at the Scaffold," 145.

21. Silas Told, *An Account of the Life and Dealings of God with Silas Told, Late Preacher of the Gospel: Wherein Is Set Forth the Wonderful Display of Divine Providence towards Him When at Sea; His Various Sufferings Abroad; Together with Many Instances of the Sovereign Grace of God, in the Conversion of Several Malefactors under Sentence of Death, Who Were Greatly Blessed under His Ministry* (London: W. Cowdroy, 1806), 93, 98.

22. Ibid., 66–67.

23. Michelle Alexander, *The New Jim Crow: Mass Incarceration in the Age of Colorblindness* (New York: The New Press, 2010). 526,000

African American men were serving time in state or federal correctional facilities in 2013. That is 37 percent of the overall 1.5 million imprisoned men. The National Council on Crime and Delinquency identified similarly disturbing statistics for Native Americans' incarceration rates, which are often under reported by mainstream media. Native Americans are incarcerated at two times the rate of whites in the United States. This is higher than any other ethnic group except African Americans. Christopher Hartney and Linh Vuong, "Created Equal: Racial and Ethnic Disparities in the US Criminal Justice System" (National Council on Crime and Delinquency, 2009), 3, accessed December 9, 2016, http:// www.nccdglobal.org/sites/default/files/publication_pdf/created-equal .pdf. For research questioning the extent of racial injustice in the criminal justice system in America, see Barry Latzer, *The Rise and Fall of Violent Crime in America* (New York: Encounter Books, 2016).

24. *Evangelii Gaudium: Apostolic Exhortation on the Proclamation of the Gospel in Today's World* (Rome: Holy See, 2013).

25. Told, *Account of the Life and Dealings*, 79.

26. Cited in Yrigoyen, "'I Was in Prison,'" 21.

27. John Wesley, *The Works of John Wesley*, 3rd ed., vols. 11–12 (Grand Rapids, MI: Baker Books, 2002), 179–82.

28. Ibid., 180–81.

29. Told, *Account of the Life and Dealings*, 84, 89.

30. Kenneth L. Carder makes precisely this argument in "Castle Prison and Aldersgate Street: Converging Paths on the Methodist Way," 3.

31. For more information about Kairos Prison Ministry International, see http://www.kairosprisonministry.org.

32. Kairos Prison Ministry International, "Kairos Outside," accessed December 9, 2016, http://kairosprisonministry.org/kairos -outside-womens-program.php.

33. This excerpt is taken from Wesley's sermon "On Zeal," cited in Randy Maddox, "'Visit the Poor': John Wesley, the Poor, and the Sanctification of Believers," in *The Poor and the People Called Methodists*, ed. Richard P. Heitzenrater (Nashville: Kingswood Books, 2002), 72–73.

34. Told, *Account of the Life and Dealings*, 107.

35. Ibid., 105–9.

36. John Wesley, *The Works of John Wesley*, 3rd ed., vols. 1–2 (Grand Rapids, MI: Baker Books, 2002), 516.

37. Catherine E. Stoichet, "Immigrants and Crime: Crunching the Numbers," CNN, July 8, 2015, http://www.cnn.com/2015/07/08/politics/ immigrants-crime/.

38. Detention Watch Network, "Immigration Detention 101," accessed December 9, 2016, http://www.detentionwatchnetwork.org/issues/detention-101.

39. Paul Shukovsky, Brad Wong, and Kristen Millares Bolt, "22 Stowaways Nabbed at Port of Seattle," *Seattle Pi*, accessed April 5, 2006, http://www.seattlepi.com/local/article/22-stowaways-nabbed-at-Port-of-Seattle-1200407.php.

40. See "Celebrating World Refugee Day: Serving Detainees in Seattle," accessed December 9, 2016, http://www.worldrelief.org/blog/celebrating-world-refugee-day-discipling-detainees-in-seattle.

41. David Hempton, "Jabez Bunting: The Formative Years, 1794–1820," *Religion of the People: Methodism and Popular Religion, c. 1750–1900* (New York: Routledge, 1996), 107.

42. Ibid., 100. The Luddites were a group of workers who, among other things, sought to sabotage industrial equipment, which they perceived caused them to be put out of work.

43. Ibid., 101.

44. McConville, *History of English Prison Administration*, 58.

IV ECUMENICAL CONSIDERATIONS

16

THE PROBLEM OF EMPTY PEWS

Mass Incarceration as a Church-Dividing Issue

Matthew D. Lundberg

In 1960, the evangelist Billy Graham repeated what was even at that time a common observation, that Sunday morning is the most segregated hour in American life.[1] Still more famously, Martin Luther King Jr. put his own rhetorical stamp on the point while deepening it theologically: "As a minister of the gospel, I am ashamed to say that eleven o'clock on Sunday morning—when we stand to sing 'In Christ There is No East Nor West'—is the most segregated hour of America, and that Sunday school is the most segregated school of the week."[2] While times may have changed somewhat, with more exceptions today, congregations still tend to be racially homogeneous.[3] It is not uncommon, for example, for predominantly Latina/o, white, and black congregations to exist just blocks from one another, separate and separated, living the Christian life in parallel, with relatively few intersections.

Who we worship with and who is worshipping apart from us tells us something about what is going on in the churches. The observations made by King and Graham suggest that this is true *between* congregations, although we need to be nuanced in the conclusions we draw (more on this in a moment). It is also true as we look *within* individual congregations. For there we see another kind of separation that divides the churches, one with a related racial element.

In some congregations—disproportionately those populated by people of color—there are glaring gaps in the pews, as members and friends of the congregation who would probably be there

255

have been taken away by the American system of incarceration. Whether it be a father, sister, cousin, husband, or friend, there are many absent from the worship life of the church. Some undoubtedly are imprisoned for justifiable reasons, perpetrators of violent crimes who pose a genuine risk to public safety and well-being. As prison critic and theologian James Logan writes, "Incapacitating and controlling socially destructive persons is a legitimate social aim for any society wishing to preserve itself. Indeed, it would be naïve to deny that in a highly complex society at least some minimum system of justice is necessary."[4] This point must be taken seriously: Some who are in prison ought to be there, as their actions have harmed people and endangered society. But we must also deal forthrightly with the fact that the forces of racism in America have, at both conscious and unconscious levels, targeted the nonwhite population for arrest, prosecution, and imprisonment, often for nonviolent crimes that pose little risk to public safety. And this part of the nation's population includes within it a portion of the American church. What affects nonwhite churches and their members at disproportionate rates may often barely register on the radar screen of the white churches, even though it involves factors and forces closely related to them.

In the American church as a whole, we thus have a huge disparity in the way in which congregations tend to be affected by mass incarceration. In some, blissful ignorance, willing complacency, and even active participation prevail. In others, empty pews, guilt, despair, and anger about injustice are the norm. In some, undoubtedly, a complex mixture of these elements is present. The American church and the American churches, in short, are divided by the system of mass incarceration. It is not only an issue of social and racialized injustice, though it is that. It is also a force that tears at the unity of Christ's Body in this country.

Let us reflect on just two dimensions of mass incarceration as a church-dividing ecumenical problem.

I

A first dimension is the presence of Christians at all levels of the criminal justice system in the United States. Just as the Christian church is present in significant ways in the various spheres and strata of American society, so also the church is represented in noticeable ways in all dimensions of the criminal justice and prison system. As mentioned already, Christians are among the prisoners.[5] This is true across the American racial spectrum, including in a predominantly white, middle-class congregation like my own. I remember a Sunday worship service early in our family's time at the church when our pastor included in her prayer, "We pray for the four members of our church family who are in prison," followed by their names. They had been unknown to me (a relative newcomer), and perhaps often forgotten by other parishioners, but certainly a painful absence in the hearts and minds of family members and friends, former Sunday School teachers and youth leaders. Given the statistics about racial dynamics in American incarceration rates, however, how much more must this be the case in some African American congregations, whose pews are likely to have many more conspicuously empty seats.[6]

Yet in the churches we also have police officers, prosecuting attorneys, corrections officers, judges, prison administrators, and politicians, as well as church members who work for businesses or in industries whose success depends upon the prison system and a continuing supply of prisoners. If societies require at least some system of criminal justice, then personnel, supplies, and services are needed for the system to function. And across the racial spectrum, some Christians experience a sense of calling in relation to these vocations—that God has brought them to the point where keeping society safe is part of their life's work. Some of this work, moreover, involves difficult decisions, risks to their safety, and tough moral dilemmas. At a more practical level, for anyone who works in the system at whatever level, the system provides their job and livelihood, something that communities come to depend upon, especially in uncertain economic times. But from a Christian vantage point, the existence of crime and therefore prisons is lamentable; incarceration is a regrettable necessity rather than a positive good.

The two sides of the situation can and do coexist within congregations, with police officers and families of the incarcerated worshipping together. But it is more often the case that they cluster in separate congregations with differing preponderant skin tones.

Some churches reflect more of the people of God's participation in the power structures of the system, while others experience the Body of Christ's relative powerlessness in the face of the system's momentum.

This state of affairs is not altogether different from the sociological realities of the church in other areas of life and in relation to other problems of the world. Most of the wars of the past half millennium in the West have featured confessing Christians on both sides of the conflict and the trenches.[7] Similarly, in today's global economy, Christian purchasing power among the so-called "haves" is often supplied by resources and products either mined or assembled in parts of their world where Christianity is booming among the "have-nots." Though this dynamic does not always involve exploitation, it sometimes does, often unbeknownst to us.

It is therefore not a unique phenomenon that disciples of Jesus may be found at every turn in the intricacies of the prisoner control system. It remains striking, though, if we allow ourselves to reflect upon the phenomenon, that there is a Christian face to both the power and powerlessness, the financial benefit and financial loss, the means to support a family and the rupturing of family dynamics, the satisfaction and despair that coexist symbiotically in this system.

We must not overlook, of course, the role that some Christians in the industry play in providing Evangelical leaven in a cold and bureaucratized system where people can be reduced to a prison number and identified with the offenses for which they were convicted (or to which they pled guilty). Given that prisons are a regrettable necessity for society due to dangerous offenders who pose a risk to social safety, we should not underestimate the importance of Christians striving to bring genuine humanity to the prison system by, for example, honoring the dignity of those whom they guard, or taking great care in providing high quality food to prisoners, or creating genuine educational opportunities for those inside the system, to say nothing of deciding more equitably when to arrest or prosecute and when not to.

What we have here, in short, is a situation in which the Christian churches may provide a measure of Christlike grace, mercy, justice, and dignity to the hurts and harshness of the prison industry, but also contribute, whether actively or tacitly, to the brutality, injustice, and pain of the system. While we have reason to give thanks when the Christian presence in the world of the American prison brings some light, grace, and truth, we also have ample reason to apply Jesus' prayer to ourselves: "Forgive us for we know not what we are doing" (see Luke 23:34).[8]

II

A second church-dividing dimension of the problem of mass incarceration is the role of Christians in the politics that have produced the problem. Ian Haney López argues that mass incarceration is one result of what he and others have dubbed "dog whistle politics."[9] Haney López charts the rise of coded racial messaging in American politics from the famed "Southern strategy" to the present. When it became less culturally acceptable to use overtly racist labels, the Republican Party in the United States found that it was remarkably easy and effective to appeal to the racial prejudices of white voters in ways that were not explicitly race based, but nevertheless conveyed such messages at a subconscious level that resonated with existing fears and biases. Just as "states' rights" was used as a thinly veiled yet putatively more dignified code for slavery, so also things like "busing," "welfare," "crime," and "immigration" have been used—not just by Republican politicians, but also by Democrats—to convince white citizens to lend their votes to causes based on fears and attitudes about darker-skinned Americans. To be sure, words such as *welfare* and *crime* refer to legitimate political questions about important issues across the ideological and racial continuums—for example, what responsibility does society have to care for the poor and unemployed in ways that do not create undue dependency; what should we do about the crime that afflicts communities, including forms of drug use that correlate with violent behavior? At the same time, according to Haney López, these terms were frequently used in public discourse as a coded way to suggest that racial minorities as such were threats to the well-being of white Americans.

This is what Haney López dubs "strategic racism," in distinction from three other more familiar faces of racism: hate, implicit bias, and structural racism.[10] *Hate* is the most obvious and uncomplicated of the forms of racism—hateful attitudes toward people due to their race or ethnicity. *Implicit bias* refers to the usually unacknowledged and unwitting expectations, assumptions, and prejudices that people often have about others based on race. *Structural racism*, of course, involves the systems of privilege and oppression that have been constructed and have accrued over the course of time, making things like employment and wealth building generally easier for white people and pronouncedly more difficult for Americans of color. *Strategic racism*, according to Haney López, is the deliberate act of preying upon the other forms of racism, especially implicit bias, "in pursuit of political power and (especially once big-money conservatives got behind the tactic) material wealth." Strategic racism is, in his words, "racism's most poisonous core—because it legitimizes, energizes, and stimulates the entire destructive project of racial divisions."[11]

Following Michelle Alexander's acclaimed *The New Jim Crow*, Haney López argues that the "wars" on crime and drugs from the 1970s to the present have been, at their heart, a new form of strategic racism. Given the success of strategic racism in garnering votes, politicians explored ways to "take the most punitive stand against minorities," emphasizing how they destabilized "law and order." Since darker-skinned Americans were typecast as "welfare cheats or criminals, illegal aliens or terrorists," this naturally gave rise to "racialized mass incarceration."[12] This means that even though, as just mentioned, issues such as welfare, crime, and immigration are legitimate political questions for leaders and the populace to debate and answer, the dimensions of those issues that received most attention (and attention from law enforcement) were those that concerned minorities (for example, certain kinds of drug crimes rather than date rape on university campuses). He writes, "Since the Southern strategy took hold, we have built up a massive carceral apparatus on a scale unprecedented in our history or among the world's nations."[13] Even though—controlling for poverty and age—research indicates that white Americans are just as or more likely to commit crimes, "young men of color are far, far more likely than young white men to be swept into the maw of the American crime control system."[14] From Richard Nixon through Ronald Reagan to Bill Clinton, "crime" became code for race in campaign efforts to lure voters. Then policies were enacted (such as the "War on Drugs" and "Three Strikes" laws) to follow through on those campaign efforts in quest of future votes, laws that Alexander shows have been enforced with decided racial disparity.[15] As Haney López writes, "Campaign slogans did not stay at rallies or remain in commercials; they quickly morphed into get-tough policies with real human consequences...that over decades spawned the prison system we stagger under today."[16] By comparing incarceration rates between the United States and the highest rates in Europe, Haney López estimates that as many as 80 percent of those imprisoned are there as an indirect result of "strategic racism." Even if this estimate is inflated, it suggests that millions of ruined lives—primarily in communities of color—have been the collateral damage of a breathtakingly cynical method of courting (white) voters.

If Haney López's analysis is largely correct, here is where the white Christian churches of the United States have the responsibility to take a hard look at themselves. This is, of course, a generalization, and there are plenty of counterexamples, but it nevertheless appears that we lighter-skinned Christians—extended through multiple generations—have often given in to the temptation to nurture racialized anger and fears. In one sense, of course, some slack could rightly be cut to the white Christian electorate—as there were, until recently, few clearly presented alternatives to mass incarceration. But if we are honest, it seems that we have also allowed our implicit bias and cultural prejudice, those sinful elements of our individual and communal selfhood that most need to be changed, to be hijacked in a way that has harmed many of our Christian brothers and sisters, those whose lives and well-being have been sacrificed for votes, power, and money.

It is important to remember Haney López's distinction between the architects of the rhetoric and the white populace. The former were aware of what was going on in a way that the latter were not, with their anger and fears being co-opted in a subtle and subterranean way—hence the "dog whistle" metaphor. At the same time, the white electorate proved to be remarkably receptive to those "dog whistle" messages. It is striking how quickly the tactic of strategic racism paid dividends, as white Americans, Christians among them, were ripe for such a subtle racial appeal. We may, then, have something akin to schism in the American churches, a schism that begins at an elusive spiritual level of our being but culminates in destructive material consequences. If Haney López is right, the white Christians of the United States have been all too easily convinced to support politicians and policies that have resulted in injustice and suffering among the nonwhite communities of our country. And some of those victimized have thereby been absent from their congregations' pews on Sunday morning, unable to serve on their church councils, not allowed to hear the Lord's Word proclaimed, barred from being a daily witness in their churches, communities, and families. We have submitted all too willingly to the incarceration of part of Christ's Body in this country.

The *white* Christian church, moreover, has also been harmed by the situation of mass incarceration. Haney López makes the argument that this is true in material terms—that the increasingly conservative policies enacted by the United States in the twentieth- to twenty-first-century age of "strategic racism" have harmed the middle class across the board, even while having a particularly devastating effect on poorer communities of color (almost as a self-fulfilling prophecy). But even if it turns out that he is not fully correct on policy grounds, this harm is certainly true spiritually. We have allowed our worst fears and biases—that we should be seeking to transform into the "fruits of the Spirit"—to be used for nefarious gain, which in turn cultivates more deeply the very vices that are being seized upon. We have been complicit in damage done to the lives of so many with whom we are, in Christ in a mystical yet theologically true way, *one* and yet so often without feeling the pain.

With the verve of a preacher, Michelle Alexander writes the following about the spiritual condition of the American nation in relation to racialized incarceration:

> The reality is that, just a few decades after the collapse of one caste system [legalized segregation], we constructed another. Our nation declared a war on people trapped in racially segregated ghettos—just at the moment their economies had collapsed [in the late 1970s]—rather than providing community investment, quality education, and job training when work disappeared. Of course

those communities are suffering from serious crime and dysfunction today. Did we expect otherwise?...Clearly a much better set of options could be provided to African Americans—and poor people of all colors—today....We could choose to be a nation that extends care, compassion, and concern to those who are locked up and locked out or headed for prison before they are old enough to vote. We could seek for them the same opportunities we seek for our own children; we could treat them like one of 'us.'...The economic collapse of inner-city black communities could have inspired a national outpouring of compassion and support. A new War on Poverty could have been launched....Instead we declared a War on Drugs....Almost overnight, black men found themselves unnecessary to the American economy and demonized by mainstream society. No longer needed to pick cotton in the fields or labor in factories, lower-class black men were hauled off to prison in droves.[17]

Replace Alexander's "we" and "our nation" with "Christians" and "the church" and we have a soul-shattering indictment that should cut to our spiritual core. Where the *Book of Common Prayer*'s confession states, "We have failed to love our neighbor as ourselves," we should intensify the point: "We have failed to love our *sisters and brothers* as ourselves." In relation to so many of our fellow disciples on the hard journey of faith, "we have left undone those things which we ought to have done, and we have done those things which we ought not to have done."[18]

III

Though it seems almost blasphemous to move too quickly to this point, at the heart of the Christian gospel is the proclamation that in Christ there is forgiveness, that we are not bound to our old ways, that the Holy Spirit is at work convicting us and renewing us. What might it look like to testify to this reality in a credible way?

We might start by reflecting upon two important affirmations of Pauline theology: (1) "if anyone is in Christ, there is a new creation:

everything old has passed away; see, everything has become new" (2 Cor 5:17); and (2) "there is no longer Jew or Greek, there is no longer slave or free, there is no longer male and female; for all of you are one in Christ Jesus" (Gal 3:28).

If the analysis here is anywhere near the mark, then a large portion of the American church—especially among white Christians—needs to recognize that our complicity in the strategic racism that has constructed mass incarceration has led us to contradict affirmation 2. Through our fears and sinful biases, we have permitted our votes, our actions, our ignorance, and our silence to be funneled toward a system where there *are* slave and free in our society, relabeled and justified by only the thinnest of legal veneers. Just as the American churches have to confess their role in the historic evils of slavery, convict leasing, and segregation that have egregiously and with historical longevity wounded not only our neighbors but our brothers and sisters in faith, so also we must confess our role in the justification, enactment, and perpetuation of the racialized criminal justice system. In other words, the first step in walking toward our renewal in Christ—affirmation 1—is through the honest and painful acknowledgment of our role in this evil.

Let us return briefly to the situation of racially segregated congregations that we began with. While, following Graham and King, there may be a prima facie sense in which this situation is obviously troubling in light of the Christian message of reconciliation (e.g., Eph 2:11–22), calls to change the situation are fraught with difficulty. On the side of white churches, the call for more diverse congregations often brings with it the tacit understanding that "we" want "them" to join "us," with the white "we" continuing to dominate the leadership, style, and direction of the congregation. And it is frequently the case that in their call for integration, white congregations easily remain blind to the history and structures of white racism, going back to slavery and continuing to mass incarceration, in creating the situation of segregated Christianity in the first place. On the side of black congregations, it is rather understandable that such calls for integration sometimes ring hollow and that the pressures of societal racism may make the prospect of a predominantly African American church home quite desirable.[19] In other words, we should recognize that the reasons for racially homogenous congregations often look strikingly different on different sides of the racial divide, but with white racism as the structural bedrock of it all.

"Racial reconciliation" can all too easily suggest two parties of different races with roughly equivalent wrong, or at least estrangement, on both sides. But that is not the full story here. Congregational segregation along racial lines is largely the result of policies, structures, attitudes, and the history of white racism, including the strategic racism that Haney López documents. Moreover, such structures and strategies of racial inequity and blame have through collusion with the systems and industries of mass incarceration created more empty pews, absent brothers and sisters, than there would otherwise be in black congregations across America. While reconciliation and integration may be the goal, they are not the first step; if anywhere, they stand at the end of a long and difficult road.

Prior to reconciliation, repentance is in order, especially for white Christianity in America.[20] In biblical terms, *repentance* (*metanoia*) is a changed mind that takes us in a new direction. It involves a transformed mindset that the Western theological traditions have associated with two simultaneous movements—*against* our sin and its soul-crushing and systemic effects and *toward* new attitudes and patterns of life. Simultaneously, as the Spirit works to kill our old sinful selves, the Spirit is at work to bring forth in us renewed, changed ways of being.

If mass incarceration is a church-dividing issue, one whose divisions fall both *along* racial lines and predominantly *within* Christian communities of color, then hopeful talk of unity can only begin with repentance. Only with confession and changed patterns of life will it be possible to prove to Christians and churches who have been harmed by the unjust systems of criminal control that we are genuinely interested in reconciliation and Christian unity. The blessing of forgiveness, should it be granted, can only be honored and received by means of a consistent and growing movement of Christian insistence on equitable prosecution, fair sentencing, just policing, and the costly meeting of needs of individuals and communities whose lives and future generations have been crippled by our society's disease of incarceration.

This call for justice on the policing and prosecution side of the system intersects with the notion of restorative justice that is currently in vogue in Christian ethics and in denominations across the ecumenical spectrum. For prisoners who *do* deserve to be in prison because of clear crimes for which they bear genuine responsibility and which have created real harm for society, *restorative* means tailoring the experience of punishment so that it facilitates change and prepares the person to return to society. From one angle, such an idea may seem impossibly naïve and idealistic, but from the angle of Christian hope, it may be an obligatory attitude to cultivate. But for those prisoners who—if we're being honest—really do *not* deserve to be incarcerated, those who have been the victims of political strategies rooted in the various forms of racism, restorative justice means getting them out. And getting them out in a truly restorative way, after months or years of their life have been taken from them and their families, will require providing recompense, assistance, and opportunities on the outside, to make a flourishing life possible.

Notes

1. Billy Graham, "Why Don't Our Churches Practice the Brotherhood They Preach?" *Reader's Digest* (August 1960): 53.

2. Martin Luther King Jr., *A Testament of Hope: The Essential Writings and Speeches of Martin Luther King, Jr.*, ed. James M. Washington (New York: HarperCollins, 1986), 107–8; also see 101, 270.

3. See Kevin D. Dougherty, "How Monochromatic Is Church Membership? Racial-Ethnic Diversity in Religious Community," *Sociology of Religion* 64 (2003): 65–85.

4. James Samuel Logan, *Good Punishment? Christian Moral Practice and U.S. Imprisonment* (Grand Rapids, MI: Eerdmans, 2008), 9.

5. The religious affiliation of inmates in American prisons has not been rigorously studied. A survey of prison chaplains conducted by the Pew Forum on Religion & Public Life produced the estimate that 66.3 percent of the prison population self-identify as some form of "Christian." See "Religion in Prisons: A 50-State Survey of Prison Chaplains," 48, accessed November 17, 2015, http://www.pewforum.org/files/2012/03/Religion-in-Prisons.pdf. Such an estimate, of course, does not speak to religious affiliation upon entering prison.

6. While white men have a 1 in 17 likelihood of being incarcerated, black men have a 1 in 3 and Latino men a 1 in 6 likelihood. Sixty percent of prisoners are people of color. See the helpful summary of recent statistics from The Sentencing Project: "Trends in U.S. Corrections," 5, accessed

September 10, 2015, http://sentencingproject.org/doc/publications/inc
_Trends_in_Corrections_Fact_sheet.pdf.

7. For example, reflecting on his experience as a soldier, C. S. Lewis famously observed (with a rather unbecoming glibness): "I have often thought to myself how it would have been if, when I served in the First World War, I and some young German had killed each other simultaneously and found ourselves together a moment after death. I cannot imagine that either of us would have felt any resentment or even any embarrassment. I think we might have laughed over it." C. S. Lewis, *Mere Christianity*, rev. ed. (New York: Collier, 1960), 107.

8. On this point I am indebted to a sermon by Dr. Randy Gabrielse.

9. Ian Haney López, *Dog Whistle Politics: How Coded Racial Appeals Have Reinvented Racism and Wrecked the Middle Class* (New York: Oxford University Press, 2014).

10. Ibid., 41–48.

11. Ibid., 49.

12. Ibid., 50.

13. Ibid.

14. Ibid., 51.

15. Michelle Alexander, *The New Jim Crow: Mass Incarceration in the Age of Colorblindness*, rev. ed. (New York: New Press, 2012), 187–90.

16. Haney López, *Dog Whistle Politics*, 52.

17. Alexander, *New Jim Crow*, 217–19.

18. The Episcopal Church, *The Book of Common Prayer* (New York: Church Publishing, 1979), 79, 41–42.

19. That said, we should recognize that African American churches that pride themselves on their black identity generally strive to be inviting to visitors and new members, whatever their race. A horrific yet impressive example is Emanuel African Methodist Episcopal Church in Charleston, South Carolina, where on June 17, 2015, fourteen members of a Bible study opened their doors and hearts to the (white) stranger who entered their midst, unaware of his murderous intentions.

20. See Matthew D. Lundberg, "Bitter History on the Journey of Mission," in *Unity in Mission: Theological Reflections on the Pilgrimage of Mission*, ed. Mitzi J. Budde and Don Thorsen, Faith & Order Commission Theological Series (Mahwah, NJ: Paulist Press, 2013), 153–71.

17

COMMON MORAL GROUND
Can Ethics Be Church Uniting?

Mitzi J. Budde

Bilateral and multilateral theological dialogues made great advances in the twentieth-century ecumenical movement, but the dialogue process has been challenged and at times stymied by differences in Christian stances on specific ethical questions, for example, same-sex marriage and ordination, abortion, genetic engineering, and just war/peacemaking. Now, some of the dialogues are discovering common ground on the principles of moral decision-making and witness. Episcopal priest Jared Cramer has written, "A careful analysis of the new polarities and streams arising across denominational lines, streams that are already present in the pews if not recognized by the leadership of communions, could yield remarkable fruit for a new unity that seems to be breaking out among Christians."[1] The present essay seeks to explore the theological and practical dimensions of this outbreak of new unity through the lens of the moral issues surrounding mass incarceration and human trafficking. It will articulate how the churches in dialogue are addressing ethical issues, advocacy, and action; identify eight challenges to this work; and posit six characteristics of morally serious ecumenical communities, with the goal of encouraging the churches to aspire to be these kinds of communities.

A different version of this essay was previously published as "Lived Witness," *Journal of Ecumenical Studies* 50, no. 3 (Summer 2015): 391–416. It has been rewritten and reprinted with permission.

DIALOGUES ON ETHICAL ISSUES

Many ecumenical dialogues have sought to bring together the doctrine of the church and the nature of the moral life in Christ. In a paper for the North American Academy of Ecumenists presented in Washington, DC, in 2009, Michael Root provided a comprehensive survey and analysis of how various ecumenical dialogues have addressed issues related to ethics. He found the ecumenical literature on ethics to be extensive, compiling a list of all the dialogues that have addressed ethical matters in any way.[2] One of the most significant is the World Council of Churches' study on Ecclesiology and Ethics (1992–96) that resulted in three reports, all issued on January 1, 1997: *Costly Unity*,[3] *Costly Commitment*,[4] and *Costly Obedience*.[5] *Costly Commitment* asserts that ethics is part of the church's essential identity, its *esse*,[6] and *Costly Obedience* defines this more fully: "The church as intrinsically a 'moral community'…not only *has* an ethic but *is* an ethical reality in itself."[7] It is "a community 'formed' as the gospel 'resonates' across the divisions of confession, space and time, a community whose flourishing koinonia is marked both by its growing agreement in matters of faith and church life, and by its common ethical commitments."[8] These three World Council of Churches (WCC) reports provided vital ecclesiological grounding for the ensuing bilateral work on moral concerns.

At its best, ecumenical work for moral action and advocacy bridges the traditional division between Life and Work (social action and advocacy) ecumenism and Faith and Order (formal theological dialogue) ecumenism, becoming a both/and proposition rather than the either/or paradigm it has often been. Perhaps this historic division in the ecumenical movement can be overcome by engaging in mission together for the sake of the world and for the good of humanity. Bearing a unified witness to the gospel can reinforce and strengthen efforts for justice, peace, and the welfare of all.

The relationship between Christian unity on theology and ethics can be seen in the 2013 WCC convergence document on ecclesiology, *The Church: Towards a Common Vision* (*TCTCV*). It includes a chapter on "The Church: In and for the World,"[9] which draws together doctrine and ethics, faith and order, and life and work. *TCTCV* asserts that "discipleship demands moral commitment" and upholds the theological basis for united action on moral matters. *TCTCV* encourages the churches to continue to dialogue on specific divisive moral questions, as well as the differing perspectives on whether these moral matters are church-dividing. The document also encourages the churches to work together for a just social order, to advocate peace; to defend human dignity; to seek the transformation of unjust societal structures; to care for creation; to care for the poor, needy, and marginalized; and "to serve God in the ministry of reconciling those divided by hatred or estrangement," in solidarity with all of God's people.[10]

Shared community in Christ involves "unity in faith, unity in sacramental life, and unity in service" at "two altars: one in the Church and the other among the poor, the suffering and those in distress," *TCTCV* asserts.[11] This requires confrontation of the sinfulness of the fallen human condition and the broken structures of society. As Arleon Kelley has written in his in-depth study of the history of local ecumenism in the United States, *A Tapestry of Justice, Service, and Unity*: "The sin that is dealt with most often in the ecumenical context is not personal, but rather the evil that is imbedded in institutional inertia and complex systems....The future will require sophisticated understandings of the nature of evil by institutions whose mission is to transform that evil into goodness. Local ecumenism is in position to be a part of this transformation."[12] This transformation is what the lived witness of the church seeks to address theologically, ecclesiologically, and receptively. This is the sort of transformation that is needed in mass incarceration situations. In her book *The New Jim Crow*, Michelle Alexander calls for the transformation of the racial caste system in the United States, seeking "to cultivate an ethic of genuine care, compassion, and concern for every human being—of every class, race, and nationality—within our nation's borders."[13]

Of the bilateral ecumenical dialogues that have attempted to address moral and ethical issues, the Anglican-Roman Catholic dialogue has been preeminent in this field ever since the international Anglican-Roman Catholic dialogue statement *Life in Christ: Morals, Communion, and the Church* was released in 1994.[14] The 2014 U.S. Anglican-Roman Catholic statement, *Ecclesiology and Moral Discernment* (*EMD*),[15] builds upon the differentiated-consensus approach of *Life in Christ*. It analyzes the differences between the two traditions in moral decision-making and moral teaching, identifies basic agreement in core moral values, and then assesses how those general moral values play out moral discernment on the issues of immigration and same-sex marriage. *EMD*'s mandate is "to address questions of ethics and the Christian life in the context of ecclesiology,"[16] and the document asserts that contextual theological agreements on moral principles (how we approach ethical decision-making) can be achieved even when disagreement persists on the content or application of those principles to a specific moral question (such as same-sex marriage). *Ecclesiology and Moral Discernment* has identified a way to move forward ecumenically and collegially. Agreement on moral matters does not need to be all-or-nothing to advance ecumenically. Ecumenically, we can uphold the centrality of shared moral witness, moral decision-making, and moral formation, even while continuing to work nimbly on the specific moral and ethical questions that challenge our world and even our theological relationships as churches.

The Church: Towards a Common Vision asserts, "It is on the basis of faith and grace that moral engagement and common action are possible and should be affirmed as intrinsic to the life and being of the Church....As churches engage in mutual questioning and affirmation [on ethical decisions], they give expression to what they share in Christ."[17] This, then, impels the ecumenical community to come together in a particular place to make a community that is more just, to work in solidarity against injustice and for racial reconciliation.

MASS INCARCERATION AND HUMAN TRAFFICKING—MORAL WITNESS AND ADVOCACY TOGETHER

Mass incarceration and human trafficking are two areas in which the Christian community can work together with a united voice for moral witness and advocacy. Michelle Alexander points out that "the term *mass incarceration* refers not only to the criminal justice system but also to the larger web of laws, rules, policies, and customs that control those labeled criminals both in and out of prison....Like Jim Crow (and slavery), mass incarceration operates

271

as a tightly networked system of laws, policies, customs, and institutions that operate collectively to ensure the subordinate status of a group defined largely by race."[18] A June 20, 2015, article in *The Economist* provided compelling statistics on the extent of the problem of mass incarceration: the United States has more than 2.3 million people in prison, "including 1.6m in state and federal prisons and over 700,000 in local jails and immigration pens.... At any one time, one American adult in 35 is in prison, on parole, or on probation. A third of African American men can expect to be locked up at some point."[19] Of the 2.3 million incarcerated, an estimated 400,000 have some form of significant mental illness. Prison may be "the largest mental health facility in the country."[20] For-profit prisons earn $3.3 billion annually, usually with contracts that require a 90 percent or above occupancy rate. "The nation is, in effect, commoditizing human bodies for an industry in militant pursuit of profit....The influence of private prisons creates a system that trades money for human freedom, often at the expense of the nation's most vulnerable populations: children, immigrants and the poor."[21] Writing in *Christian Century*, John Buchanan says, "The system is both a moral failure and a fiscal disaster."[22]

The National Council of Churches of Christ, USA (NCCC), Christian Churches Together (CCT), and the U.S. Conference of Catholic Bishops (USCCB) are working individually and collaboratively to address this issue of mass incarceration. This moral issue encompasses questions around social structures, social justice, human dignity, racial equality, immigration, and class, as well as the needs of individuals who are caught up in the American prison system. "The redeeming power of the cross needs to find deeper, and more effective, expression, in which the realities of human wickedness and guilt, on the side of both the offender *and* the judiciary, are creatively addressed."[23]

The USCCB was an early leader in the work for mass incarceration justice, with the statement, "Responsibility, Rehabilitation, and Restoration: A Catholic Perspective on Crime and Criminal Justice," in 2000 and a position paper, "Criminal and Restorative Justice and Sentencing Reform," in 2016. The NCCC has taken a newly integrative approach toward this complex topic, bringing together the work of all its convening tables to address various facets of mass incarceration. Each convening table seeks to use the five justice lenses of race, gender, ability, economics, and age in this work. Within the Theological Dialogue and Matters of Faith and Order Convening Table, three study groups spent over two years (2013–16) studying mass incarceration justice: a biblical foundations group; a study group on "How Theology Informs Justice," which analyzed what the churches' theological presuppositions are when it comes to how we view those who are incarcerated and addressing theologically themes of violence, marginalized peoples, and justice issues; and a study group on "How Justice Informs Theology," which addressed justice as a practical theological concept lived out in the world. The Faith and Order Convening Table also contributed a workshop on the theological foundations for the justice work on mass incarceration as part of the Ecumenical Advocacy Days event, "Breaking the Chains: Mass Incarceration and Systems of Exploitation," April 17–20, 2015, in Washington, DC. Another theological workshop, "Exploring the Theological Basis for Lifting the Voices of the Marginalized," was offered for the 2016 Ecumenical Advocacy Days event, "Lift Every Voice! Racism, Class and Power." The papers of this book are products of these three years of collaborative ecumenical work from the NCCC.

For its own part, Christian Churches Together in the U.S.A. has also encouraged awareness and education on the issues of mass incarceration. In October 2014, it issued a set of "Principles on Mass Incarceration," including the shared humanity of all people made in the image of God, the racial and economic dimensions of mass incarceration, the need for systemic change to provide both safety to the community and restoration for violent offenders, and the call for churches to work collaboratively in this effort to seek healing and stop mass incarceration.[24]

In short, the reality of mass incarceration in the United States has become a unifying moral issue for creative, new, multilateral, ecumenical approaches to this issue in American society. Through their ecumenical commitments, the churches have become convinced that they have a voice, a role, and a calling to work together to speak prophetically against unjust societal structures and to advocate for justice and reconciliation in the U.S. penal system. Antonios Kireopoulos stated, "Herein lie the twin aims of ecumenism made real: to provide a common witness to justice in everyday contexts of injustice even as we seek unity to proclaim the Gospel of reconciliation in all its fullness."[25] Together, the ecumenical community is incarnating the love of Christ and taking concrete actions to achieve justice for society, offenders, victims, families, and all others affected by mass incarceration.

In terms of human trafficking, however, the need for united Christian witness and advocacy is great. The Global Slavery Index asserts that "an estimated 45.8 million men, women and children around the world are today trapped in modern slavery, 20% more than previously estimated, whether through human trafficking, forced labour, debt bondage, forced or servile marriage, or commercial sexual exploitation."[26] Joint moral work against human trafficking and modern slavery has given Anglican-Roman Catholic relations a renewed vitality and a new vision. Despite increased tensions in the two churches' relationship due to differences in teaching on sexual ethics and the ordination of women, a partnership called the Global Freedom Network has been forged by Pope Francis and the Archbishop of Canterbury, Justin Welby. Inaugurated in March 2014, this joint initiative was created to enable Anglicans and Roman Catholics to work together to combat modern human trafficking, trade in migrants and prostitutes, human exploitation, and modern slavery. The Global Freedom Network seeks to persuade fifty multinational companies to ensure that by 2020 no one in their supply lines is enslaved, to gain endorsement of the campaign by 162 countries, and to convince the Group of Twenty to adopt an antislavery initiative.[27]

When the pope and the archbishop met in June 2014, the pope described the renewed relationship as one of "prayer, peace and poverty" and said to Welby, "We must walk together."[28] Francis selected this moral issue as his emphasis for the World Day of Peace, January 1, 2015, with the theme, "Slaves no more, but brothers and sisters," calling slavery "a fatal running sore on the flesh of Christ!"[29] This movement against trafficking has been called "the defining civil rights struggle of our time."[30] This Roman Catholic-Anglican ecumenical initiative has now expanded to an international, interreligious accord with world religious leaders who signed a historic "Joint Declaration of Religious Leaders against Modern Slavery"[31] on December 2, 2014. Hindu, Buddhist, Muslim, and Jewish leaders joined Francis, Welby, and Emmanuel, Metropolitan of France (on behalf of the Orthodox Ecumenical Patriarch Bartholomew), in signing the statement of common intention to seek spiritual and social action to eliminate human slavery.

Movements such as these are challenging the churches to work collaboratively to identify and address such issues in local communities. The Archbishop of Canterbury has called upon all churches to be "at the forefront of this new abolitionist movement" and to observe the United Nations' Day against Trafficking in Persons. He declared October 19 Freedom Sunday: "a day of worship, prayer and action on human trafficking…[to] join together to raise awareness of the crime of human trafficking and show the world our compassion for the men, women and children who are trafficked and exploited."[32] According to the website Stop the Traffik, more than twenty denominations and faith-based groups have collaborated in the development of Freedom Sunday resources.[33] Christians, churches, and parishes now need to put these resources to use. This ecumenical and interreligious work against human trafficking and slavery is both global and local.

CHALLENGES TO THE WORK OF ECUMENICAL DIALOGUE ON MORAL MATTERS

Citing these positive examples of collaborative ecumenical work on moral matters is not intended to ignore the deep divisions between the churches on specific ethical stances. As Kelley writes,

> Over the past few decades healing toward unity has been taking place among the churches in many communities across America. Because of the work of the bilateral and the multilateral relationships developed in ecumenical bodies,…many churches developed covenantal relationships, only to see the denominations and their local churches re-denominate, or re-fragment, around views about sexual orientation, political ideology, theology, race, or culture, but in the end, mostly about power and who should be in and who is to be excluded.[34]

In short, there are real and urgent challenges to this work of ecumenical dialogue on moral matters. Let us explore eight of these challenges: methodology, will, goal, the changing nature of the issues, the weight of moral differences, new issues that arise, time sensitivity, and shifting alliances between and among church bodies.

Methodology: The methodology presented in *Life in Christ* (and repeated in *Ecclesiology and Moral Discernment*) moves from shared commitment on general common principles to acknowledgment of continuing disagreement on specific moral decisions. Michael Root raises the question of the weight or priority given to a specific moral issue; for example, must churches agree on the centrality of a particular moral issue, such as peace vis-à-vis the historic peace churches, and what happens when there is "an asymmetrical evaluation of the ethical difference?"[35] He asserts that finding shared commitment on general moral principles is not enough, and that a differentiated consensus on a specific moral issue must include "a variety of elements: basic values and specific rules, comprehensive visions and concrete practices."[36] Clearly the questions around how much unity is sufficient in the practice of specific ethical issues will continue to be a methodological challenge for these dialogues. And behind the methodological challenge is the deeper theological question of what is the unity to which Christ calls us.

Will: It is far easier for the churches that find themselves on opposite sides on a significantly divisive moral issue to condemn each other than to stay in dialogue together. To seek dialogue is to be open to the theological thinking of the other and, at least theoretically, to be open to having one's own approach changed or varied by the encounter. Some Christians and churches do not want to agree or find common ground with those who differ in moral judgments. There is often reluctance, or even overt hostility, to the perceived agenda of ecumenism. It is far easier to reject the other as immoral, too liberal, or too conservative—that is, wrong— than to seek out areas of consensus. In his chapter in this volume, "The Problem of Empty Pews: Mass Incarceration as a Church-Dividing Issue," Matthew D. Lundberg thoughtfully describes the ways that predominantly white churches have a different will and perspective on mass incarceration in comparison to predominantly black churches.

Goal: Churches differ on their perception of the goal of ecumenical dialogue on moral/ethical matters. Episcopal ethicist Timothy F.

Sedgwick titled the first chapter of *Sex, Moral Teaching, and the Unity of the Church* "It's Not about Who's Right." Therein, he argued eloquently that the question, "Who's right?" is the wrong question, while "How should we teach and why?" is the more foundational question.[37] However, for many Christians and churches, the debate over "who's right?" remains the central dividing question, and dialogue about how we should teach is, for them, a derivative, second-level question. Questions around the nature of moral truth will persist.

The changing nature of the issues: Ethical disputes are usually around flash points of controversy in society and are multivalent in nature. Look at how frequently and quickly cultural norms of acceptance in American society have shifted around the question of gay marriage. It is difficult for serious ethical thinking to keep up with and respond to changing societal mores within an individual church body, much less in ecumenical dialogues among the churches. A 2016 *Washington Post* blog points to the slight decline in the number of people under criminal justice supervision as "evidence that mass incarceration continues to unwind in the United States,"[38] an assertion that most in the field would strenuously dispute.

The weight of moral differences: Denominations persist in their distinctive approaches to moral teaching and moral decision-making regarding the specific questions around what differences in morality can be tolerated and the weight given to the moral discernment of the conscience of the individual believer. Some denominations consider agreement on moral matters to be definitive for group affiliation; others allow or tolerate a wider range of individual expression in moral matters. These differences in the assessment of the significance of moral decisions for denominational affiliation and ecumenical accord add another layer of complexity beyond the presenting moral issue.

New issues that arise: As individual denominations discern new paths that they believe to be faithful to the gospel, their ecumenical dialogue partners may find these new paths to be new obstacles in the relationship between the churches. *EMD* cites some specific examples of this between Anglicans and Roman Catholics: "the ordination of persons living in openly acknowledged same-sex relationships, as well as the blessing of such relationships, and other persisting problems of moral theology, including questions about abortion, divorce and remarriage, and contraception."[39] For many predominately white churches, the issues around mass incarceration and human trafficking are awakening issues that have not long been on their ethical or social justice agendas. The assertion that mass incarceration is a new form of systemic societal racial control over black bodies, as persuasively argued by Michelle Alexander in her seminal book *The New Jim Crow*, is a new and challenging perspective for many white Christians and churches.

Time-sensitivity: Hot moral issues in society demand a kind of nimbleness from the churches if a response is going to be timely and relevant. This is directly in tension with the traditional ecumenical dialogue process, which has the churches working together to agree upon a topic for study, then each church respectively appoints specialists to the dialogue team, which then meets once or twice a year to present papers on the topic in question and work toward an agreed statement. This careful and lengthy process is often not congruent with the volatile nature of moral matters, yet a rushed process is often not conducive to thoughtful, theologically grounded ecumenical work. For ethical issues that resist short-term solutions, such as mass incarceration and human trafficking, churches and ecumenical organizations must determine how long to spend working on specific theological aspects of the issue, how they might effect change, and when their work has been able to accomplish some achievable, measurable outcome. Is it possible to make a substantial contribution on such immense, intractable, and ever-changing issues of morality and social justice?

Shifting alliances between and among church bodies: Church bodies that are utterly at odds with one another on a specific moral question may subsequently find themselves in profound theological accord on a different moral matter. For example, other church bodies filed friends of the court briefs on behalf of the Episcopal Church in its recent property lawsuits with congregations that have left the denomination over the issue of allowing practicing, same-gender-loving persons to serve as clergy and bishops. *Amici curiae* briefs were filed by institutions and officers of the United Methodist Church, the African Methodist Episcopal Church, the African Methodist Episcopal Zion Church, the Worldwide Church of God, the PCUSA, the Seventh-day Adventists, the ELCA's Metropolitan Washington, DC, Synod and Virginia Synod, and the

Virlina District Board of the Church of the Brethren. Most of these churches would disagree with the Episcopal Church on its moral teaching on ordaining practicing, same-gender-loving persons, but they supported the national church's moral and legal claim to the congregations' properties.

MORALLY SERIOUS ECUMENICAL COMMUNITIES

In view of these difficult challenges, the question presents itself of what kinds of church communities will be up to the task of taking on tough issues like mass incarceration and human trafficking in concert with one another? In his book *Do Morals Matter? A Guide to Contemporary Religious Ethics*, theologian Ian Markham proposed the concept of the "morally serious person," referred to as an "MSP" throughout the book: "This is a person who takes ethical discourse seriously and strives to live in a positive and constructive way….[and is] motivated by the quest for a position that is life enhancing and committed to the care of others."[40] Markham described seven features of an MSP as "(1) responsible citizenship, (2) intolerance toward discrimination, (3) obligation to be empirically informed, (4) disciplined reflection on the cultivation of virtue, (5) consciousness of our sociological conditioning, (6) an ordered interior life, and (7) commitment to moral conversation."[41]

Adapting this model and drawing upon the serious theological work of the Anglican-Roman Catholic ecumenical statements discussed above, *Life in Christ* and *Ecclesiology and Moral Discernment*, I would suggest that there are also characteristics of morally serious ecumenical communities that will contribute to forward progress on ecumenical moral decision-making, witness, and formation. These characteristics will bridge the unhelpful faith and order/life and work divide of twentieth-century ecumenism and bring them together into coordinated, collaborative dialogue, action, and advocacy.

Morally serious ecumenical communities are not communities that have it all figured out. In speaking about individual churches, Paul Avis astutely observed,

A moral community is not the same as a virtuous community. To call a certain body "a moral community" does not mean that it is a "highly moral" community, a paragon, a shining example of the virtues that should pertain between the members. A moral community is a body of people that is held together and motivated by a shared recognition of certain moral imperatives—the fabric of the community consists partly of moral issues and obligations held in common—but they may not all be good and right ones, and they will be argued over within that community. A moral community may be fraught with moral tensions.[42]

I would assert that Avis's observation is also true of morally serious ecumenical communities—that these are communities that seek together to understand moral matters more deeply and fully by engaging the moral tensions of theological dialogue and living out their faith together, despite those tensions, in shared common action.

Ecumenism at its best in the twenty-first century is characterized by unity in worship (*latreia*), proclamation (*kerygma*), community (*koinonia*), witness (*martyria*), and service (*diakonia*).[43] Morally serious ecumenical communities live out this unity in concrete ways that make unity a visible, shared witness. Specifically, I propose that the six characteristics of morally serious ecumenical communities are the following: the mutual recognition of baptism in the triune God; discerning the call to common mission; openness to the work of the Spirit, changing minds and hearts in *koinonia*/community; joint work for justice and service to those in need; building upon past ecumenical achievements to move toward new agreements; and prayer for Christian unity.

A. Mutual Recognition of Baptism in the Triune God

Recognition of the baptism of other churches in the triune God is the foundation for ecumenical life. Being clothed in Christ in baptism means to be united in "one Lord, one faith, one baptism" (Eph 4:5) and thus with Christ's church in all its expressions, across divisions and across denominations. "When baptismal unity is realized in one holy, catholic, apostolic Church, a genuine Christian witness can be made to the healing and reconciling love of God."[44] Christian baptism in the name of the Trinity is the sacrament of unity, grounding Christian life in Jesus Christ and in the community of faith that is the church catholic.[45]

The U.S. Conference of Catholic Bishops and four Reformed churches (the Christian Reformed Church in North America, the Presbyterian Church [USA], the Reformed Church in America, and the United Church of Christ) in 2010 completed an ecumenical dialogue on baptism and signed an agreed statement mutually recognizing one another's baptism when conducted with water and the scriptural trinitarian formula.[46] For most churches, the goal of the ecumenical movement—full communion—derives from mutual recognition of baptism. Full eucharistic sharing is founded upon exchangeability of membership and clergy and recognition of each other as true church. Mutual recognition of baptism is the foundation of ecumenical relations and can lead to shared catechesis and joint social advocacy.

I would assert that the claim of baptism on Christians is grounded in the understanding of every human individual as created in the image of God. There can be no "us" and "them" in Christ's eyes. Seeing every person through the eyes of Christ, as a brother or sister of worth and created in the image of God, should transform one's approach to every person who is incarcerated or trapped in modern slavery. This transformation should, in turn, transform the church's approach to the broader societal issues around mass incarceration and human trafficking and inspire Christians and churches to work for equal justice for individuals and for transformative justice within the penal system.

B. Discerning the Call to Common Mission Together in Christ

Baptism commissions Christians for a life of witness. Ecumenical agreements derive from the common mission that all Christians share with the communion of saints and with all faithful Christians, ordained and lay. Through a united witness made visible to the world, the Spirit continues to heal the breaches in the church. The churches have found much common ground, for example, in a shared commitment to ecological justice, led and inspired by Ecumenical Patriarch Bartholomew I, often called the "Green Patriarch" for his passionate advocacy for the environment as a Christian and ecumenical vocation. Another example might be how Pacific Lutheran Seminary and Church Divinity School of the Pacific (Episcopal) share a joint appointment of a professor of Christian Ethics, a position currently held by Dr. Cynthia Moe-Lobeda, an expert in globalization and moral agency around issues of race, gender, and culture.

The work of the churches together on these pressing moral issues of our day can spur political and governmental action. On July 31, 2016, the new prime minister of the United Kingdom, Theresa May, pledged that the eradication of human trafficking would be an urgent focus of her government. She indicated that, "as Prime Minister, I am setting up the first ever government task force on modern slavery," and asserted that "this is the great human rights issue of our time, and as Prime Minister I am determined that we will make it a national and international mission to rid our world of this barbaric evil."[47] This breakthrough is consistent with the Global Freedom Network's international ecumenical and interfaith Joint Declaration of Religious Leaders against Modern Slavery, signed by leaders of the world religions in December 2014.

C. Openness to the Work of the Spirit, Changing Minds and Hearts in *Koinonia*/Community

Christians and churches find ecumenical dialogue and accord only through recognition that their unity with each other is based on their unity in the triune God. Christian community (*koinonia*) is grounded in Christ. The WCC convergence document, *The Church: Towards a Common Vision*, makes the theology of *koinonia* central to the churches' ecumenical ecclesiology: "In the Church, through the Holy Spirit, believers are united with Jesus Christ and thereby share a living relationship with the Father, who speaks to them and calls forth their trustful response. The biblical notion of *koinonia* has become central in the ecumenical quest for a common understanding of the life and unity of the Church."[48] *TCTCV* goes on to explore how our participation as Christians in the life of the

Trinity leads believers to serve and witness together as an expression of Christ's call to go forth into the world.

Through the guidance of the Holy Spirit, Christ challenges Christians and churches to learn how to live in the presence of sharp disagreements on deeply important matters and to abide together in the face of serious disagreement—whether those disagreements center on theology, or on ethical issues such as same-sex marriage or differing views of racism. The Christian call is to seek *koinonia*/communion with the whole people of God, including the incarcerated, perpetrators of crime, police, judges, and victims of crime or human trafficking. Even those who perpetuate modern slavery are individuals made in the image of God, called by the Spirit to repentance, redemption, reconciliation, and transformed lives. In his book *The Executed God: The Way of the Cross in Lock-Down America*, Mark Lewis Taylor calls upon "Jesus-followers" to "create communities of action that nurture tactical resilience for transforming social and political life in opposition to Lockdown America."[49] Taylor calls for the "decarcerating of the U.S.A.," by which he means "the process of ceasing to organize society for the confining of bodies—in jails, prisons or other detention facilities—as a mode of punishment or social control." He admits that this would require "comprehensive social and political change."[50] The Christian call is the call to the churches to be prayerfully discerning change agents in Christ.

D. Joint Work for Justice and Service to Those in Need

Following Christ's example and teaching, morally serious ecumenical communities will see Christ in one another and serve others in mutuality and love. They will "live in love, as Christ loved us and gave himself up for us, a fragrant offering and sacrifice to God" (Eph 5:2). In so doing, they will find ways to work together for the issues of justice in society, religious freedom, the human dignity of all persons, and the care of creation. Collaborative work to address the individual needs of the incarcerated, the enslaved, the oppressed, the persecuted, the marginalized, the poor, the sick, the hungry, and all who suffer in local communities is also a hallmark of morally serious ecumenical communities. At the national church level, bilateral dialogue partners work collaboratively through the structures provided by full-communion agreements to bear common witness on moral issues and to advocate for moral action. In the United States, for example, the Episcopal Church and the ELCA share a staff position in Washington, DC, a Legislative Representative for International Affairs, whose responsibilities include advocacy for both churches on federal policies and legislation and building shared advocacy coalitions.

Calling mass incarceration "the key civil rights struggle of our time," James Kilgore asserts that imprisonment has been used unethically and unjustly in American society. He writes, "Mass incarceration is actually one of this country's key strategies for addressing problems of poverty, inequality, unemployment, racial conflict, citizenship, sexuality, and gender, as well as crime."[51] Kilgore offers Christians and churches concrete ways to act for justice on this issue. He describes how the approaches of restorative justice and transformative justice can be effective agents for addressing the systemic social issues, while also advocating an unwavering focus on the needs of the individual caught in the social machine of mass incarceration.[52] Morally serious ecumenical communities could effectively educate themselves on this issue and equip themselves for action and advocacy together through an ecumenical study of Kilgore's book.

E. Building upon Past Achievements to Accomplish New Agreements

Morally serious ecumenical communities draw upon the accomplishments of the ecumenical movement to date in both Faith and Order and Life and Work in order to move toward new levels of agreement. Agreement for the future will entail theological insight, moral will, and commitment to action. The WCC convergence document, *TCTCV*, raises several specific questions for dialogue among the churches to move toward deeper convergence on moral matters, in "a spirit of mutual attentiveness and support," asking, "How might the churches, guided by the Spirit, discern together what it means today to understand and live in fidelity to the teaching and attitude of Jesus? How can the churches, as they engage together in this task of discernment, offer appropriate models of discourse and wise counsel to the societies in which they are called to serve?"[53] A notable model would be the Anglican-Roman Catholic international ecumenical dialogue, which has been stressed in recent years over ethical disagreement on the ordination of women and gays. Reinvigorated, perhaps, by their joint work on human trafficking, the two communions are now in direct dialogue about ethical discernment in the context of the church as communion.

F. Commitment to Prayer for Christian Unity—and for Justice

To participate in prayer for Christian unity is to participate in Christ's own prayer "that they may all be one" (John 17:21). The Most Rev. Sir David Moxon, the Archbishop of Canterbury's Representative to the Holy See and the Anglican co-chair of the Anglican-Roman Catholic International Commission (ARCIC) III, recently suggested, "Perhaps a gift of grace we can offer the world is the capacity to live with a measure of difference and yet hold each other in prayerful love."[54] Grounded in the common life in the gospel, Christians and churches are called to pray for each other as individuals, for each other's denominations, and for the united witness of the church catholic. The Samuel DeWitt Proctor Conference report, *Bearing Witness: A Nation in Chains*, challenges Christians and churches: "The places we sing, pray, teach, and preach about 'Amazing Grace' should be where people who have been affected by mass incarceration can find affirmation, not condemnation."[55] Grace and justice, prayer and moral witness are integrally linked for ecumenical Christians.

CONCLUSION

Ecumenists are demonstrating a way forward in these challenging ecumenical times for Christians and churches to work together in creative and collaborative ways to reveal life in Christ lived in social action, in moral decision-making, and in moral witness. The Samuel DeWitt Proctor Conference report, *Bearing Witness*, suggests five specific ways in which faith communities might advocate for fairness in the criminal justice system and make a difference in the lives of those caught in that system, recommending that churches (1) provide welcome and healing to those who have been incarcerated and their families; (2) be "models of safe and sacred spaces where formerly incarcerated persons can gather to lead and address the situations they confront, the causes and effects of choices they made, the organization of the criminal justice system and next steps of strategic action"; (3) advocate for "a more equitable and humane criminal justice system in the courts, in prisons and as related to post-release treatments and supports for rehabilitation and restorative justice"; (4) provide "literacy centers and mentoring programs" for children; and (5) "institutionalize life skills, jobs and entrepreneurial training programs for formerly incarcerated persons."[56] No church can do this alone; these suggestions are prime examples of ways in which churches could partner together to effect change and to witness to the gospel of Jesus Christ ecumenically. The kinds of churches that are morally serious in the way they approach these issues in an ecumenical context will need to reflect the six characteristics explained in the previous section.

Morally serious ecumenical communities work in tandem to reveal the deep unity given in Christ in gentleness and love to reflect in their lives and actions the wisdom of God that the world so desperately needs. In accord with James 3, they "show by [their] good life that [their] works are done with gentleness born of wisdom" (3:13). Ecumenists and ethicists continue to work at the reconciliation of ongoing moral and ethical disputes, while Christians and churches continue this work together because Christ is already there. I believe that our work together ecumenically on the pressing ethical questions of our time, such as human trafficking and racial justice, is a practice of ecumenical moral discernment that will empower fruitful theological dialogue on ethical matters. The Holy Spirit can make a way where there seems to be no way. "In the end we need ecumenical expressions of Church because the world needs to see what Christianity living in harmony looks like."[57] And Christians working together in harmony can effect change for good in this world, in response to the call of Christ, empowered by the Holy Spirit.

Ecumenically minded Christians and churches seek to engage the world faithfully, to bear witness to Christ, and to present a united voice and united effort to address oppression and injustice in society. Faith, hope, and love are one in action. Faith gives hope, which teaches us to love, revealing Christ's active presence, which is working through the Spirit on behalf of humanity. Whether that evil manifests itself as systemic injustice in the penal system, human trafficking, or religious persecution, the community of faith seeks to speak out with a united voice for just treatment, for safe haven, and for the dignity of every human being made in God's image.

Notes

1. Jared Cramer, "Choosing Death or Life: Reflections on 21st Century American Ecumenism in Light of the NCC's 2014 Christian Unity Gathering," *Care with the Cure of Souls Blog*, May 20, 2014, http://carewiththecure.blogspot.com/2014/05/choosing-death-or-life -reflections-on.html.

2. See Michael Root, "Ethics in Ecumenical Dialogues: A Survey and Analysis," *Journal of Ecumenical Studies* 45 (Summer 2010): 357–75.

3. Available at https://www.oikoumene.org/en/resources/docu ments/commissions/faith-and-order/vi-church-and-world/ecclesiology -and-ethics/costly-unity.

4. Available at https://www.oikoumene.org/en/resources/docu ments/commissions/faith-and-order/vi-church-and-world/ecclesiology -and-ethics/costly-commitment.

5. Available at https://www.oikoumene.org/en/resources/docu ments/commissions/faith-and-order/vi-church-and-world/ecclesiology -and-ethics/costly-obedience.

6. See Thomas F. Best and Martin Robra, eds., *Ecclesiology and Ethics: Ecumenical Ethical Engagement, Moral Formation, and the Nature of the Church* (Geneva: WCC Publications, 1997), 39, 51.

7. Ibid., 50, 2; emphases in original.

8. Ibid., xi.

9. World Council of Churches, *The Church: Towards a Common Vision*, Faith and Order Paper 214 (Geneva: World Council of Churches, 2013), nos. 58–66; hereafter, *TCTCV*.

10. Ibid., no. 66; see nos. 64–66.

11. Ibid., no. 67.

12. Arleon L. Kelley, "The Body of Christ and the Family of God: A Theological Reflection," in *A Tapestry of Justice, Service, and Unity: Local Ecumenism in the United States, 1950–2000*, ed. Arleon L. Kelley

(Tacoma, WA: National Association of Ecumenical and Interreligious Staff Press, 2004), 433.

13. Michelle Alexander, *The New Jim Crow: Mass Incarceration in the Age of Colorblindness*, rev. ed. (New York: The New Press, 2012), 18–19.

14. Available at http://www.vatican.va/roman_curia/pontifical _councils/chrstuni/angl-comm-docs/rc_pc_chrstuni_doc_19930906_life -in-christ_en.html.

15. The Anglican-Roman Catholic Theological Consultation in the U.S.A., *Ecclesiology and Moral Discernment: Seeking a Unified Moral Witness* (2014), available at http://www.usccb.org/beliefs-and-teachings/ ecumenical-and-interreligious/ecumenical/anglican/upload/arcusa-2014 -statement.pdf; hereafter, *EMD*.

16. Ibid., "Preface from the Co-Chairs."

17. *TCTCV*, nos. 61 and 62.

18. Alexander, *New Jim Crow*, 13.

19. "Jailhouse Nation: Justice in America," *The Economist*, June 20, 2015, http://www.economist.com/node/21654619.

20. John M. Buchanan, "Repenting for Our Prisons," *Christian Century* 132, no. 19 (September 16, 2015): 3.

21. Michael Cohen, "How For-Profit Prisons Have Become the Biggest Lobby No One Is Talking About," *The Washington Post*, April 28, 2015, https://www.washingtonpost.com/posteverything/wp/2015/ 04/28/how-for-profit-prisons-have-become-the-biggest-lobby-no-one-is -talking-about/.

22. Buchanan, "Repenting for our Prisons," 3.

23. Timothy Gorringe, *God's Just Vengeance: Crime, Violence, and the Rhetoric of Salvation* (Cambridge, UK, and New York: Cambridge University Press, 1996), 270; emphasis in original.

24. See Christian Churches Together in the U.S.A., "Principles on Mass Incarceration," available at http://christianchurchestogether.org/wp -content/uploads/2014/12/CCT-Principles-on-Mass-Incarceration.pdf.

25. See chap. 3 above.

26. "45.8 Million People Are Enslaved across the World," May 30, 2016, http://www.globalslaveryindex.org/45-8-million-people-are-enslaved -across-the-world/.

27. See Robert Pigott, "Archbishop and Pope Join Forces to Tackle People-Trafficking," BBC News, June 16, 2014, http://www.bbc.com/ news/uk-27861907?print=true.

28. "Address of Pope Francis to His Grace Justin Welby, Archbishop of Canterbury and His Entourage, Monday, 16 June 2014," available at

http://w2.vatican.va/content/francesco/en/speeches/2014/june/
documents/papa-francesco_20140616_arcivescovo-canterbury.html.

29. "Slavery to Be Theme of 2015 World Day of Peace," Vatican
Radio News, August 22, 2014, http://www.news.va/en/news/slavery-to
-be-theme-of-2015-world-day-of-peace.

30. Gordon Brown, "Good News: We Brought Back Some of Our
Girls. Do We Have as Much Courage as Them?" *The Guardian*, October
14, 2014, http://www.theguardian.com/commentisfree/2014/oct/14/news
-bring-back-our-girls-nigeria-gordon-brown.

31. Available at http://www.news.va/en/news/declaration-of-reli
gious-leaders-for-the-eradicati.

32. "Archbishop's Statement on the First UN Anti-Trafficking
Day," July 30, 2014, http://www.archbishopofcanterbury.org/articles
.php/5379/archbishops-statement-on-the-first-un-anti-trafficking-day.

33. See "Freedom Sunday: What's It All About?" http://www
.stopthetraffik.org/campaign/freedomsunday.

34. Kelley, "Body of Christ," 429–30.

35. Root, "Ethics in Ecumenical Dialogues," 366.

36. Ibid., 370.

37. Sedgwick, *Sex, Moral Teaching, and the Unity of the Church: A
Study of the Episcopal Church* (New York: Morehouse, 2014), 8.

38. Keith Humphreys, "Here's Another Sign the Era of Mass
Incarceration Is Slowly Coming to an End," The Washington Post
Wonkblog, January 1, 2016, https://www.washingtonpost.com/news/
wonk/wp/2016/01/01/the-era-of-mass-incarceration-is-unwinding/.

39. *EMD*, 9.

40. Ian S. Markham, *Do Morals Matter? A Guide to Contemporary
Religious Ethics* (Malden, MA: Blackwell, 2007), 2; emphasis in original.

41. Ibid., 182.

42. Paul Avis, *Reshaping Ecumenical Theology: The Church Made
Whole?* (London and New York: T&T Clark, 2010), 147.

43. See "Ecumenism in the 21st Century: Final Report of the Continuation Committee on Ecumenism in the 21st Century, Geneva, 2012,"
in *Ecumenical Visions for the 21st Century: A Reader for Theological Education*, ed. Mélisande Lorke and Dietrich Werner (Geneva: World Council
of Churches Publications, 2013), 380.

44. World Council of Churches, *Baptism, Eucharist, and Ministry*,
Faith and Order Paper 111 (Geneva: World Council of Churches, 1982),
no. 6.

45. For more on the ecumenical significance of the mutual recognition of baptism, see Mitzi J. Budde, "Baptism: Sacrament of Unity,
Sacrament of Mission," in *Unity in Mission: Theological Reflections on the*

Pilgrimage of Mission, ed. Mitzi J. Budde and Don Thorsen (New York: Paulist Press, 2013), 90–109.

46. See USCCB and Four Protestant Communities, "Common Agreement on Mutual Recognition of Baptism," *Origins* 40 (November 25, 2010): 390.

47. Theresa May, "Defeating Modern Slavery," *The Telegraph*, July 31, 2016, https://www.gov.uk/government/speeches/defeating-modern-slavery-theresa-may-article.

48. *TCTCV*, no. 13.

49. Mark Lewis Taylor, *The Executed God: The Way of the Cross in Lockdown America*, 2nd ed. (Minneapolis: Fortress Press, 2015), 322.

50. Ibid., 375.

51. James Kilgore, *Understanding Mass Incarceration: A People's Guide to the Key Civil Rights Struggle of our Time* (New York: The New Press, 2015), 1.

52. Ibid., see chap. 13, "Changing the Mind-Set," 199–217.

53. *TCTCV*, no. 63, italicized section.

54. David Moxon, "Prayer, Poverty, and Peace," *The Director's Blog*, June 23, 2014, The Anglican Centre in Rome, June 22, 2014; no longer available online.

55. Samuel DeWitt Proctor Conference, *Bearing Witness: A Nation in Chains: Findings from Nine Statewide Justice Commission Hearings on Mass Incarceration* (Chicago: Samuel DeWitt Proctor Conference, Inc., 2014), 45.

56. Ibid., 32.

57. Kelley, "Body of Christ," 439.

V EXPERIENTIAL AND PRACTICAL PERSPECTIVES

18

THE VOICES OF TOO MANY PEOPLE ARE SILENCED

Kenneth Q. James

It was my privilege to be invited to share on this panel. Upon receiving the invitation, naturally I was excited at the opportunity. I was even more ecstatic and further motivated when I read the opening paragraph of the letter of invitation: "In a major U.S. election year when lives, votes and the global economy are at stake, followers of Christ ask, 'Who has a voice?' The response is, 'Everyone!' But in our neighborhoods, cities, and around the world, the voices of too many people are silenced."

These words caught my notice: "the voices of too many people are silenced." I wondered why. We should engage this idea. Discuss it. Ask hard questions about it.

To begin, I must pay homage to the historical significance of the day on which this conversation took place. April 15, 2016, as all serious baseball fans and anyone interested in the significance of the history of the day would know, was the sixty-ninth anniversary of the day that Jackie Robinson broke the color barrier in Major League Baseball. That makes this day special not only for fans of "America's pastime," but also for those who have watched the progress of our nation. There is little doubt that the entry of Jackie Robinson into the ranks of baseball in 1947 is one of the seminal events in our nation's history. Some have even suggested this event may have been the beginning of the modern civil rights movement.

I mention the beginning of the career of Jackie Robinson here because my deep love of baseball combined with my devotion to

---

A version of this paper was delivered as part of a panel presentation at Ecumenical Advocacy Days on April 15, 2016.

politics will shape this essay. The issue or topic of mass incarceration is a moral and political issue, and it seems that the forthright courage of a man like Jackie Robinson can be a benchmark by which we chart our course. These factors (my love of baseball and politics) qualify me, I suppose, to being something of a "political junkie." I follow politics almost as closely as I follow baseball and the New York Mets. You may not understand how much that means. To put my devotion for politics into context, it is a statement of my profound and serious interest in politics to say that I follow politics as closely as I do baseball and the Mets. I have been a lifelong Mets fan, and I have visited and seen a game in every stadium in major league baseball. I think that fact qualifies me as a "serious baseball fan." In many ways, we find that life intersects. It does for me here. I recognize that some people prefer to eliminate sports from politics or religion, but I guess I don't easily see such clear divisions or separation, perhaps because I believe there is a special responsibility (fair or not) placed upon any athlete or celebrity who is representative for a marginalized group to not accept such otherwise facile segmentation.

But lately my interest in following politics has been severely challenged. I have listened to one candidate for president engage in some disgraceful rhetoric that refers to Mexicans as "drug dealers, criminals, and rapists" although he allows that some may be "good people."[1] Another candidate for the highest office in our nation once commented that what the United States Senate really needed was "100 more [senators] like Jesse Helms."[2] I am only hoping, though I cannot be sure, that the candidate must not have been aware how chilling a comment that is to hear by those who have suffered from the policies and efforts of the senator from North Carolina during his tenure of service. On another occasion, this candidate said that the #BlackLivesMatter movement was "literally suggesting and embracing and celebrating the murder of police officers."[3] Yet another candidate for president, during a recent town hall meeting, was asked about criminal justice reform. He decided to change the subject to comment about infant mortality, and offered the comment that "the minority community is going to have to have a better partnership with all of us to begin to solve that problem."[4] This comment is troubling for two reasons: (1) it seems to presume that infant mortality is of no concern to

the so-called "minority community"; and (2) the candidate con-
veniently ignored the fact that in the state where he is governor,
the funding of the main organization that addressed the problem
of infant mortality in his state was cut under his administration.
And on the other side of the political aisle, what pleasure we have
enjoyed watching the recent internecine bickering between two
candidates about who is "qualified" to be president.[5] All this just
about made my head spin.

Now I cannot say accurately or with certainty that any of
these factors have anything to do with why "the voices of too
many people are silenced," but for my part, this political season
has made this self-described "political junkie" want to check in to
rehab! That's why I am grateful for this opportunity for the kind
of serious engagement that can serve to refocus the conversation.
We need to redirect the conversation now to talk about the things
that really matter.

I recognize there is difficulty and tension when discussing
politics in any arena, and how this tension increases and becomes
even more problematic when combining the incendiary topic of
politics with the equally provocative theme of religion. So let me
be up front and honest by stating my premeditated intention. I am
going to make every effort to offend some readers. If I really do a
good job, maybe I will end up offending all readers. It is my calculated desire to cause more than a few of us to move in the direction
of outrage. I take this approach in the spirit of what I often find is
the tone of Older Testament prophets.

Yes, outrage. Why not? Outrage is surely what many people
felt when Dr. Jeremiah Wright, former pastor of Trinity United
Church of Christ in Chicago, in a video clip of a sermon that went
viral, proclaimed "God damn America."[6] His comment, or the
clips[7] most of us have seen (which, by the way, have been taken
wildly out of context because it was a part of a larger sermonic
point), dared to challenge the notion of so-called "American
exceptionalism" (a phrase freely tossed around in political discussions and on television and talk radio). The notion of America as
an "exceptional" nation in the political terms in which it is used is
arguably dubious and should not go unchallenged by Christians
if we hold to the claim that God loves all humankind. Reinhold
Niebuhr seems to raise doubts concerning such a premise:

295

For, from the later Puritans to the present day we have variously attributed American prosperity to our superior diligence, our greater skill or (more recently) to our more fervent devotion to the ideals of freedom....Any grateful acceptance of God's uncovenanted mercies is easily corrupted from gratitude to self-congratulation if it is believed that providence represents not the grace of a divine power, working without immediate regard for the virtues or defects of its recipients (as illustrated by the sun shining "upon the evil and the good and the rain descending upon the just and the unjust"); but rather it represents particular divine acts directly correlated to particular human and historical situations.[8]

So why not outrage? It is the feeling, certifiable or not, among many that "outrage" to some degree seems to be motivating a large swath of the electorate in 2016. So while this outrage is being expressed, what are people of faith to do—shall we just sit passively by, watching as the good creation intended by God's plan is ruined? This may well be the outcome if "the voices of too many people are silenced."

One example of why I know outrage is possible was witnessed by viewers and fans of the ESPN show *Mike and Mike*. On their show airing April 7, 2016,[9] sports commentator Bomani Jones wore a T-shirt intended as a parody of the uniform of the Cleveland major league baseball team. The shirt upset quite a few people. Instead of carrying the name "Indians" on the front, with a caricature of Native American culture showing a man with a feather on his head, the shirt Jones wore depicted a caricature of a white man with a dollar sign on his head and the word *Caucasians* emblazoned on the front. As you can imagine—can't you?—the social media universe and many of its commentators were absolutely beside themselves with infuriation.

Now I want to ask that we stop and think about this for a minute. Native Americans have been protesting for decades about how offensive the imagery of a so-called "Indian" is when used as a mascot, but the larger culture has generally dismissed and ignored their concerns. But let someone use that same idea in the imagery of a white person and it causes all kinds of disruption and trouble—

not to mention threats of physical harm or economic retaliation. It should not come as a surprise to anyone that more than a few persons called for the firing of Bomani Jones. The reason this kind of outrage occurs is because of how groups tend to view things through the comfortable lens of privilege. I had a member of the church I pastor (a white member, by the way), ask me, "Why do we have to say #BlackLivesMatter? Why can't we say 'All Lives Matter?'" I responded to her by sharing with her that there is currently a popular meme that to me best explains this current attitude of discomfort, if not outrage: "When you're accustomed to privilege, equality feels like oppression."

It is something to be examined in the depths of our hearts that we find it so uncomfortable to declare that black lives matter. Some people think it is unnecessary to say in the first place. It has been the defense of those who reject the mantra that no one has ever said otherwise. I'm guessing that depends on what you hear said and how you interpret the silence when nothing is said. In the din of words or the absence of them, it is left to those who are receiving the situation to determine its meaning.

The problem we must address is that in the main, we culturally have little to no sympathy for the daily "microaggressions"— those encounters described by Cory J. Sanders and Angela Yarber as "brief, everyday exchanges that send denigrating messages to certain individuals because of their group membership"[10]—that so many otherwise invisible persons in our world suffer. Sanders and Yarber also comment that "it is vital to note that microaggressions derive their power to injure largely from their invisibility to perpetrators."[11] Could it be that this is at the very least a contributing factor as to the reason "the voices of too many people are silenced?" Suffering people are marginalized by poverty, race, gender, and class. And often, these people are the persistent and unrelenting victims of police brutality, economic and class warfare, poverty, and discrimination of all kinds.

Like me, you may well have heard the same retort that I often hear when I attempt to discuss the issues of poverty, race, gender, class, police brutality, class warfare, and discrimination. Somehow, for some head-scratching reason, people think it helpful to compare tragic stories—"Your people/group are not the only ones who have suffered." In response to this now hackneyed rejoinder,

I have found the words of James Baldwin helpful: "People are continually pointing out to me the wretchedness of white people in order to console me for the wretchedness of blacks. But an itemized account of the American failure does not console me and it should not console anyone else."[12]

There are voices that are silent or have been silenced. Now it's time for the community of faith to speak up, to be prophetic, to raise our voices, to refuse to be silenced. But where are the voices of the "prophets"? Who speaks for the marginalized and ostracized among us? Howard Thurman wrote,

> To those who need profound succor and strength to enable them to live in the present with dignity and creativity, Christianity often has been sterile and of little avail. The conventional Christian word is muffled, confused, and vague. Too often the price exacted by society for security and respectability is that the Christian movement in its formal expression must be on the side of the strong against the weak. This is a matter of tremendous significance, for it reveals to what extent a religion that was born of a people acquainted with persecution and suffering has become the cornerstone of a civilization and of nations whose very position in modern life has too often been secured by a ruthless use of power applied to weak and defenseless people.[13]

How desperately we need the voices of prophets! Granted, it will be difficult to hear their message through the din about "making America great again" (really that is a new refrain on an old chorus). But the true prophet sees things differently—others brag about the "greatness" of a nation, and "the world is a proud place, full of beauty, but the prophets are scandalized, and rave as if the whole world were a slum."[14]

I wish to suggest two perspectives that I hope will motivate us to speak up and speak out, to let our voices be heard and not be silenced.

First, let us remember the words of the Older Testament Prophet Isaiah (Isa 61:1), and of Jesus (Luke 4:18): "*The Spirit of the Lord GOD is upon me, because the LORD has anointed me to bring good news to the poor; he has sent me to bind up the brokenhearted, to pro-claim liberty to the captives, and the opening of the prisons to them that are bound.*"[15] I offer here questions that I trust will guide our path forward as we raise our voices: How does "good news to the poor" sound? What do we who enjoy comparative well-being need to know or do in our attempts to "bind up the brokenhearted?" What is the message of "liberty" that those who are "captives" need and wait to hear? As we share this message, let us be aware that if we ask those who are currently in any kind of prison to simply exchange one type of prison for another, we have done them no service.

Sometimes we must admit that we are guilty of (or comfort-able with) "blaming the victim" for their current circumstance or sit-uation, be it crime, poverty, or unemployment. Even if the condition of those we encounter is of their own making, that does not alleviate the responsibility of those of us who are called to do the Lord's work in the spirit of Isaiah and Jesus to set them free. This is why mass incarceration must be seen as tragic and antithetical to our message of hope and grace. We operate in the futile attempt or assumption that warehousing human beings will make us safe. This is a myth that serves no one well, and is not working; mass incarceration is a scourge on the testimony of those who advocate for liberty and a blight on the witness of those who claim to be God-fearing people.

The voices of too many people are silenced. But we, people of faith, are their voice! We cannot speak in soft tones, and our silence is tantamount to consent, for we realize that "it is the aim of every totalitarian effort to stop the language of newness."[16] Let us raise our voices on behalf of those who are brokenhearted, captive, in prison, and bound, mindful that "it is the task of the alterna-tive prophetic community to present an alternative consciousness that can energize the community to fresh forms of faithfulness and vitality....It is the task of prophetic imagination and ministry to bring people to engage the promise of newness that is at work in our history with God."[17]

The second perspective I would offer is an appeal based on my personal experience. I grew up in New York City, in Harlem, to be exact. And during my formative years, on a regular basis I saw persons who were referred to as "junkies." Junkies were drug addicts, men or women we used to pass by, still in the throes or waning stages of a drug- or alcohol-induced stupor on Sunday mornings as my grandmother led my brother, sister, and me to church at the Mother AME Zion Church on 137th Street. These people must have been invisible to the rest of the world because I don't recall (and no history or record proves me wrong) any push for a "War on Drugs" or a "Just Say No" campaign when drugs were mostly affecting and damaging residents of Harlem or other ghettos or barrios, those sections within a section of the city of New York or other cities where people were ignored, marginalized, and often forgotten—out of sight, out of mind.

It seems we lacked the courage to do what needed to be done to address these concerns. And courage is what we needed, and what we still need. Arguably, however, courage is neither easy to come by nor especially abundant in a selfish culture when we are called to do what is right. How sad that this lack of courage is an indictment of the church as well as the larger society. We are challenged by the words of Paul Tillich who said, "There should be no question of what Christian theology has to do in this situation. It should decide for truth against safety, even if safety is consecrated and supported by the churches."[18]

If we lack courage, by which I mean that if we choose what Tillich warns us against, safety rather than truth, we will do nothing. Then, sadly, one day in the not very distant future, the problem will hit home, and trust me, sooner or later, it will. And so my favorite and saddest example of this is my own recollection of how the larger community ignored the drug problem as an issue that only impacted delinquents and ne'er-do-wells in the ghettos and the barrios. But then in 1969, the daughter of Art Linkletter committed suicide, a death that Mr. Linkletter blamed on an overdose of LSD. In 1970, singer Janis Joplin died of an overdose of heroin. And in 1984, the son of the late Senator Robert Kennedy, David Kennedy, reportedly died from a multiple ingestion of cocaine, Demerol, and thioridazine. And (almost) suddenly, wouldn't you know, America realized it had a drug problem. Surely by now we are all likely aware of the drug issue that has been reported and focused upon in this election cycle in—of all places—New Hampshire, in what has been described by Manchester, New Hampshire, Police Chief Nick Willard as a heroin "apocalypse."[19]

Why do I bring this up? Drugs are just one example, but it is to our national peril that we ignore these issues of poverty, race, gender, and class, as well as issues of police brutality, economic and class warfare, discrimination of all kinds, including the issue of mass incarceration and how it is carried out both in policy and practice. These issues affect us all, however we might think or pretend that it does not. My friends, if we think these issues are only a problem in "poor" or "minority" areas or communities, and if we think that so long as we build these incarceration centers in areas that do not intersect with "good" neighborhoods so that "good" citizens don't have to deal with the fallout or traffic or danger of those we warehouse there, essentially putting them "out of sight, out of mind," we miss a very salient point. The point is that evil has no respect of boundaries. The problem or issue you ignore today will soon be coming to a neighborhood near you. And this is why we cannot let our voices be silenced.

We cannot allow the matter of mass incarceration to force us into an attitude of resignation and helplessness, to seep ever so slowly into the neighborhoods where we never imagined it might go and therefore to become normalized. History is replete with examples of how this happens, repeatedly. People who look like me—black, brown, so-called "minorities"—cannot be the only ones who raise a voice of complaint. If we are going to insist on incarcerating large segments of our population for whatever reason we think it is best, it won't be long before we all end up in a prison of some kind, whether it has bars or not.

We can face this challenge now, and perhaps even change the course of history, because we can act on the belief that God wants more—and better—for us all. And so, to conclude:

> Notwithstanding the fact that there is no easy formula for knowing how and to what immediate ends God is moving in the restless flux of happenings, the Christian confesses that the hand of God is behind, within, and against whatever transpires in the universe. [We] seek therefore, to discern, through the binoculars of faith, what it is precisely that God is doing to accomplish that which pleases [God] and then to join [God] at that place and time with the human instrumentalities at [our] disposal.[20]

Notes

1. Kerry Eleveld, "Trump Calls Mexican Immigrants 'Drug Dealers' and 'Rapists,' Crickets from the GOP Field," *Daily Kos*, June 17, 2015, http://www.dailykos.com/story/2015/06/17/1394019/-Trump-calls-Mexican-immigrants-drug-dealers-and-rapists-crickets-from-the-GOP-field.

2. Jennifer Bendery, "Ted Cruz: 'We Need 100 More like Jesse Helms' in the Senate," *The Huffington Post*, September 11, 2013, http://www.huffingtonpost.com/2013/09/11/ted-cruz-jesse-helms_n_3909610.html.

3. Kira Lerner, "Cruz: Black Lives Matter Is 'Literally Suggesting and Embracing and Celebrating the Murder of Police,' *Think Progress*, October 14, 2015, https://thinkprogress.org/cruz-black-lives-matter-is-literally-suggesting-and-embracing-and-celebrating-the-murder-of-police-6ebbce111126#.wir2lr7wn.

4. Laura Clawson, "John Kasich Blames 'the Minority Community' for Ohio's Sky-High Infant Mortality Rate," *Daily Kos*, March 31, 2016, http://www.dailykos.com/story/2016/3/31/1508458/-John-Kasich-blames-the-minority-community-for-Ohio-s-sky-high-infant-mortality.

5. Julie Ellperin and Anne Gearan, "Clinton Questions Whether Sanders is Qualified to Be President," *The Washington Post*, April 6, 2016, https://www.washingtonpost.com/news/post-politics/wp/2016/04/06/clinton-questions-whether-sanders-is-qualified-to-be-president/.

6. Brian Ross and Rehab El-Buri, "Obama's Pastor: God Damn America, U.S. to Blame for 9/11," *ABC News*, March 13, 2008, http://abcnews.go.com/Blotter/DemocraticDebate/story?id=4443788&page=1.

7. See https://www.youtube.com/watch?v=UnlRrxXv-v8.

8. Reinhold Niebuhr, *The Irony of American History* (Chicago: The University of Chicago Press, 1952), 48–49, 50.

9. Jordan Heck, "Bomani Jones Makes Statement on Indians Logo with 'Caucasians' Shirt," *Sporting News*, April 7, 2016, http://www.sportingnews.com/mlb/news/bomani-jones-caucasians-shirt-mike-and-mike-chief-wahoo/16152j6vrfvhp1jhp12moxc1we.

10. Cory J. Sanders and Angela Yarber, *Microaggressions in Ministry: Confronting the Hidden Violence of Everyday Church* (Louisville, KY: Westminster John Knox Press, 2015), 12.

11. Ibid.

12. James Baldwin, *Nobody Knows My Name* (New York: Vintage International Books, 1961), 60.

13. Donna Schaper, ed., *40-Day Journey with Howard Thurman* (Minneapolis: Augsburg Books, 2009), 34.

14. Abraham J. Heschel, *The Prophets* (New York: Harper & Row, 1962), 3.

15. Author's translation.

16. Walter Brueggemann, *The Prophetic Imagination*, 2nd ed. (Minneapolis: Fortress Press, 2001), xxiii.

17. Ibid., 59–60.

18. Paul Tillich, *The Courage to Be* (New Haven and London: Yale University Press, 1952), 141.

19. Kevin Johnson, "Heroin Apocalypse Shadows New Hampshire Primary," *USA Today*, February 8, 2016, http://www.usatoday.com/story/news/politics/elections/2016/02/08/heroin-new-hampshire-primary/79720402/.

20. Gayraud S. Wilmore, *The Secular Relevance of the Church* (Philadelphia: Westminster Press, 1962), no. 37.

19

WHITE PRIVILEGE
My Journey with Segregation

Frank Lesko

If you ask me what it feels like to be white in America, the first thing I would ask for is some time to formulate an answer.

I don't feel like a white person very often. Most days I just feel like a person. I feel like a man. I feel like a forty-one-year old. I may feel my small-town roots or my Catholic upbringing, but I don't feel like a white person very often.

It is difficult to admit this. My first impulse after writing it is to want to apologize. I don't mean to sound flippant or flaunt this privilege at all. My goal here is simply to describe it as plainly as possible to show how people experience race so differently in this country. My racial identity has not seemed directly relevant throughout most of my life, and thus I have rarely had to think about it—I can *choose* to think about race, but I very rarely *have to*.[1]

I feel like a white person only when I am around people of different races. Those times were few and far between growing up in a small, rural, mostly white town in the Midwest. Even though my musical selections and TV viewing featured many African Americans, I could probably count on my fingers the number of in-person interactions I had with African Americans before going to college.

Since then, I have intentionally worked hard to engage with people from diverse races and cultures. Because of those efforts, it has been easy to reassure myself that I no longer live in a white culture bubble. Those efforts have indeed been meaningful. However, if I am honest with myself, I realize that those engagements have remained few and far between. Having friends from other races and having experienced intense periods of cross-cultural immersion have not dislodged me from the underlying reality of living in a mostly white world.

I am, therefore, writing this piece with incredible trepidation. Being a white American writing about race, I feel compelled to list a string of disclaimers: I want to apologize preemptively in case I say anything unintentionally insensitive. I don't want to beat myself up to win the approval of the liberal community or admit things I am not ready to admit out of fear of backlash. I may say some things poorly on the path toward developing a more enlightened racial consciousness. Many white liberals would not hesitate to crucify me on the altar of white guilt to show their superior racial savvy. Writing this piece is like walking through a minefield, and that is exactly why I am doing it—we can't continue to avoid these discussions, even if they are uncomfortable.

I will tell the story of what it feels like to be white from my perspective as a nonexpert on race. It is the story of one person, but I think it might help tell the story for many others.

GROWING UP AS A SYMPATHETIC OBSERVER

I grew up watching documentaries of the civil rights struggle on TV. My heart burned with righteous anger when I read about the atrocities of slavery in history classes. I beamed with pride for the African American community in the enormous achievement of the civil rights movement. Few other groups in history have been so thoroughly oppressed only to rise out of those circumstances so proudly. Had I the chance, I hoped that I would have been brave enough to stand first in line behind Martin Luther King Jr. in the struggle for freedom and the recognition of human rights.

The sheer scope of the problem of racial oppression stirred my passions, empathies, and compassions like few other issues. As a young person steeped in comic books, I often fantasized I could go back in time, free the slaves, and punish the slave owners like a hero in some action movie. (It bears mentioning that this was before my commitment to nonviolence.) Yet, the phenomenon of racism today failed to move me in the same way.

Yes, there was the lingering devastation from centuries of slavery and decades of Jim Crow-era discrimination and persecution.

I was keenly aware that the fallout from those two horrors, such as multigenerational poverty (to name one of many examples),[2] might take many decades or even centuries to heal. But I thought we were on the mend—the dragon of racism at the heart of the problem had been slain, and it was simply a matter of cleaning up the damage—extensive damage, no question. I was confident each generation was more inclusive than the ones prior. We were moving in the right direction. After all, we had an African American president!

In a hushed whisper, I might even admit that I observed moments of racial overcompensation. I saw this as a sign we were not only wrapping things up but were potentially replacing one discrimination with a reverse discrimination (something to be expected as the pendulum of injustice swings back and forth before eventually settling over time in the middle). I mostly saw progress. Count me among the folks who assumed we were in a postracist society. However, many of these conclusions were based on assumptions and inferences that I had reached in an unreflective way. I did not study the issue in any great depth. The examples of racism and acts of discrimination that I directly observed often left me unconvinced that racism was still a deep-seated issue for our society.

SEGREGATION AND COGNITIVE DISSONANCE

I worked at a restaurant during college in the late 1990s. My white coworkers were mostly single moms living in a rural town. The restaurant was a mildly upscale, old country inn. It was a popular spot for folks from Cleveland, Ohio, to visit, especially after a long country drive on the weekends.

African American patrons would arrive on Sunday afternoons in church vans. An elaborate racial dance would sometimes ensue. If there was a perceived delay in service or poor quality of food, some of the African American patrons would subtly—but clearly—imply racial bias. I remember a charged atmosphere. The overworked waitresses did not look forward to this. It made them less enthusiastic about engaging with our African American customers. I didn't think this was due to race. They may or may not have had racial biases, but I suspected their hesitations were simply the result of wanting to avoid a tense situation.

To the waitstaff, it seemed these encounters were coming out of nowhere. They had very few interactions with people from other races. They assumed these African American groups came in looking for a confrontation. The waitresses seemed to ask through their facial expressions, "Can't you see that everyone is getting a delay in service on a busy Sunday afternoon?"

I never did ask the perspective of the African American patrons. I was far too nervous to attempt that. I just watched from the sidelines as a busboy and tried to be as polite as I could to everybody.

This example is painful to recall. Now I see the enormous disconnect it represents. I am hesitant to put words into anyone's mouth, but I believe these African American patrons were expressing the tensions they were living with every day. They were telling us something about their lives, their history, and the world they live in. Racial struggle was an ever-present reality to them. To white folks in the rural North, racial struggles were something we mostly experienced on TV or in books, if at all.

Even if the white waitstaff believed themselves to be innocent bystanders who had no responsibilities in the struggle against racism, these patrons were demanding both our involvement and response—to heed the call from Scripture to wake from slumber (Isa 26:14; Eph 5:14) and wade into the racially charged waters (Ezek 47:3–5) that our brothers and sisters live in every day. The waitstaff did not see it that way. In this scenario, I suspect that both sides felt unfairly treated and resented it.

The result is sad: If this was a moment when white and African American citizens could have entered a meaningful dialogue with each other about race, it did not happen. Instead of shedding more light, it was more polarizing. Some white folks I knew became less sympathetic to the struggle for racial equality after instances like this.

For better or for worse, this story encapsulates the racial disconnect that was prevalent in our society during the 1990s and early 2000s. Before the story of mass incarceration and #BlackLivesMatter broke into the mainstream, the discussion about race in America had largely dried up—at least according to many in the white community. There was a significant gap between the lack of racism that was perceived by white people and the racism that was articulated by the African American community. Looking back, it is horrifying to realize that people were screaming and few could hear. Cornel West describes this as "sleepwalking."[3]

I saw this same disconnect in social justice circles when people were asked, "What are the prevailing issues of injustice in the United States?" Most white folks would think for a bit and answer with little emotion: "The environment," "health care," or "vegetarianism," for example. The words were cognitive sounding and seemed to come from a headspace.

When African Americans would respond, their answer was almost always visceral, consistent, and immediate: "Racism." It came from the gut and it came with urgency. This did not resonate with my experiences. If white folks mentioned racism at all in their list of urgent social issues, they would almost invariably include it much farther down their list—maybe in their top ten, but rarely in their top five.

The Roman Catholic peace organization, Pax Christi USA (of which I have been a member of a local chapter), had been continually refocusing its efforts in recent years to include dismantling racism more front and center in its mission.[4] I remember scratching my head and wondering what all the fuss was about. I worried they were abandoning their traditional focus on disarmament and other anti-war efforts in favor of an issue that was not as relevant to the needs of the world today.

I began to hear murmurings about mass incarceration. The frequency in which I heard about racism was starting to increase. I received email alerts that the annual Ecumenical Advocacy Days (EAD) conference had selected the theme of "Breaking the Chains: Mass Incarceration & Systems of Exploitation" for its 2015 conference.[5] I had always loved EAD, but was lukewarm about the upcoming topic.

I confess, I thought the black community might be going through a multigenerational experience of post-traumatic stress disorder (PTSD). I have personally experienced PTSD. I know its rhythms and its lingering impact. Imagine someone who has been in a tragic automobile accident or another who has been physically attacked. Many years after the incident, a person's palms may sweat and heart start racing while looking in the rearview mirror if an approaching car doesn't slow down with ample leeway. A person may cringe if a stranger stands too close or makes abrupt movements. These feelings are real and healing certainly needs to happen. A person may *feel* violated by all these examples, but it is important to differentiate between the feeling and the current reality. The attacks are no longer happening, but the ghosts from the past can linger for so very, very long.

With no disrespect intended toward the African American community, I thought something like this might be going on. It was the only way I could reconcile the racial concerns I was hearing from African Americans with my failure to see any evidence for racism.

Unfortunately, both are probably true: PTSD is, no doubt, a lingering struggle, but so is the reality of ongoing racism, which is very much alive.

MY CONVERSION

I must thank Ecumenical Advocacy Day 2015 for my profound conversion on this issue. Justice-minded folks and organizations from across the Christian denominational spectrum gathered to pray, study, and act on mass incarceration. Numerous speakers, small table conversations, and informal talks in session after session detailed with overwhelming evidence and anecdotes a new understanding of racism in America. Somewhere between the nationally recognized speakers and the informal comments overheard in the elevators and coffee lines, the truth finally broke through to me. I usually disdain clichés, but this one is so very appropriate: the scales fell from my eyes, and I could finally see what had been right in front of me the whole time.

It was a true conversion in every sense of the word. What I had been hearing consistently from African Americans suddenly came together and started making sense: Racism is indeed alive and well in the United States—and not just in certain pockets. It is an endemic problem that seeps into our pores and swims deep in our unconscious minds. It colors everything we see, no pun intended. Discrimination is an ongoing reality.

The evidence was too strong to dismiss: mass incarceration; police brutality; disproportionate treatment by the criminal justice system; the #BlackLivesMatter movement; voter suppression; racial profiling; the overwhelming, constant, sickening resistance to our first African American president. Others in this book and elsewhere can and will do a far better job describing the phenomena. My point: I finally got it, in a huge way.

With Michelle Alexander's book *The New Jim Crow*, we finally had a new paradigm to describe what she calls the new "racial caste system"[6] with data to back it up. Discriminatory treatment could no longer be seen as a string of seemingly isolated incidents. It could now be described as the enduring, systemic problem of racism.

I remember being chilled to my bones. I had to ask myself the horrifying but very necessary questions: Has the situation of racism in America improved *at all*? Or have we simply replaced one group of discriminatory behaviors, practices, and laws with others? Given the progress I thought we had made from the emancipation of slavery through the civil rights movement, that prospect brought me nearly to despair. Whether the answer to those questions is yes or no, we must be brave enough to ask. Only the truth will set us free (John 8:32), even if it first seems too much to bear.

What I feel the worst about is that, while the evidence and language around mass incarceration broke the logjam inside of me, all it really did was help me see what African Americans have been saying all along. That information, however, was already there long before I heard about mass incarceration. I just couldn't see it. Like any conversion, there is always the element of divine mystery as to why it happens for certain people at certain times. Grace has an essential role to play. I wish I could translate my experiences into a formula that could be replicated. While I don't know how to do that, I can say that people of faith continuing to talk about racism and mass incarceration with increasing frequency and urgency played a significant role in this process for me.

HOW DID I MISS IT?

I have been an activist for social justice for much of my adult life. I focused on Catholic social teaching when I earned my master's in theology. I worked very hard to be close to the suffering of the world, to hear the cry of the poor and respond from my heart. I have deeply immersed myself in works of charity and justice.

That someone like myself who cares so deeply about human flourishing could completely miss the persistence and urgency of racism in the United States says something about the incredibly sinister nature of the problem. I tried to tune in and hear the voices of the marginalized, and yet I could not hear the cries of racism in America.

I plan to spend a good deal of effort understanding why I didn't get it sooner. Maybe I have had a huge blind spot. Maybe the sting of white guilt compelled me to insulate myself and avoid the topic. Maybe there were subtle layers of racism inside of me that I have yet to identify. I want to suggest, however, that something else may be at fault. To blame me as an individual could cause us to miss another glaring reason: segregation. The way we refer to segregation these days is "white privilege." White privilege has created a system whereby white people experience life very differently from African Americans and may have little awareness that this is happening at all.

I had evaluated the situation of race based simply on what I saw and experienced. Nothing convinced me that racism was anything other than an old problem in its final death throes. All the indicators I observed showed that we were moving in the right direction in terms of race in America. After all, we had an African American president. The discriminatory laws of Jim Crow were off the books. The civil rights movement was a big "win" and ready for the history books. Being called a "racist" has become one of the worst things anyone wants to be called. I saw law enforcement and the criminal justice system as inherently fair. Segregation in the form of white privilege made sure I didn't see it any other way.

There was one glaring exception to this: I was aware that African Americans were regularly saying that racism was an ongoing and serious problem. This was a piece of information that should have challenged my narrative that we were moving in the right direction. When a new piece of information comes along to challenge a commonly held perspective, it creates a feeling of discomfort known as cognitive dissonance. People often simply push the new information aside to avoid the discomfort of challenging their worldview. I think this is what I did. I now know it takes ongoing vigilance and a commitment to honesty to resist this tendency.

I take only slight comfort in knowing that I am not alone in having failed to recognize the reality of ongoing racism for so long. "How did we miss it?" asks my Glenmary colleague, Catholic priest Fr. John Rausch. Even Michelle Alexander confesses to believing at one time that racism in the United States was largely a phenomenon of the past.[7]

SUBATOMIC RACISM

So, having acknowledged the reality of racism today, how can we best understand it? This analogy from the natural sciences helps me to put modern day racism in perspective:

The lions, tigers, and bears that are the subjects for a zoologist can be clearly seen with the human eye. Microbiologists can also visibly see the cells and microbes that are the focus of their work, even though they need a high-powered microscope to do so. Chemists hone in on still smaller particles, but most of those can also be seen or evidence for them directly observed. However, going still deeper, atomic and subatomic particles simply cannot be seen. However, we know these particles exist because we can observe their influence. We can see their "reflections." Their small size does not correspond with their importance, however. Their role in shaping our world is even more foundational than the lions, tigers, and bears who more easily capture our attention.

I think it is helpful to think about racism today using this subatomic analogy. Even well-intentioned people simply cannot see it. Even people directly affected by it often doubt it. The latter may feel it in their bones, but the evidence of their eyes seems to contradict it. We can know racism today through its contradictions—for example, criminal sentence lengths and incarceration rates that correlate to skin color. The lighter the skin color, on average, the smaller chance of arrest, the smaller chance for a conviction, and the greater chance for the shortest of sentences.[8] Blackness is under constant scrutiny and suspicion, even by people who wholeheartedly profess colorblindness. Most people do not think they treat white or black people differently. Yet studies show they do.

Segregation in 2016 does not look like segregation in 1956. Back then the lines were clearly, and often very literally, drawn. Public drinking fountains were labeled *colored* and *white*. People could have argued whether segregation was a positive thing or not, but it was nearly impossible to deny that it was happening. Jim Crow segregation was literally the law of the land in the South.

The impact of racism today is perhaps just as dire, but the segregation that undergirds it is so hidden it often cannot be seen directly. A white man and a black man can live in the same neighborhood, go to the same schools, apply for the same jobs, and still have an enormously different experience of life. That kind of segregation is hard to wrap our minds around. Yet we know that it *does* happen, as studies have repeatedly shown. I don't know *how*. It's hard to believe a judge sentencing two men guilty of the same crime would give one a longer sentence based solely on the darkness of skin. We can't see this discrimination happening in real time. Each decision may seem fair and reasonable at the moment. It isn't until we pool the data over a period and find that the primary factor that correlates with sentence length is skin color.

At some point in the decision-making process, in some neural pathway buried deep in the brain, something compels the judge to decide accordingly. Is it that black lives are not valued? Is it that blackness is seen as a threat that must be tightly controlled?

It is important for people to hear that this is not an indictment on their individual character. Even African Americans have been found to support racist structures unconsciously in their behaviors and preferences through implicit bias.[9] Racism is simply endemic in our culture. The best we can do is to commit ourselves continually to identifying and unpacking all those layers inside ourselves and our culture. Untangling ourselves from a culture of racism and privilege in which we are immersed takes time, effort, and continued focus. A negative spin has been so deeply attached to blackness in our culture that even black people themselves will make decisions accordingly.

Negative spin is an appropriate term: Imagine if a role-playing game like Dungeons & Dragons placed automatic penalties based on the color of each character's skin. For example, a very dark-skinned man may have a –10 penalty on each roll; a lighter brown-skinned man may have a –5. All characters have a chance at either good or negative outcomes. They are rolling the same dice and playing by the same rules. However, the darker-skinned characters have a drag that keeps them down. A white player can still bottom out and a dark-skinned player can still beat the odds and excel, but the game is rigged to make those outcomes rare. The fact that they do occasionally happen make it seem that the game is fair and that success or failure is purely a function of individual achievement and ability.

How do these mysterious penalties play out in real life? Lighter skin color equates to easier treatment, more benefit of the doubt, and more trust in a variety of settings: police stops, criminal trials, job interviews, housing opportunities, and even shopping at retail establishments. This does not fully describe the racial caste system we live in, but it does help explain some racial bias along the way.

Even though racism is at that unseen "subatomic" level, Kenneth Q. James and Reginald Broadnax write in "On the Other Side of the Divide" that there is one sure way of *experiencing* the divide: "Engage someone from another culture other than your own living in America about any one of these three issues and you will see what I mean." They list the shooting at Mother Emmanuel AME Church in Charleston, South Carolina, flying the Confederate flag, and the #BlackLivesMatter movement. My experience with this follows.

FROM RESISTANCE TO LISTENING

A mentor of mine says that there is a very significant difference between disagreeing with someone and resisting them. Resistance is always a key to something deeper.

People do not simply disagree with taking down the Confederate flag or the #BlackLivesMatter movement, for example. No, they resist it. They deny it. They use all sorts of stall tactics and rhetoric designed to redirect the conversation to literally anything else. They are extremely quick to anger and offer no quarter.

An example is the reaction to a blog piece I wrote about the decision of the Southern Baptist Convention in June 2016 to repudiate the use of the Confederate flag.[10] I praised that decision wholeheartedly and offered supporting views. Within a few days of posting the article, I had 253 comments on Facebook, some so nasty I had to delete them.[11] This was unusual for social media pages that typically average only a few polite comments on each post. While there were some reasonable exchanges, most of the comments were overwhelmingly negative, insulting, and racially charged. It wasn't just that folks disagreed—the level of resistance and nastiness spoke volumes. While in this case the racism was often blatant, often the only way to see racism is to hold up one discussion next to another discussion about another topic and see the contrast. Some of the comments could be seen as reasonable disagreements, but the ways the disagreements were communicated were vastly different from how disagreements on another topic would be treated. What accounts for the difference? Racism.

So instead of talking about the pain behind the rallying cry, "black lives matter," we instead spend endless time debating the merits of "all lives matter." As long as people fall for it and allow themselves to be pulled off topic, the diversion will work. "All lives matter" is more of that subatomic racism at work. On the surface, there is nothing wrong with saying it. In fact, if there is any insight that comes out of the Judeo-Christian understanding of human nature and our relationship with God, it is precisely this: all lives, all the time, everywhere, have dignity. We are all created in the image and likeness of God (Gen 1:27). This is a truth at the foundation of Christian morality and anthropology. What is wrong with this statement is more about what is not being said. To paraphrase Jesus in John 18:36, If this were the kingdom of God, we would all be acting differently.

When people shout out, "Black lives matter," the rest of society should ask those speaking to come forward. We should invite them: "Tell us your pain. Share your experiences. We want to know what we have not seen or experienced. Let's share perspectives and get on the same page." All of society should ask forgiveness for having missed it—not because we are bad people, but we still must take responsibility for our part in social sins, even our blind spots. We did not hear the cry of the poor and marginalized. That's a sin and that's on us, even if our blindness can be understood given the complex social structures around us. Responding to "black lives matter" with "all lives matter" is not a kingdom response. It's not what love looks like. It's a form of resistance to a message and not regard for it. It does not consider what is being said and why before offering a vague rebuttal.

Each member of society does not have to agree with all the assertions of the #BlackLivesMatter movement or any other effort to confront racism. Reasonable people can and will disagree on the details. The problem is that much of society is not even willing to listen to them. Much of society has its fingers in its ears, attempting to drown out the cries of "black lives matter" with louder cries of "all lives matter."

Desmond Tutu says, "If an *elephant* has its foot on the *tail of a mouse* and you say that you are neutral, the mouse will not appreciate your neutrality."[12] Let me be so bold as to build off that: If an *elephant* has its foot on the *tail of a mouse*, we could run the risk of wasting valuable time hearing the elephant offer an explanation that this was not done on purpose and that he's not intentionally discriminating against mice. All of that could be true. In the meantime, however, his foot is still on the mouse's tail, the mouse is still hurting and disadvantaged, and the very fact that we are focusing on the elephant's feelings supports the oppressive structure due to the fact that the elephant's foot has not moved off the mouse's tail. We need to get the foot off the tail, attend to the mouse, and then we'll have plenty of time to hash out where the responsibilities lie afterward.

An essential demand of love is that we take the expressed concerns of our fellow brothers and sisters seriously. A truly Christian expression of love would be patient, kind, polite, and bearing of all burdens, to name a few characteristics listed in 1 Corinthians 13:4–8.[13] That is what we are not seeing with the national discussion around racism, mass incarceration, and especially the #BlackLivesMatter movement. In fact, as a national exercise, it would be wonderful if we were to hold up the public discussion of racism against the criteria in 1 Corinthians 13:4–8 as a checklist. How are we doing in light of that?

When someone says, "Black lives matter" and someone refutes that with, "All lives matter," that is not a rational exchange but rather a rhetorical red herring. By the definition found in 1 Corinthians 13:4–8, that is not what love looks like. Love is, after all, the primary commandment given by the man Christians profess to be God—Jesus Christ (see, e.g., John 13:34–35; Mark 12:28–34; Luke 10:25–37; and Matt 22:34–40).

Imagine someone hurrying to the emergency room. This person is screaming, "My foot is broken!" However, the nurses and doctors reply with, "All body parts matter." Yes, all body parts *do* matter. And *because* they all matter—not despite that—we have to attend to the one that is hurting *right now*. It is good and holy to single out certain parts of God's creation to celebrate individually, especially in times of trauma.

#BlackLivesMatter leader DeRay Mckesson provides this stirring comparison in a recent CNN interview: "I would never go to a breast cancer rally and yell out 'Colon cancer matters!'"[14] As Mckesson says in that interview, there is "unique trauma" in the experiences of the African American community that needs to be addressed directly and specifically by name. Sadly, much of America refuses to hear why people are taking to the streets shouting, "Black lives matter." The refusal to dialogue about black lives in our society is evidence, if not downright proof, of the sin of racism. It is simply not what love looks like.

FROM AVOIDANCE TO TOUCH

In addition to resistance, another response by much of white America is avoidance. Perhaps subconsciously, much of white America sees discussions of race in high-risk, low-reward terms. A poorly thought-out statement or offhanded comment could abruptly end a career or damage a reputation permanently, even if racial bias were far from the intention. The perception is that talking about the subject will do little to help race relations in America but could potentially damage individuals. As a result, many folks do everything they can to avoid it.

Yet, we need to talk about race. Those thoughts—the good, the bad, and even the ugly—need to stand before the healing light of day.

I have held underdeveloped opinions on all sorts of topics. I have often been amazed to discover that those thoughts did not make as much sense when spoken out loud as they did in my mind.

The community was there to correct me if I didn't realize that myself. We limit those corrective moments when we don't talk about a subject.

I strongly support high standards for what is acceptable in civil, public discourse. But like anything, political correctness has come with its share of negatives. For example, the way we have appropriated it has contributed to a climate where negative thoughts are potentially swept under the rug. The 2016 U.S. presidential race has shown that racism did not go away with political correctness; it just went into disguise. I do not believe that white America is oppressed under the tyrannical yoke of political correctness as some claim. It is worth asking, however, whether political correctness has changed racist attitudes or whether it has just created an environment where we are less likely to talk about them and thus make it more difficult to address. I believe we have suppressed some of the external symptoms of racism, but the disease has continued to gain strength in the body.

If we really do want to move toward a postracist society, that's going to involve the input and the unique genius of everybody. Not every accusation of discrimination is accurate, as it may be coming from a limited perspective. The important thing is that every concern is given a fair hearing and that every feeling is validated. We should not resist accusations of racism. Our resistance to hearing what some have to say only strengthens the case that there must be legitimacy to their concerns.

A crucial Christian call is to be present to each other, just as Christ shared in our humanity. Jesus walked into messy situations of racial and cultural tensions. He recognized the full dignity of everyone and paid little heed to social caste, even as everyone around him was scrambling to situate themselves according to social hierarchy and custom. We too must be willing to wade into someone else's pain with all the turbulence and trauma that could potentially be in there—even better if we can do that without trying to be the hero of the story.

The way to heal a wound is to touch it. Jesus taught us that. So whether I've been impacted by racism or have perpetuated it in any way, it's important to touch the issue by first talking about it. We don't have to be experts, we just have to enter the conversation from wherever we happen to be. Being committed to dialogue about race, to listen, to continually reflect on my own hidden biases and to touch our nation's racial wounds, are what I believe to be my first responsibilities as a white man today. Modifying my behavior in light of what I learn in this process must follow quickly afterward. This essay is my attempt to put one foot forward on this path. I invite others to reflect on race, tell their own story, listen deeply to others, and be open to the transformation that may come as a result.

Notes

1. I recommend contrasting this portrait with the depiction of rage by Kenneth Q. James and Reginald Broadnax in "On the Other Side of the Divide" in this volume. I was inspired to write this reflection after reading theirs. Their descriptions of living with a constant awareness of their racial identity are in sharp contrast to my experiences as a white man, and I wanted to show the contrast.

2. Michelle Alexander, *The New Jim Crow: Mass Incarceration in the Age of Colorblindness* (New York: The New Press, 2012), 3.

3. Cornel West, foreword to Alexander, *The New Jim Crow*, ix–xi.

4. For a noteworthy example, see "STATEMENT: 'Walking together as brothers and sisters,' a Pax Christi USA official statement on a national dialogue on race," Pax Christi USA, January 17, 2011, originally issued March 18, 2009, https://paxchristiusa.org/2011/01/17/statement-walking-together-as-brothers-and-sisters-a-pax-christi-usa-official-statement-on-a-national-dialogue-on-race/.

5. See "EAD 2015—Breaking the Chains: Mass Incarceration & Systems of Exploitation," Ecumenical Advocacy Days, http://advocacydays.org/2015-breaking-the-chains/.

6. Alexander, *New Jim Crow*, 2, 40–58.

7. Ibid., 2–4.

8. James Kilgore, *Understanding Mass Incarceration: A People's Guide to the Key Civil Rights Struggle of our Time* (New York: The New Press 2015), 54–55.

9. See Theodore R. Johnson, "Black-on-Black Racism: The Hazards of Implicit Bias," *The Atlantic*, December 26, 2014, http://www.theatlantic.com/politics/archive/2014/12/black-on-black-racism-the-hazards-of-implicit-bias/384028/.

10. Frank Lesko, "Enough Is Enough: Southern Baptists Vote against Confederate Flag," *The Traveling Ecumenist Blog*, last modified June 14, 2016, accessed August 18, 2017, http://travelingecumenist.blogspot.com/2016/06/enough-is-enough-southern-baptists-vote.html.

11. See discussion at https://www.facebook.com/evangelicals.and.catholics/posts/698987620241783.

12. See quote by Desmond Tutu in Gary Younge, "The Secrets of a Peacemaker," *The Guardian*, May 22, 2009, https://www.theguardian.com/books/2009/may/23/interview-desmond-tutu.

13. "Love is patient; love is kind; love is not envious or boastful or arrogant or rude. It does not insist on its own way; it is not irritable or resentful; it does not rejoice in wrongdoing, but rejoices in the truth. It bears all things, believes all things, hopes all things, endures all things. Love never ends. But as for prophecies, they will come to an end; as for tongues, they will cease; as for knowledge, it will come to an end" (1 Cor 13:4–8).

14. DeRay Mckesson, "All Lives Matter," *CNN*, July 18, 2016, https://business.facebook.com/cnn/videos/10155050255046509/.

20

PREACHING TO BRIDGE PEOPLES ON ISSUES OF RACE

Joyce Shin

None of us can experience everything. As a preacher, I assume that one of my tasks is to bridge the gaps among peoples' experiences so that compassion and understanding can be expanded and other people's causes can become common causes. The church's unique resource for bridging gaps among persons who have lived different experiences is Scripture. Literally Scripture puts people on the same page. Through one of its primary functions, that of preaching the Word, the church has enormous potential to help people of good will, but of different life experiences, to work for the common good on issues of race, class, mass incarceration, etcetera. This paper consists of excerpts from sermons I have preached—sermons intended to help people mine their own life experiences, to bridge their life experiences with others' life experiences, and to show what may be theologically at stake in this work. It is divided into three biblical themes that I think have significant bridging potential: (1) that God created the world and called it good; (2) that Christ commands us to put ourselves at the mercy of other people's hospitality; and (3) that the Spirit works relationally.

This chapter was first delivered as part of a preconference workshop at the Ecumenical Advocacy Days in Washington, DC, on April 15, 2016. The chapter's reflections are drawn from sermons preached by the author on various occasions.

TRUSTING GOD AND THE WORLD TO BE GOOD

You might not think about it this way, but there is a fine line between pessimism and optimism, between preparing for the worst and hoping for the best. Try as we might to walk this line, each of us probably tends to step on one side of the line more than the other. Which side of the line we tend to walk on probably has a lot to do with our upbringings, our life experiences, as well as our hardwiring. Most of the time, we may not even be aware that we tend to walk on one side more than the other, until we trip over it.

I have become more aware of the need to walk the line since becoming a parent. As a parent, I need to equip my daughter with a heavy dose of realism and idealism, with pessimism and optimism, with street smarts and a carefree attitude. She will need all of this to navigate life with resilience.

When we moved to Chicago, Sophia was just two years old. She wanted, of course, to walk on her own two feet rather than to be carried everywhere, and with the wonder that is typical of a toddler, everything along her path fascinated her. As her parent, I was also her protector, and there were times, when we would arrive home at sundown and have to park on the street some distance from our apartment, that I knew it wouldn't be in our best interest to dawdle at every dandelion. And yet, not wanting to alarm her, I got into the habit of saying, "Sophia, we have to walk with a purpose, not like a porpoise."

In a book titled *Raising Resilient Children*, leading clinicians in child development and psychology, Robert Brooks and Sam Goldstein, write on the theme of resilience as the key to helping children cope with everyday challenges, adversity, and trauma. Having worked with many children over the course of their careers, they have concluded that the mindset of resilient children has to do with two things: first, how children view themselves and, second, how they view the world.[1] I think we are all aware of the first: that children must view themselves as having worth. But have you given thought to the second—that children must view the world as benign, not harmful, as friendly, not threatening?

In the book *Between the World and Me*, author Ta-Nehisi

Coates writes a letter to his fifteen-year-old son. Mr. Coates is a black man who grew up in Baltimore, and in this letter, he shares with his son the story of his own awakening to the truth about his place in the world.

Every parent wonders how much and when we should tell our children about the world. We wonder how we should expose them to it. Should we speak of its dangers, or should we speak of it as benign, even benevolent? In the letter to his adolescent son, Ta-Nehisi Coates deals with this dilemma. As a parent of a black child, on the one hand, he knows that it is a risk not to speak of racism in the world; his child's survival depends on knowing about it. On the other hand, to speak of racism is also a risk; it risks raising fear, anger, cynicism, pessimism, hopelessness, and defensiveness, emotions that will stand between his child and the world. To his son he writes,

> I am afraid. I feel the fear most acutely whenever you leave me. But I was afraid long before you, and in this I was unoriginal. When I was your age the only people I knew were black, and all of them were powerfully, adamantly, dangerously afraid. I had seen this fear all my young life....It was always right in front of me.[2]

Coates goes on:

> The fear was there in the extravagant boys of my neighborhood, in their large rings and medallions, their big puffy coats and full-length fur-collared leathers, which was their armor against their world....I heard the fear in the first music I ever knew, the music that pumped from boom boxes full of grand boast and bluster....I felt the fear in the visits to my Nana's home in Philadelphia....I barely knew her, but what I remember is her hard manner, her rough voice. And I knew that my father's father was dead and that my uncle Oscar was dead and that my uncle David was dead....My father was so very afraid. I felt it in the sting of his black leather belt, which he applied with more anxiety than anger...as if someone might steal me away, because that is exactly what was

happening all around us....I would hear it in Dad's voice—"Either I can beat him, or the police."[3]

Because of racism, generations of people have grown up in fear. They have grown up to view the world with suspicion, cynicism, and the resulting defensiveness. That is why racism is not just a social and moral issue that religious communities need to address. Racism is itself a religious issue. It strikes at the core of religion because racism fundamentally threatens a person's capacity to trust.

Over the course of his life, American theological ethicist H. Richard Niebuhr wrote extensively about the experience of faith. He distinguished between two fundamental existential orientations to the world—an orientation of fear and an orientation of trust.[4] The latter, he explained, is what we experience as faith. Faith is a basic confidence that the world is ultimately good and therefore trustworthy. Faith allows us to live in hope, even when things are not going well for us, when things do not make sense to us, or when we suffer. In contrast, an orientation of fear toward the world, Niebuhr wrote, leads to defensiveness, which is the source of all evil.[5]

As a theologian, Niebuhr further recognized that how we conceive of God profoundly shapes our existential orientation toward the world.[6] If, for example, we conceive of God as a loving and benevolent parent, we may perceive the world as gracious. If we conceive of God as just, we may perceive the world as governed by justice. In such cases, we would be able to take a trusting stance toward the world. If, however, we conceive of God as vengeful, we may perceive the world as exacting and punitive. If we conceive of God as stingy, we may perceive the world in terms of scarcity. If we conceive of God as capricious, we may perceive the world warily. In all such cases, we would take a defensive stance toward a hostile world.

Here I look to the biblical story of Job as an example. In the story of Job, we find that he is undergoing an existential crisis. He used to be a man who, like his friends, conceived of God as a just God and thought that the world was governed by justice. But when he suffers unjustly, when everything is taken from him—his home, wealth, children, and health—Job can no longer make sense of the world as he used to. Having lived a righteous life, he does not understand why he is now suffering. His former trust in a world that he thought was governed by justice begins to crack. Furthermore, the trust Job once had in God begins to falter, not only because God is not acting justly, but also because he cannot find God. More than anything, Job wants to make his case before God, but God is nowhere to be found. Job complains,

> If I go forward, he is not there;
>   or backward, I cannot perceive him;
> on the left he hides, and I cannot behold him;
>   I turn to the right, but I cannot see him....
> God has made my heart faint;
>   the Almighty has terrified me."
>
> (Job 23:8–9, 16)

From trust to fear, Job undergoes a crisis of faith.

Can you imagine no longer being able to say, as the Apostle Paul does, "If God is for us, who is against us?" (Rom 8:31) and, instead, saying, "With God against you, what hope can you possibly have?"

Job is a man badly in need of consolation, but the conventional wisdom with which his friends try to console him does not suffice. They try to console him by drawing upon the proverbs and formulas that people have been using over the centuries to explain the way the world operates and how human beings fit into the overall order of things. A righteous man like Job would have lived in accordance with such wisdom and he would have done so expecting that by living wisely he would live well. His suffering is made all the greater precisely because he cannot fall back on the conventional wisdom on which he had always relied and with which his friends now try to console him. The wise know, they say, that a good person will be rewarded with success and a bad person punished with failure. Having no other explanation to fall back on, Job's friends assume that Job, or his sons, must have done something wrong. But Job maintains that he has lived a righteous life, and we know from the first two chapters of the Book of Job that this is, in fact, true.

Sometimes true consolation must come in the form of the sublime. By chapter 37, everyone has spoken, that is, everyone except

God. The debate over the meaning of Job's suffering has exhausted explanations and conventional wisdom. At last, in chapter 38, God intervenes. "Out of the whirlwind" God speaks, and though he is angry, God's speech is no argument. God doesn't argue with Job. God doesn't answer Job's questions or address Job's charges of injustice. God's speech is, instead, a parade of questions:

> Who is this that darkens counsel by words without
>   knowledge?
> Gird up your loins like a man,
>   I will question you, and you shall declare to me.
>
> Where were you when I laid the foundation of the
>   earth?...
> Who determined its measurements...
>   who laid its cornerstone
> when the morning stars sang together
>   and all the heavenly beings shouted for joy?
>
> Or who shut in the sea with doors
>   when it burst out from the womb?
>
> (38:2–8)

God gets so caught up marveling at his great cosmic acts and then contemplating the vast variety of creatures he has made that he seems to forget his anger. And we notice that God's speech leaves the very vocal Job stunned into silence. God has stunned Job with the sublime. With question after question, God silences Job, and God reorients Job.

When Job does speak again, he has very little to say—just six verses—and yet his brief response makes it all too clear that he is a changed man. The tone, the brevity, and the words of Job's response portray a man who has been transformed. Not only does Job reengage himself in relationships and in the business of living, but he also reorients his existential quest. Job has been consoled. Not by conventional wisdom. Not by reasoned argument. But by meditation on the sublimity of God and the multitudinous composition of life!

There are times in life when things are so wrong and conditions are so unjust that we feel like even God is against us. But we must nevertheless engage the world and go about the business of living. When the officer who shot Michael Brown in Ferguson, Missouri, was not indicted, Ta-Nehisi Coates observed his son watching the news coverage. Without expressing his own opinion about the guilt or innocence of the officer, Coates writes about that night in his letter:

> It was not my expectation that anyone would ever be punished. But you were young and still believed. You stayed up till 11 p.m. that night, waiting for the announcement of an indictment, and when instead it was announced that there was none you said, "I've got to go," and you went into your room, and I heard you crying. I came in five minutes after, and I didn't hug you, and I didn't comfort you, because I thought it would be wrong to comfort you. I did not tell you that it would be okay, because I have never believed it would be okay. What I told you is what your grandparents tried to tell me: that this is your country, that this is your world, that this is your body, and you must find some way to live within all of it.[7]

How do we walk the line between planning for the worst and hoping for the best? How do parents raise their children to be resilient—to trust that the world is ultimately a benign place? Conventional wisdom doesn't always help us to overcome attitudes of fear and suspicion toward the world. Perhaps those are the times when we need more than ever to marvel at, to be struck by, God's great multitudinous world. Perhaps at those times when fear and suspicion stand between the world and ourselves, and there is nothing anyone can say to make sense of it, the consolation we so badly need can come by way of the sublime.

AT THE MERCY OF OTHERS' HOSPITALITY

In his book *On God's Side*, Jim Wallis, a preacher, social activist, international commentator on ethics and public life, as well as president and CEO of Sojourners, writes about our shared responsibility to work for the common good. He laments that the term *social justice* stirs up so much controversy in American politics.

The term has become so politicized that people who speak of social justice are sometimes even accused of being socialists. The way Jim Wallis uses the term, and the way it makes sense also to me, is simply to say that to be concerned about social justice means that we use justice *as a lens* by which we see society. "Part of the job of each new generation, part of the vocation of young people, and part of the faith obligation of Christians," he writes, "is *to learn to see* what is wrong, unfair, cruel, and unjust in the world around them....*Paying attention to* what is wrong, and then figuring out how to make it right—that's exactly what people of faith are supposed to do."[8]

The problem, of course, is that we all have blind spots that prevent us from seeing what is wrong, unjust, and unfair. Unfortunately, as blind spots, we need to have them pointed out to us, and it is no fun when someone else points out what we were unable to identify about ourselves. We get defensive and sometimes even deny that they exist.

One of the things that I like so much about Jim Wallis is that he seems to enjoy when other people point out his blind spots, to the point that he goes out in search of such people. Usually they are people that are outside what he calls his "tribe." He writes that he has learned the most about the world, that he has learned to see the world more clearly, by being with "outsiders," that is, by being with people who were not of his race, socioeconomic class, Evangelical Christian community, etcetera. From being with people outside the groups into which he had been born, he learned the true meaning of the gospel, and he writes, "I think that's why God is always telling his people to welcome the strangers, the foreigners, the poor—the outsiders."[9]

I would like for Jim Wallis to go an important step further. It is not enough for us to welcome "outsiders" and learn from "outsiders." We ourselves need to know and learn from the experience of *being* an outsider. When God commanded the Israelites always to welcome the stranger amidst them, he never failed to remind them that they too had been strangers in a foreign land. God reminded them that they too knew how it felt to be at the mercy of others' hospitality, others' power, and others' privilege. Likewise, when Jesus sends his disciples to go out, he instructs them to take no gold or silver or copper; no bag, extra tunic, sandals, or staff. He instructs them to be at the mercy of those who receive him.

What blind spots might be identified and removed, if we were to leave our comfort zones and venture out of the "tribes" into which we were born? I'll never forget how brave I thought my college roommate was when she told me that she had decided to spend a year in Kenya. She returned, and of all the many things she told me about her experience, most memorable to me was when she said, "I had never before been so aware of my skin, how white I am."

My mother's father had been governor of a province in Korea. As his seven children grew older and decided, one by one, to come to the United States not only for further education, but to stay and make lives for themselves here, my mother's parents decided that they too would immigrate to the United States. They were already older, and I can only imagine that the decision to leave Korea brought with it significant losses: loss of command of language, loss of a social circle, loss of social status and the privileges that went with being a former governor. From time to time, I wonder what my grandparents learned from being immigrants, from being at the mercy of others' hospitality, power, and privilege.

I will always remember the time when my sister's college boyfriend met almost our entire extended family. It was winter break, and our extended family had gathered at the home of my aunt and uncle in Pennsylvania. My sister's boyfriend drove a long distance to meet everyone and to take my sister out on a date. I observed the kindness with which everyone received him, and I overheard the heated discussion that ensued after he left. My uncles and aunts challenged my parents with their decision to allow their daughter, the eldest child of the second-generation of our extended family living in the United States, to date someone who was not Korean. What kind of example would this set for all my sister's younger cousins living in this country? What would happen if their children grew up to marry people who weren't Korean? Every now and then my grandmother would gently say, "As long as he believes in our Lord Jesus Christ, that's all that really matters." Out of respect for her, I guessed nobody told her that he was Jewish. For hours into the night, I overheard my elders expressing their tribal fears and proudly watched my parents staking our ground outside the tribe.

The stories that I can tell mostly concern race and religion, but there are other kinds of tribes as well—tribes delineated by gender, class, and groupthink. As Jim Wallis says, stepping outside of our own tribes—whatever they may be—is a necessary step. But beyond this, the next step is the step *into* a group unlike our own. It is only by joining groups outside our comfort zone, by being at the mercy of their hospitality, at the mercy of their norms and their ways of doing things, that we can see for ourselves what our blind spots have been, how they have made others feel, and the damage they have done. It is only then that we can start to remove our blind spots so that we can see society in ways that we couldn't see it before—through another's lens. That is the start on a path toward social justice.

The church is called to this work. From the beginning, God has been calling his people to leave their tribe and to put themselves at the mercy of others. The story of the church is the story of God's people wrestling with that call. Will we, like Abraham and Sarah, be willing to leave our home, our kin, and our comfort zone to follow God into a land unknown to us? Will we, like Moses, be willing to leave the power and privilege of Pharaoh's palace? Will we, like Israel, be willing to be led by God into a foreign land, and will we never forget what it feels like to be foreigners? Will we, like Jesus' disciples, put ourselves at the mercy of others' hospitality? Whenever Christians answer yes—whenever Christians step away from their tribes, out of their comfort zones, and into groups in which they become the outsiders—the church learns how *to see* things it couldn't see before. Then, and only then, does the church have prophetic vision, seeing God's world through the lens of justice. Then, and only then, can we get to work on making things right.

THE PUBLIC RELATIONAL WORK OF THE SPIRIT

In the classic book *Roots for Radicals*, community organizer Ed Chambers put pen to paper and delivered a body of social knowledge that he had accumulated over years and years of relating to people from all walks of life—men and women who raise children, run businesses, lead organizations, stay at home. It is a pragmatic "know-how" book about how people from different races, religions, classes, political parties, and neighborhoods can overcome real differences to work together for the common good.

In it, Chambers carefully distinguished between an ideological approach and a relational approach.

Let's look at the distinction he made. A relational approach, he wrote, "is not a search for those who share our faith, class, politics, or other views. Ideologues on the right or left tend to seek consistency and certainty." Describing the dynamics of our day, he went on to name "the increasing insularity and narrowness of far-out liberals and right-wing conservatives." Both groups end up preaching to their people, using their own language, sometimes fabricating their own theology, and sticking to their single agendas. "Both extremes communicate, 'If you want to join us, you must be like us—follow the party line.'"[10]

In contrast, a relational approach does not depend on demographic or partisan dissections of the public. Instead, it requires the discovery of the wholeness, complexity, and spirit of people. In our relationships, we discover what makes the other person tick, what matters to the other person, and why it matters. In these relationships, we can raise possibilities and aspirations.

If you and I are fortunate, we've all had relationships like this—relationships that go to the root of who we are and what we care about. These relationships may not be with the people with whom we grew up; they may not be with people we see every day or with people who share our background. They may not be our most intimate relationships. Yet they are the relationships out of which we can imagine a new social reality being created. Chambers called these "public relationships."[11] When people connect with one another at the level of their core values, a *public* relationship is formed, one that transcends the narrower limits of family, clan, and class.

Our public relationships are different from our private lives. The truth is, in our private lives, we aren't given a choice about the family, the race, the history into which we are born. Whether we like it or not, our original identities are often shaped by conditions that we didn't choose for ourselves. So it is in our public relationships more than in our private lives that we actually have greater opportunity to exercise our freedom and choice, our imagination, and most of all our compassion. As counterintuitive as it may seem, in the public realm, more than in our private lives, we can be our whole, most complex, and most spirited selves.

I came across a beautiful example of this when I read the spiritual autobiography of actor Sidney Poitier. His book *The Measure of a Man* is an account of both his private life and the public relationships he formed.[12] It was in the work of acting, because of the roles he chose to play, that Poitier had the opportunity to form public relationships with fellow actors with whom otherwise he would have shared very little in common. In their movie roles, he and his fellow actors were freer than they were in their personal lives to imagine, role-play, and create social realities that were ahead of their time.

Take, for example, the film *Guess Who's Coming to Dinner*, in which Poitier played a young black doctor who had academic credentials a mile long and who was the charming suitor of the white daughter of Spencer Tracy and Katharine Hepburn. This movie came out in 1968, the year when both Martin Luther King Jr. and Robert F. Kennedy were assassinated. It was also the year when the protests at the Democratic National Convention in Chicago turned violent. Against that backdrop, Poitier had several box office successes. Given the volatile social currents of that year, he writes, "There was more than a little dissatisfaction rising up against me in certain corners of the black community."[13] This dissatisfaction crested a few years later when the *New York Times* published an article titled "Why Do White Folks Love Sidney Poitier So?" According to Poitier's assessment, "The issue boiled down to why [he, as a black man] wasn't more angry and confrontational."[14]

When he thinks back to the making of *Guess Who's Coming to Dinner*, Poitier remembers how risky the movie really was. Here's how he tells the story of meeting Miss Hepburn for the first time:

> Clearly she was going to check me out....When I arrived at her door and that door opened, she looked at me and didn't say a word and didn't crack a smile.... After the longest while she said, "Hello, Mr. Poitier," and I said, "Hello, Miss Hepburn," and the conversation began. I could tell that I was being sized up every time I spoke, every response I made. I could imagine a plus and a minus column, notations in her mind. That's how big a step this was for her....The truth of the matter is that the formation of this business relationship was

almost a literal "pre-enactment" of the situation in the film we were about to make. The black man was coming for dinner, and we didn't usually do that.[15]

So Poitier asks, "Should I have been angry and confrontational?... All I can say is that there's a place for people who are angry and defiant, and sometimes they serve a purpose, but that's never been my role."[16]

In his autobiography, Poitier writes as nonideologically, compassionately, and *relationally* as I have ever read on the topic of racism in America. While he acknowledges the hard reality that we shouldn't expect those in power to crumble willingly, he also leaves room for imagination, compassion, and freedom—the freedom to forgive, not get stuck, and to re-create.

The public reception that Pope Francis received when he visited the United States was extraordinary and historic. Those who weren't usually "followers" of the Pope, even people of all faiths, found it remarkably easy to be moved by him. As nearly every commentator noted, part of the reason for this seems to be that Pope Francis refuses to be pigeonholed. Instead of taking political sides or drawing ideological lines, Pope Francis crosses thresholds.

Not everyone gets an opportunity to be received at the White House and to speak to a joint session of Congress at the Capitol. During the days of his visit, given the statement made by a presidential candidate that he could not vote for any Muslim ever to be president, we know that we still have a long way to go before all Americans can imagine their religious leaders being welcomed with an open spirit.

It's when an open spirit is lacking that we need even more to look for or to create an opening for the Spirit. It may not be that every front door opens. It may be that the route of the Spirit is not the straightest, most direct, expected, or typical path. It may not be Pennsylvania Avenue that opens. No, I have a feeling that the Spirit takes whichever path is lined with people who have open hearts and minds. We know the Spirit is relational, and if the Spirit is pragmatic too, perhaps the Spirit takes the path of least resistance.

When you follow the path of the Spirit, you never know whom you'll meet or through whom you'll end up where you need to be.

In the Spring of 2015, I attended the annual Christian Unity Gathering of the National Council of Churches. The National Council of Churches includes thirty-seven member communions. A special guest of the NCC at that gathering was the Reverend Olav Tveit, the secretary general of the World Council of Churches. Addressing a room full of church leaders representing different Christian denominations, Rev. Tveit shared his sense that the ecumenical movement is now reemerging out of a long winter. After his talk, I asked Rev. Tveit what he thought was responsible for this reawakening of ecumenism. His hypothesis was the same as mine: that the world's pressing need for interreligious cooperation has made a unified Christian witness even more important.

As I thought further about the relationship between ecumenical and interfaith work, it became more apparent to me that surprisingly, perhaps ironically, ecumenical relationships today have been facilitated by interreligious relationships. Let me explain what I mean. For years, I have been participating in interfaith gatherings. I cannot tell you how commonplace it has now become that my Muslim interfaith partners will introduce me to their Roman Catholic or Methodist partners and that my Jewish interfaith partners will introduce me to even other Presbyterians. If I trace the path that led to my involvement in ecumenical work in the first place, I know that the path was lined by Muslim and Jewish partners. Because of their open hearts and minds, the Spirit found a way to connect me, one Christian, to other Christians. Could it be that wherever there is a spirit of openness, the Body of Christ may be strengthened?

To his disciples, Jesus said, "Whoever is not against us is for us" (Mark 9:40). He didn't name one by one who is a follower and who is not. What he tells us is not to spend our time and energy drawing lines and taking sides. We don't know whose hearts and minds are open until we get to know one another, until we learn what makes the other person tick, what matters, and why. Taking the path of least resistance is not simply the pragmatic thing to do; it is, I believe, the way of the Spirit, re-creating the world one whole, complex, spirited person at a time.

Notes

1. Robert Brooks and Sam Goldstein, *Raising Resilient Children: Fostering Strength, Hope, and Optimism in Your Child* (New York: McGraw-Hill, 2002).

2. Ta-Nehisi Coates, *Between the World and Me* (New York: Random House, 2015), 14.

3. Ibid., 15–16.

4. H. Richard Niebuhr, *The Responsible Self: An Essay in Christian Moral Philosophy*, Library of Christian Ethics (Louisville, KY: Westminster John Knox, 1999), 118–21.

5. Ibid., 99–100.

6. H. Richard Niebuhr, *Radical Monotheism and Western Culture* (New York: Harper & Row, 1960), 47.

7. Coates, *Between the World and Me*, 11–12.

8. Jim Wallis, *On God's Side: What Religion Forgets and Politics Hasn't Learned about Serving the Common Good* (Grand Rapids, MI: Brazos, 2013), 247 (italics added).

9. Ibid., 127.

10. Edward T. Chambers, *Roots for Radicals: Organizing for Power, Action, and Justice* (New York: Bloomsbury, 2010), 52.

11. Ibid., 72–79.

12. Sidney Poitier, *The Measure of a Man: A Spiritual Autobiography* (New York: HarperCollins, 2000).

13. Ibid., 118.

14. Ibid.

15. Ibid., 121–22.

16. Ibid., 122, 124.

21

LORD, MAKE MY TROUBLES LIGHT

A Historical and Spiritual Reflection
on Quaker Work in Prisons

Philip Caroom, Rachel Guaraldi, and Ann K. Riggs

> "I was naked and you gave me clothing, I was sick
> and you took care of me, I was in prison and you
> visited me."
>
> —*Matthew 25:36*

The Religious Society of Friends (Quakers) as a religious movement emerged during a time of great religious upheaval. In defi-
ance to church and government politics in 1650s England, many
Friends were imprisoned for their beliefs. This experience of
imprisonment was formative for the movement and for denominational development. From the start, Friends took the instructions
of Matthew 25 literally—they clothed and tended the imprisoned
and began a legacy of prison visitation.

Friends held regular Meetings for Sufferings, meetings where
the Quaker community came together to discuss how to clothe and
feed those who had been imprisoned, whether to pay fines accrued
by these prisoners, and how to support the families of those imprisoned while they were away. While at the time, the care that was
provided to prisoners was only to those of the Friends community imprisoned, experiences both in the prisons and in visiting the
prisons incited Friends' involvement in prison reform throughout
the eighteenth and nineteenth centuries.

One well-known nineteenth-century Friend, Elizabeth Fry,
visited Newgate Women's Prison in London and was shocked to
discover so many women and children without adequate clothing,

bedding, or food under the age-old prison practice that required prisoners to provide such things for themselves. Appalled by these conditions, Fry pursued a fierce and organized campaign—with many groups eventually consolidated to form the "British Ladies' Society for Promoting the Reformation of Female Prisoners"—to provide clothing, bedding, and food for all the poor women and children imprisoned, regardless of religious affiliation. Other Friends took up the ministry and extended it to other prisons and jails throughout the United States and England.[1]

With establishment of Pennsylvania by Friend and nobleman William Penn, Quakers had the chance to decide for themselves the corrections policies of this new colony. Penn saw typical punishment of the day as a violation of God's command to love one another—ongoing practices included capital punishment, whipping, hard labor, public humiliation in stocks, and deportation to penal colonies. Creating what was later termed the "Quaker experiment," Penn abolished corporal punishment and the death penalty for crimes except for premeditated murder. He instituted bail for minor offenses and made opportunities for prisoners to learn a trade while doing time. Unfortunately, Penn's experiment was temporary and within a generation, English criminal law had won out and corporal punishment and the death penalty were reinstated on a wide scale.

In response, some Friends latched on to a Calvinist proposal to create prisons with solitary confinement cells. They hoped, for a time, that prisoners' Quaker-like silent penance for their crimes, rather than torture or death, might serve as a viable means of rehabilitation. Although Friends did not find unity—Elizabeth Fry adamantly opposed the penitentiary system—Pennsylvanian Friends built and ran the first penitentiary in Philadelphia on the theory of solitary confinement. The dangers of solitary confinement and its effect on prisoners soon became apparent, but it was well into the nineteenth century before the Friends began to oppose this view. Since then Friends have been involved with abolishing the practice and have returned to advocating for better prison conditions and shorter sentences.

"The spirit of the Lord is upon me, / because he has anointed me to bring good news to the poor. / He has sent me to proclaim release to the captives / and recovery of sight to the blind, to let the oppressed go free, / to proclaim the year of the Lord's favor" (Luke 4:18–19). This passage from the Gospel of Luke is part of what is thought to be the first written-down sermon of Jesus. It emphasizes not just the call to visit those in prison, but that prison work itself is deeply rooted in social justice, social transformation, and liberation. Like Isaiah's words in Isaiah 61, on which the Lukan passage draws, Jesus called for his disciples to begin the process of social reform from the ground up, in profound and pervasive renewal. Drawing on their understanding of these pivotal biblical passages in *Beyond Prisons: A New Interfaith Paradigm for Our Failed Prison System*, a report prepared for the American Friends Service Committee, Laura Magnani and Harom Wray write, "Radical justice redistributes resources among the people and creates space for the people both to define the changes that are required and to demand that they be implemented."[2]

During the twentieth century, many Friends again gained familiarity with the U.S. prison system from a place of defining and demanding change. During World Wars I and II, the Korean War, and the Vietnam War, some Quakers who resisted being drafted into military service participated in recognized alternative service programs, while others were imprisoned. Civil rights protests in the 1940s, 1950s, and 1960s also led to lived experience in U.S. prisons. Some, such as African American Quaker Bayard Rustin, had experienced both. He was imprisoned from 1944 to 1946 for his pacifist refusal of military service and, in 1947, served on a chain gang for violating Jim Crow laws.[3]

"Conscientious objector" status and alternative service sometimes were granted during the wars. Quakers founded the American Friends Service Committee (AFSC) in June 1917 to coordinate their nonviolent relief efforts and provide alternative service placement. AFSC and its British counterpart were recognized for such service in receiving the Nobel Peace Prize in 1947. But many draft boards prided themselves for imprisoning Friends. This renewed personal experience of imprisonment, the stories of Friends and the stories of the people Friends met during imprisonment, revitalized Friends' interest in reform of prison conditions and sentences.

Beginning in December 1943 and continuing through 1947, Friends established the Prison Service Committee (PSC) who, like

Elizabeth Fry, ministered to needs of imprisoned conscientious objectors and their families. The PSC also strove to educate the public about those who shared the Quaker aspiration to live, in the words of pivotal early Quaker George Fox, "in the virtue of that life and power that [takes] away the occasion of all wars."[4] Years later, when the PSC laid down its prison work, the issue again was taken up by AFSC as well as several other newly formed Quaker organizations including the following: the Friends Committee on National Legislation; Prisoner Visitation and Support; Alternatives to Violence Project; and by other Friends Meetings on a local basis.

Quaker prison work broadened over time from prison visitation and support for people imprisoned for social conscience to include issues such as prison conditions, excessive incarceration, and discriminatory sentencing (particularly for those in federal prisons). Friends Committee on National Legislation (FCNL) worked on the government level on lobbying congress while other Quaker organizations worked at the grassroots. Recently, in 2015, FCNL set up a weekly conferencing network of "advocacy teams" in different regions targeting support for the bipartisan Sentencing Reform and Corrections Act of 2015.

Prisoner Visitation and Support (PVS) was established by Quakers in 1968 primarily for Vietnam protest inmates, and it was expanded over time to become an interfaith project with hundreds of volunteers permitted by the Federal Bureau of Prisons and the Department of Defense to offer support and guidance to inmates in all 102 federal and 4 military prisons across the United States. This prison visitation work continues the tradition of Elizabeth Fry and the early Friends, and has become an inspiration for other kinds of visitation programs, including visitation programs for immigrant detainees.

Working more on the grassroots level, Alternatives to Violence Project (AVP) was founded in the early 1970s from a collaboration between inmates in New York's Green Haven Prison and local Quakers who had conducted nonviolence training around antiwar demonstrations. AVP is based on the belief in the transformational power of love and the ability for prisoners, perpetrators of violence, and their victims to grow out of a place of hatred and violence into a place of love and peace. One Friend, Martin Krafft, vice president and public relations/outreach committee co-chair of the Alternatives to Violence Project USA, wrote for inclusion in this essay,

> AVP is the manifestation of my Quaker faith. I connect with Quakerism because of its model of action out of silence and stillness. For me, AVP is both the action and the silence. The silence is the space made for people to come together, reflecting on their lives and on the lives of those in the group. The action comes from the creation of a sense of community and the desire to change one's life for the better. AVP is founded on Quaker values, in seeing everyone's capacity to make good in the world, and figuring out how to support and nurture each person's capacity for good....Growing up at the Annapolis Friends Meeting, I saw but did not comprehend the extent of the activist efforts of adults at the Meeting. As an adult myself now, I am inspired by the call for justice of those who have gone before me. I define my faith through action.[5]

AVP is known as a restorative justice program and in some prisons is seen as a major step toward parole. AVP in its development was first offered to prisoners, but has since expanded its work to youth, communities, and even warring parties. As AVP training has gained recognition, it has spread now to thirty-five U.S. states and over forty other countries.

"Take my yoke upon you, and learn from me; for I am gentle and humble in heart, and you will find rest for your souls. For my yoke is easy, and my burden is light," writes Matthew in 11:29–31. Some Friends find inspiration for prison-related ministries in associating "light" in this passage with the Divine Light that enlightens every human person (John 1:9) and the soteriological processes of discovering, confessing, and being released from sins and errors (1 John 1:7–9). The approach intimately connects prison ministries with central Quaker doctrines and expectations for spiritual development in both the imprisoned and those in ministry with them.[6]

As Friends have moved in their work away from traditional prison visitation models, they have been inspired by challenges offered by other groups to look at the systemic causes of mass incarceration and related injustices.

One effective call to action for educating and organizing in recent years, Friends have found, is Michelle Alexander's book *The New Jim Crow: Mass Incarceration in an Age of Colorblindness (NJC)*.[7] Published in 2010, *NJC* invites readers to take a fresh look at the statistics of the U.S. "War on Crime" and "War on Drugs" policies that led to a tripling of American prison populations between 1980 and 2010 without substantial improvement in crime rates. Just as important, although studies show blacks and whites abuse illegal drugs at similar rates, black citizens are arrested, convicted, and incarcerated for drug offenses at more than three times the rate of whites. Many Friends have used *NJC* "book club" groups to join a growing movement from study to political action, seeking to reduce the overuse of incarceration. Quaker *NJC* book groups are reported in Florida, Georgia, Indiana, Maryland, Massachusetts (and other New England meetings), Nevada, New Jersey, New York, North Carolina, Pennsylvania, Washington, DC, and elsewhere.

In Maryland, for example, Quakers transitioned from an *NJC* book club to found a statewide, interfaith network: Maryland Alliance for Justice Reform (MAJR). Within two years, MAJR has successfully supported passage in 2015 and 2016 of two major pieces of prison reform legislation to reduce mass incarceration and to encourage diversion and sentencing alternatives. Patience Schenck, one of the most active participants in the Maryland Alliance for Justice Reform, expressed her faith understanding that informed that work:

> Believing that there is something of the divine (that of God) in every person, we don't believe in giving up on people. We believe people deserve second chances. We believe in forgiveness. In the area of criminal justice, we believe in helping the person return to wholeness and heal broken relationships, if possible. That means drug or mental health treatment over incarceration. It means providing mediation and community conferencing services, so people can be held responsible for their actions in a way that is meaningful and healing. It

means helping persons gain skills to be self-supporting and to developing economic opportunities, especially in neighborhoods with few such opportunities.

I believe incarceration has three purposes: to protect the public, to make crime unattractive, and to punish. Protecting public safety is important, but for those who can't be trusted outside prison walls, more compassionate prisons (like in Europe) serve as well. The threat of incarceration is of limited use in dissuading people from committing crimes; offering more community opportunities and services is more effective—and ultimately cheaper. And as for punishment, "Judgment is mine, saith the Lord"; unless punishment is restorative, it is of limited usefulness. William Penn said, "Let us then try what Love will do." We Quakers challenge ourselves to find that way of love.[8]

Schenck's reference to the thought of William Penn is particularly helpful in seeing the biblical roots characteristic of Quaker theological and spiritual perspective and action. She has quoted one of Penn's maxims from *Some Fruits of Solitude* (1682): "Let us then try what Love will do: For if Men did once see we Love them, we should soon find they would not harm us."[9] In this quote and its surrounding passages, Penn paints a vision of a beautiful, fearless life of love based especially in passages from two New Testament epistles: "And now faith, hope, and love abide, these three; and the greatest of these is love" (1 Cor 13:13) and "There is no fear in love, but perfect love casts out fear; for fear has to do with punishment, and whoever fears has not reached perfection in love" (1 John 4:18). Many centuries later, this way of life, this spirituality based in trying what love can do, continues to be central to a Quaker religious view of everyday life and of aspirations for a more just justice.

Over the centuries, prisons, incarceration, and faithful responses to the needs of the imprisoned, through advocacy and direct contact and programs, have been favored locations for this way of life, for both historical and eschatological reasons. It is participation in this life of power, virtue, and beauty that Friends have understood to be the goal and the reward for being Friends of God on earth as in heaven. Within the Quaker community, there is a living memory of life in the jails and prisons. This in turn has led to a living memory of satisfaction and achievement in making love real and present in visiting and serving the imprisoned and in proclaiming liberty to captives and release to prisoners.

Notes

1. Averil Douglas Opperman, *While It Is Yet Day; The Story of Elizabeth Fry* (Leominster Enterprise Park, UK: Orphans Publishing, 2015).

2. Laura Magnani and Harmon L. Wray, *Beyond Prisons: A New Interfaith Paradigm for Our Failed Prison System*, A Report by the American Friends Service Committee Criminal Justice Task Force (Minneapolis: Fortress Press, 2006), 12.

3. Devon W. Carbado and Donald Weise, eds, *Time on Two Crosses: The Collected Writings of Bayard Rustin* (San Francisco: Cleis Press, 2003), 1–57.

4. George Fox, *Journal*, originally published in 1694 and reprinted numerous times, including Norman Penney, ed., *Journal of George Fox* (London: Friends Tract Society, 1901), 68ff.

5. Martin Krafft, unpublished digital correspondence with the authors, April 26, 2016.

6. The clearest exposition remains Robert Barclay's "Proposition V" in his *Apology for the True Christian Divinity* first published in English in 1678 and reprinted numerous times, including in 1827 by the Trustees of Obadiah Brown's Benevolent Fund, available in the Christian Classics Ethereal Library, accessed January 6, 2017, https://www.ccel.org/ccel/barclay/quakers.vii.v.i.html.

7. Michelle Alexander, *The New Jim Crow: Mass Incarceration in an Age of Colorblindness*, rev. ed. (New York: The New Press, 2012).

8. Patience Schenck, unpublished digital correspondence with the authors, April 26, 2016.

9. William Penn, Maxim no. 545 in *Some Fruits of Solitude in Reflections and Maxims*, originally published in 1682, reprinted numerous times, and included in a variety of collections, including Charles W. Eliot, ed., *The Harvard Classics*, vol. 1, part 3 (New York: P. F. Collier & Son, 1909–14), accessed January 6, 2017, http://www.bartleby.com/1/3/170.html.

22

AN INTRODUCTORY PROPHETIC CRY AGAINST INEQUITIES IN THE AMERICAN MASS INCARCERATION SYSTEM

David J. Fekete

When I showed a draft of this article to a friend of mine, her first response was, "Are those facts true?" She was referring to the statistics that clearly demonstrate a disproportionate representation in prisons from racial minorities and the economically disenfranchised. For those who have been working to reform the American mass incarceration system, my friend's statement may seem hard to believe. But not everyone is aware of injustices in the American prison system, as there is a startling lack of information among the public.

With such a lack of information in mind, this chapter was originally written for members of my Swedenborgian denomination, but has relevance for other traditions as well. It is intended to alert and inform congregations and clergy of some of the basic issues of injustice structured into the American mass incarceration system. But this chapter is also biblically based, drawing on the prophet Amos against the backdrop of the Covenant Code in Exodus 20:19—23:33. I draw on Amos because his prophetic utterances are clear in their call for reform in his day. Amos criticized his society for forgetting the principles of justice as found in the early Covenant Code.

Jesus stands firmly in this prophetic tradition. In like manner as the Covenant Code and the prophet Amos, Jesus teaches consideration for the vulnerable in society. Those who call themselves by Christ's name are likewise called to consideration of vulnerable groups in society.

Who will fulfil the prophetic role in today's world? On the one hand, in certain respects, the press is a watchdog on government and a voice exposing society's ills. However, the press is a consumer-driven institution and has some vested interest in not speaking truths that would offend their readership. The church, on the other hand, has a time-honored role in keeping society mindful of God's ways. This may mean an unpopular decrying of social ills. It may mean bespeaking wrongs that people don't want to hear about. It may mean being a voice for people who do not have a voice.

The issue of mass incarceration is one social problem the church must speak out about. There are too many inequities in American society that result in disproportionate incarceration dependent on race, poverty, and education. The prophetic voice of the church calls for America to repent and rectify the inequitable demographics of mass incarceration. The church must challenge American society to ask whether we have turned from godly ways, whether society has abandoned the norms of freedom, equity, and justice. It is hoped that a clear statement describing the basic facts of injustices in the American mass incarceration system, in conjunction with scriptural exhortations to protect vulnerable segments of society, will move Swedenborgians and the wider Christian community to take practical action to reform and ameliorate problems in the American mass incarceration system.

THE PROPHETIC VOICE AND AMERICAN MASS INCARCERATION

Letting society know when they had strayed from God's ways was the function of prophets in ancient Israel. Accordingly, the prophet Amos was a harsh critic of his society, which had strayed far from God's ways. They had strayed from the old Covenant Code (Exod 20:19—23:33). The Covenant Code is the earliest articulation of God's intent, and is at the heart of the Law. The Covenant Code advocates clearly and forcefully for the disenfranchised in Israelite society: widows, orphans, foreigners, and the poor; and Amos draws on it heavily in his prophetic critique of his society. Compassion for the disenfranchised was part of what it meant to be God's people. But in Amos's day, society had turned from Yahweh and worshipped other gods. As a result, society in his day was corrupt and constructed to favor the rich while exploiting the vulnerable.

The Covenant Code is clear that persons who were ethnically different from the dominant Israelite tribes, but living among them, are not to be oppressed: "You shall not wrong or oppress a resident alien, for you were aliens[1] in the land of Egypt" (Exod 22:21). In American society, minority races who are ethnically different from the dominant white race can be perceived as modern-day equivalents of "resident aliens." Minority races find disproportionately greater representation in prisons: "A Black boy born in 2001 has a 1 in 3 chance of going to prison in his lifetime; a Latino boy a 1 in 6 chance; and a White boy a 1 in 17 chance."[2] This is the kind of injustice that Amos decried in his own society, and would decry in American society were he here today: "Ah, you that turn justice to wormwood, / and bring righteousness to the ground!" (Amos 5:7). Regarding the disproportionate representation of minority races in prisons, is Amos talking to us? Harsh as his words are, do we "bring righteousness to the ground"?

According to Israelite law, the minority "resident aliens," the *gerim*, were accorded special protection. They were excluded from certain rituals such as Passover, but were not to be taken advantage of or oppressed. However, if they wished to join Israelite society and partake of their holy feasts and celebrations, they could be circumcised, which granted them full participation in the life of the Israelites: "There shall be one law for the native and for the alien who resides among you" (Exod 12:49). Echoes of this concern for equity can be found in American law. According to the spirit of the United States Constitution and the Fifth and Fourteenth Amendments, no person shall be denied "equal protection of the laws," regardless of race, creed, ethnic origin, or gender. But can we say that this spirit is practiced in the case of mass incarceration? Perhaps further legislation, inspired by the Covenant Code, is called for to establish special protection for the "aliens" in our society.

The disproportionate representation of minority races in prison is driven by economic forces. Poverty is the largest factor leading to mass incarceration, thus leading to the metaphor of a "cradle-to-prison pipeline."

> Poverty is the largest driving force behind the Pipeline crisis, exacerbated by race. Black children are more than three times as likely as White children to be born into poverty and to be poor, and are almost four times as likely to live in extreme poverty. One in 3 Latino babies and 2 in 5 Black babies are born into poverty. More than 3 in 10 Latino children and 1 in 3 Black children are poor.[3]

The Covenant Code exhorted Israelites to be compassionate to the economically disenfranchised. It called for special care and consideration to ensure that the poor would not be singled out and exploited. If the poor cry out to Yahweh, Yahweh will hear; Yahweh is compassionate:

> If you lend money to my people, to the poor among you, you shall not deal with them as a creditor; you shall not exact interest from them. If you take your neighbor's cloak in pawn, you shall restore it before the sun goes down; for it may be your neighbor's only clothing to use as cover; in what else shall that person sleep? And if your neighbor cries out to me, I will listen, for I am compassionate. (Exod 22:25–27)

Amos forcefully echoes this call to protect the economically disenfranchised. He castigates "[those] who trample the head of the poor into the dust of the earth, / and push the afflicted out of the way" (Amos 2:7). God will remember the injustices of those who oppress the poor: "Hear this, you that trample on the needy, / and bring to ruin the poor of the land.... / The LORD has sworn by the pride of Jacob: / Surely I will never forget any of their deeds" (Amos 8:4, 7).

It may be an overgeneralization to say that law courts show partiality and favor the wealthy, or those who can pay for top lawyers. But statistics indicate that the poor are more likely to become incarcerated than those who are economically comfortable. This does indicate a perversion of justice, as the Covenant Code describes it. It points to a systemic injustice in American society.

347

The author of the Covenant Code is aware of the potential for this kind of inequity to arise, and, accordingly, denounces such inequities: "You shall not follow a majority in wrongdoing; when you bear witness in a lawsuit, you shall not side with the majority so as to pervert justice; nor shall you be partial to the poor in a lawsuit" (Exod 23:2–3).[4]

Poverty and instability of home life, often from single parent households, lead to difficulties in education and healthy childhood development. Then, being deprived of a solid education makes employment difficult, as undereducated individuals lack the skills needed to compete in American society.

> Studies have shown that children who do not get the early intervention, permanence and stability they need are more likely to act out and fail in school because they lack the skills necessary to succeed. Researchers of early childhood emphasize the importance of early childhood nurturing and stimulation to help the brain grow, especially between birth and age seven, and even beyond and thus help children to thrive and to be on a positive path toward successful adulthood.[5]

The Covenant Code recognizes the vulnerable position of widows and orphans, and, accordingly, zealously calls for their special protection. In Israelite society, widows were powerless and poor, and orphans were equally so, not having the power that adult males held in their world. In American society, the equivalent of Israelite widows and orphans would be single-parent families—which usually means families headed by a single woman—and children brought up in homes in which they are not able to receive the nurture necessary for healthy socialization and mental development. "You shall not abuse any widow or orphan. If you do abuse them, when they cry out to me, I will surely heed their cry" (Exod 22:22–23).

I ask, are not these injustices indications of a spiritual malaise in American society? Can Americans feel secure in houses of worship and remain complacent with the status quo when race and socioeconomic factors are predestining certain populations to incarceration? Would Amos decry American society, as he did his own?

Alas for those who are at ease in Zion,
    and for those who feel secure on Mount Samaria,
the notables of the first of the nations,
    to whom the house of Israel resorts!...

Alas for those who lie on beds of ivory,
    and lounge on their couches,
and eat lambs from the flock,
    and calves from the stall;
who sing idle songs to the sound of the harp,
    and like David improvise on instruments of music;
who drink wine from bowls,
    and anoint themselves with the finest oils,
    but are not grieved over the ruin of Joseph!
                    (Amos 6:1, 4–6)

Is this a spiritually healthy society pleasing to God? Is our worship meaningful while these inequities persist? Or are our prayers hollow and our worship empty as we ignore the injustices of the "cradle-to-prison pipeline"? Are Amos's words appropriate for contemporary American society as he prophesies against the religious rituals of his day, while his society fails to "let justice roll down like waters, and righteousness like an ever-flowing stream"?

Come to Bethel—and transgress;
    to Gilgal—and multiply transgression;
bring your sacrifices every morning,
    your tithes every three days;
bring a thank offering of leavened bread,
    and proclaim freewill offerings, publish them;
    for so you love to do, O people of Israel!...
                    (4:4–5)

I hate, I despise your festivals,
    and I take no delight in your solemn assemblies.
Even though you offer me your burnt offerings and
    grain offerings,
    I will not accept them;

and the offerings of well-being of your fatted animals
　I will not look upon.
Take away from me the noise of your songs;
　I will not listen to the melody of your harps.
But let justice roll down like waters,
　　and righteousness like an ever-flowing stream.

(5:21–24)

Jesus stands firmly in the prophetic tradition of Amos and the other prophets calling for social reform and liberation of the oppressed. In fact, Jesus claims to be the fulfillment of such a prophecy in Isaiah:

The Spirit of the Lord is upon me,
　because he has anointed me
　　to bring good news to the poor.
He has sent me to proclaim release to the captives
　and recovery of sight to the blind,
　　to let the oppressed go free,
　to proclaim the year of the Lord's favor.

(Luke 4:18–19; cf. Isa 61:1, 2; 58:6, 7)

And Jesus follows the voice of the Covenant Code and Amos in making special provision to protect and help the poor, racially different (stranger), and incarcerated:

"For I was hungry and you gave me food, I was thirsty and you gave me something to drink, I was a stranger and you welcomed me, I was naked and you gave me clothing, I was sick and you took care of me, I was in prison and you visited me." Then the righteous will answer him, "Lord, when was it that we saw you hungry and gave you food, or thirsty and gave you something to drink? And when was it that we saw you a stranger and welcomed you, or naked and gave you clothing? And when was it that we saw you sick or in prison and visited you?" And the king will answer them, "Truly I tell you, just as you did it to one of the least of these who are members of my family, you did it to me." (Matt 25:35–40)

Jesus has harsh words for religion, or religiosity, practiced with an indifference to justice and mercy: "Woe to you, scribes and Pharisees, hypocrites! For you tithe mint, dill, and cummin, and have neglected the weightier matters of the law: justice and mercy and faith. It is these you ought to have practiced without neglecting the others" (Matt 23:23; cf. Luke 11:42).

It is the place of Christian religion to speak prophetic words, when needed, and to act to rectify injustices. Jesus calls us to be attentive to vulnerable demographics of society—the stranger, the poor, widows, and orphans. This general call to be sensitive to the marginalized in society is especially important in the issue of mass incarceration in America. The church needs to speak and act to rectify the injustices of the American mass incarceration system.

NEXT STEPS

What interventions can individuals, families, and groups take now to remedy some of the problems associated with mass incarceration? The recidivism rate, that is, the percentage of released inmates who return to crime and are incarcerated again, is high. The National Institute of Justice cites a study covering released prisoners from thirty states that indicates the grim realities of recidivism:

- Within three years of release, about two-thirds (67.8 percent) of released prisoners were rearrested.
- Within five years of release, about three-quarters (76.6 percent) of released prisoners were rearrested.
- Of those prisoners who were rearrested, more than half (56.7 percent) were arrested by the end of the first year.
- Property offenders were the most likely to be re-arrested, with 82.1 percent of released property offenders arrested for a new crime compared with 76.9 percent of drug offenders, 73.6 percent of public order offenders, and 71.3 percent of violent offenders.[6]

However, visits from caring individuals have been shown to reduce recidivism rates.[7] Visits from siblings, in-laws, fathers, and clergy are most effective. Ideally, visits can help to provide support systems outside the prison walls. Such supports can help establish positive relationships in the community to which they are released.[8] Here church communities can provide a role in aiding the transition back into society. Some churches have been known to create ceremonies for welcoming people back into their community.[9]

Care needs to be exercised in the way religious support is provided. Positive messages based on love, forgiveness and purification, partnership with God—the belief that God is helping the person through their difficulties—and a sense that God is a source of power greater than self-will are most effective in helping to establish healthy attitudes.[10] Religion is not effective when it emphasizes fear, emotional appeals, and shaming. Clergy are particularly effective when they have undergone formal training in counseling. Taking a Clinical Pastoral Education unit focusing on prison chaplaincy would be advantageous. For clergy and laity, working with prison chaplains is highly recommended.

As helpful as visitation may be in reducing recidivism, intervening before incarceration is much more effective. Providing support to children and youth who appear to be in "the pipeline" can help to prevent incarceration to begin with and supply the support that such children need to flourish in society. The Children's Defense web page provides many suggestions for individuals, families, communities, and organizations—including churches—to take on in order to remove the stressors that generate the cradle-to-prison pipeline. Some of the suggestions they offer speak volumes about early social conditions that can lead to criminal behavior later in life.[11]

Some of the interventions suggested may prove challenging for Christian communities. Individuals, for instance, can volunteer with children who are homeless or in foster care. Communities can ensure that at least one caring community member attends every public school student suspension meeting or court hearing. Communities and churches can also generate a "cradle roll" that links at-risk children with families or an adult mentor to keep the child on track and intervene if they stray. Churches can work with school systems to start after-school programs to keep educational standards at appropriate levels. Recall that students who drop out of school, or fail to meet the standards for their age, will not be able to compete effectively in the job market. Those who are unprepared to compete in the job market are more likely to turn to crime than are those who have stable home lives and a good education. The interventions listed above suggest that some children lack the kind of stability and family support that many take for granted. Churches can provide just the necessary supports that at-risk children require if churches work with school counselors and social service agencies. Families, as well, may wish to consider becoming foster parents.

There are also positive interventions for less acute situations. Individuals can mentor an at-risk child. One can invite youth to events at the next educational level, such as taking a high school student to a college basketball game. One can volunteer at schools to mentor and tutor students who are falling behind. Families or individuals can babysit for single-parent families, offer transportation, or invite them to activities with their own family.

Many of these interventions are sensitive and require that individuals, families, and churches work with professional agencies. Laws that are designed to protect children mean that well-meaning individuals may need to undergo background checks at times, interviews by social service agencies, and other requirements. Also, prison visits require protocols, some of which can be invasive, such as strip searches, walking through metal detectors, and the like. Working with prison chaplains and the prison administration will be necessary. Helping in this area of social justice may require serious personal commitment, and individuals need to be prepared to persevere in the face of legal and bureaucratic requirements. My intention is not to discourage individuals from taking up the challenge to rectify a seemingly unjust system. Rather I wish to encourage individuals, families, groups, and churches to rise to the occasion, and commit themselves to do what it takes to interrupt the cradle-to-prison pipeline. "Just as you did it to one of the least of these who are members of my family, you did it to me" (Matt 25:40).

CONCLUDING REMARKS

This chapter is an introductory alert to the inequities in American mass incarceration. The statistics that this article has broached show that there are serious inequities in the system of mass incarceration in America. Racial minorities and the poor are far more likely to be incarcerated than are the majority white race and the economically comfortable. The Covenant Code, the prophet Amos, and Jesus decry such abuses of the poor, the stranger, the orphan, and the widow. So must the church. The inequities of justice in American mass incarceration need to be remedied. It is an issue that cannot be ignored any longer by persons of conscience. The next steps I have listed above are important interventions that can make a difference in the lives of children and in the lives of incarcerated individuals. Amos heard God's call to social justice in his day. Do we hear a similar divine injunction to rectify the structural injustices that lead to disproportionate incarceration based on race, economic status, family, and neighborhood?

Notes

1. Interestingly, the Hebrew word used here for "resident alien" is *ger*, not *goy*. The word *ger* refers to a person from a different country who lived among the Israelites. So the NRSV translates *ger* as "resident alien." Clearly, the *gerim* were recognized as ethnically distinct from the Israelites. They are not allowed to partake in the Passover feast unless they have been circumcised (Exod 12:48). The Israelites themselves were "resident aliens," *gerim*, when they were in Egypt. When God promises Canaan to Abram, God says that Canaan is a land of Abraham's "sojournings," *maguwr*; which has the same root as *ger*: *guwr*. This suggests that even in Canaan, the Israelites were still "resident aliens."

2. "Children's Defense Fund Cradle to Prison Pipeline Fact Sheet," October 2009, accessed March 7, 2016, http://www.childrensdefense.org/library/data/cradle-to-prison-pipeline-overview-fact-sheet-2009.pdf.

3. Ibid.

4. The issue of just distribution of wealth is beyond the scope of this introductory article. But I would call attention to the issue as a deepseated difficulty in American society. Even now, politicians are using it in their election campaigns.

5. "Children's Defense Fund Cradle to Prison Pipeline Fact Sheet."

6. Office of Justice Programs, *National Institute of Justice*, "Recidivism," accessed May 22, 2016, http://www.nij.gov/topics/corrections/recidivism/Pages/welcome.aspx.

7. Minnesota Department of Corrections, "The Effects of Prison Visitation on Offender Recidivism," November 2011, accessed August 18, 2017, https://mn.gov/doc/assets/11-11MNPrisonVisitationStudy_tcm 1089-272781.pdf.

8. Emily Brault, "Pastoral Care in Prison: What Works?" *Journal of Pastoral Care* 68, no. 3 (September/December 2014): 2.

9. Ibid., 8.

10. Ibid., 6.

11. Children's Defense Fund, Cradle to Prison Pipeline Campaign, "Key Immediate Action Steps," accessed May 24, 2016, http://www.childrensdefense.org/campaigns/cradle-to-prison-pipeline/. More information on how to get involved may be found at the above website.

CONTRIBUTORS

Peter Althouse* (Society for Pentecostal Studies) is Professor of Religion and Theology at Southeastern University in Lakeland, Florida.

W. Scott Axford* (Unitarian Universalist Association) is Pastor of the First Universalist Church in Providence, Rhode Island, and Ecumenical Representative of the Council of Christian Churches within the UUA.

Reginald D. Broadnax* (African Methodist Episcopal Zion Church) is Professor and Chair of the Department of Religion at Clinton College in Rock Hill, South Carolina, and Pastor of Mt. Olive AME Zion Church in Durham, North Carolina.

Mitzi J. Budde* (Evangelical Lutheran Church in America) is Head Librarian and Professor at Virginia Theological Seminary in Alexandria, Virginia.

Greg Carey* (United Church of Christ) is Professor of New Testament at Lancaster Theological Seminary in Lancaster, Pennsylvania.

Philip Caroom (Friends) is a former Maryland trial judge, prosecutor, and defense attorney. A member of the Annapolis Friends Meeting for many years, he is also a founding board member of the Maryland Alliance for Justice Reform.

David J. Fekete* (Swedenborgian Church of North America) is Pastor of the Church of the Holy City in Edmonton, Alberta, and Senior Editor of the denominational online journal *Our Daily Bread*.

Douglas A. Foster* (Churches of Christ) is Professor of Church History in the Graduate School of Theology and Director of the Center

---

* An asterisk indicates an officially named representative of his or her church or other sending body to the National Council of Churches USA's Convening Table on Theological Dialogue and Matters of Faith and Order. The church traditions of other contributors are listed for identification purposes only. All essays reflect the authors' own theological perspectives and not necessarily those of their traditions or communities.

for Restoration Studies at Abilene Christian University in Abilene, Texas.

Rachel Guaraldi (Friends) is an interfaith hospital chaplain, Quaker minister, and spiritual director.

Benjamin Hartley* (The United Methodist Church) is Associate Professor of Christian Mission in the College of Christian Studies of George Fox University in Newberg, Oregon, and an ordained deacon in the Oregon-Idaho Annual Conference.

Kenneth Q. James* (African Methodist Episcopal Zion Church) is Pastor of Memorial AME Zion Church in Rochester, New York.

Antonios Kireopoulos (Orthodox) is Associate General Secretary for Faith & Order and Interreligious Relations & Collaboration at the National Council of Churches USA.

Gayle Gerber Koontz* (Mennonite Church USA) is Professor Emerita of Theology and Ethics at Anabaptist Mennonite Biblical Seminary in Elkhart, Indiana.

Frank Lesko (Roman Catholic) is Director of Catholic-Evangelical Relations at Glenmary Home Missioners in Fairfield, Ohio.

Matthew D. Lundberg* (Christian Reformed Church in North America) is Professor of Theology in the Department of Religion at Calvin College in Grand Rapids, Michigan.

Loida I. Martell* (American Baptist Churches USA) is Professor of Constructive Theology at Palmer Theological Seminary of Eastern University in St. Davids, Pennsylvania.

Madelon Maupin (Church of Christ, Scientist) is a member of the national team of Ecumenical Affairs of the Church of Christ, Scientist in Boston, Massachusetts, and a member of the Faith and Order Commission of the Southern California Christian Forum.

Glen Alton Messer, II* (The United Methodist Church) has taught at Boston University and Yale University, and served for several years as the ecumenical and interfaith staff person responsible for theology and dialogue for the United Methodists.

Kirsten Sonkyo Oh* (The United Methodist Church) is an ordained elder and Associate Professor of Practical Theology at Azusa Pacific University in Azusa, California.

Shirley Paulson* (Church of Christ, Scientist) is Head of Ecumenical Affairs of the Church of Christ, Scientist in Boston, Massachusetts.

CONTRIBUTORS

Michael C. Richardson (Nondenominational) is an elder who serves at Oasis of Faith in Philadelphia, Pennsylvania. He is an invited guest contributor to this collection.

Ann K. Riggs (Friends) is the former director of the Faith and Order Commission at the National Council of Churches USA, and the former principal of the Friends Theological College in Kaimosi, Kenya. She also represents Friends on the Central Committee of the World Council of Churches.

Joyce Shin (Presbyterian Church [USA]) serves as Pastor at Swarthmore Presbyterian Church in Swarthmore, Pennsylvania.

Felicia Y. Thomas (American Baptist) is an ordained minister and Assistant Professor of History at Morgan State University in Baltimore, Maryland.

Don Thorsen* (Independent) is Professor of Theology in the Azusa Pacific University Seminary in Azusa, California, and represents the Wesleyan Theological Society.

Michael Reid Trice* (Evangelical Lutheran Church in America) is Associate Professor of Theological Ethics and Constructive Theology and Associate Dean of Ecumenical and Interreligious Dialogue at the School of Theology and Ministry, Seattle University, in Seattle, Washington.